W9-CPO-213

Evidence-Based Educational Methods

This is a volume in the Academic Press
EDUCATIONAL PSYCHOLOGY SERIES

Critical comprehensive reviews of research knowledge, theories, principles, and practices

Under the editorship of Gary D. Phye

Evidence-Based Educational Methods

Daniel J. Moran

*MidAmerican
Psychological Institute
Joliet, Illinois*

Richard W. Malott

*Department of Psychology
Western Michigan University
Kalamazoo, Michigan*

ELSEVIER
ACADEMIC
PRESS

Amsterdam • Boston • Heidelberg • London
New York • Oxford • Paris • San Diego
San Francisco • Singapore • Sydney • Tokyo

Elsevier Academic Press
525 B Street, Suite 1900, San Diego, California 92101-4495, USA
84 Theobald's Road, London WC1X 8RR, UK

This book is printed on acid-free paper. ∞

Library of Congress Cataloging-in-Publication Data
Application submitted

British Library Cataloguing in Publication Data
A catalogue record for this book is available from the British Library

ISBN: 0-12-506041-6

For all information on all Academic Press publications
visit our Web site at www.academicpress.com

Printed in the United States of America
04 05 06 07 08 09   9 8 7 6 5 4 3 2 1

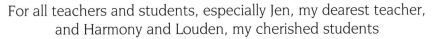

For all teachers and students, especially Jen, my dearest teacher,
and Harmony and Louden, my cherished students

DJM

For Fred and Lillian Malott

RWM

Contents

Contributors   xix

Preface   xxiii

Introduction to Evidence-Based Educational Methods

1. THE NEED FOR EVIDENCE-BASED EDUCATIONAL METHODS
Daniel J. Moran

2. REVIEWING THE OUTCOMES AND PRINCIPLES OF EFFECTIVE INSTRUCTION
Laura D. Fredrick and John H. Hummel

3. A REAL SCIENCE AND TECHNOLOGY OF EDUCATION

R. Douglas Greer and Dolleen-Day Keohane

2

Precision Teaching

4. PRECISION TEACHING: FOUNDATIONS AND CLASSROOM APPLICATIONS

Charles Merbitz, Doreen Vieitez, Nancy Hansen Merbitz,
and Henry S. Pennypacker

5. PRECISION TEACHING: APPLICATIONS IN EDUCATION AND BEYOND

Charles Merbitz, Doreen Vieitez, Nancy Hansen Merbitz, and Carl Binder

$$\boxed{3}$$

Direct Instruction

6. DIRECT INSTRUCTION: THE BIG IDEAS

Timothy A. Slocum

7. TEACHER-MADE SCRIPTED LESSONS

John H. Hummel, Martha L. Venn, and Philip L. Gunter

8. THE COMPETENT LEARNER MODEL: A MERGING OF APPLIED BEHAVIOR ANALYSIS, DIRECT INSTRUCTION, AND PRECISION TEACHING

Vicci Tucci, Daniel E. Hursh, and Richard E. Laitinen

4

Computers and Teaching Machines

9. EFFECTIVE USE OF COMPUTERS IN INSTRUCTION

Marcie N. Desrochers and G. David Gentry

10. ADAPTIVE COMPUTERIZED EDUCATIONAL SYSTEMS: A CASE STUDY

Roger D. Ray

11. SELECTED FOR SUCCESS: HOW *HEADSPROUT READING BASICS*™ TEACHES BEGINNING READING

T. V. Joe Layng, Janet S. Twyman, and Greg Stikeleather

5

Personalized System of Instruction

6

Significant Developments in Evidence-Based Education

14. THE MORNINGSIDE MODEL OF GENERATIVE INSTRUCTION: AN INTEGRATION OF RESEARCH-BASED PRACTICES

Kent Johnson and Elizabeth M. Street

18. TRAINING PROFESSIONALS USING SEQUENTIAL BEHAVIOR ANALYSIS

Tom Sharpe, Daniel Balderson, and Hosung So

19. GRAMMAR AND WRITING SKILLS: APPLYING BEHAVIOR ANALYSIS

Marilyn B. Gilbert

Contributors

Daniel Balderson (335), Department of Educational Leadership, University of Nevada—Las Vegas, Las Vegas, Nevada 89154

Yvonne Barnes-Holmes (277), Department of Psychology, National University of Ireland Maynooth, Maynooth, County Kildare, Ireland

Dermot Barnes-Holmes (277), Department of Psychology, National University of Ireland Maynooth, Maynooth, County Kildare, Ireland

Carl Binder (63), Binder Riha Associates, Santa Rosa, California 95404

Guy S. Bruce (267), Community Psychology, Behavior Analysis Program, St Cloud State University, St Cloud, Minnesota 56301

Mapy Chavez-Brown (295), Columbia University Teachers College and Graduate School of Arts and Sciences, New York, New York 10027

Marcie N. Desrochers (127), Bachelor's Program in Behavioral Psychology, School of Human Studies and Applied Arts, St Lawrence College, Brockville, Ontario, Canada, K6V 5X3

Eric J. Fox (201), Arizona State University, Tempe, Arizona 85281

Laura D. Fredrick (9), Department of Educational Psychology and Special Education, Georgia State University, Atlanta, Georgia 30303

Grant Gautreaux (295), Columbia University Teachers College and Graduate School of Arts and Sciences, New York, New York 10027

G. David Gentry (127), Department of Psychology, College of Charleston, Charleston, South Carolina 29424

Marilyn B. Gilbert (361), The Performance Engineering Group, Bainbridge Island, Washington 98110

R. Douglas Greer (23, 295), Columbia University Teachers College and Graduate School of Arts and Sciences, New York, New York 10027

Philip L. Gunter (95), College of Education, Valdosta State University, Valdosta, Georgia 31698

John H. Hummel (9, 95), Department of Psychology and Counseling, Valdosta State University, Valdosta, Georgia 31698

Daniel E. Hursh (109), Department of Advanced Educational Studies, West Virginia University, Morgantown, West Virginia 26506

Kent Johnson (247), Morningside Academy, Seattle, Washington 98109

Dolleen-Day Keohane (23, 295), Columbia University Teachers College, New York, New York 10027

Richard E. Laitinen (109), Tucci Learning Solutions, Inc., Aptos, California 95003

T. V. Joe Layng (171), Headsprout, Seattle, Washington 98102

Richard W. Malott, Western Michigan University, Kalamazoo, Michigan 49008

Toby L. Martin (223) University of Manitoba, Winnepeg, Manitoba, Canada R3T2N2

Katherine Meincke (295), Columbia University Teachers College and Graduate School of Arts and Sciences, New York, New York 10027

Charles Merbitz (47, 63) Institute of Psychology, Illinois Institute of Technology, Chicago, Illinois 60616

Nancy Hansen Merbitz (47, 63), Private Practice, Glen Ellyn, Illinois 60137

Daniel J. Moran (1), MidAmerican Psychological Institute, Joliet, Illinois 60432

Carol Murphy (277), Department of Psychology, National University of Ireland Maynooth, Maynooth, County Kildare, Ireland

Joseph J. Pear (223), University of Manitoba, Winnepeg, Manitoba, Canada R3T2N2

Henry S. Pennypacker (47), MammaCare, Gainesville, Florida 32601

Jo Ann Pereira (295), Columbia University Teachers College and Graduate School of Arts and Sciences, New York, New York 10027

Roger D. Ray (143), Department of Psychology, Rollins College, Winter Park, Florida 32789

Tom Sharpe (335), Department of Educational Leadership, University of Nevada—Las Vegas, Las Vegas, Nevada 89154

Timothy A. Slocum (81), Utah State University, Logan, Utah 84321

Hosung So (335), Department of Kinesiology, California State University—San Bernardino, San Bernardino, California 92407

Greg Stikeleather (171), Headsprout, Seattle, Washington 98102

Elizabeth M. Street (223), Department of Psychology, Central Washington University, Ellensburg, Washington 98926

Vicci Tucci (109), Tucci Learning Solutions, Inc., Aptos, California 95003

Janet S. Twyman (171), Headsprout, Seattle, Washington 98102

Martha L. Venn (95), Department of Special Education, University of Colorado, Colorado Springs, Colorado 80918

Doreen Vieitez (47), Department of Education, Joliet Junior College, Joliet, Illinois 60431

Lynn Yuan (295), Columbia University Teachers College and Graduate School of Arts and Sciences, New York, New York 10027

Preface

The age of accountability is affecting a wide array of cultural practices. Society is asking for verification of the effectiveness and efficiency of corporations, health agencies, and governmental organizations. Society is also asking for verification of the effectiveness and efficiency of instructional practices provided by the institutions of education. The *No Child Left Behind Act of 2001* clearly indicates a nationwide interest in improving student education, and it suggests that this goal will be met by using instructional methods developed from scientific research, in other words, instructional methods whose effectiveness and efficiency have been verified. The appeal for evidence-based educational methods comes not only from this legislation but also from teacher organizations, administrators, parents, community agencies, and even the students themselves. The educational community and the legislation pose an important challenge to the scientific community: the research community must develop and refine effective and efficient educational methods.

Evidence-Based Educational Methods answers the challenge by presenting scientific principles and applications aimed at improving human learning. Decades before the current era of accountability, researchers were developing strong assessment and educational methods based on the science of behavior analysis. Precision Teaching (PT), Direct Instruction (DI), Computerized Teaching (Computers), Personalized System of Instruction (PSI), and other unique applications of behavior analysis (e.g., Peer Tutoring and Generative Instruction) are all informed by the scientific principles of learning, They have been tested successfully in the laboratory, and many have also been tested successfully in the field.

This book is divided into five sections regarding each of the four aforementioned approaches: PT, DI, Computers, and PSI, and another section for additional applications. It is important to note that the principles and applications from all five sections can be synthesized into a cohesive whole. Each of the sections has much in common with the others, but each also brings different perspectives and techniques to evidence-based education. In addition, the chapters are authored by leading educational researchers from each domain.

Individuals and agencies responsible for executing instruction that leaves no children behind will find this book an important resource for achieving that important goal. Not only can teachers and administrators use this book as a valuable guide to improving education, but involved parents, community leaders, and PTA groups can use it as a model of how educational goals can be formulated and accomplished. In addition, student-teachers can use it as a text showing the blueprint for the evidence-based education systems being planned for the future.

This book is a compendium of empirically verified instructional methods that can be seamlessly integrated into most general and special education curricula. The book is unique in that it unites separate educational domains by looking at those domains with a common vision, a common educational philosophy, and common principles of learning.

Society has demanded more efficient and effective education, and our government has legislated it. The evidence-based educational methods in this book meet those demands because these methods have evolved from a long line of scientific, behavioral research aimed at developing efficient and effective educational methods.

Daniel J. Moran
Richard W. Malott

Introduction to Evidence-Based Educational Methods

CHAPTER

1

The Need for Evidence-Based Educational Methods

DANIEL J. MORAN

MidAmerican Psychological Institute

INTRODUCTION

The twenty-first century has introduced an era of accountability, with a demand for advocates of important social and cultural activities to "prove" the "facts" they promote, so that decisions affecting the public will lead to consistent, socially valuable goals. "Evidence-based medicine" has emerged, for example, to answer these questions: "Are these medical procedures proven to promote health?" and "Is it a fact that this is the most effective and efficient treatment for this patient?" One current trend in clinical psychology is the promotion of "empirically supported treatments" to answer a similar question: "Is this therapy proven to be effective and efficient?" The turn of the century has become an era in which practitioners are being held increasingly more accountable for the time and money being spent to address important issues.

Education, perhaps a culture's most important issue, is witnessing a similar surge of interest in evidence-based practice. Educators, parents, taxpayers, and students all ask the same question: "Are the educational practices used in schools actually effective and efficient?" This desire for proof that the student is being well educated goes beyond the pre-K to 12th-grade classrooms. University settings, vocational schools, and training sites of all kinds search for economical and successful methods for imparting skills to their students. This demand for responsible educational practices led to the establishment of the No Child Left Behind Act (NCLB) of 2001, which legislates that pedagogical practices must demonstrate measurable effects on the learning of America's children.

NO CHILD LEFT BEHIND

On January 8, 2002, President George W. Bush signed the No Child Left Behind Act (Public Law 107–110) in an effort to encourage the use of proven pedagogical techniques that can meet the growing demand for increased accountability with regard to the outcomes of education. The legislation puts "special emphasis on determining which educational programs and practices have been proven effective through rigorous scientific research" (U.S. Department of Education, n.d.), and it suggests that federal funding will be available for educators to learn new and successful pedagogical techniques. In the crucible of this cultural change, the need for *evidence* is made clear, and the term *evidence-based education* steels and shines.

Black's Law Dictionary defines *evidence* as "that which tends to produce conviction . . . as to the existence of a fact" (p. 489), and it supports the outcome of making reliable, valid, and valued decisions. Grover J. Whitehurst, Assistant Secretary for Educational Research and Improvement in the U.S. Department of Education, defines *evidence-based education* as "the integration of professional wisdom with the best available empirical evidence in making decisions about how to deliver instruction" (Whitehurst, 2003). So, prudent educational pursuits are guided by both "empirical evidence" and "professional wisdom." Empirical evidence leads to an objective report about which teaching methods reliably lead to scholastic gains and which of these work in a shorter amount of time or with fewer resources expended. Professional wisdom is required so that each empirically supported method is appropriately adapted to the current scholastic environment. This wisdom can also guide the decision process when research data are absent. In effect, Whitehurst suggests that evidence-based education occurs when educators select teaching methods supported by reliable and valid data from scientific experiments and then judiciously synthesize these methods into a functional curriculum for a given setting.

When accumulating research evidence, investigators must consider both methodological and philosophical issues. An extensive literature about these critical scientific concerns focuses on what constitutes reliable and valid observations, how to collect and synthesize data, and how to interpret and report the findings. A thorough review of basic science is beyond the scope of this chapter, but the definition that the legislation provides is a practical guide to the critical questions of educational research. An excerpt from the No Child Left Behind Act reads as follows:

The term 'scientifically based research'—

(A) means research that involves the application of rigorous, systematic, and objective procedures to obtain reliable and valid knowledge relevant to education activities and programs; and

(B) includes research that—

    (i) employs systematic, empirical methods that draw on observation or experiment;

    (ii) involves rigorous data analyses that are adequate to test the stated hypotheses and justify the general conclusions drawn;

    (iii) relies on measurements or observational methods that provide reliable and valid data across evaluators and observers, across multiple measurements and observations, and across studies by the same or different investigators;

    (iv) is evaluated using experimental or quasi-experimental designs in which individuals, entities, programs, or activities are assigned to different conditions and with appropriate controls to evaluate the effects of the condition of interest, with a preference for random-assignment experiments, or other designs to the extent that those designs contain within-condition or across-condition controls;

    (v) ensures that experimental studies are presented in sufficient detail and clarity to allow for replication or, at a minimum, offer the opportunity to build systematically on their findings; and

    (vi) has been accepted by a peer-reviewed journal or approved by a panel of independent experts through a comparably rigorous, objective, and scientific review. (pp. 126–127)

So, the NCLB legislation has established an important challenge for social and behavioral scientists, but decades before this legislation and the era of evidence-based practices, scientists in the field of behavior analysis had been working within the rigors of the aforementioned guidelines.

BEHAVIOR ANALYSIS AND EDUCATION

Behavior analysis is a science that investigates the functional interrelations between stimuli in the environment and relevant behavioral responses. Its vast literature contains meticulously controlled experiments demonstrating effective, valuable techniques for behavior change in a range of areas, including industry, health, safety, social welfare, and education. Behavior analysis was founded by B.F. Skinner and has developed a large, dedicated community of researchers and practitioners. Applied behavior analysis addresses systematic, pragmatic methods of behavior change in the everyday world. And, despite all the definitions and theories of *learning*, when a college student takes a course called "Learning" a significant majority of the topics will be from the literature of behavior analysis.

The basic characteristics of this science of behavior include empiricism, parsimony, scientific verification, and the assumption that behavior is lawful (Cooper, Heron, & Heward, 1987). In other words, the pursuits of applied behavior analysis require the practice of objective data collection (empiricism), the assumption that explanations are more useful when they are simple and logical (parsimony), the practice of controlled experimentation as a method of investigation, and the consideration (and accumulating evidence) that the relations between the environment and behavior are orderly. The educational methods described in this book answer the current call for evidence, and they draw on years of literature to support their claims.

This journey toward establishing "proven" effective interventions is arduous, and each of the pedagogical methods that follow is supported by various levels of research. Most of the techniques are based on behavioral principles from well-replicated laboratory and field research. For example, one instructional method, Direct Instruction, was investigated in Project Follow Through, the largest and most expensive educational research project in history (Adams & Engelmann, 1996). In 1967, Congress initiated Project Follow Through to determine which methods of instruction delivery were most effective in promoting various areas of learning and achievement. At a cost of approximately $1 billion, this research indicated that, when contrasted with the other comparison methods, Direct Instruction produces the most significant outcomes for basic scholastic skills (*i.e.*, math computation or spelling), cognitive skills (*i.e.*, math, problem solving, or reading comprehension), and affective outcomes (*i.e.*, adjustment or self-concept). Yet, to the detriment of the children, Project Follow Through research is largely ignored, as the mainstream schools rarely use Direct Instruction (see Chapter 6 for more information). Fortunately, charter schools and private programs retained the methodology and continue to collect field research data, and Direct Instruction is being promoted in the literature of the No Child Left Behind Act (U.S. Department of Education, 2000).

Most of the educational methods described in this book have not had the benefit of the type of research and funding associated with Project Follow Through, but most of these instructional techniques have been developed using the basic scientific principles of behavior derived from the extensive literature on the experimental analysis of behavior and applied behavior analysis. Much can be gleaned from this literature to inform educators about how people learn and how behavior changes after an instructional experience.

Herbert Spencer, philosopher and sociologist from the Victorian era, wove this often-cited quote: "The great aim of education is not knowledge but action." Action is the behavior of individuals. Educational environments are designed to change an individual's behavior, and the measure of the educator's impact is in the measurable change in the individual's behavior, whether that behavior be reciting the ABCs or writing a thoughtful, coherent, critical analysis of a poem. Instructional methods derived from the science of behavior have focused on such measurement issues—not only measuring the frequency of correct responses but also measuring the concurrent reduction of incorrect responses, as well as the rate or "speed" of those responses. In certain domains of behavior analysis, measurement of *fluent* responding is a gold standard. This focus on fluency in education by Precision Teachers has yielded impressive scholastic gains (see Section 2 for more information), but Direct Instruction and Precision Teaching represent only a fraction of the pedagogical techniques associated with behavior analysis. Computer-aided learning, instructional design, and generative instruction are all parts of the interrelated core of pedagogical techniques that are accumulating evidence of effectiveness.

Education aims to facilitate the development of a student–culture relationship. Society provides the support of an educational environment to first assess each individual's current abilities, then this environment must bolster those abilities while remediating skill limitations, recruit the individual's abilities toward a constructive contribution, and deploy those abilities in a functional manner that promotes social growth and well-being. Education is for the good of the student and the good of society, and it deserves to be executed with wisdom and scientifically supported methods. This book provides many of the evidence-based educational methods we need to ensure that no child is left behind; now we must all apply those educational methods wisely.

Acknowledgments

I would like to thank Marilyn B. Gilbert and Dick Malott for their editorial remarks on this chapter, and Kurt Salzinger for his early support for this book project.

References

Adams, G. L., & Engelmann, S. (1996). *Research on direct instruction: 25 years beyond DISTAR*. Seattle, WA: Educational Assessment Systems.

Black, H. C., & Connolly, M. J. (1979). *Black's law dictionary*, 5th ed. St. Paul, MN: West Publishing Company.

Cooper, J. O., Heron, T. E., & Heward, W. L. (1987). *Applied behavior analysis*. Englewood Cliffs, NJ: Prentice Hall.

No Child Left Behind Act of 2001 (2002). Public Law 107–110, 107th Congress of the United States of America. (http://www.ed.gov/legislation/ESEA02/107–110.pdf).

U.S. Department of Education. (2000). *Early implementation of the comprehensive school reform demonstration (CSRD) program*. Washington, D.C.: U.S. Department of Education, Office of the Under Secretary, Planning and Evaluation Service, Elementary and Secondary Division (http://www.ed.gov/programs/compreform/csrdimprpt.doc).

U.S. Department of Education. (n.d.) *Proven Methods* (http://www.ed.gov/nclb/methods/index.html).

Whitehurst, G. J. (2003). *Evidence-based education* (http://www.ed.gov/admins/tchrqual/evidence/whitehurst.html?exp=0).

CHAPTER 2

Reviewing the Outcomes and Principles of Effective Instruction

LAURA D. FREDRICK
Georgia State University

JOHN H. HUMMEL
Valdosta State University

INTRODUCTION

Education is an entitlement in our society. Every child is entitled to an excellent education, yet not every child receives such an education (Barrett et al., 1991). We provide schools, transportation to the schools, teachers for the classrooms, and administrators to run the schools, making it possible for every child to attend, but we do not make it possible for every child to receive an excellent education. The difference between attending school and receiving an excellent education lies in the instruction students receive while in school. That instruction is a combination of the instructional methods and programs used and the skills of the teachers. In this chapter, we examine the outcomes of effective instruction and why those outcomes are important. We also delineate principles of effective instruction and their importance in producing the outcomes all children deserve. Finally, we introduce four pedagogical approaches that incorporate principles of effective instruction and we examine how these approaches produce the outcomes that are the entitlement of all children.

Definitions of effective instruction are as numerous as the scholars who study instruction. Most definitions include some aspect of students being able to do something new after instruction that they could not do before the instruction, as well as some aspect of efficiency in learning. Our definition of effective instruction guides our discussion and uses concepts from Cartledge (2001) and Kozloff (2002): *Effective instruction is instruction that enables students to demonstrate, maintain, and generalize competency on prespecified learning outcomes faster than students would be able to accomplish this either on their own or with less effective instruction.*

The ultimate outcome of effective instruction is that students become lifelong learners. To become lifelong learners, students must learn both content and how to learn independently. It is not possible, nor is it the responsibility of education, to teach everything students will ever need to know. However, if critical content such as reading, math, and writing is taught, and it is taught in a way that teaches students how to learn, students are prepared to be lifelong learners. It is not our intent in this chapter to consider what the particular content is that students need to learn; rather, our concern is with the outcomes and the principles of effective instruction. The outcomes of effective instruction (Kozloff, 2002) are that students are fluent in the content they learn; that they can combine and apply various simple skills to solve complex problems; that they can maintain these skills over time; that they can generalize their learning to new, similar situations and problems; and that they can work independently.

Fluency, one of the outcomes of effective instruction, is a measure of accuracy and time. A student who reads 100 words correctly in one minute is more fluent than a student who reads 50 words correctly in the same time. Similarly, the student who correctly writes the answers to 50 math facts in the same time it takes another student to correctly write the answers to 20 math facts is more fluent. It is especially important that students are fluent in tool skills, the skills necessary for higher-order learning and complex problem solving. Every content area has tool skills; they are the basics, the critical components for that content. In reading, tool skills include decoding and blending sounds into words; in math, they are the math facts and order of operations; in writing, they are the parts of speech and agreement between subjects and predicates. To be fluent in tool skills is to be able to use the tool skills automatically without thinking about them so that students can focus on the big picture, allowing them to comprehend what they are reading, solve math problems, or write a coherent essay. Students who correctly read 100 words per minute are more likely to understand what they read than students who correctly read 50 words per minute. Similarly, students trying to solve a complex math problem are more likely to be successful if they are thinking about the problem rather than trying to remember that 6 times 9 equals 54. If instruction is effective, students become fluent.

A second important outcome of effective instruction is that students can apply what they learn. Students who are fluent are more likely to be able to combine skills and apply them. Consider addition problems with renaming.

If, when adding the 1's column, the total is more than 9, then the student has to make a set of 10 to be included in the 10's column and put the remaining number of 1's in the 1's column. This can continue across the problem, if, for example, the 10's column totals more than 9, etc. Similarly, if a student is demonstrating mastery of the content of an American history course by taking an essay exam, consider the importance of combining and applying writing skills and being able to organize and present course content to demonstrate mastery.

The remaining three outcomes of effective instruction—maintaining skills, generalizing skills, and being able to work independently—are all important and related. Because there is so little time to teach all that students need to know, students cannot afford the luxury of forgetting and then relearning. Effective instruction provides enough review and high-level application of information that students maintain what they learn. Similarly, it would be impossible to teach students every situation in which a particular response or behavior would be appropriate; therefore, it is essential that students learn to generalize their learning to new situations when appropriate. For instance, the math facts used to solve math problems are the same math facts used to solve chemistry problems, and when instruction is effective students readily see the appropriate applications. The final outcome, being able to work independently, is critical if students are to succeed and to continue to learn beyond the classroom. Ultimately, to be lifelong learners, students need to be able to work independently with what they have already learned and they need to be able to continue to learn new information on their own. These outcomes of effective instruction are the essence of mastery.

The key to achieving these outcomes lies in the principles of effective instruction. *Effective instruction begins with clearly stated behavioral objectives; provides accurate, competent models; provides many opportunities for active responding; delivers immediate feedback about the accuracy of responses; allows self pacing; teaches to mastery; reinforces accurate responding; and frequently and directly measures responding that is explicitly tied to the behavioral objectives, using the outcomes of those measurements to make instructional decisions.* A brief examination of these principles of effective instruction highlights their importance. Effective instruction is not possible unless we know exactly what we want students to learn. As behavior analysts, we insist that students demonstrate what they learn, so we write behavioral objectives that let students know what they will be able and required to do when they are at mastery. These objectives provide goals for students, as well as a guide for the day-to-day instructional decisions teachers must make.

Once we know what we want students to be able to do, it is efficient to provide a model of that behavior. When we are teaching letter sounds and we point to the letter *m*, we tell students the sound that is appropriate for that letter. We do not provide a list of words that begin with the letter *m* and then have students guess how those words are the same; some students will be successful with this indirect approach, but it lacks efficiency, an important component of effective instruction. Having students imitate the models is very efficient and reduces the number of errors students make while learning. Although it is possible to learn from errors, it is not always the most efficient method because errors waste valuable instructional time, and once students make an error they are likely to make the same error again. It is far more effective to eliminate as much as possible the errors students make, and providing models accomplishes this.

Effective instruction provides many opportunities for students to respond so they can make the response a part of their repertoire. Watching a competent model is informative and helpful, but students become competent when they actually practice the responses themselves. Imagine learning cursive writing by watching someone else write and never writing yourself. It would be much like trying to learn to sink a three-point basketball shot by only watching others do it. The responding that students practice needs to be active and it needs to be the same type of responding that will be necessary to apply the learning. Solving math problems typically requires students to write numerals; therefore, they need to practice and become fluent in writing math facts in addition to just verbally stating them.

It is critical for students to receive immediate feedback about the accuracy of the responses they are practicing. When students respond correctly and receive feedback that they are correct, it can serve to motivate students to continue; when they receive feedback that their response is incorrect, they can make immediate changes rather than continuing to practice the incorrect response. An important aspect of this immediate feedback is the information teachers provide for incorrect responses. To only tell students their response is incorrect gives students very little information; they know not to make that response in this situation in the future, but they do not know what response to make. To provide a long explanation of why their response is incorrect is to provide more information than students can typically process in a short time and can function as punishment to the extent that some students will stop responding. The most efficient feedback for incorrect responses is to tell students the response is incorrect and then to provide the correct response and ask the students to repeat it. Providing the correct response allows the students another opportunity to imitate the model correctly and to receive feedback that confirms their response. Effective instruction continually presents the correct response as a model at the outset of instruction, as a confirmation of the students' correct response, or as a correction for the students' incorrect response.

Providing frequent immediate feedback that lets students know if they are correct is of little value if students are required to continue in the instructional sequence when they learn they are incorrect. To be effective, instruction must allow self pacing. Not all students learn at the same rate and even some who learn at similar rates will not necessarily all learn the same content at the same rate. Students need to be allowed to continue to practice and to work with information until they demonstrate mastery and only then continue in the instructional sequence. Without this opportunity, students who do not master requisite skills before moving on will be unlikely to master the course objectives. Effective instruction teaches to and requires mastery, a prerequisite for students to become independent learners.

When students are at mastery, their behavior comes in contact with the natural reinforcement that will maintain the behavior. As students are learning new skills, however, their correct responses need to be extrinsically reinforced until they are at mastery and contact the natural reinforcement. Extrinsic reinforcement is most often a simple confirmation of a correct response; it may be accompanied by a nod, a smile, a thumbs-up, or some other gesture that lets students know they have the correct response and that the teacher is pleased with their performance. These are very powerful reinforcers for most students. The ultimate reinforcement, however, is being able to accomplish something new with what students are learning and to experience the natural reinforcement that comes from engaging in that behavior. The natural reinforcement for reading is the information and/or pleasure one receives from reading. However, students with poor or underdeveloped reading skills do not get information or pleasure from their reading; at this level, reading is not naturally reinforcing and will not be maintained. One of the best ways to become a better reader is to read more. Reading more, though, is the last thing a poor reader wants to do, so we must provide effective instruction and extrinsically reinforce all the small steps in learning to read until eventually students are reading connected text fluently and comprehending what they are reading so that reading is naturally reinforcing because of the information and/or pleasure it is providing.

The final principle of effective instruction is to provide frequent direct measures of student learning tied to the behavioral objectives and to use the outcomes of these measures to make instructional decisions. Students know from the behavioral objectives what is required of them, what they need to be able to do to demonstrate mastery. Every time students respond, teachers have an opportunity to measure learning and to make instructional decisions. Possibly unique to behavioral instruction is that there is no penalty for incorrect responses when teachers are measuring achievement. Students are not blamed if they respond incorrectly; rather, it is assumed that the instruction or the delivery of the instruction is inappropriate and the instruction is changed.

In this chapter we introduce four behaviorally based instructional approaches: Precision Teaching, Direct Instruction, Programmed Instruction, and Personalized System of Instruction. With these approaches, teachers can help all students achieve their educational entitlement. After the introduction of each approach, we examine how that approach incorporates the principles of effective instruction delineated above.

PRECISION TEACHING

Precision Teaching (PT), founded by Ogden Lindsley, is designed to evaluate instruction (West, Young, & Spooner 1990) and can be used in conjunction with any instructional approach. The basic aim or goal of PT is to achieve fluency in the tool skills associated with academic content (Kame'enui et al., 2002). PT requires students to frequently (usually daily) practice, measure, and report an appropriate overt response associated with each academic subject. The measurement unit utilized in PT is *rate of responding*: the count or frequency of the target behavior divided by the time taken to emit the target behavior. The rate is charted by students on a semilogarithmic chart (Fredrick, Deitz, Bryceland, Hummel, 2000); this chart is referred to as a *Standard Celeration Chart* in PT circles. Student performance depicted on the chart is used to modify instruction, which reflects the most important tenet of PT: "The student knows best, or in other words, the student's behavior can tell us better than anything else whether or not instruction has been effective" (West et al., 1990, p. 8).

In PT classrooms, teachers may present content using a variety of methods. Teachers select the appropriate performance measures, and students count and record the data on their semilogarithmic chart. The individual data for each student are typically analyzed one or more times each week. If the data slope shows that the student's fluency is increasing, instruction continues. If the slope is flat or negative, the teacher alters the instruction.

Precision Teaching often employs tutoring. Students typically spend a few minutes each day in each subject working with another student and focusing on areas of performance where the students are not yet fluent. Part of these tutoring sessions has one student counting the frequency of a particular response within a specified time, often one minute. The response may be reading words aloud, spelling words on paper, solving math problems, or any other responses that require fluency. The students chart their data and then they reverse roles. The data for each student are then used as the basis for altering teaching (pedagogy, pacing, remediation, etc.) and tutoring and for determining what the students should focus on during the coming week.

Precision Teaching is an educational tool that can be used in any subject at any grade level with any instructional method. Teachers need to have clearly stated learning outcomes and identify overt performance measures associated with each. In daily tutoring sessions, which can precede or follow the class's regular instruction, students work on specific skills that the teacher has identified based on each student's performance as shown on the semilogarithmic charts.

Although PT is primarily an assessment procedure rather than an instructional procedure, it incorporates the principles of effective instruction, because assessment is a critical component of instruction. Teachers rely on clearly stated behavioral objectives to determine which responses students will practice during PT, and tutors provide accurate, competent models for each other. Students have many opportunities to actively respond when they take on the role of the tutee, and when they are the tutor they must be especially focused on the accuracy of the tutee's responses. The tutor provides immediate feedback about the tutee's responses, and those responses determine the pace at which the student will continue through the program. Mastery is evidenced by the acceleration of the data, and if mastery is not forthcoming then instruction is changed until students ultimately master the objectives. Recording data points to show an acceleration in learning is a powerful reinforcer for correct, improved performance. Finally, PT is an evaluation tool to help educators objectively judge student progress and the effectiveness of instruction.

DIRECT INSTRUCTION

The Direct Instruction (DI) we present is the commercially available Direct Instruction sold by SRA and originally developed by Sigfried Engelmann. The late 1960s saw the first widespread dissemination and research on DI when Public Law 90–92 authorized Project Follow Through (PFT). DI was one of nine curricular programs evaluated on three dimensions (basic skills, cognition, and affective), and the DI model produced the highest average performance in all dimensions (Watkins, 1988). All nine of the PFT curricula were originally developed as approaches to address the needs of students who were at risk for school failure. Interestingly, instruction that works well for students who are at risk also works well for other students, including students in gifted programs (Ginn, Keel, & Fredrick, 2002).

Direct Instruction programs are available for reading, writing, spelling, and math. All programs provide scripted lessons based on faultless communication, with placements in instructional groups determined by each student's current achievement. Extensive logical analysis makes clear the skills students need to learn to become competent in different content areas. Placement tests for the DI programs are designed to determine the skills students have already mastered so that instruction begins with the necessary prerequisite skills and progresses in a logical sequence. Students are easily moved from one group to another as they master particular skills.

Direct Instruction lessons rely on choral responding so that during each lesson all students have many opportunities to respond rather than the one or two opportunities each student has or the multiple opportunities a few students have in more traditional classes. The teacher presents the lesson from a script that often begins with the teacher modeling the answer. This is followed with a request for students to make the same response, a couple seconds to think about the response they are going to make, and a signal to respond. The students respond in unison. If their response is correct and everyone responds together, the teacher confirms the response by repeating it. If even one student does not respond correctly, the teacher immediately provides a correction by saying the correct response and asking the students to try again. If students do not respond in unison, the teacher requires the students to try again until they all respond together on signal. All students need to respond in unison so the teacher knows that all the students know the response and that some students are not just echoing the response after hearing the group.

Direct Instruction programs reflect a "bottom-up" philosophy in that outcome behaviors are thoroughly analyzed to identify their critical components and then the instruction is designed to explicitly teach each of these components in carefully sequenced lessons. For example, sounds are introduced before the symbols for those sounds are introduced so that students are fluent in producing a sound correctly before the symbol for that sound is presented. At that point, the student only needs to learn the symbol that goes with the sound the student already knows. Mastery of one lesson provides the students with the requisite skills to master the next. The lessons are designed to provide sufficient practice so that students become firm on all skills, applying them often in subsequent lessons until those skills become automatic and are subsumed within more complex skills (Engelmann, 1999).

Conceptually, one can view the content of a DI program as a stairway (Engelmann, 1999). Each student "steps" onto the stairway at the student's entry skill level and, through teacher-directed activities while on that step, masters its content. Each step is approximately equal in terms of the amount of time and effort required, and each higher step is associated with increasingly more complex behaviors, although they are not necessarily "more difficult" because the previous steps provide the students with the background skills and knowledge needed for success.

The inclusion of principles of effective instruction is evident in all DI programs. The programs begin with empirically established objectives that measure outcomes aligned with state and national standards for public schools. Accurate, competent models are provided by the teacher throughout the programs. Typically, the teacher models the response and then asks the students to give the same response. Because of the choral responding, all students have extensive practice responding throughout the lessons, and all responses are followed by immediate feedback. The feedback is either a confirmation of a correct response, which the teacher typically repeats, or a very direct correction that provides a model of the correct response. In an effort to teach as much as possible in the allocated instructional time and to keep students focused and engaged, teachers keep DI lessons moving at a quick pace; however, it is always student performance that determines when the teacher moves on to new activities in the lesson. After the choral responding, students receive individual turns to be sure all are firm before moving on to the next instructional activity. DI programs require mastery throughout, for all activities and all content. If students are not at mastery, the teacher provides correct models, remediation, and additional practice until mastery is achieved.

Teachers reinforce correct responding by confirming and repeating the response. Ultimately, because the programs have been so carefully analyzed, the instruction so explicit and systematic, and mastery a requirement for progressing, students quickly come in contact with the natural reinforcers associated with being competent. Finally, the principle of effective instruction that calls for frequent measures of responses tied to objectives and then used to make instructional decisions is evident throughout DI programs. After each activity the teacher provides individual turns to assess the responses tied to specified objectives, and student performance on these individual assessments determines subsequent instruction.

PROGRAMMED INSTRUCTION

The initial development of Programmed Instruction (PI) is credited to B. F. Skinner. Skinner (1954, 1968) cautioned that educators had overlooked several critical components required for learning and that these components can be addressed by implementing what he called teaching machines.[*] Teaching machines and today's computers, with all their attendant software and variations, are especially useful in providing two of Skinner's critical components of effective instruction. Students need to make thousands of responses and receive feedback for these responses if they are to acquire complex academic learning. Teaching machines can provide for both and as a result can shape complex verbal responses as well as teach subtle discriminations.

While Skinner's teaching machine was one of the first applications of programmed instruction, most often the technology is thought of as textual materials in book form. Programmed instruction consists of sequenced frames, typically organized into sets of three. Each set of three frames follows an ABC approach. In this approach, the A frame is the antecedent, usually a small piece of information. The B (behavior) frame requires the student to make an overt response to a question based on the information in the previous A frame. The last frame in the set, C, allows the student to check the accuracy of the response made in the B frame (*i.e.*, confirmatory consequence). With carefully constructed frames, students are not likely to make many mistakes. Students who make an incorrect response are instructed either to start the three-frame set over or to go back several sets and repeat the instruction. This illustrates *linear* programmed instruction.

The majority of current programmed instructional materials reflect what is known as *branching* programs. Students continue working through the frames in sequence until they make an error. When students make an error, the program breaks out of the original sequence into a branch designed to remediate and

---

[*] Sidney Pressey of Ohio State University developed "automated learning machines" in the 1920s.

reteach the information on which students made the mistake. Once the error is corrected, the branch returns to the original sequence of frames. The main distinction between linear and branching PI materials involves how errors are corrected. In the linear programs, students simply repeat sets of frames they have already completed. In branching programs, students are introduced to new frames.

With the advent of personal computers becoming widely available in the late 1980s, PI became the basis for virtually all forms of computer-aided instruction. Computer-based examples of PI can be accessed through the Internet by opening a search engine such as Internet Explorer and searching for programmed instruction. Thousands of examples can be sampled. For example, the Center for Programmed Instruction's website (http://www.centerforpi.com/) offers a PI tutorial, tutorials on creating computer-based PI courses, one on preparing for the Behavior Analysis Certification Exam, and another on the field of behavior analysis. There are also hundreds of PI sites devoted to engineering and science. In addition, the Internet Encyclopedia (http://www.freesoft.org/CIE/Course) has a tutorial designed to teach people how the Internet works.

Used as either a supplement to other instruction or as the original source of content and skills, PI clearly incorporates the principles of effective instruction. Frames are written based on behavioral objectives that specify measurable outcomes. Models are provided in the first frame, students make an overt response in the second frame, and they receive immediate feedback in the third frame. If students are correct, they receive confirmation of their correct response; if they are incorrect, they are provided additional frames to learn the content. In this way, PI is self paced and teaches to mastery. Students advance only when their responses are correct. To keep students working toward mastery, reinforcement (the opportunity to continue with the next frame) is provided for correct responding. Enough correct responding brings students to the end of the program and they find they have new skills. Some programs also deliver points for correct responding. Students may accumulate these points and exchange them for a preferred reinforcer. All responding is a direct measure of the objectives, and the accuracy of each response is used to make instructional decisions to continue in the program, to repeat some of the frames in a linear program, or to branch to supplemental frames in a branching program.

PERSONALIZED SYSTEM OF INSTRUCTION

Personalized System of Instruction (PSI) was originally designed for use in the college classroom; however, since its introduction into the college classroom over 30 years ago, it has been used to deliver effective instruction in elementary, middle, and high school, as well as in business. PSI is also commonly known as the Keller Plan, after Fred S. Keller, one of its designers. The five defining feature of PSI are that it emphasizes the written word, allows self-pacing, requires mastery, relies on proctors, and provides lectures for motivation or reinforcement.

Emphasis on the Written Word

The content for a PSI course is presented in units. Each unit includes objectives, often in the form of study questions, and a set of readings. These readings must provide all the information necessary for students to master the unit objectives. Teachers typically include readings they develop as well as journal articles and book chapters. Students work through each unit by reading the materials provided and checking their learning against the objectives or study questions. Students may work with these materials in the classroom during regularly scheduled class time or at any time outside the classroom. They may work independently or they may form study groups. Once students have studied the readings and are confident that they have mastered the objectives, they ask to complete an assessment for that unit. The assessment is typically a short test administered by the proctor. As soon as the student completes the assessment, the proctor grades it and provides feedback to the student. This feedback includes clarification for any items missed, an opportunity for the student to ask additional questions, and notification of whether the student demonstrated mastery. Students who do not demonstrate mastery on any unit assessment restudy the reading materials and take an alternate form of the assessment. This continues until students demonstrate mastery of the unit. At this point, students are permitted to begin the next unit.

Self Pacing

Given that not all students will demonstrate mastery on all units at the same time and mastery is necessary for students to be able to continue, self pacing is critical in a PSI course. Students' prior knowledge, their other commitments for the semester, and their intrinsic motivation to finish all affect the speed with which they master units. Ideally, there is no deadline by which all units must be completed; however, many institutions require that coursework be completed within a specific time period. When this is the case, instructors often limit the number of required units so that if students complete at least one unit each week they will complete the course within the academic term. Compared to traditional courses taught by the same instructor, PSI courses often have higher withdrawal rates because students procrastinate. While this is a negative aspect of self pacing, self pacing is essential for mastery. Creative methods to reduce student procrastination have been implemented to help reduce withdrawals from PSI courses.

Mastery

The mastery feature requires that students continue to study the content of a particular unit until their assessment score equals or exceeds a predetermined standard, often between 80% and 90%. If students do not demonstrate mastery, they are required to continue to work on the unit and then to take another form of the assessment for the unit. They may continue to do this as many times as they need to until they demonstrate mastery. There is no penalty for taking multiple forms of the assessment before demonstrating mastery. When students demonstrate mastery, they may begin work on the next unit.

Proctors

Self pacing makes the mastery requirement possible and proctors make self pacing possible. Keller (1968) originally viewed proctors as being students who had already finished a particular PSI course and assisted in the class for additional course credit. Their assistance included administering and immediately scoring unit assessments, providing corrective feedback to students about their scores on the assessments, tutoring students having difficulty with particular objectives, and helping to make the learning experience more personal for the students. According to Johnson and Ruskin (1977), proctors fall into two categories—external and internal—both of which work equally well. External proctors generally fit the description of proctors given above, while internal proctors are often students who are currently enrolled in the class. Internal proctors typically work only with students who are involved with units that the proctor has successfully completed.

Lectures for Motivation or Reinforcement

In PSI courses, lectures are used as a motivational tool rather than as a source of course content. Students are not permitted to attend lectures unless they have mastered particular units. The lectures are an opportunity to learn exciting things that are not included in the course units. Students are not accountable for the information so the lecture can be heard and processed without the burden of taking notes and thinking about how one might have to know this information for a test. Further, these lectures are an opportunity to pique students' interest in issues and research beyond the course requirements. The lecture may be offered by a noted researcher or expert who is not the professor for the course (*i.e.*, it could be someone students typically would not have an opportunity to hear).

The defining principles of effective instruction are evident in PSI. All PSI courses begin with behavioral objectives that the instructor uses to design the course and the students use to guide themselves through the content of each unit and to prepare themselves to demonstrate unit mastery. Proctors serve as models as they have already mastered the content and they can model correct responses to help students who are struggling. While students are encouraged to study actively, take notes, and discuss the readings with others who are studying the same unit, there is no requirement for this behavior built into PSI. However, to demonstrate mastery, students must actively respond to a unit assessment. Their feedback is immediate. The proctor grades the assessment immediately and shares the results with the student. Accurate responses are reinforced and remediation is provided as needed. Self pacing and mastery, two principles of effective instruction, are two defining features of PSI. Students may spend as much or as little time as they need on each unit and they are permitted to continue only after they demonstrate mastery. Frequent measurement of objectives occurs throughout the course as objectives are assessed for each unit. Instructional decisions are made based on these assessments; that is, the student is allowed to advance to the next unit or the student must restudy and complete another assessment.

SUMMARY AND CONCLUSION

In this chapter we introduced four instructional approaches based on behavioral principles and we demonstrated how each incorporates the principles of effective instruction. That is, they all begin with clearly stated behavioral objectives; provide accurate, competent models; provide many opportunities for active responding; deliver immediate feedback about the accuracy of responses; allow self pacing; teach to mastery; reinforce accurate responding; and frequently and directly measure responding that is explicitly tied to the behavioral objectives, using the outcomes of those measurements to make instructional decisions. Using instructional approaches that incorporate these principles of effective instruction gives all students access to the education that is their entitlement.

References

Barrett, B. H., Beck, R., Binder, C., Cook, D. A., Engelmann, S., Greer, D. R. *et al.* (1991). The right to effective education, *The Behavior Analyst*, 14, 79–82.

Cartledge, G. (2001). *Culturally responsive instruction for urban learners: Effective instruction* (http://www.coe.ohio-state.edu/gcartledge/urbaninitiative/effectinstruction.htm).

Engelmann, S. (1999). *Student-program alignment and teaching to mastery*. Paper presented at the 25th National Direct Instruction Conference, Eugene, OR (http://www.nifdi.org/MasPapr99DI-Conf.pdf).

Fredrick, L. D., Deitz, S. M., Bryceland, J. A., & Hummel, J. H. (2000). *Behavior analysis, education, and effective schooling*. Reno, NV: Context Press.

Ginn, P. V., Keel, M. C., & Fredrick, L. D. (2002). Using reasoning and writing with gifted fifth-grade students. *Journal of Direct Instruction*, 2, 41–47.

Johnson, K. R. & Ruskin, R. S. (1977). *Behavioral instruction: An evaluative review*. Washington, D.C.: American Psychological Association.

Kame'enui, E. J., Carnine, D. W., Dixon, R. C., Simmons, D. C., & Coyne, M. D. (2002). *Effective teaching strategies that accommodate diverse learners*, 2nd ed. Upper Saddle River, NJ: Prentice Hall.

Keller, F. S. (1968). "Good-bye, teacher . . ." *Journal of Applied Behavior Analysis*, 1, 79–89.

Kozloff, M. A. (2002). *Three requirements of effective instruction: Providing sufficient scaffolding, helping students organize and activate knowledge, and sustaining high engaged time*. Paper presented at the PaTTan Conference, Pennsylvania Training and Technical Assistance Network, Pittsburgh, PA.

Skinner, B. F. (1954). The science of learning and the art of teaching. *Harvard Educational Review*, 24, 86–97.

Skinner, B. F. (1968). *The technology of teaching*. New York: Appleton-Century-Crofts.

Watkins, C. L. (1988). Project follow through: A story of the identification and neglect of effective instruction. *Youth Policy*, 10(7), 7–11.

West, R. P., Young, K. R., & Spooner, F. (1990). Precision teaching: An introduction. *Teaching Exceptional Children*, Spring, 4–9 (http://www.teonor.com/ptdocs/files/West1990.doc).

CHAPTER 3

A Real Science and Technology of Education

R. DOUGLAS GREER

Columbia University Teachers College, and Graduate School of Arts and Sciences

DOLLEEN-DAY KEOHANE

Columbia University Teachers College

INTRODUCTION

In the last two decades, discussions on technology and education have been restricted to the promise of new hardware, ranging from the personal computer to web-based instruction. These new innovations in hardware and software, like the introduction of the overhead projector in an earlier era, were hailed as the solution to educational problems. Even though these innovations have drastically altered the delivery of instruction, substantive changes are needed that address the real scientific and technical problem for most schools—*the lack of a science and technology of pedagogy* (Keller, 1968, 1978; Skinner, 1968). Without a science of teaching, these new technologies can only deliver a proliferation of teaching as an art. The approach to teaching as an art has been in vogue over the last several centuries but has not met the challenge of education for *all* children any more than alchemy met the challenge of human disease in earlier centuries. President George W. Bush has called for an education system that "leaves no child behind." That can be a reality only with the wholesale application of a science and technology of teaching.

An important book on this issue, *The Technology of Education*, was published over 35 years ago (Skinner, 1968). In that book, B. F. Skinner explained and proclaimed how the science of behavior (really a science of the behavior of the individual) could replace the art and craft of teaching with a technology of pedagogy. While the book did not lead to immediate solutions, it did set the stage for the development of an applied science and technology of teaching. The importance of the development of teaching as a science is not just an argument for the halls of academe, because the development of a science of teaching is as critical to the prognosis for children and society as the mapping of genes is for the future promise of the medical sciences for individuals and our species. Few would argue that effective education is a necessary component of any solution to the problem of poverty and its byproducts of crime, disease, risk-taking behaviors, malnutrition, high incidences of teenage pregnancies, and high unemployment. It is equally evident that the shortage of adequately educated individuals for a knowledge-based society is related to ineffective approaches to learning. While Skinner's book introduced the basic principles and promise that programmed instruction could provide the basis for a science of teaching, the necessary applied research and demonstration base for realizing a technology of education remained to be accomplished.

We argue that a systems technology and a related strategic science of instruction are now available. We have described the research base and the demonstrations of practice in several articles and we shall not repeat those here (Greer, 1991, 1992, 1994a,b, 1997a,b). What we shall do in this chapter is describe two components of what is especially new about a science of schooling: (1) a new sophisticated science of pedagogy, and (2) the behavioral systems technology that results in the development and maintenance of high quality instruction. These two components resulted in model teaching schools that produce from four to seven times more learning for students than is possible in a system that treats teaching as an art. Several of the schools that use this scientific approach to teaching have populations of students with behavioral disorders (*e.g.*, children with autism spectrum disorders, students without developmental disorders but with self-destructive and oppositional problems), learning delays, and conduct disorders, as well as students with academic delays of more than 2 years who are from impoverished communities. However, the fact that a science-of-teaching approach has been used on a school-wide basis mostly with populations that an art-of-teaching approach could not serve in no way limits the applicability of the system to all children.

Parents in well-to-do communities may be happy with schools that treat education as an art. Well-educated parents with adequate incomes provide much of the critical instruction that children need to progress through schools that treat education as an art (Hart & Risley, 1996). When students learn good self-management skills at home and have a home environment in which the parents make the time to provide critical language instruction, parents can provide much of the necessary instruction needed by children. In the latter case, exposure to interesting educational material may be all that is needed for the acquisition of minimal repertoires; however, children who are from less advantaged communities, the children who are being left behind, require and deserve the kind of accelerated instruction that only a science of teaching can provide. Some would argue that all is not well in schools in upper-income neighborhoods either, as students' performance is not as up to par as the national and international studies suggest. But, we will not pursue that argument herein; however, we do want to address the need for a science of teaching for the disabled, the economically disenfranchised who are the children left behind, and all students and parents who need or want superior and accountable instruction for themselves or their children. We will not solve the problems of crime, health, disability, our economy nor can we save the children left behind, unless we implement a science and a technology of pedagogy on a wide-scale basis.

THE NEED FOR A STRATEGIC SCIENCE OF INSTRUCTION

Our science and technology of teaching is predicated on the belief that effective education is *necessarily* individualized instruction. There are several reasons for this.

- First, the basic and applied sciences that serve as the foundation of our pedagogy are *sciences of the behavior of individuals.*
- Second, disparities in skills, language deficits, variations in native languages, and cultural differences that characterize students today require comprehensive individualization of instruction. It is not enough to drop information on a school desk or web page and leave it to the student to grab and run.
- Third, our science of pedagogy is a science that has identified both best practices for initial instructional efforts and tactics (derived from research) for idiosyncratic learning difficulties that arise for all students at different points in their education.

Thus, the application of teaching as a science to individual students is a complex task requiring sophisticated measurement and analysis as part of the process of instruction. Of course, the use of measurement and analysis as part of the process is characteristic of any real technology, including medicine or engineering, to name two technologies that provide the means to our survival.

Teachers encounter students with wide ranges of repertoires and deficits in repertoires. We use the word *repertoires* because the term indicates learning that can be used whenever it is needed; it is *not inert knowledge (e.g.,* something stored in a hypothetical mind). Repertoires consist of *behaviors occurring in and controlled by antecedent and subsequent events and their contexts.* Repertoires are bundles of behaviors and environments that the individual can use as needed. The source for the difference in repertoires presented by students is tied to the communicative behaviors that students do or do not bring to school. The critical need for the student is acquisition of the functional use of language, including mathematics as language, regardless of disability label, educational deficit, developmental category, or socioeconomic level. Individuals who do not have functional communicative repertoires are at a disadvantage, and when that facility is severely lacking and not effectively dealt with, the individual and society pay enormous human and monetary costs. For example, Hart and Risley (1996) have documented the differences in incidental language instruction that occurs in the homes of preschool age children who are from different socioeconomic classes. Impoverished children receive one-third of the language interactions that children from professional families receive, often because there is simply not enough time for children in homes where economic survival is a day-to-day gamble.

Greenwood and his colleagues found that these communicative deficits are exacerbated annually when these children go to school, in a multiplier effect (Greenwood, Hart, Walker, Risley, 1994). That is, the students' lack of communicative functions results in those students receiving less instruction from teachers than do their peers. The attention these children do receive often comes as disapproving consequences or nagging. The students simply do not have the repertoires to obtain reinforcement for academic responding. Their source of reinforcement in the class comes from misbehaving, which results in attention from their peers and teachers. The lack of and ever-diminishing opportunities to receive effective instruction results in the eventual categorization of these children as developmentally disabled by the time they are in the fourth grade (Greenwood et al., 1994). The deficits in classroom reinforcement for these children for academic responses relegate those who have not received adequate instruction to sources of reinforcement for behaviors that work for them in the streets. Behaviors reinforced in the culture of the streets are not in the best interests of these children or society. Ultimately, this leads to incarceration and the acquisition of behaviors that work at the margins of society. These marginalized children then become the teenage parents of still a new generation that is economically and instructionally impoverished. The numbers of those suffering from deficits in communicative learning opportunities are likely to grow without the systematic use of extraordinarily effective pedagogy. The fact that these students receive less instruction proportionate to their lack of communicative repertoires does not mean that their teachers are uncaring. More likely their teachers are devoted to teaching and do their best; they are simply trapped in the coercive cycle that perpetuates the problem. Unfortunately, teaching as an art does not provide teachers with the necessary skills to teach these children such that the language deficits are overcome.

Another group of children suffer from native communicative deficits rather than lack of communicative instructional opportunities. These are children with disabilities acquired before birth, at birth, or in childhood. They suffer from real native deficits, unlike the children who suffer from learning opportunity deficits. However, the well-informed and more economically privileged parents of this latter group, particularly parents of children with autism spectrum disorders, have demanded the right to effective education for their children, not just the right to an education (O'Brian, 2001). Currently, universal education for typically developing children simply means the provision of *services*, not the provision of *accountably effective education*. Evidence is growing of the promise of effective education for children with autism who receive the appropriate kind of intervention that improves their prognosis drastically (U.S. Surgeon General's Report, 2001; Autism and Pervasive Developmental Disabilities, 1999). Moreover, there is adequate evidence that early and scientifically based education for students with disabilities is cost effective for society (see research literature) (Greer, 1994b). In the case of children with autism, two forces have driven innovations in educational effectiveness: (1) the advent of portions of the science and technology of instruction, and (2) the political advocacy of economically and educationally advantaged parents (O'Brian, 2001). In effect, instruction from behavior analysis has provided interventions that overcome native disabilities.

The children and the parents of children from impoverished homes and communities have not had, and will not have, the political influence that has served the children with disabilities so well. Instead, other forces in society must provide that advocacy, if the major ills of our society are to be alleviated. Society must do this in the best interests of individuals and groups as a whole. Part of that advocacy will come only when the benefits of a science of teaching for impoverished children are made apparent in terms of human and monetary costs, as they have been for children with disabilities. Thus, data-based demonstration schools that show the feasibility of comprehensive and effective individualized instructions like those that have occurred in our systems-wide behavior-analytic schools are critical to that effort (Greer, 2002).

In the Hart and Risley book (1996), the authors state that behavior-analytic and non–behavior-analytic educational interventions that they had tried in the 1970s were not enough to overcome the lost opportunities for language interactions in the homes of young children from economically depressed homes. The intervention done by the Kansas Behavior Analysis Approach was one of the two most effective interventions in the $50 million follow-up on the Project Follow Through research effort. Most attempts of the Head Start effort (there were 13 of them) were based on teaching as an art, not a science of teaching, and they were not effective; however, one of the two science-based models, Direct Instruction, was shown to be dramatically effective and continues to produce exceptional outcomes (Becker, 1992). Despite the outcomes of that research, teaching as an art continues as standard practice (Greer, Keohane, & Healy, 2002).

Much of the behavior-analytic–based science of teaching has developed since the 1970s, and there is great promise for a science-based schooling effort to accelerate the education of the disenfranchised. Thus, while the call of Hart and Risley for interventions in the home are well founded, such interventions are only one among many components that lead to effective schooling. Pre-schools and primary schools that apply comprehensive and up-to-date appli-cations of behavior analysis to education can produce four to seven times more learning than teaching as an art, as well as provide for teaching parents to use effective procedures with their children. In fact, instruction for family members is a key part of the new behavior analytic schooling practices (Greer, 2002). Unfortunately, schools that provide a real science and technology of instruction addressing all necessary components have been developed in only a few special places.

COMPONENTS OF AN ADVANCED AND SOPHISTICATED SCIENCE AND TECHNOLOGY OF INSTRUCTION

Our new science and technology of instruction has several major components. These include continuous measurement of instruction as it occurs, reliable assessment of entering repertoires, visual summaries of the measurement of instruction, use of *functionally* valid curricula, and the application of these components by teachers who can provide best-fit tactics from the research on an individualized basis addressing the moment-to-moment needs of the students.

The first and essential component is the use of measurement. Indeed, measurement is the distinguishing characteristics of both a science and a technology (Bushell & Baer, 1994). Before instruction begins, a reliable assess-ment of the student's existing repertoires across the range of repertoires that the child needs for effective living (the "whole child") must be done to fix initial instruction. This initial determination of what the child can do and under what conditions the child can do it requires continual updating to determine the student's progress in common and valid curricula. We refer to this assessment as an *inventory of student repertoires*. Such an inventory is not a standardized test that determines a child's placement in the school according to a bell-shaped curve, although that is useful, too. Rather, the inventory is all about where the child is now and what is needed to progress. Once the needed instruction is determined and begins, teachers need to collect continuous, valid, and accur-ate measurement of the important outcomes of instruction as that instruction occurs for individual students (Bushell & Baer, 1994; Greer, 1994b; Greer & Hogin-McDonough, 1999). That is, the response of the student to each basic instructional unit needs to be reliably recorded.

These measures are then summarized continuously in visual displays of the progress of the students to determine: (1) where the student is on the continuum of instruction, (2) whether the particular pedagogical tactic or technology that is in use at the moment is working or needs to be replaced, (3) what has and has not been successful in the past, and (4) the costs and benefits of the procedures. The following figures are representative of the importance of measurement, not only of each student as described, but for entire schools. Measures are made for each student on numbers of learn units received across all curricula, state standards, and short-term objectives achieved. These are then summarized for each classroom and for the total school (Fig. 1, top panel). Measures of the numbers of learn units required by students to meet objectives are shown in Fig. 2. Teachers' accuracy for a cumulative number of presentations of learn units is summarized across the school year in Fig. 3. A summary of the cumulative number of tactical decisions made by teachers across the school is shown in Fig. 4. These measures are crucial to effective education.

The instructional goals need to be logically and empirically derived curricula that result in functionally effective repertoires, not inert ideas (Skinner, 1957; Whitehead, 1929). We group curricula according to four large categories or *repertoires*: (1) academic literacy, (2) self-management, (3) problem-solving, and (4) an enlarged community of interests or reinforcers (Greer, 2002). Students' instructional needs relative to curricula and pedagogy are determined by the existing repertoires of verbal behavior that, in turn, set the

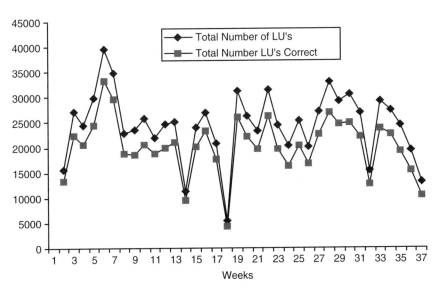

FIGURE 1

Weekly numbers of learn units (LUs) taught by teachers and their students' correct responses to LUs in all classrooms of a CABAS® middle school for the academic year 2002/03.

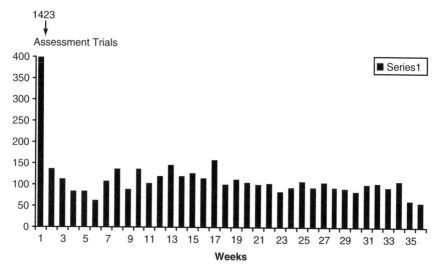

FIGURE 2
Weekly mean numbers of learn units to criteria at a CABAS®
middle school for the academic year 2002/03.

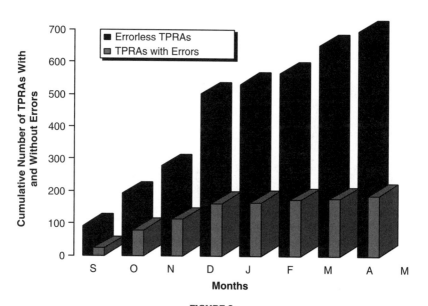

FIGURE 3
The cumulative numbers of supervisors' observations of teachers' instructional
sessions with and without errors at a CABAS® middle school for the 2002/03
academic year. The measure includes both inter-observer agreement for
students' responses and accuracy of teacher presentation of learn units
(learn units predict student outcomes).

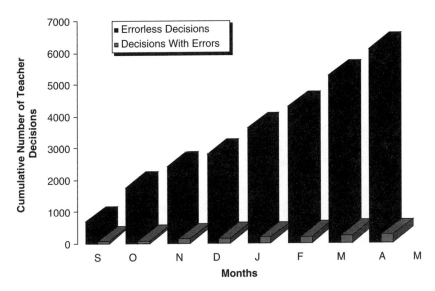

FIGURE 4

The weekly cumulative numbers of accurate and inaccurate strategic and tactical decisions made by teachers at a CABAS® middle school for the 2002/03 academic year. Accurate decisions predict student learning in the research.

subsequent target repertoires to be taught. Thus, students are categorized according to their repertoires of verbal behavior for instructional purposes rather than developmental and disability categories. Students fall into broad categories of pre-listener, speaker, speaker/listener, reader, writer, and writer as own reader (self-editor). Within the reader and writer categories, students are subdivided according to whether they are verbally governed (*i.e.*, they can respond accurately to written or spoken verbal behavior) and whether they have repertoires that allow them to verbally direct others (vocally or in written form).

Curricular goals also must be arranged according to national and state curricular standards and empirically validated standards. These standards act as the community's consolidated goals and are surprisingly common across several countries (New York State Standards of Education, K–6, 1998; Department of Educational Excellent, 1998). These in turn must be converted into verbally functional repertoires, rather than structural categories. Structural categories are currently used to characterize standards, but standards that consist of the structure of the knowledge do not tell us how to use that knowledge to teach and measure the presence or absence of the goal in a student's repertoire. Structural goals need to be converted to statements of how the students use the standards or repertoires in order for the goals to be true repertoires of behaving including thinking as behaving. In our school curricula, we have converted the structural standards to functional standards. Thus, our instruction and measurement of the attainment of standards are measures of a student's use of knowledge. When a student uses the knowledge reliably, such that it works for the student, we refer to this as a repertoire. For example, teaching a student to write sentences that are grammatically correct is a structural goal, while teaching a student to write such that the student's writing affects the behavior of a reader is a functional goal.

Once the appropriate places in the curricula are located for each child, the instruction proceeds along a continuum driven by the individual progress of the student. The progress of the children is apparent in visual displays that serve as the basis for deciding the tactics that are needed by the children at any given stage in their education. We have identified over 200 tactics in the literature that may be fitted to the instructional needs of the child (see Chapters 4 to 6 in Greer, 2002). What is relatively new is that the process of determining when and what tactics are needed has itself become a strategic science. The evidence for the effectiveness of this strategic science of instruction has accrued quickly. We now know that, when teachers have these analytic repertoires, the progress of students is significantly enhanced (Keohane, 1997; Nuzzola-Gomez, 2002). Moreover, we can teach new professionals to use these sophisticated and strategic instructional repertoires rapidly via a systems-wide behavior analysis approach (O'Brian, 2001). A key component of developing expertise in teaching as a science includes teaching professionals to use the learn unit context and a research-based protocol or decision tree, as shown in Figs. 5 and 6. Figure 5 shows the learn unit context for both the teacher and the student, and Fig. 6 shows the decision process related to strategic and tactical analysis used by our teachers and how the decisions are measured by our supervisors. This measure ensures that students make optimal progress because their instruction includes the tactics that work for them.

Teachers are the key. When teaching is an art, a good teacher is an accident. When teaching is a science, good teaching can be replicated by many professionals in a reliable fashion (Greer, 1994a, 2002). Our research program, data from the existing body of applied behavior analysis, and 22 years of application of teaching as a strategic science to teach the whole child in our demonstration schools clearly show that the advancement of teachers in the components of what we term *teaching as a strategic science* determines the rate of student progress (Greer, 1994b). Thus far, we have identified three categories or repertoires of teaching that predict student progress: (1) the vocabulary of the science or *verbal behavior about the science*, (2) classroom practice or *contingency-shaped repertoires of instruction*, and (3) analytic decisions or *verbally mediated repertoires* for identifying and solving instructional problems. Within these three repertoires, there is a progression from basic to advanced performance. Teachers with advanced repertoires in all three categories produce better outcomes with their students than those who have beginning skills, and those with beginning skills produce better outcomes then teachers who have no repertoires in the science

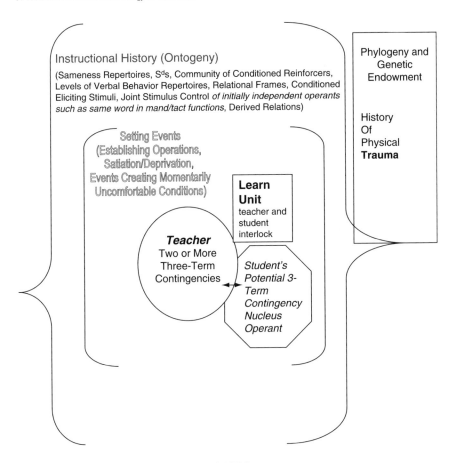

FIGURE 5

The learn unit and its context, including the student's potential operant,
the teacher's operants, the teacher–student interlocking operants
(or learn units), the setting events or immediate context,
instructional history, and the phylogenic history.

and technology of teaching (Greer, 2002; Greer & Hogin-McDonough, 1999;
Greer et al., 2002; Ingham & Greer, 1992; Keohane, 1997; Lamm & Greer, 1991;
Nuzzola-Gomez, 2002). These repertoires are the ones that have made the
difference for those children who suffer native deficits and provide the means
to overcome learning opportunity deficits for the children who are left behind
when teaching is an art!

Teachers need the vocabulary or verbal behavior of the science to characterize or describe teacher and student behaviors and curricula scientifically.
Instructional operations and student performance that are precisely identified

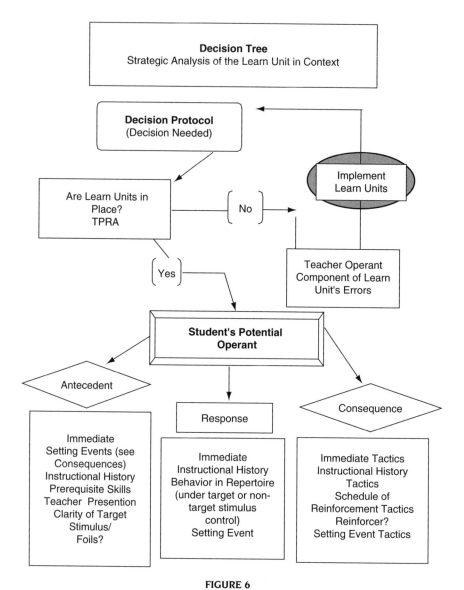

FIGURE 6

The decision protocol involving the learn unit context as it is used by the
teacher and measured by supervisors.

scientifically lead to better outcomes for students than when teachers use non-
scientific terms (Nuzzola-Gomez, 2002). When teachers can accurately describe scientifically what is happening, can verbally mediate or analyze instruction, and can teach in ways that the science has identified as effective,

students learn from four to seven times more than when the teachers do not do so (Greer et al., 2002; Selinske, Greer, Lodhi, 1991; Lamm and Greer, 1991). These teaching practices are contingency shaped when they are automatic, rapid, and errorless (Ingham and Greer, 1992).

One of the key ways we teach and monitor these practices is through measurement of instructional practices, or learn units (see Fig. 5 for a diagram of the learn unit in context). The presence of learn units predicts student learning, and their absence predicts delays in progress or the lack of progress (Greer & Hogin-McDonough, 1999). Again, learn units are the instructional units that characterize effective student and teacher interaction and are basic measures of effective teaching. The use of learn units also predicts better outcomes when instruction is automated, as in the case of computerized instruction (see Emurian, Hu, Wang, Durham, 2000, for research on the learn unit in computerized instruction). Learn units specify what, when, and how the teacher or an automated instructional device is to interact with the student.

When visual displays show that the student is not progressing in an optimum fashion, teachers and their mentors draw on verbally mediated repertoires using a scientific decision tree that leads to decisions about the sources of a given learning or instructional problem (Fig. 6). Strategic decisions made by teachers then occasion the determination of which of the existing 200-plus tactics from the research literature are likely to solve the learning plateau (see Chapters 5 and 6 in Greer, 2002, for a list of those tactics derived from behavior analysis). Teachers who are well trained in strategic decision-making produce better student outcomes than those who are not (Greer, 2002; Keohane, 1997). Teachers and their supervisors learn to determine whether the problem is in: (1) the students' instructional histories, (2) the current motivation conditions, (3) teacher behaviors, (4) instructional history, (5) faulty curricula, or (6) some phylogenic or physiological conditions (*e.g.*, hearing impairment, poor vision). We have subjected each of these instructional repertoires to experimental tests devoted to testing the relationship of teacher repertoires or components of teaching by automated means to student outcomes, and in each case we have found functional relationships between these teaching practices and student learning. Also, we have found that we can teach teachers to accurately use these repertoires, using instructional procedures that are themselves experi-mentally tested (Greer, 1994a,b, 1997a, 2002).

We have replicated the training of teachers who are strategic scientists of instruction in several schools in this country, as well as in Ireland, Italy, and England (Greer et al., 2002; Lamm & Greer, 1991). For example, in 4 years a CABAS® (Comprehensive Application of Behavior Analysis to Schooling; see discussion below) pilot project in Ireland resulted in the country moving from having no trained behavior analysts and no applied behavior analysis schools to having three schools (in Cork, Dublin, and Drogheda) with over 80 trained staff, over 70% of whom have achieved CABAS board certification at the level of at least one teacher rank and several who have achieved Master Teacher and

Assistant or Associate Behavior Analyst ranks. We have taught teachers to function as strategic scientists of instruction as part of a university graduate curriculum that involves both daily instruction in demonstration schools and university courses. We have also taught teachers to perform as sophisticated scientists of instruction directly in our schools without instruction in the university (O'Brian, 2001). The repertoires learned by the teachers are the same, although those who are in graduate programs in teaching as behavior analysts proceed at a significantly faster pace in acquiring them than those we have trained in the school setting only. It is important to note that, in our graduate program, the teacher trainees spend the day in our model schools and the evenings in graduate classes tied to practices in the schools.

Parents are also key performers in our system of educating students; indeed, parents are the most important teachers of children (Hart & Risley, 1996). In our demonstration schools, which use teaching as a science for all instruction, we provide parents with basic and key instructional repertoires to teach and manage their children using *positive and non-coercive procedures derived from the science* (Latham, 1996). Parents learn to use learn units to teach their children new skills and to use language effectively, to teach their children to behave effectively in the home and community, to interact with their children in ways that lead to better outcomes for the children, and to develop positive home environments. Typically, we teach parents very basic vocabularies and contingency-shaped repertoires. They learn how to interact in their homes and communities across a wide of range of learning opportunities to maximize learning opportunities for their children and to extend instruction from school to home and occasionally from home to school (Greer, 1997a). Individuals who are not familiar with our science often think that schools like those we describe are cold and unfeeling. In fact, the opposite is the case. Schools based on positive reinforcement and adequate individualized instructions are happy and productive community centers (it is not unusual for our preschoolers to cry when it is time to go home).

The strategic science we have described is not a technology that can be learned in a workshop or even a series of workshops. Rather, the repertoires needed by teachers are based on a science and must be taught using the same principles and techniques used to teach the children and much of what teachers learn must be taught *in situ*—in the classrooms in which they are used. A science consists of a verbal community that has a specialized vocabulary and special meanings that are distinct from non-scientific approaches. True scientific terms are not jargon; rather, scientific terms specify the world in ways that can be characterized as *uncommonly good sense*. Attempting to describe scientific phenomena in the common-sense terminology of the layperson is certainly useful for the popular reporter of science but will not do for practitioners. Reinforcement is not the same as reward, and precision is needed in the analysis of learning and instruction, as it would be in any science. Moreover, those scientific verbal terms must correspond with instructional practices (*i.e.*, doing and saying must correspond). We have researched instructional procedures to teach professional repertoires over the last 22 years, and we have researched ways to ensure the maintenance of quality instruction on a daily basis across many years. The findings of this body of research have led to the system that we describe next.

CABAS®: A SYSTEMS TECHNOLOGY OF SCHOOLING AND A STRATEGIC SCIENCE OF PEDAGOGY

The conversion of the science of the behavior of the individual to a technology of education is not currently a process of simply packaging what we know into a delivery system that requires no scientific repertoires on the part of teachers. The technology consists of at least 200 research-based *tactics*—tactics that are useful for different situations (Greer, 2002). Thus, tactics such as the following are all components of teaching as a strategic science: Echoic to Mand Training, Programmed Instruction, Picture Exchanges, Simultaneous Prompts, Classwide Tutoring, and Trained Tutoring, Verbally Governing Scripts, Personalized Instruction, Fast Rate Training, Peer Mediation, Self-Monitoring, Contingency Contracts, Learn Unit Presentations, General Case or Multiple Exemplar Training, Speaker or Writer Immersion, Increased Learn Units To Decrease Aberrant Behavior, Conversational Units, Interruptions of Behavior Chains, Brief Motivational Procedures, Captured or Incidental Learn Units. These are not separate or independent methods; rather, they are individual tactics that are useful under different instructional circumstances. Teachers need to analyze learning problems using the verbal behavior of the science and select a potentially successful tactic from the research for the problem at hand using a scientific decision tree. The process of fitting needed tactics to presenting problems cannot be relegated to a simplistic process that can be taught in one or, indeed, a series of workshops. The process is a complex and strategic science. Thus, systemic effective education is not a matter of making the procedures user-friendly to non-scientific teachers but rather an approach that requires the very reform of educational practice if we are truly to leave no child behind.

The identification of scientifically based repertoires for teachers and the use of scientifically based repertoires to teach teachers is a major step in an educational science and technology; however, simply identifying those repertoires scientifically is not enough. How does one produce a school in which teachers and parents learn the repertoires? How does one monitor, improve, and maintain instruction on a day-to-day basis? How does one deliver a science and technology of education that requires hard work and sophisticated repertoires? To do this, one needs a systems approach. The system needs to be self-correcting and self-maintaining and it needs to be a science and technology itself. Over the last 20 years, several of us have been engaged in developing a database and demonstrations of a systems science of schooling. The particular system that we have developed is called the Comprehensive Application of Behavior Analysis to Schooling, or CABAS®.

In our system, behavior analysis is applied strategically to all of the components of schooling that we have identified to date (Greer, 1992, 1994b, 1997a). They include the roles of students, teachers, parents, supervisors or teacher mentors, administrators, the university training program, and the organization as a whole (see Fig. 5). We draw on the existing 65 years of basic and applied research in behavior analysis and our own systems behavior analysis (Greer, 1997b; Skinner, 1938; Sulzer-Azaroff et al., 1988). Research drives behavior management, instruction, and curriculum for the students and the training and monitoring of teachers, parents, supervisors, and the overall system performance (Greer, McCorkle, Williams, 1989). Research in behavior analysis provides tactics and basic principles for organizational management, teacher training, supervisor training, administrative training, and parent education (Cooper, Heron, Heward, 1987). Measurement of the performance of all components results in data on all of the components and provides a systems-wide summary (Greer, 1994a). These data direct the use of other behavioral tactics to fix or maintain performance at the teacher, supervisor, parent, or system levels. The CABAS® system is outlined briefly in Fig. 7.

The training of teachers requires a comprehensive and ongoing curriculum for teaching the three repertoires we have described. Behavioral tactics from a Personalized System of Instruction (Selinske et al., 1991; Keller, 1968) are used to organize the curriculum and to teach the research-derived repertoires to a criterion-referenced standard of quality. Classroom or contingency-shaped performance is taught in the classroom using a research-based observation protocol called the Teacher Performance Rate/Accuracy Protocol (Greer et al., 1989; Ingham & Greer, 1992). Verbally mediated repertoires or analytic repertoires are taught using the Tactic Decision Protocol together with the learn unit context analysis (Keohane, 1997) (see Figs. 3, 4, and 6). Verbal behavior about the science is also taught to teachers using supervisor learn units. Teachers' use of precise scientific vocabularies is directly tied to student progress (Nuzzola-Gomez, 2002).

Teacher and parent mentors, who are behavior analytic supervisors and professors, are professionals who have acquired advanced repertoires not only in teaching students but also in teaching teachers and parents. They, too, have a curriculum that provides continuous training and advancement in teaching and supervision as a strategic science. This education team continually provides new research that is immediately disseminated across all the schools before the research reaches the publication stage.

All of the data on students and teachers as well as school-wide performance are graphed on a continuous basis and used to determine needed school-wide interventions as well as a means of improving and maintaining daily

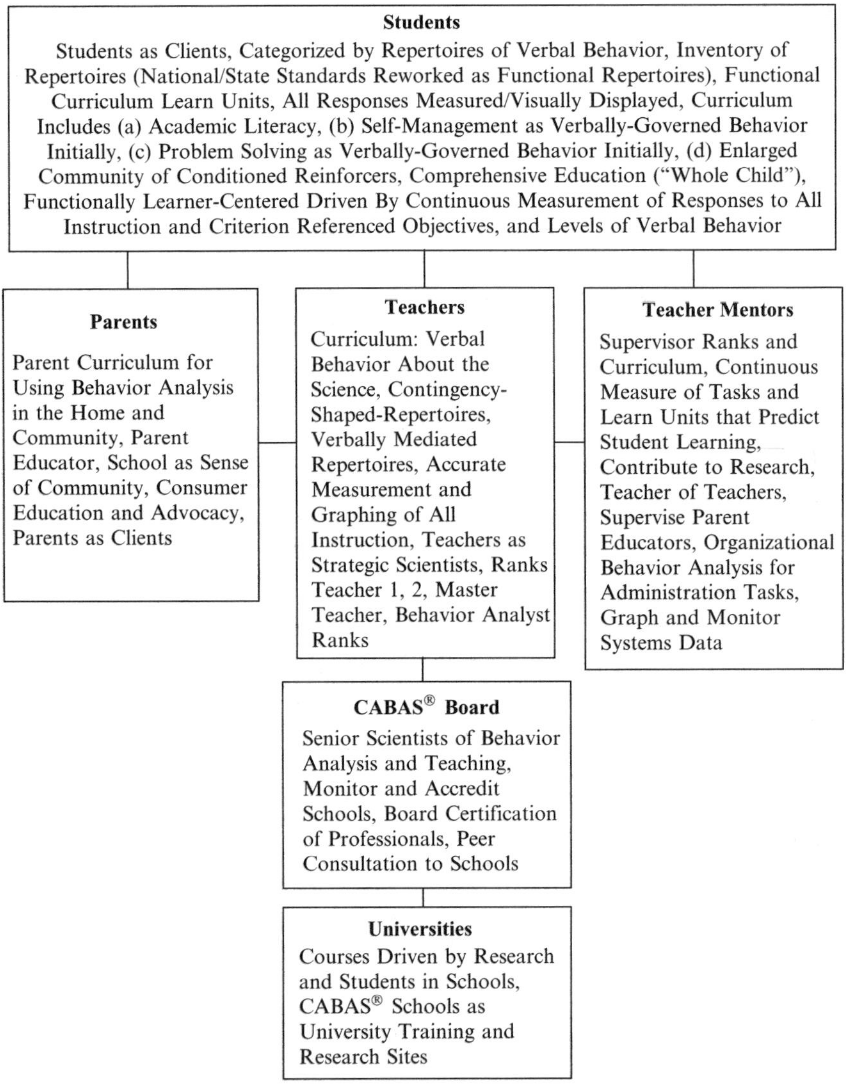

Students

Students as Clients, Categorized by Repertoires of Verbal Behavior, Inventory of Repertoires (National/State Standards Reworked as Functional Repertoires), Functional Curriculum Learn Units, All Responses Measured/Visually Displayed, Curriculum Includes (a) Academic Literacy, (b) Self-Management as Verbally-Governed Behavior Initially, (c) Problem Solving as Verbally-Governed Behavior Initially, (d) Enlarged Community of Conditioned Reinforcers, Comprehensive Education ("Whole Child"), Functionally Learner-Centered Driven By Continuous Measurement of Responses to All Instruction and Criterion Referenced Objectives, and Levels of Verbal Behavior

Parents

Parent Curriculum for Using Behavior Analysis in the Home and Community, Parent Educator, School as Sense of Community, Consumer Education and Advocacy, Parents as Clients

Teachers

Curriculum: Verbal Behavior About the Science, Contingency-Shaped-Repertoires, Verbally Mediated Repertoires, Accurate Measurement and Graphing of All Instruction, Teachers as Strategic Scientists, Ranks Teacher 1, 2, Master Teacher, Behavior Analyst Ranks

Teacher Mentors

Supervisor Ranks and Curriculum, Continuous Measure of Tasks and Learn Units that Predict Student Learning, Contribute to Research, Teacher of Teachers, Supervise Parent Educators, Organizational Behavior Analysis for Administration Tasks, Graph and Monitor Systems Data

CABAS® Board

Senior Scientists of Behavior Analysis and Teaching, Monitor and Accredit Schools, Board Certification of Professionals, Peer Consultation to Schools

Universities

Courses Driven by Research and Students in Schools, CABAS® Schools as University Training and Research Sites

FIGURE 7

The organizational flow chart of the CABAS® system, which provides a learner-driven science of pedagogy and schooling.

performance (Greer, 1997a). This systems-wide measurement provides up-to-the-minute information on where each student is (learn units received, cumulative objectives, achievement of repertoires in the inventory), where each teacher is (learn units taught, cumulative objectives, repertoires mastered by the teachers' students, repertoires of the science mastered by the teacher), where each supervisor is (learn units, objectives, and repertoires achieved across the school; supervisor learn units with teachers, rate of administrative tasks, progress in the curriculum), and where the parent is (learn units, object- ives, and repertoires taught to children; parent repertoires mastered). Learn units and objectives are converted into costs and used for cost–benefit analyses for boards of education and the community (see Greer, 1994b, for a cost comparison). For example, a comparison of the costs per learn unit and costs per instructional goal between a CABAS® school and a similar school showed that in the CABAS® schools the cost per learn unit was about 60 cents and the cost of an objective was about $30, while in the comparison school the cost per learn unit was well over $60; we are unable to estimate costs per objectives for the comparison school because it had no reliable measures of the objectives that the children achieved in that school (Greer, 1994b).

University programs in our system design and modify courses based on the changes in the science of behavior and the science of schooling. They are driven by the needs of students in the schools and the graduate students who train in them and subsequently lead to the application of teaching as a strategic science.

External and internal political issues create problems from time to time with results that are not unlike the damage that occurs when viruses invade software systems. These invasions call for additional system design and interventions that counteract the viruses, such as the development of CABAS® accreditation of schools and board certification of professional expertise. Also, the acquisi- tion of an intellectual trademark for CABAS® as a means of controlling quality has made possible another level of checks to be in place to deter potential invasions. While we encourage all educators to use the components of the model to improve their instruction, we reserve the name CABAS® for those programs and individuals trained to meet the standards that we have set. These standards take the form of criterion-referenced board certification of over six levels of expertise. These and other developments accrued as a result of attacks on the integrity of the model. They have improved the system. Other problems will occur from time to time, and they too will require new system designs.

A recent book describes the strategic science of teaching and a behavioral system to develop and maintain the system (Greer, 2002). The book details strategies and tactics of the science and brings together the research studies and demonstration efforts that have gone into the development of a systems- wide approach to teaching as a science. Tutorial handbooks and related inventories of repertoires will follow to describe in detail each of the protocols and systems that we have developed. As these are disseminated and improved by those who use them, we can hope for better educational outcomes. A real science and technology of education promises solutions to the problems that beset education and society. The basic science and technology are here now; it remains to use our science to spread the word to consumers. Selinske et al. (1991) showed that students who received CABAS® learned four to seven times more (as measured by correct responses and instructional objectives) than teaching as usual, and that was with a much less sophisticated science than we now have. An independent study of a CABAS® classroom for students with autism showed that in a 4-month time period, the CABAS® children gained on average 11 months of learning, and the comparison classes gained less than 2 months (Greer, 1997a, b).

CONCLUSION

CABAS® has been implemented in several demonstration or professional training schools in the USA, Ireland, and England. These schools or centers of excellence have worked for children with autism, conduct disorders, learning disabilities, developmental disabilities, hearing impairments, and blind and visual impairments. We currently have a middle-school model for students from impoverished communities and failing school systems. These students are the ones who were left behind, but even at that late date in their schooling we have made significant gains (Figs. 1 and 2). Several hundred professionals have been trained to various levels of expertise in the science, including numerous graduate students who have received their doctorates and masters in teaching and supervision as a strategic science. We have shown that a strategic science of teaching and schooling exists, and that it can be developed and maintained in the real world, and we have shown how to do it using a research-based approach. We have revised schooling around what the science tells us works and the needs of individual students. Our CABAS® system schools are also centers of inquiry for all involved in the education process. Currently, the system is complex and requires a sophisticated training system, but we are getting better at creating sophisticated professionals much faster, and our expertise about what those professionals need to know grows. We are sure our system and other systems will become more effective as research is disseminated and more research accrues. Following the lead of B. F. Skinner, we have researched and demonstrated how a system can work and the basic processes that can be used to develop better systems—a real science and technology of teaching. Yes, we can have a school system that truly leaves no child behind; however, these schools will need to be based on systems-wide science and technology of education. This will require a paradigm shift in education, but surely it is as doable as mapping human genes—a comparable effort in education would make the expression "no child left behind" more than a platitude.

References

Bushell, Jr., D. & Baer, D. M. (1994). Measurably superior instruction means close continual contact with the relevant outcome data. Revolutionary! In Gardener III, R., Sainato, D. M., Cooper, J. O., Heron. T. E., Heward, W., Eschelman, J. W., & Grossi, T. A. (Eds.), *Behavior analysis in education: Focus on measurably superior instruction*. Pacific Grove, CA: Brooks/Cole.

Cooper, J. O., Heron, T. E., & Heward, W. L. (1987). *Applied behavior analysis*. Columbus, OH: Merrill.

Department of Educational Excellence (1998). *Standards of excellence for English schools*. London: Department of Educational Excellence.

Donoghue, V., The Minister for Education and Science and the Irish Attorney General, No. 602p/2000, The High Court, March 2, 2001.

Emurian, H. H., Hu, X., Wang, J., & Durham, D. (2000). Learning JAVA: A programmed instruction approach using applets. *Computers in Human Behavior*, 16, 395–422.

Greenwood, C. R., Hart, B., Walker, D. I., & Risley, T. (1994). The opportunity to respond and academic performance revisited: A behavioral theory of developmental retardation. In Gardener III, R., Sainato, D. M., Cooper, J. O., Heron. T. E., Heward, W., Eschelman, J. W., and Grossi, T. A. (Eds.), *Behavior analysis in education: Focus on measurably superior instruction*. Pacific Grove, CA: Brooks/Cole.

Greer, R. D. (1991). The teacher as strategic scientist: A solution to our educational crisis? *Behavior and Social Issues*, 1, 25–41.

Greer, R. D. (1992). The education crisis: Issues, perspectives, and solutions. *Journal of Applied Behavior Analysis Monograph*, 25 (1 and 2), 1–89.

Greer, R. D. (1994a). A systems analysis of the behaviors of schooling. *Journal of Behavioral Education*, 4, 255–264.

Greer, R. D. (1994b). The measure of a teacher. In Gardener III, R., Sainato, D. M., Cooper, J. O., Heron. T. E., Heward, W., Eschelman, J. W., & Grossi, T. A. (Eds.), *Behavior analysis in education: Focus on measurably superior instruction*. Pacific Grove, CA: Brooks/Cole.

Greer, R. D. (1997a). The crisis in education: Contributing factors and solutions. Thyer, B. & Mattaini, R. (Eds.), *Problems in society and solutions from the science of behavior*. Washington, D.C.: American Psychological Association.

Greer, R. D. (1997b). Acting to save our schools (1984–1994). In Cautela, J. & Ishaq, W. (Eds.), *The science of behavior and the human condition*. New York: Praeger.

Greer, R. D. (2002). *Designing teaching strategies: A behavioral systems approach*. New York: Academic Press.

Greer, R. D. & Hogin-McDonough, S. (1999). Is the learn unit the fundamental measure of pedagogy? *The Behavior Analyst*, 20, 5–16.

Greer, R. D., McCorkle. N. P., & Williams, G. (1989). A sustained analysis of the behaviors of schooling. *Behavioral Residential Treatment*, 4, 113–141.

Greer, R. D., Phelan, C. S., & Sales, C. (1993). *A costs–benefits analysis of a graduate course*. Paper presented at the International Conference of the Association for Behavior Analysis, Chicago, IL.

Greer, R. D., Keohane, D., & Healy, O. (2002). Quality and CABAS. *The Behavior Analyst Today*, 3(2) (http://behavior-analyst-online.org).

Hart, B. & Risley, T. (1996). *Meaningful differences in the everyday life of america's children*. New York: Paul Brookes.

Ingham, P. & Greer, R. D. (1992). Changes in student and teacher responses in observed and generalized settings as a function of supervisor observations. *Journal of Applied Behavior Analysis*, 25, 153–164.

Keller, F. S. (1968). "Goodbye teacher . . ." *Journal of Applied Behavior Analysis*, 1, 79–90.

Keller, F. S. (1978). Instructional technology and educational reform: 1977. *The Behavior Analyst*, 1, 48–53.

Keohane, D. (1997). A functional relationship between teachers' use of scientific rule governed strategies and student learning, Ph.D. dissertation, Columbia University, 1990, *Dissertation Abstracts International*, 57.

Lamm, N. & Greer, R. D. (1991). A systematic replication of CABAS in Italy. *Journal of Behavioral Education*, 1, 427–444.

Latham, G. I. (1996). *The power of positive parenting*. North Logan: P&T, Inc.

New York State Department of Education (1998). *Educational Standards: K–12*. Albany, NY: New York State Department of Education.

New York State Department of Health (1999). *Clinical practitioner guideline report of recommendations: Autism and pervasive developmental disorder, assessment and intervention for young children* (Publ. No. 4215). Albany, NY. New York State Department of Health (http://www.health.state.ny.us/nysdoh/eip/index.html).

Nuzzola-Gomez, R. (2002). The effects of direct and observed supervisor learn units on the scientific tacts and instructional strategies of teachers, unpublished Ph.D. dissertation. New York: Columbia University.

O'Brian, C. (2001). Pilot project: A hope for children with autism. *The Irish Examiner*, July 7, p. 7.

Selinske, J., Greer, R. D., & Lodhi, S. (1991). A functional analysis of the comprehensive application of behavior analysis to schooling. *Journal of Applied Behavior Analysis*, 13, 645–654.

Skinner, B. F. (1938). *The behavior of organisms*. Cambridge, MA: B. F. Skinner Foundation.

Skinner, B. F. (1968). *The technology of teaching*. New York: Appleton-Century-Crofts.

Sulzer-Azaroff, B, Drabman, R. M., Greer, R. D., Hall, R. V., Iwata, B. A., & O'Leary, S. G. (1988). Behavior analysis in education [reprint]. *Journal of Applied Behavior Analysis*, Lawrence, KS: Society for the Experimental Analysis of Behavior.

U.S. Surgeon General's Report. (2001). *Mental disorders in children and adolescents* (http://www.surgeon-general.gov/library/mentalhealth/chapter3/sec.6html#autism).

Whitehead, A. E. (1929). *The aims of education*. New York: Mentor Philosophy Library.

Precision Teaching

Precision Teaching: Foundations and Classroom Applications

CHARLES MERBITZ
Illinois Institute of Technology

DOREEN VIEITEZ
Joliet Junior College

NANCY HANSEN MERBITZ
Private Practice

HENRY S. PENNYPACKER
MammaCare

"The learner is always right."

WHY PRECISION TEACHING?

A public school implements a limited Precision Teaching (PT) program, and dramatically raises the standardized test scores of its elementary and middle school students, such that the majority of them eventually qualify for advanced placement courses. Private PT schools and learning centers reliably raise student performance by an entire grade level in 20 hours or less of instruction (Barrett, 2002). A fourth grader with school phobia and poor attendance comes to a PT learning center twice a week, quickly improves reading and math performance, and begins attending school with enthusiasm. A middle-aged man of Mexican-American heritage who cannot get a driver's license because he cannot read receives 1 hour per week of instruction with PT, and within 2 months has finished grade-I-level materials; he begins planning the jobs he can apply for once he reads well enough to take the driver's exam. Two dedicated and enterprising PT teachers begin working with students with autism and their parents, and within a year they are so swamped with requests that they initiate a nationwide consulting and training service. Parents report that children who were written off are learning to speak, converse, and read. A private school accepts students with diagnoses of learning disability who are behind academically and failing, and within 2 years most improve enough to return to general education classes in public schools, get good grades, and keep up with their peers.

Proponents of every teaching approach provide stories and testimonials, and it is the individual success stories that move our hearts and pique our interest as educators. What each of us hopes to find as we learn about yet another approach is that its benefits can be repeatedly demonstrated across a variety of learners and settings, that the benefits are large and lasting, and that it can be implemented in our setting. It is hoped that, in this chapter, those who are interested in Precision Teaching will find enough supporting information to spur them to read further, ask questions of PT teachers, try the methods, and see results for themselves. Please note that our goal here is not to teach PT, but to introduce PT and provide sufficient information for readers to decide if they wish to invest the time it takes to learn PT skills. The next PT chapter provides additional information, references, and examples.

The motto of Precision Teachers—"The learner is always right"—succinctly expresses both its mode of operation and its behavioral heritage. More implications of this aphorism are spelled out below, but underlying all of them is the concept that it is what the learner *does* that guides and informs the teacher. The founder of PT, Ogden Lindsley, discusses PT as "a system of strategies and their tactics for the self-monitoring of learning" (G. Hrga, personal communication, 1997). Rather than a curriculum, method of, or approach to classroom instruction, PT is a measurement and decision-support system, a way for teachers to analyze and understand their effects on students. Use of this system of self-knowledge also has generated a growing set of techniques with known outcomes, some of which we outline in the two chapters in this section.

Precision Teaching is an astonishingly powerful technology. In one of its early implementations in the late 1970s at Sacajawea School in Great Falls, MT, students in lower grades used PT in addition to their standard curricula for 15 to 30 minutes each day. Their scores rose from average to the top of the Iowa Test of Basic Skills, while the rest of the district remained average. This was in spite of the fact that special education students at Sacajawea were tested along with general education students, while special education students in the rest of the district were excused. By the end of the 4-year project, the Sacajawea students were so skilled that they overwhelmed the middle and high school advanced placement classes, as the schools were not organized for classes in which the average student performed at the advanced placement level (McManus, 2003; see also Beck & Clement, 1991). These gains were made using curriculum materials developed by the teachers. Now, with the benefit of several decades of curriculum and procedure testing and development, even greater gains are routinely made. PT centers can confidently promise to increase a student's performance by an entire grade level in 20 hours of instruction, and many adult learners can achieve such gains in fewer than 10 hours (Barrett, 2002).

THE CHART

The hallmark of PT is the blue, 140-calendar-day Chart, which was invented by Ogden R. Lindsley in the 1960s and subsequently refined by him and his students. This Chart provides a uniquely unbiased and helpful way to visualize the history and the future of a person's behavior over time. The Precision Teacher reads the Chart to see how the learner has responded to past events, so that the instructional conditions that were associated with more progress can be provided again, and conditions associated with less progress can be avoided. Thus, the motto reminds us that, whatever the learner's performance in the past, it is our responsibility to provide the instruction under which that learner will make progress in the future. The daily Chart worked so well that a new set of Charts was developed, ranging from minutes (session Charts) to days, weeks, months, and years, and many types of events have been plotted in addition to those of interest in classrooms.

The process of PT begins with determining where each learner is, and the learning outcomes are measured primarily in terms of progress from this baseline to true mastery. The motto reminds us to look for things we can influence to facilitate progress and not to blame the learner or focus too long on diagnoses and factors that cannot be changed (such as socioeconomic status or parent's educational level). It also reminds us when to *stop* teaching; PT offers a truly effective way to know when the learner has mastered something (has it right), and we can move on. It reminds us that learning is personal: While we cannot forget the whole class, if we teach each individual, we will teach the class (and the reverse is not true). PT allows each child to practice what is needed and only what is needed, thus providing functional individualization. The motto reminds us that our goal is empowerment of the learner through honest evaluation and feedback about performance, and that the learner becomes truly engaged through this process. Finally, it reminds us that whenever a learner does something that is contrary to our theories of education or learning, it is the theory that should be ignored, not the learner. Thus, PT is the quintessential form of data-driven decision making (Cromley & Merbitz, 1999; van der Ploeg & Merbitz, 1998).

EXAMPLE OF PRECISION TEACHING
IMPLEMENTATION

As we noted earlier, one constant element of PT is the display of learner performance frequencies on a standard Chart to monitor improvement. In most cases, it is best and most empowering to have learners count, time, and chart their own performances. Here are few examples of things measured in schools: reading words or sentences correctly and incorrectly, generating positive adjectives that describe themselves, making factual or inferential statements about concepts from a passage, saying the steps they use in solving complex problems, or answering math problems orally or in writing. Selection of what is measured depends on the goals of the learner, but it must be countable and repeatable. In academic activities, analyzing learn units (see Chapter 3; Greer, 1999) that occur in current instruction is a good place to start.

Our first figure (Fig. 1) shows data from Lynn, a graduate student in an introductory course on special education. Lynn charted her SAFMEDS performance, a PT strategy for learning concepts and facts that Lindsley developed (Graf, 1994). SAFMEDS is an acronym for *Say All Fast a Minute Every Day Shuffled*. SAFMEDS cards resemble flash cards. Each card has a visual prompt on one side, such as a definition or problem, and the desired response on the other side, such as a term or answer.

In this course, the students were given a deck of 180 cards with special education definitions on the front side and terms on the back. They were instructed to study the definitions and terms each day (*i.e.*, look at the definitions on the front of the cards and say the terms on the backs of the cards before turning them over). Next, they conducted one-minute timings, going through as many cards as they could and saying the answers out loud, then separating correct and incorrect responses in different piles and counting their correct and incorrect responses. Finally, they charted their timed responses (including corrects and errors) and shuffled the cards for the next timing. In timings conducted in class, the goal was to answer correctly at least 30 SAFMEDS per minute from a shuffled deck. Note that different classes use different SAFMEDS criteria, and the frequency also depends on the length of the stimulus to be read (*i.e.*, briefer stimuli and answers are generally quicker when going through a SAFMEDS deck).

READ A CHART

Let us now review Lynn's Chart in detail (see Fig. 1). What you see is a computer-generated version (http://people.ku.edu/~borns/) of Lynn's Chart. While some elements of the original paper Chart were removed to maintain clarity during

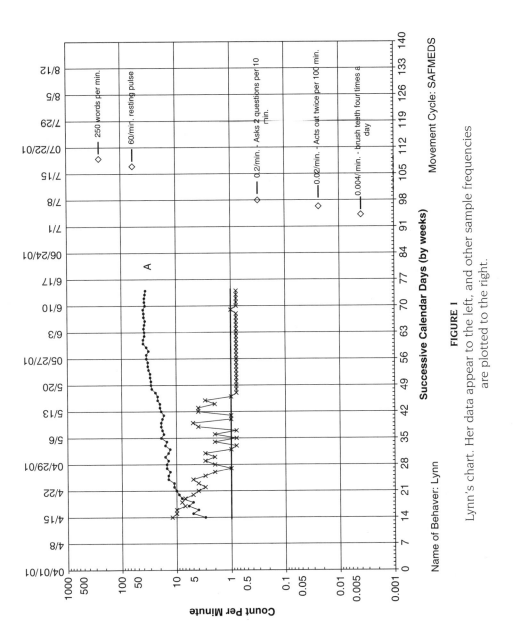

FIGURE 1

Lynn's chart. Her data appear to the left, and other sample frequencies are plotted to the right.

printing, like any Chart this one tells us the scientific story of who was doing what when and what happened. Lynn's data are on the left half of this Chart. Even before we orient you to the features of the Chart, it is easy to see the compelling story told by Lynn's data. The line of dots going up and to the right show her number of correct answers getting higher over 9 weeks. The X's show her errors decreasing and finally dropping to virtually none. The uppercase A indicates the level and target date of her goal frequency, which she exceeded early.

Now, let us discuss the standard features of this Chart. The units of time on the horizontal (x) axis are successive calendar days. The bold vertical lines are Sunday lines, so the chart begins on a Sunday and ends on a Sunday, for a total of 140 days. Each fourth Sunday is dated. Day lines are represented as vertical lines on paper Charts and can be seen as tic marks in our figures. This student began her timings on 15 April 2001. Note that this is a typical PT convention; this style of using day, month, and year provides clear date communication to all readers. Note also the date of the first Sunday; most North American schools use the same Sundays in Fall and January to synchronize their Charts, but Lynn's quarter started later, so all of the Charts in her class started on 1 April 2001. These conventions facilitate fast and accurate interpretation by making it easy to see right away when the work took place relative to the current date, what absences or other events occurred, and so forth.

CHART FEATURES

The unique features of the Chart are important because they allow much faster, more accurate, and easier communication among chart readers (skilled teachers read 6 to 12 Charts per minute). Imagine a group of third-grade teachers gathered to talk about how their students are doing with multiplication tables, and all of the teachers in the room have transparencies of Charts from their students. Each teacher can show Charts, and all can see the rate of progress for the groups and the individuals. So, rather than spending time interpreting individually constructed graphs that have various scales for both time units and behavior, the teachers' time can be better spent analyzing data to make appropriate instructional decisions and more time is available to plan what to do next. Thus, the student's behavior can continuously guide educational decisions.

What features of the Chart allow for this quick and reliable interpretation of learners' progress? Looking at Fig. 1, we see that the vertical (y) axis has horizontal lines for frequency, or count per minute. This axis is one of the key features of the Chart. It is a multiply (or logarithmic) scale including six cycles; for example, one of the cycles encompasses frequencies from 1 to 10, another from 100 to 1000, and so forth. (The horizontal (x) axis is not logarithmic, thus the Chart is *semi-logarithmic*). Note that within each cycle on the vertical axis the lines become more closely spaced from the beginning to the end of that cycle. This seemingly esoteric convention of the Chart is in reality a critical feature that enhances its everyday utility. It confers at least three major advantages over the conventional "square" (non-log) graph paper commonly used: (1) prediction, (2) relative emphasis, and (3) wide-range display.

PREDICTION

Because most behavior changes, including academic learning, are proportional, a traditional square graph of behavioral change produces a curved line as behavior increases or decreases (the *learning curve*). When one looks at such a curve taking shape while the behavior changes, it is nearly impossible to predict future rates of behavior; however, the Chart displays behavioral changes in straight lines (or rather, as data through which a straight line can be drawn to summarize the overall trend). Such a line can be extended visually (or with a straight-edge) into future days and weeks for a quick and accurate estimate of rates in the future if current trends persist. It allows more accurate tracking and predicting of a learner's change in performance, thus supporting more rapid and accurate judgments about learning and hence better decisions.

RELATIVE EMPHASIS

On a common square graph, the distance between counts of 80 per minute and 85 per minute is the same as the distance between 10 per minute and 15 per minute. In a teaching situation, when a child progresses from 10 words read aloud per minute to 15 words, it is a more significant event than going from 80 to 85 words per minute. A graph with frequency on a multiply scale reflects the relatively greater importance of small gains when the initial baseline frequency is low. This feature also means that the teacher can see instantly the bounce (variability) in data points from day to day and know when the day's performance is a peach (unusually good) or a lemon (bad). Seeing when a performance is a peach or a lemon allows the teacher to follow up and find potentially critical information about how to repeat it (peach) or prevent it (lemon). Because of the Chart's arrangement, peaches and lemons can be seen regardless of the frequency of the behavior and regardless of the goal (such as accelerating pro-social skills or decelerating harmful or dangerous behavior). Virtually anything of educational interest (such as arithmetic problems, out-of seats, reading, and absences) can be plotted with the same frame of reference or even on the same Chart, so the reader can make rapid and easy comparisons. Also, it makes for easy and fast communication between PT people reading the Chart. This helps in consultation and problem solving. Finally, children readily learn to read it, so they become empowered to manage their own learning, with the teacher as guide and coach.

WIDE-RANGE DISPLAY

With a logarithmic *y*-axis, a huge range of frequencies can be recorded within the confines of one display, from low-frequency events such as daily attendance at school to high-frequency events such as words read silently before answering comprehension questions. Thus, these can be compared and the teacher can assess the effectiveness of procedures across a huge range of behaviors. Fortunately, it is not necessary to know the properties of logarithmic scales in detail use to the Chart effectively. The important skill is to learn to count up the vertical axis. Maloney's (1982) little rhyme can help students remember: "Big number in the margin that starts with one/ tells you what to count by and what to count from."

A dot at the exact middle line of the Chart (on the line marked 1) would indicate 1 per minute. The next heavy line going up is for 5 per minute, and then 10 per minute. Thus, beginning with the frequency line for 1, we count by ones until, going up the axis, the next "big number that starts with one" we see is at the 10 frequency line. From that point, we know to count by 10s to the 100 line. An example of a frequency in that range is resting pulse; your resting pulse might be a dot around 60 if you are in good shape or maybe 70 to 80 per minute if not. We have added some examples of these to the space on the right side of Lynn's Chart, after Day 100. At the frequency line for 100, we count by 100s to the 1000 line. A nice reading speed of 250 words per minute would fall between the 200 and 300 lines (see the diamond on Lynn's Chart).

Similarly, if we start at the bottom of the Chart, .001 per minute indicates something happening at a rate of 1 per 1000 minutes, or about 1 per waking day, such as going to school or making the bed. If you brush your teeth four times a day, your dot would be at the .004 line, like the diamond on the Chart. Then, further up at .01, we are in the range of 1 per 100 minutes, or 10 to 100 a day. An example might be weights lifted at the gym or (among examples of behaviors to be reduced) it might be acting out with self-injurious behaviors (another diamond on the Chart). Above .1, we are in the range of 1 per 10 minutes, or 100 to 1000 a day. As we reach the "1" line we are back in the range of events that may occur at a very high rate per day or may be performed many times within a brief practice period.

The Chart allows every kind of countable event to be expressed in the same language (by its count per minute), whether the target event is counted over the course of a day or within the span of 20 seconds. Note that Precision Teachers adjust the practice period to the material and learner, but they often use brief practice periods of 1 minute or less to great effect.

An important convention is that frequencies we want to accelerate (*e.g.*, correct answers) are always denoted with dots (blue or green, if color is used) and incorrect and other deceleration frequencies are denoted with X's (red or orange). Lynn's Chart shows that on her first timing (Sunday, 14 April 2001), she correctly said the term for three definitions and either did not know or said the incorrect term for 12 definitions. She performed her last timing on Thursday, 14 June 2001, a week prior to the end of the class. Lynn performed at a rate of 37 correct per minute with no errors during her final timing. An "AimStar" (upper-case A) on the Chart points to the goal rate of 30 per minute and the goal date of Thursday, 21 June 2001, the final day of the course. Her highest rate was 40 correct per minute, which she hit several times. We can also tell how long Lynn performed each day. The time bar is a dash mark placed at 1 per minutes observed. For Lynn, these are at the "1" frequency line, as 1/1 minute is 1. Hence, the longer the observation interval, the lower the time bar. Note that some of Lynn's Xs are placed below the time bar, because on those days she made no errors during the timing.

An interesting pattern on Lynn's Chart is the crossover that occurred on the sixth day of recording when the correct responses became more numerous than the errors. From that point, errors remained below correct responses, and correct responses steadily increased, forming what some students have called a "Jaws" learning picture. A dozen types of "learning pictures" have been defined (for further information see www.members.aol.com/johneshleman/ index.htmlr). Also, as with learning pictures, PT includes other standard conventions that, within the small space of one Chart, provide much information that skilled Chart readers can size up quickly. For those readers interested in learning more, sources are listed in this and the following chapter.

Other interpretations can be made rapidly from Lynn's Chart. She performed last on 14 June 2001 (Day 74). She stopped making errors about Day 47, but her correct responses still accelerated, so she was still improving even though she was at 100% correct. After Day 60, when she achieved 40 per minute, she was high above the aim of 30 but her corrects did not accelerate further. Looking at the course overall, classes started on Thursday in the first week and ended on Day 81 in the twelfth week, but all of Lynn's progress accrued between Day 14 and Day 60. So, with respect to the SAFMEDS part of the course, she achieved 12 weeks of learning in only 7 weeks!

ANOTHER CHART EXAMPLE: MIDDLE SCHOOL

Now let us compare Lynn's Chart with Becki's Chart (Fig. 2). Becki was in middle school when her Chart was made. She was also studying SAFMEDS, but these were made up by her teacher to address the U.S. and Illinois Constitutions and government. She took the cards home and studied them. In class, the teacher did timings. He paired each student in the class, and one student in each pair shuffled the deck. Each student had 1 minute to respond rapidly to the prompt on the front of the cards while the other student sat opposite and counted any errors in spoken response compared to the answer printed on the back of each card. "Corrects" went in one pile (minus any errors) and "skips" in another; students doing SAFMEDS always are encouraged to skip any card

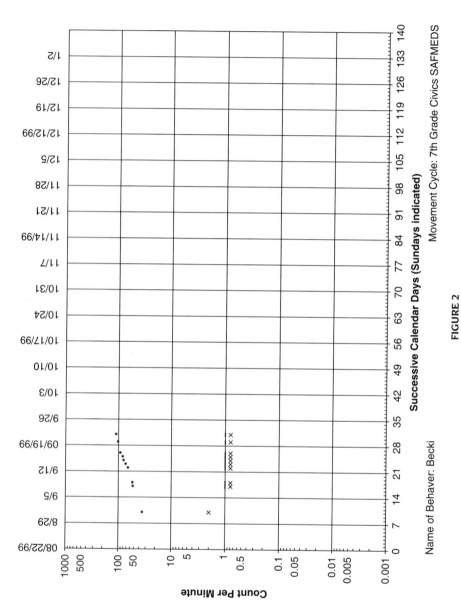

FIGURE 2

Becki's SAFMEDS Chart. Note her outstanding final performance—over 100 per minute correct.

for which they cannot summon a quick response. At the end of 1 minute, each student counted the cards in the piles, plotted "corrects" and "errors plus skips" on their personal Charts, and then switched roles as listener and performer.

If you look at Becki's Chart, you can see a trail of dots going up and to the right. Again, each dot shows her correct performance on 1 day, and the Xs show errors and skips. You can see when she was working and when she was not. Also, let your eyes draw a line through the dots. PT calls such a line a *celeration line* (adapted from *accelerate* when successively doing more or *decelerate* when doing fewer per minute). A strong, universal, and quantitative definition of learning is celeration (mathematically, count per time per time—on these Charts, count per minute per week). However, to see and compare celerations (and hence learning), we do not need to do the math. Just look at the Chart. On Becki's Chart, we did not have to actually draw the celeration line; however, we can take any straight-edge and draw a line that best goes through the dots to see the celeration line. A steeper celeration always means more learning; a flatter one always means less learning. Celeration is thus a universal definition of learning that can be applied to any situation in which frequencies can be obtained, and it allows precise comparison across all learners and all situations. Even very young elementary students can look at the celeration line and know that they are learning when it goes up and that they should talk to the teacher if it is flat or goes down. Also, it is not difficult to teach elementary students to chart; for example, Maloney (1982) describes teaching Charts about 20 minutes per day for 1 week, after which elementary-aged students usually are successfully charting their own data.

For our purposes, we can now compare the celerations that Lynn and Becki achieved, as well as the initial and ending frequencies. Obviously, Becki was *performing* faster, at over 100 per minute compared to Lynn's 35 to 40 per minute, but the celeration lines let us see who was *learning* faster, because steeper lines mean faster learning. Lynn tripled her performance in the first week, but after that accelerated more slowly than Becki. Also, with Charts from some more students, we can compare the SAFMEDS with other curricula just as easily as we compared the students—either in terms of performance or learning. Next, we will discuss other things that make Becki's case interesting.

First, recall that she was doing her SAFMEDS very quickly and by the end she reached over 100 per minute. Observing her being timed, one saw a relaxed, happy girl who was the picture of confidence, and she could discuss the concepts as well as do the SAFMEDS. Second, her teacher reported that the entire class was ready for the Constitution tests much more quickly than usual, and all students passed the first time. The State unit, which usually takes a class 5 to 6 weeks to complete, took about 4 weeks, and the U.S. unit, which usually requires 9 weeks, was completed in 7 to 8 weeks. (B. Bennett, e-mail communication, May 5, 2000). So, the State unit showed a 20% to 33% saving of classroom time, and the U.S. unit showed a 10% to 20% savings. These gains were achieved by a teacher who had about a year of part-time experience with the Chart, who managed about 120 Charts in 6 classes, and who made up his own SAFMEDS.

Imagine if we could save even 10% of the education budget by helping all teachers apply this sort of effective, efficient teaching. One secret is that a focus on celeration (the rising line) lets both student and teacher arrange things to help learning. Another is that in this particular case the room had periodic "Chartshares" in which the students would briefly present their data to the class on transparencies and problem-solve about doing better. Because they learned faster, over time their cumulative learning was truly impressive, and they took fewer days to reach mastery than a non-PT class. The effects of celeration are like compounding interest; the higher the interest rate, the greater the amount that accrues, and it builds faster and faster as it compounds.

LEARNING/CELERATION

Recall that the Chart actually shows *learning*. At its root, we infer learning from a change in performance between two (or more) measurement points. Technically, because frequency is count per time, learning (*e.g.*, change in frequency) can be expressed as count per time per time, or celeration. But, while the Chart was constructed using exact math, to read it we do not need the same level of mathematical sophistication. We simply look at the dots (or Xs) and try to draw a line that best describes the trend. If there is too much bounce (variability) in the dots, we will not see a good line. If the dots are too far apart, data should be taken more often. It sounds basic, but having too few data or too much bounce compromises our ability to make an accurate inference. The Chart lets us know right away how solid our information is, so we can better judge what is really likely to be best for that learner.

Comparison of celerations is easy. All Charts are carefully constructed such that the same angle means the same celeration, regardless of frequency. For example, any celeration parallel to a line that goes from the lower left corner of the chart to the top right corner indicates a X2 (*i.e.*, times 2) celeration, or a doubling in frequency of behavior each week. A X2 (times 2) celeration in performance is generally accepted as a significant change, and an appropriate goal for classroom performance. The celeration line on Lynn's Chart shows a X1.4 (times 1.4) change in behavior per week, while Becki's almost doubles each week. For more details on how to use the Chart and additional Charting conventions, see Graf and Lindsey (2002), Pennypacker, Koenig, & Lindsley (1972), Pennypacker, Gutierrez, & Lindsley (2003); or White and Haring (1980) or visit the Standard Celeration Society webpage (www.celeration.org) to sign up for the SCS listserv, which can lead to finding someone who can help you learn PT.

PRECISION TEACHING'S PLACE IN TEACHING
AND EDUCATION

Precision Teaching is unique among approaches and methods of teaching and education. It has no fixed curriculum, subject-matter areas, types of students, or grade levels. It has been successfully applied with an incredible diversity of students, settings, and learning situations. PT does demand measuring the definition frequency (count per unit time) of each learner's performance, displaying those data on a Chart, and making instructional decisions based on the data. Precision Teachers select and change curricula to optimize performance of individual students, and they discard ineffective curricula and practices. Thus, many PT classrooms use Direct Instruction methods and curricula (see Section 3) simply because they work and then supplement them with PT-designed practice materials because the students learn better. Similarly, many customary procedures and practices in standard classrooms do not really help students learn, and as Precision Teachers examine what they do the data help them reduce wasted time and gravitate toward more effective, learning-enhancing, and time-conserving methods. Also, because anyone who can read a Chart can understand the rationale for decisions, Precision Teachers can rapidly share effective curricula, techniques, suggestions, and consultation and can easily and completely test and personalize their application in a new classroom.

Another difference between PT and other educational theory may be its new vocabulary (*e.g.*, celeration, bounce). Lindsley, the founder of PT, and other developers of PT have made a strong effort to use plain English words instead of jargon in developing a vocabulary for PT (Graf & Lindsley, 2002); however, the real differences of PT from other educational theories (and the secrets of its success in fostering learning) lie in its motto ("The learner is always right") and the use of learner's Charts to guide teacher efforts.

Persons who do not practice data-driven decisions and instruction may have a difficult time understanding how Precision Teachers can verify that a given curriculum is or is not effective in their classrooms. School curricula typically are selected according to theoretical fads or political expediency, and data-driven evaluation of curricula is superior to those arbitrary processes. Data-driven decision-making also affects the decision of when to present the next new topic within a curriculum. Look at Becki's Chart again. Where the celeration line flattens, Becki's progress slowed, and because she was already performing with great speed and accuracy we could have given her the final test right then, instead of continuing to work on the SAFMEDS. When time is saved in the classroom, teachers can decided what to add to the current semester and how to change plans for the future semesters (which can affect the plans of other teachers).

When first hearing about PT, many educators cannot imagine how they could operate such a truly individualized system with a whole class of students, even if the students did their own charting. Many think their students could not possibly chart themselves. Yet, many classrooms have successfully used PT, and many students have charted their own performances. Calkin (2000) estimates that over 1 million Charts have been completed, many by students. It is certainly true that adding PT to what is currently happening in a classroom involves adding timings, Charting, and prep time. It is also true that the strong, well-organized teacher gets better results than a weaker, less well-organized one. Typically, though, added time is soon dwarfed by the increased learning, and even more time is saved when less efficient and less informative methods of assessment are discontinued.

The first step to making these improvements is to read more about PT, perhaps by consulting some of the Internet resources listed herein. Then, think through the curriculum and arrange for practice materials that are appropriate for the subject and students. For example, Becki's teacher used the available subject texts and made sets of SAFMEDS. Some of the resources listed in the next chapter provide worksheets and curricula, particularly for math and reading; Precision Teachers use a variety of materials other than SAFMEDS. As you develop or obtain PT materials, you will want to set the performance criteria for mastery. In PT, such decisions about goal setting are often discussed in terms of fluency, a topic described in detail in the next chapter. Roughly speaking, *fluent* describes a performance that is smooth, accurate, and sufficiently rapid and does not decay in the presence of distractors or in novel applications. You may be able to find fluency standards for your material within the available PT literature; if not, a few timings with adults who have already developed competence with that skill can provide a rough guide. Next, learn to chart and teach the learners to chart, and look at the Charts each day. Systematically search for and remove the fluency blockers that impede the learners, and put in place fluency builders instead (Binder, 1996). Finally, celebrate learning. Tell each student, "Beat your own score," and make that the standard for measuring achievement.

ETHICS AND PRECISION TEACHING MEASURES IN SCHOOLS

Precision Teaching and the measurement of learning bring us to some ethical issues in education. Some may assert that measuring student performance is emotionally damaging and argue against any timed measurement or direct feedback. Of course, any procedure can be misused, but in the typical PT situation, when students are timed each day, they and their teachers use that data together to improve teaching and learning. In a PT environment, the learner is not pressured by comparisons to others who may be ahead, nor embarrassed by unwelcome use as an example to others who may be behind; instead, students have direct access to their own data over time and beat your own scores becomes the incentive. Data feedback in this type of situation is empowering and may be compared directly to athletics and music where data on personal performance are key to self-improvement when the feedback is handled in constructive ways.

Any consideration of ethics in education must include the problem of limited resources. Resources (including the students' time and the public's money) can be wasted through failure to teach. In typical educational settings, such failure is not immediately apparent, but with PT anyone who can read a Chart can tell if learning is occurring or not. Thus, administrators and parents may be encouraged to regularly view students' Charts, and the data will show if students are learning or not. Contemplating this level of true accountability may provoke anxiety, but remember that the student and teacher see the data each day, so there are many opportunities to change procedures and move forward before much time is wasted or to call for consultation and get help with the problem. The repeated assessment and rapid formative feedback of PT compares very well to the increasingly common situation of teachers and schools facing censure based on once-per-year tests and students facing the possibility of not receiving a diploma.

The teacher who honestly hones his or her practice of teaching as a craft will find PT to be an immensely invaluable tool, while a teacher who just goes through the motions or one who is intimidated by change may find many arguments against PT. Students themselves see the effects of PT procedures and how they are intended to facilitate learning. The result is a system that is student centered, facilitative, empowering, liberating, and refreshingly honest to the student.

Because the learner is always right, PT is resistant to the fads and fashions that often plague education (Grote, 1999; Lindsley, 1992). Educational innovations and theories must be tested in the crucible of the classroom, and show benefit through data from individual students over time. Those that benefit only their originators, bureaucrats, and consultants must be modified or discarded. To help people learn, there is no substitute for good data.

Acknowledgments

Preparation of this chapter occurred while the first author was supported in part by Grant H129E030003 from the Rehabilitation Services Administration. Earlier work described herein was supported in part by grants H133B8007 and G00830079 from the National Institute for Disability and Rehabilitation Research. Collaboration and support for additional projects was provided by the North Central Regional Educational Laboratory and the Rehabilitation Institute Foundation.

References

Barrett, B. H. (2002). *The technology of teaching revisited: A reader's companion to B. F. Skinner's book.* Concord, MA: Cambridge Center for Behavioral Studies.

Beck, R. (1979). *Report for the Office of Education Joint Dissemination Review Panel*, Great Falls, MT: Precision Teaching Project.

Beck, R. & Clement, R. (1991). The Great Falls Precision Teaching Project: A historical examination. *Journal of Precision Teaching*, 8, 8–12.

Bennett, B. (2000). E-mail to Charles Merbitz, May 5.

Binder, C. (1996). *Building fluency with free operant procedures*. Invited address presented at the Annual Meeting of the Association for Behavior Analysis, San Francisco, CA.

Calkin, A. B. (2000). *Chart count*. Precision Teaching/Standard Celeration Charting Listserve (http://lists.psu.edu/archives/sclistserv.html).

Cromey, A. & Merbitz, C. (1999). *PT and data driven decision making: Making it happen in public schools*. Paper presented at the 14th International Precision Teaching Conference, Provo, UT.

Graf, S. A. (1994). *How To develop, produce and use SAFMEDS in education and training*. Youngstown, OH: Zero Brothers Software.

Graf S. A. & Lindsey, O. R. (2002). *Standard Celeration Charting 2002*. Poland, OH: Graf Implements.

Greer, R. D. & McDonough, H. S. (1999). Is the learn unit a fundamental unit of pedagogy? *The Behavior Analyst*, 22, 5–16.

Grote, I. (1999). The behavior of the scientist: Epistemological tools science-makers use and games they play. *Behavior and Social Issues*, 9, 47–53.

Lindsley, O. R. (1992). Why aren't effective teaching tools widely adopted? *Journal of Applied Behavior Analysis*, 25, 21–26.

Maloney, M. (1982). Teaching the standard behavior chart: A Direct Instruction approximation. *Journal of Precision Teaching*, 2, 11–30.

McManus, R. (2003). *Morningside PT*. Precision Teaching/Standard Celeration Charting Listserve (http://lists.psu.edu/archives/sclistserv.html).

Pennypacker, H. S., Koenig, C. H., & Lindsley, O. R. (1972). *Handbook of the standard behavior chart*. Lawrence, KS: The Behavior Research Company.

Pennypacker, H. S., Gutierrez, Jr., A., & Lindsley, O. R. (2003). *Handbook of the standard celeration chart*. Gainesville, FL: author.

van der Ploeg, A. & Merbitz, C. (1998). *Data-driven decision making in classrooms: Vision, issues, and implementation*. Paper presented at the annual conference of the American Evaluation Association, Chicago, IL.

White, O. R. & Haring, N. G. (1980). *Exceptional teaching*, 2nd ed. Columbus, OH: Merrill.

CHAPTER

5

Precision Teaching: Applications in Education and Beyond

CHARLES MERBITZ
Illinois Institute of Technology

DOREEN VIEITEZ
Joliet Junior College

NANCY HANSEN MERBITZ
Private Practice

CARL BINDER
Binder Riha Associates

INTRODUCTION

In the previous chapter, we introduced some foundations of Precision Teaching (PT) and provided individual examples. In this chapter, we present some of its innovations in more detail and describe applications for special education, college classrooms, prevocational training, accommodation to disability, personal growth, and other topics. Finally, we present an annotated bibliography of PT websites and some PT resources.

In addition to many other activities, teachers problem-solve, invent, and try new things. In this arena, Precision Teachers have been especially productive, and standard Charts facilitate sharing their innovations. Because the learner is always right (see previous chapter), PT teachers test their teaching practices with every student, and with the Chart everyone can see rapidly what works and what does not. While space does not permit a full discussion of all the topics raised here, we will briefly introduce a few critical concepts and innovations used in PT. Note that the order of exposition here is not the order of discovery, and we apologize that most references to the people who discovered these are omitted to save space.

An interesting concept in PT is that of *fluency*, or a fast, comfortable, effortless performance (Binder, 1996; Graf & Lindsley, 2002; Kubina & Morrison, 2000). In PT, fluency has a specific meaning; it refers to performing at true mastery, or a level at which the skill becomes reliable and useful. The characteristics of fluency have been analyzed and widely discussed among Precision Teachers and are often presented as an acronym to facilitate understanding and retention. Various Precision Teachers have used different acronyms, but we will use SARGE—fluency is *stable* (resistant to distractions), is easily *applied* (incorporated in more complex skills or new combinations), is *retained* over long periods with little or no practice, is *generalized* to new situations, and shows *endurance* (can be performed for long durations without undue fatigue or loss of quality). Fluency means more than performing at 100% correct (see Barrett, 1977, 2002); it indicates when we should stop teaching a skill and move to another. Johnson and Layng (1992, 1994) use a different fluency acronym; they discuss "generative instruction," in which selected components of complex skills are taught to fluency such that learners *generate* other components without specific instruction. Acronyms aside, our goal of fluency means learner independence.

Celerations and frequency ranges at which fluency is observed when we test the learners with more complex skills have been discussed in the PT literature for over 20 years (Haughton, 1980). Along with fluency is the related notion of *components* of more complex *composite* behaviors (or skills). Because all visible behavior is made up of smaller behaviors, when key smaller component behaviors are performed fluently, we can easily teach the more complex composite behavior. Thus, if a learner's celeration is low when performing complex tasks, one tactic is to measure to see if *components* of that composite behavior are at fluency. If not, we may switch efforts to teach the components. For example, if a child reads slowly and makes inaccurate guesses at pronunciation, component reading skills of phonemic discrimination and decoding should be taught to fluency before much progress will be made in reading. In rare cases of disability, we may bypass a component (*e.g.*, auditory discrimination for a person with severe hearing loss) and substitute another learning stream, as discussed below.

Note that a behavior can be successfully performed at 100% correct and not be fluent. To see the difference, look for labored, effortful, and slow performances; low endurance; difficulty in learning the next more complex skill; and even escape, evasion, and tantrums when the more complex skill is addressed. For example, several early Precision Teachers worked with learners having a variety of severe disabilities. They identified the "Big Six" components of skilled hand movements: reach, touch, point, place, grasp, and release (Binder &

Haughton, 2002; Binder, Mallabello, Desjardins, & McManus, 1999; Haughton, 1980) that are the basis for useful hand function. Deficient skills on these components frustrate learners and impede or prevent acquisition of more complex skills that use the hands. For example, dysfluent hand skills will make learning math difficult and unpleasant if one has to write answers. Again, it is not that the movements are absent; they are just slower. A motor dysfluency that blocks learning of academic tasks may escape detection if frequencies are not measured.

The "Big Six" and other hand movements can be independently sampled and should be in the range of hundreds per minute. When they are that fast, making slash marks and Os with a pencil can also be taught to the rate of hundreds per minute. These simple hand skills (and some gross motor movements) will then support teaching the student to write numbers in sequence and randomly at rates of over 150 correct per minute, which in turn will support learning elementary math $(+, -, \div, \times)$ in the range of 80 to 120 digits per minute correct, which in turn will support learning fractions, geometry, algebra, and calculus. Obviously, we may fill in the slices of many curricula here, from basic mobility skills to reading, writing, and other academic and life skills. Thus, fluency provides true mastery goals as well as new tactics; when learning is stalled, we can address its components. For the learner comes confident competence. The resources listed later can guide you to curriculum slices and fluency goals devised by PT people, sometimes utilizing existing curricula (*e.g.*, Direct Instruction) and sometimes developing new material.

Precision Teaching also uses the notion of Learning Streams (earlier called Learning Channels; Lindsley, 2002) to label in plain English what learners are being exposed to and what they are supposed to do. For example, SeeSay words in context clearly use the active verbs "see" and "say" as unambiguous terms for the actions that are counted. Other Learning Streams include Hear-Write, SeePointSay, ThinkSay, and so forth. The term "comfort pairs" denotes the PT practice of counting two academic behaviors simultaneously, one to accelerate and one to decelerate, as in math digits correct and errors (or "learning opportunities"). This focus on the situation and on active verbs to describe behavior helps us to change the situation to advance the learner and to ensure that the desired effects are being achieved (Barrett, 2002; Lindsley, 1964).

An interesting PT finding is that the frequency, celeration, and bounce of a behavior are independent; interventions may affect any of these and not the others. Because PT uses the standard Chart, any effects can be seen and classified: frequency may jump up or down, celeration may turn up or down, and bounce (variability in frequency from one performance to the next) may converge, diverge, narrow, or widen. Similarly, corrects may accelerate without changing error frequency (an outcome invisible to percent-based measures). The simultaneous display of all of these distinct features makes Chart analysis quick, easy, and accurate (see Lindsley, 1992, for a concise and readable summary of learning effects).

Space precludes a full list of PT innovations, but we will mention two more powerful techniques resulting from Chart standardization. First are the *Chart-shares*, where the learners can put up transparencies of their Charts, discuss their learning, ask peers for advice, and give the results of last week's consultation. Typically, showing a Chart at a Chartshare requires only 1 to 2 minutes, and it is a heartwarming and inspiring experience to see young, previously shy and school-averse students confidently present their learning pictures. Chartshares are a dramatic way to empower learners, engage them in a search for effective study methods, and create a true and productive learning environment. Another technique is that of stacking multiple transparencies of Charts on top of each other (or, in digital versions of the Chart, viewing overlaid data from multiple Charts). In this way, a teacher, student, parent, or administrator can review data from several skills for one learner or data from one skill for several learners. Chart stacks summarize without the loss of individual data (Cooper, Kubina, & Melanga, 1998). Examples of questions that could be addressed by stacking include: On which skill did this learner show a greater celeration? Of the students in this classroom, which are showing greater celerations and which are having problems? In which of these classrooms are students making the most rapid gains? Which curricula shows a wider range of gains?

PRECISION TEACHING AND SPECIAL EDUCATION

The motto "The learner is always right" succinctly expresses why PT is appropriately used in special education. The fast and convenient measurement, decision-making, and communication of Precision Teaching help teachers arrange the educational environment to benefit each learner and allow stakeholders to assess the celeration (learning) of each student. Students are by definition placed in special education classes when their performance is sufficiently below that of their age and grade mates. Logically, if these students are ever to match the performance of their peers, they must learn at a faster rate than the peers. While the reader might question whether that is possible for many of the students in special education, the usual delivery of slow, inefficient, and watered-down instruction guarantees its impossibility. Opening doors to other possibilities requires that instruction be more intense and effective in the special education classroom, and there should be less tolerance for inefficient and ineffective procedures and curricula. However, a great strength of special education is the recognition that additional resources (such as teacher time and training) can and should be provided to these students to facilitate their learning, and PT is ideal for determining how to focus resources to accelerate learning, to document outcomes, and to communicate with caring stakeholders.

The Individuals with Disabilities Education Act Amendments of 1997 (IDEA) mandates a free appropriate public education for all children with disabilities in the United States between the ages of 3 and 21. It includes several major provisions that PT meets more effectively than other systems. Two provisions of IDEA are related to evaluation and individualized education programs (IEPs). In terms of evaluation, IDEA requires that schools: (1) use testing and evaluation materials and procedures that are not racially or culturally discriminatory or biased by a student's language or disabilities; (2) use assessment tools and strategies that provide functional and developmental information for determining the content of the child's IEP, that provide relevant information that directly assists in determining educational needs, and that provide information regarding involvement and progress in the general curriculum; and (3) not use any single procedure as the only criterion for determining whether the child has a disability or for determining an appropriate educational program for the child. The IEP is a written document provided for each child with a disability. The content of an IEP must include the child's current level of performance, measurable annual goals and short-term objectives, special education services, related services, supplementary aids, program modifications necessary for the child to make progress toward the goals, a plan for how progress toward the goals will be measured, and timelines for services.

Precision Teaching is ideally suited for meeting these requirements of IDEA (and similarly the No Child Left Behind legislation). Because PT can be used to measure learning in any curriculum or method, it does not discriminate racially or culturally, nor is it biased by language or disability. In addition, PT provides a relevant measure of a student's performance that is immediately applicable to selecting IEP content, determining educational needs, and measuring progress in the curriculum. By analyzing Charts of a student's achievement in various areas of the curriculum, teachers can easily summarize a student's current level of educational performance in each of those areas and select appropriate goals and objectives based on the student's needs and known fluencies. With celeration, teachers can evaluate the effectiveness of current methods and set an appropriate AimStar (*i.e.*, goal frequency and date) for each objective. Then, by drawing an expected line of progress from the current performance to the AimStar and comparing actual progress to the expected progress, advancement toward the objectives can be continually evaluated and programs modified as needed.

Rather than waiting for the required annual review of IEPs to determine student achievement and modify goals and objectives, PT provides an easy way to evaluate progress on a daily basis. With this daily evaluation, PT facilitates the crucial function of driving these educational decisions with data. Programs are promptly changed if progress is insufficient, and programs are kept in place when progress is being made. The nature of the Chart is to show proportional gains, which is particularly valuable when the learning is just beginning. Thus, PT avoids both wasting the child's time with ineffective curricula and wasting opportunities and teaching resources by switching students out of effective curricula when continued progress is subtle. Also, communication with other stakeholders is facilitated; parents may review charts for updates on their children's progress toward goals and objectives. Thus, PT is the perfect tool for making educational decisions that meet the requirements of IDEA and for providing a truly accountable, effective, and individualized educational program. Finally, because PT data are kept on a standardized Chart, paperwork and wasted time are kept to a minimum. Meetings can be brief and more focused on what can be tried to help the child accelerate. Also, if data are computerized and online, parents, administrators, and other authorized individuals can have ready access to student Charts.

PRECISION TEACHING FOR ADULT LEARNERS IN COLLEGE AND PRE-VOCATIONAL TRAINING

Teaching introductory courses at the college level and finding acceptable ways for students to master large numbers of new concepts is challenging, and PT techniques have been used in colleges for over 30 years (Johnston & Pennypacker, 1971). Lynn's Chart in the previous chapter (see Fig. 1 in Chapter 4) came from a contemporary course in introductory special education. In it, graduate elementary education majors used 180 SAFMEDS cards to learn special education terms and recorded their performance at www.AimChart.net (see Internet resources on pp. 74–76). They viewed their celerations on computer-generated charts. At one class session a week, students conducted 1 minute timings with a partner. After the final timing during the last class session, students completed a written quiz, which required them to write the corresponding term for all definitions listed in random order. Students received points toward their final course grade for daily charting, for their final timing, and for their score on the final written quiz. Celerations increased for all students, with all but a few reaching or exceeding the goal rate of 30 correct per minute. At the beginning of the term, students expressed some initial concern and resistance for the task. By the end of the term, however, only two students gave negative comments concerning the SAFMEDS task on the course evaluations.

A major positive aspect of the task was that, as students were learning the terms, they were able to understand and converse with professionals in the schools they visited for their clinical experiences. In addition, students continued to contact the instructor during the next school year regarding their use of SAFMEDS in their other course work and with the students they taught. The charting task also was beneficial, as indicated by student comments regarding their excitement when seeing correct rates accelerate and when crossover occurred. Figure 1 shows stacked data from this class for a few students.

Other PT projects and programs have used the power of PT to reach older students who had been unsuccessful in previous academic settings. One such program in Malcolm X College in Chicago (Johnson & Layng, 1992, 1994) has been operating successfully for over a decade, and a program with similar goals

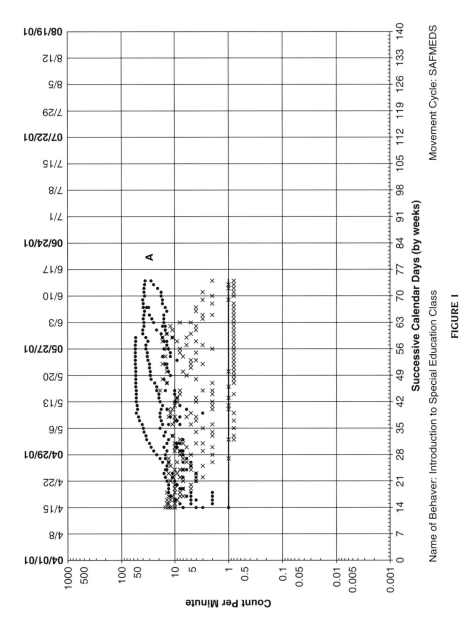

Name of Behaver: Introduction to Special Education Class   Movement Cycle: SAFMEDS

FIGURE 1

Stacked data from four students in a special education class.

at Jacksonville State University (JSU) in Alabama has been operating continuously since 1978. McDade and Brown (2001) have published a concise sampler of their PT curricula at JSU for mathematics and English language instruction, as well as two editions of a manual focused on English composition skills (Brown, n.d.).

Adult learners also are successfully taught in other venues. For example, DuPage County officials in Illinois contracted with the AimStar Precision Learning Center to teach literacy and numeracy skills to adults who were having difficulty maintaining employment. Four adults classified with learning disabilities were immediate referrals. Results of an assessment showed that, although these adults performed decoding skills at an acceptable level, they had difficulty with comprehension (including following multitask directions), lacked fluent basic math skills, and lacked the basic knowledge necessary for functioning in various environments. Using PT, direct instruction, oral comprehension lessons, practice sheets, and SAFMEDS, two teacher/consultants taught reading comprehension and basic math skills to these four adults over a 6-week period. Embedded within the comprehension lessons were opportunities to strengthen oral listening skills and basic knowledge. All students mastered many comprehension lessons and a variety of addition, subtraction, multiplication, and division facts. These adult students particularly enjoyed viewing their charts for celerations in their learning. Johnson and Layng (1994) report dramatic gains from a similar project.

PRECISION TEACHING APPLICATIONS FOR INDIVIDUALS WITH VARIOUS DISABILITIES

As can be imagined, because the PT measurement technology can be applied to any countable behavior, it offers a powerful and effective method for working with persons who have disabling conditions. In Boston, the Judge Rotenberg Center (JRC) provides such services to clients with severe behavioral and academic challenges, maintaining Charts on numerous goals for the residents in a coordinated program. The JRC website (Judgerc.org) offers current information about these programs and their effects. AimStar Precision Learning Center, located near Chicago, IL, provides services to clients with a wide range of ages, abilities, and needs. "Mindy" was an 18-year-old student with Down syndrome. Her parents had become frustrated with her public school after the school staff told them that she had reached a plateau and had learned everything that she was going to learn. Mindy's parents believed that school staff were severely underestimating her potential, so they requested services at AimStar. Mindy's assessment revealed that she could read at about the first-grade level, although not fluently, and that she was able to perform some basic math skills, primarily addition and subtraction. Observation at school showed that Mindy spent most of the school day playing computer games, listening to music, and watching movies. Given the opportunity, however, she preferred to practice reading and math skills. At AimStar, Mindy was an eager learner who was highly reinforced by mastering skills, teacher praise, and celerations on her charts. She also practiced the skills every night at home. Although her Charts showed lower than average celerations, she continues to master writing, reading, comprehension, and math skills. Hardly a plateau with no learning!

An example of PT in the rehabilitation of persons with severe brain injury is provided in an article by Merbitz, King, Bleiberg, & Grip (2000) that illustrates how PT data were used to assess medical and pharmacalogical issues as well as instructional ones. It also provides a specific example of how monitoring and charting the instructor's behaviors as well as the learner's can enable rather stunning insights to removing fluency blockers. The application of PT in rehabilitation after stroke (Cherney, Merbitz, Grip, 1986; Neely, 2002) has also been documented. Other data regarding rehabilitation (Merbitz, Miller, & Hansen, 1985) have shown that life can be stronger than our interventions; in one case, for example, PT data clearly revealed very strong effects associated with going home on a pass and partying at Christmas and New Year's. But, ultimately, good data do reflect life.

In recent years, the population of persons diagnosed with autism and autism spectrum disorders has mushroomed. Concurrently, Precision Teachers have made significant progress in working with this population of people (especially children). Building on the pioneering work of Lovaas and others (Lovaas et al., 1981), Precision Teachers found that Lovaas' discrete trial procedures often could be used to teach a new skill, but that the free operant procedures of PT were highly successful in taking it further to a point at which the skill could be considered fluent. Precision Teachers also identified fluency blockers for people with autistic behavior, such as deficiencies in components (*e.g.*, "Big Six" and other hand skills as well as social and academic skills).

In Fabrizio and Moors' highly successful programs, Charts are used to document the progress of each child as fluency is reached for each target behavior (Fabrizio, Pahl, & Moors, 2002; Moors & Fabrizio, 2002). Among all of the other instructional activities that they employ are several non-obvious tactics that spring directly from PT and bear closer examination here. One such tactic is the "Sprint"— a practice session of brief duration (such as 6 to 10 seconds) during which the child repeats the requested behavior a few times correctly, followed immediately by reinforcement. When the frequency rises, then the time bar can be lowered (increasing the timing interval) to 20, 30, or 45 seconds, while maintaining (or building up to) the desired frequency. In effect, when the child can do a short burst of correct responses, we can selectively reinforce that high frequency of performance and then gradually shape to lengthen the duration of correct responding. Finally, when the learner is at the target frequency, endurance can be built by extending the duration of the practice as appropriate for that skill (Binder, Haughton, & Van Eyck, 1990).

As a routine element of their practice, Fabrizio and Moors also systematically test achieved skills for stability and retention. Both of these checks generally occur when the learner has reached frequency and endurance goals. When a learner can perform a task correctly at the target frequency, even when a favorite video is playing, people are talking and moving about in the environment, and distracting things are happening, that task can reasonably be called stable. Similarly, a retention check also is deceptively simple: Do not present any further opportunities for practicing that particular skill for an extended period (up to a month, depending on the practical and ethical issues of not teaching in that curriculum area). Fabrizio and Moors' Charts simply show the month with no data on that skill, and then another dot. If there is no drop in frequency, instruction can move on past that goal. Charts and discussions of these and other issues can be accessed at http://students.washington.edu/fabrizio/index.htm.

When accommodations to disability are necessary within a classroom, PT offers an efficient way to manage and evaluate the effects of those accommodations, as the following example illustrates. In a combined graduate-advanced undergraduate course, Medical Aspects of Disability, students used a set of 375 SAFMEDS cards while learning medical terminology, anatomy, the functions of various body systems, and evolving concepts of health and disability. One student (Sara) had moderate impairments in visual acuity as well as severe impairments in physical strength and dexterity. She worked with the instructors to find a method of presenting the SAFMEDS that would allow her to meet the mastery criteria for an A on that portion of the course (*i.e.*, 35 cards correct per minute).

Bigger, large-print cards were tried and were not helpful. An Excel file was developed that presented the card information on her computer, and within 3 weeks she reported she was regularly reaching her aim in her home practice sessions. However, her in-class performances were still significantly slower by about 15 cards per minute. She and one of the instructors worked to identify possible fluency blockers; her first hypothesis was anxiety. Various strategies were attempted to reduce anxiety, but home practice performances continued to reach or exceed her aim, and in-class performance remained low. Next, they searched for features that might distinguish between home and in-class assessment. Because she used a portable respirator and had to coordinate her speech with the air supply, they tried having her speak her answers more softly for the instructor to conserve breath, but this did not increase her rate. As they searched for any other differences, it was determined that the screen display of the classroom laptop did not duplicate that of her home computer. The screen display was adjusted until Sara said it matched her home screen. This was immediately followed by a performance at 36 correct per minute. Figure 2 shows Sara's Chart. Dots show her SAFMEDS performance at home and diamonds show it in class. Vertical tic marks have been placed along the 100 frequency line to indicate the days on which the class met. Notice how the

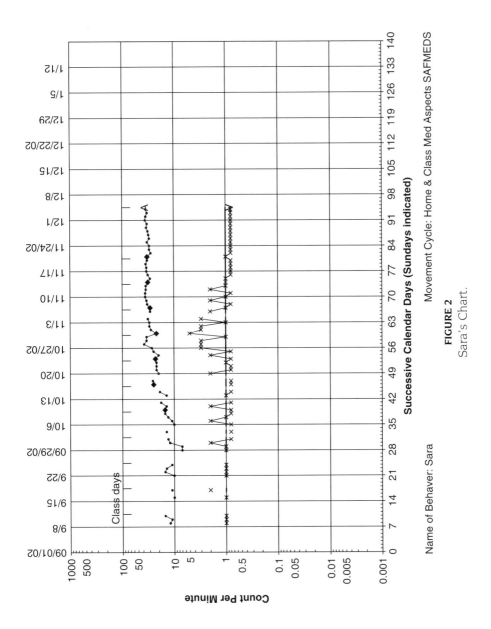

FIGURE 2
Sara's Chart.

Thursday in-class SAFMEDS rose after Day 63 to blend in with the at-home performance frequency, after the computer screen was adjusted to match her home screen.

The instructor and Sara herself initially looked for features of the learner that might set limits on performance (note the insidious "blame the learner" habit), and both had begun to consider lowering the aim before fully exploring objective features of the environment. This "solution" would have deprived her of the opportunity to demonstrate (and celebrate) her competence with the material; true accommodations to her multiple disabilities did not mean lowering standards.

PRECISION TEACHING WITH THOUGHTS, URGES, AND OTHER "INNER" PHENOMENA

Precision Teaching procedures have been used to count and chart a wide variety of important life activities. For example, mothers have charted babies' kicks before birth, and these Charts present orderly data (Calkin, 1983; Edwards & Edwards, 1971). More recently, several investigators (Neely, 2002) have charted end-of-life phenomena using PT measures with terminally ill persons. In another arena, as Calkin (1981, 1992) and others (Cooper, 1991) have convincingly demonstrated, people can use PT techniques to chart their thoughts, urges, and feelings, and the resulting data are orderly and useful; for example, they can be used as part of a plan for self-improvement, relationship enhancement, and so forth. Thus, PT has begun to grapple with some important arenas of personal life.

PRECISION TEACHING, COMPUTERS, AND INTERNET RESOURCES

Over the last three decades, a number of computerized versions of the Chart and PT data collections systems have been developed (Merbitz, 1996). The source for copies of the original, and still indispensible, blue paper Chart remains Behavior Research Company (Box 3351, Kansas City, KS 66103). While paper Charts and computer screen displays may differ in effects on the learner, the computer Charts offer some advantages for administration and long-distance sharing. With the growth of the Internet and development of more capable hardware and better software have come many more PT resources. Almost all of the sample sites listed on the following pages offer links and resources for many PT sites, such as learning centers. Because others are being developed, this list is simply a place to begin; Google listed about 2000 PT hits in 2003. Also, centralized databases of Charts are now becoming available (*e.g.*, www.AimChart.net) building on Lindsley's pioneering Behavior Bank database of the 1970s.

www.celeration.org: The official website of the Standard Celeration Society, a group that uses PT and supports its development; an active and friendly Listserv can be accessed through the website; it also has numerous links to professionals using PT and PT projects.

http://psych.athabascau.ca/html/387/OpenModules/Lindsley/: The website for David Polson's and Lyle Grant's course at Athabasca University; it contains an excellent introduction to PT.

http://www.celeration.net/: A great site by John Shewmaker, in which he collects many annotated resources for people coming to PT from the "real world."

http://www.fluencyfactory.com/PrecisionTeachingLinks.html: The Fluency Factory (Richard McManus) teaches anyone in the Boston area; site also has an annotated list of excellent PT links.

www.morningsideinfo.com: The Morningside Academy, started by Kent Johnson, is a complete school built upon PT and scientifically validated instruction; visitors can see data-driven instruction and decisions in Morningside classes.

www.tli.com: The Learning Incentive offers instructional technology as well as interesting links; it is the home base of Ben Bronz Academy, a school based on PT with a dramatic record of instructional achievements and developments in databased technologies as applied to instruction

www.judgerc.org: The website for the Judge Rotenberg Center in Boston, an organization for severely impaired persons; JRC offers both day and residential programs within which decisions are guided by PT data, operating under a computerized system.

http://members.shaw.ca/celerationtechnologies/index.html: Celeration Technologies is the source for Joe Parsons' ThinkFast computerized SAFMEDS system, an alternative to printed cards.

http://www.simstat.com/PracticeMill.html: Normand Peladeau's PracticeMill at the Simulation and Statistical Research and Consulting Centre (SimStat) supports practice sheets and SAFMEDS utilization.

www.chartshare.net: This site, developed by Jesus Rosales and a group at North Texas State University, promises support in the task of collecting large groups of Charts (metacharting) and preparing Charts for scientific publication.

www.fluency.org: Excellent site with a great collection of papers that may be downloaded; Carl Binder's 1996 review article on fluency is easily accessed here.

www.binder-riha.com: Carl Binder's site, which features applications of PT to business and industry.

www.members.aol.com/johneshleman/index.html: John Eshleman's Instructional Systems Site offers a series of tutorials on PT and data-driven instruction; see the Learning Pictures descriptions and PT References.

www.headsprout.com: An Internet-based reading system built in part on PT data and a careful analysis of steps involved in successfully teaching reading.

www.haughtonlearningcenter.com: A site presenting the highly respected Haughton Learning Center PT curricula.

www.teachyourchildrenwell.com: Michael Maloney's PT curricula and Learning Centers.

www.sopriswest.com: Sopris West publishes PT materials and offers skilled PT consultation.

http://people.ku.edu/borns/: Developed by Scott Born, this site contains a number of Excel templates that faithfully reproduce various Charts for publication and posting.

http://students.washington.edu/fabrizio/index.htm: This site, developed by Michael Fabrizio, has downloadable versions of many of his publications and presentations; a particular "must visit" for anyone interested in autism or instructional advancement.

www.teonor.com/ptdocs/: Many useful PT articles available in downloadable form.

http://home.wi.rr.com/penzky/precisio1.htm: More useful PT information and links.

www.aimchart.net: At this site, under development by the first author, you can deposit data, immediately see it on a Chart, and update the Chart whenever needed. Teachers can set up classes with a password for each student, so students can enter data and see their Charts. The teacher, however, can see all Charts and various overlays, including frequency and celeration stacks (such as this chapter's Charts). Parents can use students' passwords to see their children's data (if the child has an IEP, this feature allows parental access to the data). It also will draw a minimum celeration line to an AimStar. While many schools will opt to use traditional paper Charts, this site allows the data to be shared easily across the web. Early versions of the site were supported in part by the North Central Regional Educational Lab (NCREL).

CONCLUSIONS

With our motto, "The learner is always right," and standard Charts, it is possible to deliver learning and hence effective education. PT includes a body of techniques that are empirical and based in natural science, which makes it possible to really know what is working for your students. We hope that the resources and information provided here are useful in helping you access these techniques and improving life for you and your learners.

Acknowledgments

Preparation of this chapter occurred while the first author was supported in part by Grant H129E030003 from the Rehabilitation Services Administration. Earlier work described herein was supported in part by grants H133B8007 and G00830079 from the National Institute for Disability and Rehabilitation Research. Collaboration and support for additional projects was provided by the North Central Regional Educational Laboratory and the Rehabilitation Institute Foundation.

References

Barrett, B. H. (1977). Communitization and the measured message of normal behavior, in York, R. L. & Edgar, E. (Eds.), *Teaching the severely handicapped*, Vol. 4. Columbus, OH: Special Press, pp. 301–318.

Barrett, B. H. (2002). *The technology of teaching revisited: A reader's companion to B. F. Skinner's book.* Concord, MA: Cambridge Center for Behavioral Studies.

Binder, C. (1996). Behavioral fluency: Evolution of a new paradigm. *The Behavior Analyst*, 19, 163–197.

Binder, C. & Haughton, E. (2002). *Using Learning Channels and the Learning Channel Matrix.* Paper presented at the 15th Annual International Precision Teaching Conference, Harrisburg, PA.

Binder, C., Haughton, E., & Van Eyk, D. (1990). Increasing endurance by building fluency: Precision Teaching attention span. *Teaching Exceptional Children*, 22, 24–27.

Binder, C., Mallabello, G., Desjardins, A., & McManus, R. (1999). *Building fluency in fine and cross motor behavior elements.* Workshop presented at the Annual Meeting of the Association for Behavior Analysis, Chicago, IL.

Brown, J. M. (n.d.). *Write away, too! A precision approach to writing.* Jacksonville, AL: McLAB Pinpoint Productions.

Calkin, A. B. (1981). One minute timing improves inners. *Journal of Precision Teaching*, 2, 9–21.

Calkin, A. B. (1983). Counting fetal movement. *Journal of Precision Teaching*, 4, 35–40.

Calkin, A. B. (1992). The inner I: Improving self-esteem. *Journal of Precision Teaching*, 10, 42–52.

Calkin, A. B. (2000). *Chart count.* Precision Teaching/Standard Celeration Charting Listserve (http://lists.psu.edu/archives/sclistserv.html).

Cherney, L. R., Merbitz, C. T., & Grip, J. C. (1986). Efficacy of oral reading in aphasia treatment outcome. *Rehabililitation Literature*, 47, 112–118.

Cooper, J. O. (1991). Can this marriage be saved? Self-management of destructive inners. *Journal of Precision Teaching*, 8 , 44–46.

Cooper, J. O., Kubina, R., & Malanga, P. (1998). Six procedures for showing standard celeration charts. *Journal of Precision Teaching and Celeration*, 15, 58–76.

Edwards, D. D. & Edwards, J. S. (1970). Fetal movement: Development and time course. *Science*, 169, 95–97.

Fabrizio, M. A., Pahl, S., & Moors, A. (2002). Improving speech intelligibility through Precision Teaching. *Journal of Precision Teaching and Celeration*, 18, 25–27.

Graf, S. & Lindsey, O. R. (2002). *Standard celeration charting 2002.* Poland, OH: Grafimplements.

Haughton, E. C. (1980). Practicing practices: learning by activity. *Journal of Precision Teaching*, 1, 3–20.

Johnson, K. R. & Layng, T. V. J. (1992). Breaking the structuralist barrier: Literacy and numeracy with fluency. *American Psychologist*, 47, 1475–1490.

Johnson, K. R. & Layng, T. V. J. (1994). The Morningside model of generative instruction, in Gardner, R., Sainato, D.M., Cooper, J. O., Heron, T. E., Heward, W. L., Eshleman, J. W., & Grossi, T. A. (Eds.),

Behavior analysis in education: Focus on measurably superior instruction. Pacific Grove, CA: Brooks/Cole, pp. 173–197.

Johnston, J. M. & Pennypacker, H. S. (1971). A behavioral approach to college teaching. *American Psychologist*, 26, 219–244.

Kubina, R. M. & Morrison, R. S. (2000). Fluency in education. *Behavior and Social Issues*, 10, 83–99.

Lindsley, O. R. (1964). Direct measurement and prosthesis of retarded behavior. *Journal of Education*, 147, 62–81.

Lindsley, O. R. (1992). Precision teaching: Discoveries and effects. *Journal of Applied Behavior Analysis*, 25, 51–57.

Lindsley, O. R. (2002). *Diagramming learning streams and learning stream glossary 2002.* Invited address at the 15th Annual Precision Teaching Conference, Harrisburg, PA.

Lovaas, O. I., Ackerman, A. B., Alexander, D., Firestone, P., Perkins, J., & Young, D. (1981). *Teaching developmentally disabled children: The me book.* Austin, TX: Pro-Ed.

McDade, C. E. & Brown, J. M. (2001). *Celerating student skills: Basic and advanced.* Jacksonville, AL: author.

Merbitz, C. T. (1996). Frequency measures of behavior for assistive technology and rehabilitation. *Assistive Technology*, 8, 121–130.

Merbitz, C. T., King, R. B., Bleiberg, J., & Grip, J. C. (1985). Wheelchair push-ups: Measuring pressure relief frequency. *Archives of Physical Medicine and Rehabilitation*, 66, 433–438.

Merbitz, C. T., Miller, T. K., & Hansen, N. K. (2000). Cueing and logical problem solving in brain trauma rehabilitation: Frequency patterns in clinician and patient behaviors. *Behavioral Interventions*, 15, 169–187.

Moors, A. & Fabrizio, M. A. (2002). Using tool skill rates to predict composite skill frequency aims. *Journal of Precision Teaching and Celeration*, 18, 28–29.

Neely, M. (2002). Anna's food and stroke chart. *Journal of Precision Teaching and Celeration*, 18, 83–85.

Direct Instruction

CHAPTER

6

Direct Instruction:
The Big Ideas

TIMOTHY A. SLOCUM
Utah State University

INTRODUCTION

Direct Instruction is a systematic attempt to build a technology of effective academic instruction that includes all of the school-based components necessary to produce academic growth. Direct Instruction includes three broad components, each of which addresses a distinct set of issues that are critical to academic instruction: First, Direct Instruction includes a specific approach to determining what should be taught and how the curriculum should be organized. The driving principle is that the curriculum should be organized to teach generalizable strategies (Engelmann & Carnine, 1982). Second, Direct Instruction includes a set of specific instructional programs that are designed to systematically build skills by carefully organizing lessons, sequencing skill introduction, gradually reducing supports for student performance, providing sufficient practice, and specifying teaching procedures in specific detail. The programs cover a wide range of elementary and secondary level curricula (Marchand-Martella, Slocum, Martella, 2004). Third, Direct Instruction includes a distinct set of procedures regarding how teachers and students interact. The guiding principle is that lessons should maximize students' active and productive engagement with tasks that are at an appropriate instructional level. This chapter describes each of the three basic components, explains how the components are translated into specific instructional practice, and reviews the scientific research related to the effectiveness of the Direct Instruction approach.

TEACHING GENERALIZABLE STRATEGIES

Educators are faced with the challenge of teaching a long list of standards and objectives to a diverse set of learners in a very limited amount of time and, as a result, they must be keenly aware of the efficiency of their practices. In the Direct Instruction model, efficient and powerful instruction begins with a careful consideration of the curriculum. The goal is to identify or invent ways to organize the curriculum for efficient teaching and learning. For example, if we want to teach a student to read 1000 phonetically regular words, we could teach each of the 1000 words as a separate entity. Alternatively, we could teach the most common sound for each letter and the skill of blending sounds to form words. It would be tremendously more efficient to take the latter approach. Teaching the sounds and the ability to blend would not only enable the student to read the 1000 words in much less time, but students would also have skills that could be applied to many additional words. Learning the generalizable skill of phonetic decoding also provides a platform for learning more complex word-reading skills and even facilitates the learning of irregular words (irregular words have many phonetically regular sounds).

The key is to teach "big ideas" that allow students to go beyond the specific examples that were used in instruction and to respond correctly to new examples and in new situations that they never encountered in previous instruction. Such big ideas include skills, concepts, generalizations, and other knowledge structures that enable the student to generalize appropriately (Carnine, 1994; Kame'enui, Carnine, Dixon, Simmons, & Coyne, 2002). One of the primary challenges for instructional designers is to identify or invent powerful big ideas that can provide the foundation for efficient instruction. Phonetic decoding is, of course, a crucial big idea in early reading instruction. In elementary mathematics programs, the concept of a number family is a big idea that reduces fact memorization and provides a structure for solving story problems. The general skill of speaking in complete sentences is a big idea in preschool language development programs. Direct Instruction history programs are organized around the big ideas of a problem–solution–effect sequence and five basic types of solutions to historical problems (accommodate, dominate, move, invent, tolerate). In spelling, the big idea of dividing words into morphographs and using specific rules to join morphographs allows for highly efficient instruction. These are just a few examples of the dozens of big ideas that provide the foundation of Direct Instruction programs. For a more complete description of the big ideas in specific Direct Instruction programs, see Marchand-Martella et al. (2004).

The strategic and efficient use of big ideas is not apparent in a superficial examination of Direct Instructional materials. Like physical foundations, it is not the most obvious aspect of a structure, but it largely determines the value of the more obvious features.

INSTRUCTIONAL PROGRAMS THAT POWERFULLY AND SYSTEMATICALLY BUILD SKILLS

The big ideas that result from a careful analysis of the subject matter provide the core of the content to be taught. The next component of Direct Instruction is the *program* that organizes the content and specifies the procedures to teach this content. An instructional program is similar to a staircase that climbs from its base in prerequisite skills to its top at the program's objectives. To be effective, powerful, and inclusive, a program should enable the widest possible range of students who arrive at the start of the staircase (*i.e.*, who have the prerequisite skills) to reach the top (*i.e.*, to master the objectives). The key to creating a powerful program is to ensure that each student completes each step. Direct Instruction programs use five main strategies to make the staircase as simple as possible.

Clear and Explicit Instruction

To teach effectively and efficiently, big ideas must be conveyed to the students clearly, simply, and directly. The details of Communication depend on the learner's skills and the nature of the subject matter, but all communication is ultimately based on the use of examples. Direct Instruction programs use an elaborate and detailed analysis of communication to produce instruction that is consistent with only one interpretation. This system is described in depth by Engelmann and Carnine (1982).

When verbally stated rules are used, the instruction must carefully prepare the students to learn and apply the rule. For example, *Spelling Mastery Level C* (Dixon & Engelmann, 1999) teaches the spelling rule, "When a short word ends with a CVC [consonant–vowel–consonant pattern] and the next morphograph begins with a vowel letter, you double the last consonant" (p. 187). This rule would be worthless without careful preparation and systematic application with feedback. First, any terms or concepts used in the rule must be taught to mastery before the rule is introduced. Thus, the program includes specific instruction and practice on: (1) identifying the morphographs in words, (2) identifying whether the next morphograph begins with a vowel letter, and (3) identifying short words (less than five letters) that end with a consonant–vowel–consonant pattern. All of this instruction occurs before the overall rule is introduced. Second, the verbal statement of the rule must be explicitly taught and overtly practiced until students can say it reliably. Third, students must be carefully guided through the application of the rule. (This procedure of systematic guidance through application of a rule is illustrated in the next section.) Fourth, the rule must be implemented with the full range of relevant examples and non-examples. Thus, *Spelling Mastery Level C* provides practice that requires students to apply this rule to numerous words, including examples (*e.g.*, stopping) as well as non-examples that (1) are based on a word that is not short (*e.g.*, watering), (2) are based on a word that does not end with a CVC morphograph (*e.g.*, hoping), and (3) have an added morphograph that does not begin with a vowel (*e.g.*, runway).

Sequence of Instruction

The sequence of instruction is the order in which topics are taught, practiced, reviewed, and combined with other skills. The sequence must be carefully worked out if an instructional program are to reach a wide range of learners. Sequencing of Direct Instruction programs are based on three general guidelines. First, prerequisite skills should be taught and thoroughly practiced before students are taught the strategy that uses these skills; this guideline was illustrated with the example of teaching a morphographic spelling rule in the previous section. Second, instances consistent with a strategy should be taught and well established before exceptions to the strategy are introduced. If exceptions are introduced too early, students can make excessive errors, become confused about when to apply the rule, and guess rather than apply rules. After students have mastered a rule, exceptions can be introduced without undermining the general rule. Third, items that are likely to be confused should be separated in the sequence. Several classic learning problems are a matter of confusing similar items or processes. For example, many remedial readers confuse the similar letter-sound relations of *b* and *d*. When introducing similar items, one item should be taught and thoroughly practiced before the second item is introduced. In the Direct Instruction program, *Reading Mastery I* (Engelmann & Bruner, 2003), the letter *d* is introduced in lesson 27 and *b* is not introduced until lesson 121; this greatly reduces the confusion between *d* and *b*.

Provide Initial Support, Then Gradually Reduce Support

To create a sequence of small steps toward mastery of these complex skills, Direct Instruction programs often introduce skills with substantial support in the form of prompts from the teacher and from the written materials. Then, as students gain skills, the level of support is gradually reduced. This sequence of movement from highly supported to highly independent performance has been referred to as *mediated scaffolding* (Carnine, 1994; Kame'enui et al., 2002). For example, Table 1 shows a sequence of formats that are used to teach the rule for reading words that end with the vowel–consonant–*e* pattern (*e.g.*, hope, fire). When the rule is introduced, the teacher leads the students through its application with a series of questions (see Table 1, Format 1). As the students gain skill, the level of teacher support is reduced to that shown in Format 2, then 3, then 4. By the end of the sequence, students are able to encounter new words that end with a vowel–consonant–*e* pattern and read them correctly without any assistance from the teacher.

TABLE 1
Sequence of Formats Showing Gradual Fade of Strong Support

Format 1

1. Teacher: *Remember, when there is an "e" on the end, this letter (point to it) says its name.*

2. Teacher: *Is there an "e" on the end?* Students: *Yes.*

3. Teacher: *Will this letter* (point) *say its name or its sound?* Students: *Name.*

4. Teacher: *What is its name (or sound)?* Students: _____

5. Teacher: *What is the word?* Students: *Lake.*

Repeat steps 2 through 4 for each of the following words: fade, rot, note, bat, him, time.

Format 2

1. Teacher: *Is there an "e" on the end?* Students: *Yes.*

2. Teacher: *What sound will this letter* (point) *make?* Students: _____.

3. Teacher: *What is the word?* Students: *Lake.*

Repeat steps 2 through 4 for each of the following words: fade, rot, note, bat, him, time.

Format 3

1. Teacher: *What sound will this letter* (point) *make?* Students: _____.

2. Teacher: *What is the word?* Students: *Lake.*

Repeat steps 2 through 4 for each of the following words: fade, rot, note, bat, him, time.

Format 4

1. Teacher: *What is the word?* Students: *Lake.*

Repeat steps 2 through 4 for each of the following words: bat, float, first, toy, plane.

Format 5

Students read VCe (vowel–consonant–*e*) words in passages without previous practice on those words.

Provide Sufficient Practice and Mastery Criteria

Direct Instruction programs include the tools necessary for teachers to provide an appropriate amount of practice for a wide range of students and the provision that certain tasks should be repeated until students' responses are firm. The teacher repeats the examples in that task until the students respond correctly and without hesitation to all the items. This procedure of repeating tasks until firm is a way of adjusting the amount of practice provided in each task to the needs of the specific group. It allows the program to accommodate the needs of lower performing groups without requiring higher performing groups to work through unnecessary practice. Thus, in almost all cases, students master the particular items in a task by the end of the lesson. In addition to the adjustable amount of practice in each daily lesson and the distribution of practice across many lessons, Direct Instruction programs also include periodic mastery tests. Many Direct Instruction programs include a mastery test every five or ten lessons (*i.e.*, days). These tests provide a formal check on student mastery of skills. The programs suggest specific remedial sequences for students who fail to meet mastery criteria. Again, this system adjusts the amount of practice on each skill to ensure that students are well prepared for each new challenge in the program.

Provide Clear Instructions to Teachers

In education, as in building, plans can only be successful if they are clearly conveyed to the person who will implement them. Vague sketches with broad suggestions for building may be sufficient for creating simple structures such as a single plank spanning a creek, but complex structures such as the Golden Gate Bridge can only be constructed from detailed and specific plans. So, too, in education simple skills can be taught with relatively loose planning. This is especially true if we are working with students who bring excellent learning skills and strong prior knowledge, or if we are willing to accept a wide range of outcomes. However, if we aspire to teach complex skills to high levels of mastery with a wide range of students, then detailed and specific plans are necessary. The careful planning described in the previous sections of this chapter must be clearly conveyed to the teacher. Thus, Direct Instruction programs include scripts that specify explanations, examples, wording of rules, correction procedures, and criteria for judging mastery.

The use of scripts focuses the teacher's role in Direct Instruction. The teacher is not expected to identify big ideas, develop series of steps that build complex skills, or design sequences of examples. Instead, these tasks are the role of the program designer. In the Direct Instruction system, teachers have three main roles. First, they must present the material accurately, clearly, and with an engaging style. The teacher's presentation must breathe life into the script in the way that an actor's performance brings a dramatic script to life. Second, teachers must make numerous instructional decisions based on their understanding of each student's changing needs and abilities. The teacher must adjust the pacing the lessons, make corrections that are appropriate to the particular response, repeat activities or lessons as needed, adjust students' placement and grouping, and so on. Third, teachers must motivate the students to be engaged with the academic tasks and to apply their skills beyond the confines of the instructional session.

Scripts are an important component of the Direct Instruction system. They are intended to convey the program designer's plan to the teacher in a clear and direct manner and focus the teacher's role on making the critical instructional and management decisions that require specific knowledge of individual students (see Chapter 7 for more information).

Tracks

In most instructional programs, the teaching about a given topic is concentrated into a set of consecutive lessons—a *unit*. Because unit organization masses all the instruction on a given skill into a relatively small number of lessons, this method of organizing instruction tends to: (1) limit the time available for mastery of component skills, (2) limit the time available for introducing complex skills with strong scaffolding then gradually reducing the scaffolding as students gain competence, (3) limit the extent of application of the skills to diverse situations, (4) limit the extent of periodic review, and (5) produce lessons that are exclusively devoted to a single topic.

To solve these problems, Direct Instruction programs are organized by *tracks*. A track is the sequence of instruction on a given topic; however, no lesson is devoted exclusively to a single track. Instead, each lesson includes activities that are parts of several tracks. Track organization allows a program to prepare students for the introduction of a complex skill, to practice the skill, and to expand its application across many lessons. This form of organization supports the use of small instructional steps that build a skill across many lessons. For example, *Spelling Mastery Level C* (Dixon & Engelmann, 1999) develops the rule about doubling consonants across 69 lessons (*i.e.*, 69 days of instruction). Prerequisites for the rule are introduced in Lesson 51, and they are gradually elaborated across 40 lessons until the rule itself is taught. The rule is introduced in Lesson 91 with an elaborate format that makes the application of the rule overt. The rule is applied to numerous words, and the format is gradually simplified across the remaining 29 lessons of *Spelling Mastery Level C*.

ORGANIZE INSTRUCTION TO MAXIMIZE HIGH-QUALITY INSTRUCTIONAL INTERACTIONS

The third component of Direct Instruction is the organization of instruction in the classroom to produce high-quality interactions between teachers and students. Specifically, this component includes placing students into appropriate programs lessons, grouping students for efficient instruction, orchestrating active student engagement with the material, providing effective corrections, and ensuring that students spend sufficient time engaged with the content.

Placement

Direct Instruction programs are designed to provide a smooth sequence of steps that climb from the prerequisite skills to the program's objectives, but no instructional sequence, no matter how well constructed, can be effective if the students are not placed at a level in that sequence that is appropriate for their current skills. Students who have not mastered the prerequisite skills for the program and lesson on which they are working are unlikely to be successful in that lesson. Careful and flexible placement of students into programs and lessons is essential.

Each Direct Instruction program includes a placement test or specific placement guidelines. These assess whether the student has mastered:

(1) the program's prerequisites, (2) skills taught in various key points in the program, and (3) the program's objectives. Results from the placement test are used to determine whether the program is appropriate for the student and, if so, where in the program the student should begin. However, placement tests are not the last word on placement. Direct Instruction teachers often comment that the *real* placement test is performance on the first few lessons. When the student responds to the exercises in the lesson, the teacher can see whether that student has the skills necessary to succeed or has already mastered the material that is being taught. The teacher can then adjust the student's placement accordingly.

Even finding the ideal *initial* placement is not enough. Direct Instruction programs are designed to provide for smooth progress from beginning to end for a wide range of students; however, some students can leap ahead faster than the lessons allow and other students may progress more slowly. In both these cases, teachers must monitor daily and weekly progress throughout the programs and be alert for indications that a student's lesson placement is no longer appropriate. Thus, the concern with proper placement does not end when teaching begins; rather, it must be constantly monitored.

Flexible, Skill-Based Grouping for Efficient Instruction

Ideally, we would like to provide instruction tailored to each student's immediate needs each day, and we would like to provide the instructional step that is perfectly suited to the individual student's current skills; however, individual tutoring is rarely practical in schools. A viable alternative to individual tutoring is formation of small groups of students who have similar instructional needs. If we teach to the needs of these instructionally homogenous groups, we can come close to the effectiveness of tutoring. The success of this strategy is dependent on homogeneity of the group. If all the members of the group have very similar instructional needs, then this approach can be very successful; however, if the members of the group have diverse needs, then no single lesson can meet all their needs.

There are many instructional advantages to teaching small groups of students who have similar needs, but this method also has a potential danger. If we are not sensitive to the students' changing needs or we do not teach efficiently to every group, then the groups could impose limits on how much students can achieve. Thus, Direct Instruction programs include the means to frequently monitor student progress, and teachers must use these means to ensure that they are aware of each student's needs. A student who is capable of progressing more quickly than the rest of the group should be shifted to a more advanced group; a student who is not able to progress at the rate of the rest of the group should be shifted to a less advanced group. Thus, *flexibility* is a critical element of grouping in Direct Instruction.

Direct Instruction groups are formed on the basis of students' *current* instructional needs. Thus, the key question is what specific skills the student has and what specific skills the student needs to learn. Groups are not formed on the basis of labels such as "dyslexia," "attention deficit hyperactivity disorder," and "gifted and talented," nor are they formed on the basis of so called "general ability measures" (*i.e.*, IQ tests). It is more valid and effective to form groups on the basis of direct measures of students' initial skills (*i.e.*, placement tests) and adjust groupings on the basis of students' performance on lessons. Thus, Direct Instruction groups are based on students' current skills rather than being based on any vague, general, or long-lasting characteristic.

High Rates of Overt and Active Engagement

Students learn most when they are actively engaged with the instructional content. Active engagement means that the students *behave* with respect to the things that are being taught. In general, more engagement results in more learning. When they are engaged, students have opportunities to perform a skill, receive feedback (either from their own judgment of their responses or from an external source), and perform the skill again. Overt responses (*e.g.*, speaking, writing, gesturing) have the important advantage that teachers can observe the responses and (1) know whether students are, in fact, engaged; (2) provide confirmation or correction; (3) judge whether the group needs more practice or is ready to move on; and (4) judge whether individual students have needs that are different from the rest of the group. Thus, overt engagement is extremely important for effective and efficient instruction.

There are many ways of organizing overt engagement. Probably the most basic way is for teachers to ask questions or make requests directed to individual students. The main limitation of this approach is that while one student is engaged, all the other students may not be engaged with instruction at all. For example, if the teacher asks one direct question of each member of a 10-student group, each student makes only one overt response and may experience as much as 90% downtime. Written responses solve this problem because all students can respond simultaneously; however, written responses have the limitations of being difficult for some students and not providing the teacher with instant feedback on each student's performance.

Many Direct Instruction programs use *group unison oral responses* to promote overt engagement while avoiding the problems mentioned above. If the teacher asks oral questions and all students respond in unison, then all students can respond to each question and the teacher is made instantly aware of each student's response. If the teacher asks 10 questions with group unison responses, then each student makes 10 overt responses and experiences little, if any, downtime. The tremendous efficiency that is obtained by the use of group unison responses justifies the effort required to orchestrate them.

If all students initiate their responses at exactly the same time and makes a crisp (not sing-song or droned) response, then students do not receive hints from listening to other students and the teacher can hear a single error in a group. However, if some students answer slightly after the others or if students drone their answers, then students may receive subtle hints from hearing the others respond and the teacher cannot clearly hear any errors.

To receive the efficiency of group unison responses, the program must provide a means of coordinating the timing of student responses and teachers must use these means skillfully. Direct Instruction programs include specific signals that are used to enable all students in a group to answer together. A visual signal such as pointing is used when students are looking at the teacher or materials that the teacher is holding. An auditory signal such as a clap or finger-snap is used when the students are not looking at the teacher. With either type of signal, the teacher asks a question, pauses, and signals, and then the students answer together. An important skill for a Direct Instruction teacher is the ability to make clear signals and teach the students to respond correctly. This requires some learning on the part of teachers and students, but the return on this investment is a tremendous amount of efficiency.

Group unison responses can be tremendously efficient for providing guided practice on skills; however, they are supplemented by individual oral responses in all Direct Instruction programs and by written responses in all Direct Instruction programs in which students have the requisite skills. The mix of group unison, individual oral, and written responses varies according to the program's content and the skills assumed of students in the program.

Provide Effective Corrections

Students make mistakes during learning. The effectiveness and efficiency of error correction procedures is an important contributor to the overall success of the program. Direct Instruction teachers can make very effective error corrections because of the explicit and systematic initial presentation of instruction. In Direct Instruction programs, error corrections can refer to previously taught rules or procedures that would produce a correct response. This is a substantial advantage over less-explicit and less-systematic programs in which students may face a task without having been taught specific rules or procedures. In such a situation, the teacher must do substantial instruction in the form of error corrections, and this error correction/instruction has usually not been carefully planned in advance. This is akin to building a structure by starting with poorly planned construction, then renovating when faults become clear.

Direct Instruction programs specify the use of a variety of corrections depending on the content and the nature of the error. All corrections are variations on the basic plan in which the instructor (1) *models* the correct response, (2) *tests* the student by re-presenting the item that was missed, and then (3) performs a *delayed test* by working on some other items then returning to the item that was missed. Direct Instruction programs refer to this procedure as "model, test, delayed test." One common variation is to add a *lead* step in which the teacher makes the response along with the student, and the correction then becomes "model, lead, test, and delayed test." When students err because they did not apply a verbally stated *rule*, one or more prompts to support application of the rule are used instead of a model of the correct response, and the correction becomes "rule, test, and delayed test." When a student demonstrates a need for more practice on the corrected item, additional delayed tests are added. The correction then becomes "model, test, delayed test, delayed test, delayed test." Many other variations are used to correct specific kinds of errors.

RESEARCH RELATED TO DIRECT INSTRUCTION

Direct Instruction is one of the most thoroughly research-based and research-validated systems in education. The biggest challenge in describing the research related to Direct Instruction is organizing and summarizing the multiple streams of relevant research. We can divide the research base into two categories: (1) the indirect research base provides evidence about the effectiveness of various components, strategies, techniques, and approaches that are used in Direct Instruction programs; and (2) the direct research base provides evidence about the effectiveness of one or more specific Direct Instruction programs.

The indirect research base includes the huge body of research on teacher effectiveness (Brophy & Good, 1986; Rosenshine and Stevens, 1986) that supports many aspects of lesson organization and student-teacher interaction that are built into Direct Instruction programs. A second source of research that provides important but indirect support for Direct Instruction is research on specific subject areas that are addressed by Direct Instruction programs. For example, two recent reports summarizing research related to beginning reading instruction (National Reading Panel, 2000; Snow, Burns, Griffin, 1998) confirm the importance of phonological skills, phonic decoding, whole-word instruction on frequently occurring irregular words, and oral reading of passages. These are all core components of Direct Instruction reading programs.

An indirect research base is not sufficient, however. In order for a program to be to be empirically validated, that program must be directly subjected to research. There is also a large body of literature that directly examines the effects of specific Direct Instruction programs. This literature includes Project Follow Through and dozens of smaller studies. Project Follow Through was a massive study of the effectiveness of nine major approaches to compensatory education for students disadvantaged by poverty. The research aspect of the

project lasted 8 years (1968 to1976), involved over 10,000 students, and cost
$500 million (Adams & Engelmann, 1996). Outcomes studied included basic
skills (*e.g.*, word recognition, spelling, math computation), cognitive skills (*e.g.*,
reading comprehension, math problem solving), and affective outcomes (*e.g.*,
self-concept, attributions of success). Each of the nine approaches (or "spon-
sors") worked with multiple sites (local schools) across the country. Each site
was paired with a nearby control site that had similar demographics and was not
working with a sponsor (Stebbins, St. Pierre, Proper, Anderson, Cerva, 1977).

   Figure 1 shows the results of an overall comparison of each of the nine
approaches to control sites on the three kinds of outcomes. Each site was
compared to its control site on multiple measures. A comparison was considered *significant* if the difference was statistically significant and the effect size
was greater than .25. From Figure 1, it is clear that Direct Instruction was the
only one of the nine models that had consistently positive effects. The Direct
Instruction outcomes were vastly superior to all of the other models. Project
Follow Through produced a huge amount of data and numerous analyses.
Several good summaries of this research are available (Adams & Engelmann,
1996; Engelmann, Becker, Carnine, Gerstein, 1988; Watkins, 1997).

   In addition to Project Follow Through, dozens of reports of specific research
studies have been published. Adams and Engelmann (1996) conducted a meta-

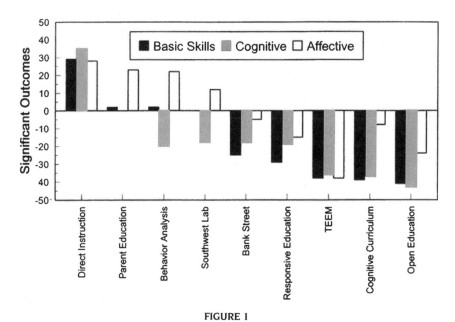

FIGURE 1

Project Follow Through results: Percent of significant outcomes
for each model. (From Adams, G. L. and Engelmann, S., *Research on
Direct Instruction: 25 Years Beyond DISTAR*, Seattle, WA: Educational
Assessment Systems, 1996. With permission.)

analysis of 37 research studies on Direct Instruction. These studies included 374 individual comparisons of groups that received Direct Instruction with groups that received some other treatment. Fully 64% of these individual comparisons found statistically significant differences that favored the Direct Instruction group, 35% found differences that were too small to achieve statistical significance, and only 1% found statistically significant differences favoring the non-Direct Instruction group. When the results of all of the studies are combined, the average effect size is .97 favoring the Direct Instruction groups. By any standard, this is a very large effect (see Chapter 9 for further information about effect sizes).

Adams and Engelmann also found that studies of general education students had an average effect size of 1.27 and studies of students in special education had an average effect size of .76. Both effects are very large. They found that studies conducted with students at the elementary level had an effect size of .84, and those at the secondary or adult level showed an effect size of 1.50. Again, both results indicate very strong positive results. They found a moderate average effect size in language (.49), a large effect size in reading (.69), and an extremely large effect size for social studies (.97), math (1.11), spelling (1.33), and science (2.44). This meta-analysis indicates that Direct Instruction has been extremely successful in research studies across general and special education, grade levels, and subject areas.

In 1998 and 1999, the American Federation of Teachers (AFT) commissioned a series of analyses of educational research literature to discover what works in various areas of education. The reports described Direct Instruction as (1) one of seven promising reading and language arts programs (AFT, 1998a), (2) one of six promising schoolwide reform programs (AFT, 1998b), and (3) one of five promising remedial reading intervention programs (AFT, 1999). One of the reports commented, "When this program [DI] is faithfully implemented, the results are stunning" (AFT, 1998a, p. 9).

The American Institutes for Research (AIR) was commissioned by the American Association of School Administrators, American Federation of Teachers, National Association of Elementary School Principals, and National Education Association to examine the literature on schoolwide reform approaches. The AIR examined 130 studies on 24 prominent models. They found that Direct Instruction is one of only three models that has "strong evidence of positive outcomes on student achievement" (Herman et al., 1999). More recently, Borman *et al.* (2002) published a meta-analysis of results from 29 comprehensive school reform models. They considered 232 studies and 1111 separate comparisons. From this large database, the authors identified Direct Instruction as one of just three models that achieved the criteria of "strongest evidence of effectiveness."

This very brief summary of research reviews related to Direct Instruction indicates that Direct Instruction (1) is consistent with effective instructional practices; (2) has been found by an independent evaluation to have strongly positive effects in Project Follow Through; (3) has been found to be effective across variations in student population, grade level, and content areas; and (4) has been judged to be well supported by research in several recent independent reviews.

References

Adams, G. L. & Engelmann, S. (1996). *Research on direct instruction: 25 years beyond DISTAR*. Seattle, WA: Educational Assessment Systems.

American Federation of Teachers (AFT). (1998a). *Seven promising schoolwide programs for raising student achievement*. Washington, D.C.: author (http://www.aft.org/edissues/downloads/seven.pdf).

American Federation of Teachers (AFT). (1998b). *Six promising school wide reform programs*. Washington, D.C.: author (http://www.aft.org/edissues/rsa/ promprog/wwschoolwidereform.htm).

American Federation of Teachers (AFT). (1999). *Five promising remedial reading intervention programs*. Washington, D.C.: author (http://www.aft.org/edissues/whatworks/wwreading.htm).

Borman, G. D., Hewes, G. M., Overman, L. T., & Brown, S. (2002). *Comprehensive School Reform and student achievement: A meta-analysis* (Report No. 59). Baltimore MD: Center for Research on the Education of Students Placed At Risk, Johns Hopkins University (http://www.csos.jhu.edu).

Brophy, J. & Good, T. (1986). Teacher behavior and student achievement, in Whittrock, M. C. (Ed.), *Handbook of Research on Teaching*, 3rd ed. New York: Macmillan, pp. 328–375.

Carnine, D. (1994). Introduction to the mini-series: diverse learners and prevailing, emerging, and research-based educational approaches and their tools. *School Psychology Review*, 23, 341–350.

Dixon, R. & Engelmann, S. (1999). *Spelling mastery level C*. Columbus, OH: SRA/McGraw-Hill.

Engelmann, S. & Bruner, E. C. (2003). *Reading mastery classic: Level I*. Columbus, OH: SRA/ McGraw-Hill.

Engelmann, S. & Carnine, D. W. (1982). *Theory of instruction: Principles and applications*. New York: Irvington.

Engelmann, S., Becker, W. C., Carnine, D., & Gersten, R. (1988). The Direct Instruction follow through model: design and outcomes. *Education and Treatment of Children*, 11, 303–317.

Herman, R., Aladjem, D., McMahon, P. Masem, E, Mulligan, I., O'Malley, A. *et al.* (1999). *An educator's guide to schoolwide reform*. Washington, D.C.: American Institutes for Research (http://www. aasa.org/ issues_and_insights/district_organization/ Reform).

Kame'enui, E. J., Carnine, D. W., Dixon, R. C., Simmons, D. C., & Coyne, M. D. (2002). *Effective teaching strategies that accommodate diverse learners*, 2nd ed. Upper Saddle River, NJ: Merrill.

Marchand-Martella, N. E., Slocum, T. A., & Martella, R. C. (Eds.). (2004). *Introduction to direct instruction*. Boston, MA: Allyn & Bacon.

National Reading Panel. (2000). *Report of the National Reading Panel: Teaching children to read: An evidence-based assessment of the scientific research literature on reading and its implications for reading instruction*. Jessup, MD: National Institute for Literacy.

Rosenshine, B. & Stevens, R. (1986). Teaching functions, in Whittrock, M.C. (Ed.), *Handbook of research on teaching*, 3rd ed. New York: Macmillan, pp. 376–391.

Snow, C. E., Burns, M. S., & Griffin, P. (Eds.). (1998). *Preventing reading difficulties in young children*. Washington, D.C.: National Academy Press.

Stebbins, L. B., St. Pierre, R. G., Proper, E. C., Anderson, R. B., & Cerva, T. R. (1977). *Education as experimentation: A planned variation model*. Vol. IV-A. *An Evaluation of Follow Through*. Cambridge, MA: Abt Assoc.

Watkins, C. L. (1997). *Project Follow Through: A case study of the contingencies influencing instructional practices of the educational establishment* [monograph]. Concord, MA: Cambridge Center for Behavioral Studies.

CHAPTER 7

Teacher-Made Scripted Lessons

JOHN H. HUMMEL, MARTHA L. VENN, and PHILIP L. GUNTER

Valdosta State University

INTRODUCTION

How one teaches course content and manages classroom behavior are often compartmentalized as separate educational issues when, in fact, research suggests that the two are interrelated (Clarke et al., 1995; Dunlap et al., 1993; Gunter & Reed, 1997; Gunter, Shores, Jack, Denny, De Paepe 1994; Kauffman, 2001). More directly, when teachers present information to students following the explicit instruction format associated with scripted Direct Instruction lessons Gunter, Hummel, & Conroy, 1998; Gunter & Reed, 1997), with scripted Direct Instruction lessons (Martella & Johnson, 2003), students' achievement increases and often their misbehavior, collaterally, decreases. In this chapter, we define explicit instruction, provide a rationale for explicit instruction, describe how teachers can employ the components of explicit instruction, and explain how its systematic use can result in both improved academic achievement and decreased undesirable behavior of students. When teachers employ well-developed scripts, students are more actively engaged with the content and, as a result, more of them master the content.

DEFINITION OF EXPLICIT INSTRUCTION

There are several different labels for what we refer to as explicit instruction. These labels include effective instruction, systematic teaching, and active teaching (Rosenshine & Stevens, 1986). Whichever label one employs, the technique involves a teacher-centered classroom where the teacher delivers content to students in a bottom-up (piece-by-piece) process, with the students actively engaged with the material presented. Conceptually, we can view this model of instruction as a specific form of what Slavin (2000) calls the *seven-step Direct Instruction (DI) lesson*. Critical features of Direct Instruction lessons include highly sequenced instruction, clear and concise directions, teacher guidance, active student participation, and assessment probes in order to practice and master new knowledge and skills. The seven sequential parts to a DI lesson are (1) gain learner's attention, (2) review prerequisites, (3) present new content, (4) probe learning, (5) provide independent practice, (6) assess performance and provide feedback, and (7) provide distributed practice and review. Explanations for each step in a DI lesson are presented within the framework of developing scripted lessons.

SCRIPTED LESSONS

Planning and implementing direct instructional lessons is important for student achievement and teacher accountability. Over the course of the year, teachers often engage in a variety of routinized schedules and activities. Frequently, these routines drive the structure of the day, regardless of whether students are actively learning new knowledge and skills. All forms of explicit instruction simply reflect highly structured teacher routine.

Commercially available Direct Instruction programs reflect explicit instruction (*e.g.*, Science Research Associates' *Reading Mastery* and Saxon's *Algebra 1/2*). We can choose, however, to develop original direct instructional lessons by scripting. Developing one's own scripted lessons is a straightforward task that practicing educators can do by themselves and has the added benefit that this powerful instructional tool can be applied to virtually any course content for all levels of students.

Typically, scripted lessons are planned for teaching academic skills that comprise a series of chained behaviors such as spelling and math computation, as well as discrete behaviors such as vocabulary terms and math facts. In essence, a teacher would plan a scripted lesson for acquisition of knowledge and skills where there are distinct steps to completing the academic task. Scripted lessons, though, should not be limited to just those academic tasks that teach concrete skills. Bloom *et al.* (1956) identified six levels of learning within a hierarchy beginning with *knowledge* (basic recall) and progressing through *comprehension* (summarizing and paraphrasing accurately), *application* (generalizing skills and knowledge to new settings and situations), *analysis* (breaking content into its pieces), *synthesis* (using learned skills and knowledge to create, for the student, something new), and *evaluation* (judging merits by comparing to standards). Teachers can also prepare scripted lessons that reflect these advanced levels of learning. In the following sections, the procedures for scripting will be integrated into the parts of a seven-step direct instruction lesson.

ORIENT AND REVIEW

New lessons begin by gaining student attention and revisiting pertinent skills and knowledge previously taught. Often, teachers accomplish this by only reviewing content covered earlier. Generally, though, an effective scripted lesson will begin with a brief overview highlighting what the day's lesson will cover to activate students' prior knowledge they possess about the content and should end with a description of the day's learning outcomes or objectives. The review (step 2 of the seven-step DI lesson) will then allow teachers to carry out several teaching functions such as focusing student attention on the task, probing student understanding of content, providing review opportunities for students, and providing opportunities for corrective feedback or positive feedback to students. In Direct Instruction, both review and new information are presented in small pieces. After each piece, students typically must make a choral response signaled by the teacher. Because information is presented in small pieces the pace is quick, and students are actively responding throughout. The fast pace of evoking student responses (9 to 12 per minute), associated with the high level of accuracy desired of those student responses (at least 90%) during review of previously learned material, also sets the stage for the response momentum phenomenon to occur when more difficult tasks (*e.g.*, questions at the higher levels of the Bloom taxonomy) are interspersed among less difficult ones (Davis, Brady, Hamilton, McEvoy, Williams, 1994). When students are on a roll (*i.e.*, correctly answering questions related to pieces of information presented by the teacher), they are also more likely to perceive (and correctly respond to) questions requiring critical thinking (*i.e.*, the higher levels of the Bloom taxonomy).

All lessons are based on clearly stated and communicated objectives that specify what the students should be able to do or say after the lesson. Formats for reviewing previous content can take many shapes. For example, teachers may plan a series of higher order questions in a sequence based the Bloom taxonomy in order to review and assess previous learning. Teachers can divide the class into two teams, and the students can then devise questions for the other team to answer based on previously learned material. A commonly used review strategy is having students check homework assignments. Remember that the goal is to review previous content, check for student acquisition, and determine whether re-teaching is required for content necessary to work with the new information or procedures to be presented.

PRESENTATION OF NEW CONTENT

A primary defining characteristic of effective instruction is that new content is presented in small steps (a bottom-up approach; see Slavin, 2000). In the following text, procedures for presenting new information are analyzed. It goes without saying that the educator's objectives should clearly state what the students are to say or do rather than employing ambiguous terms such as know or understand. Additionally, it is axiomatic that teachers must be able to do the complex outcomes specified in course objectives. Suppose one of a teacher's goals is for students to learn how to add two two-digit numbers. The objective for this could be "After the lesson on addition, students will correctly hand-compute 50 addition problems involving two two-digit numbers and regrouping with 90% accuracy in 10 minutes or less."

When the objectives have been well defined, the next step in developing an explicit lesson plan involves identifying the step-by-step progression for successfully completing the academic task. This is formally called a *task analysis* (Gagne, 1962). Conceptually, a complex activity specified in an objective is delineated into subcomponent behaviors that are placed within a sequential order. The key is to make certain that each subcomponent identifies an overt action that the students must perform. To begin a task analysis, simply list, in order, the first thing to do, the second, the third, etc., until the complex action stated in the objective is completed. It is a straightforward process but novices often make predictable mistakes. The most common mistakes include: (1) skipping steps, (2) not specifying an overt action at each step, and (3) not having enough steps.

Generally, teachers are masters of their content, and they perform the tasks associated with their objectives almost by rote because they have practiced them countless times. Because it is so easy for teachers to do complex activities, it is a good idea to double check the sequence of their academic content to ensure that critical steps have not been skipped. Once the steps are rechecked, colleagues can be asked to review them, also. Specifying an overt action at each step is vital because it provides the teacher and learner with an objective reference point, or *behavioral anchor*, to monitor progress. No one can objectively know if a person has actually acquired a skill until the person demonstrates it; when students can do the skill, it can be mastered at the level specified in the objective through practice and with feedback.

The number of subcomponents skills in a task analysis may range from 3 steps to as many as 15 or more. As Gagne (1977) pointed out, we should continue breaking down the objective's activity until the first step is a behavior that everyone in the class can do without training. Table 1 highlights examples of how to delineate the steps of adding two-digit numbers with and without regrouping, while Table 2 specifies the steps to follow to correctly use the apostrophe. Each complete task analysis is the basic starting point for the

TABLE 1

**Identifying the Subcomponents of Teaching Two-Digit Addition With
and Without Regrouping**

Step	Subcomponent
1	Copy the problem (if not already on a provided sheet), making certain that one of the numbers is above the other, the 1's and 10's place values for both numbers are aligned, and the bottom number is underlined.
2	Add the 1's place values together, and if the sum is less than 10 write their sum below the horizontal line aligned with the 1's place of the original numbers.
2a	If the sum is greater than 10, write the 1's value of the sum below the line and carry the 10's value by writing that value above the top digit in the problem's 10's place.
3	Add the 10's place values, including any carryover from the 1's sum to the left of the 1's sum and below the 10's values of the original numbers.

TABLE 2

Identifying the Subcomponents of Teaching How To Use the Apostrophe

Step	Subcomponent
1	After writing a sentence, reread the sentence aloud. If the sentence contains any contractions (*e.g.*, isn't, I'm), the omitted letter is replaced with an apostrophe.
2	In the sentence you just read, also look for nouns that denote ownership/possession. If the noun is singular, add an apostrophe *s* ('*s*) after the last letter of the noun. If the noun is plural, add an *s* followed by an apostrophe (*s*').

scripted lesson the educator develops to teach students the series of discrete behaviors identified in the complex action specified by an objective.

PRACTICE

For each subcomponent of the task analysis, the teacher provides clear instruction and explanation and models the step to provide guided practice to students. During the numerous group and individual practice opportunities, the teacher initially uses prompts to guide the student through the steps delineated in the task analysis (and later through activities composed of multiple steps) and fades this assistance as the students acquire mastery of the content. For example, suppose a teacher had recently taught students how to show possession by using apostrophes. While these students complete a worksheet that requires them to correct sentences illustrating possession, the teacher might verbally prompt them to use "apostrophe *s*" for singular cases, and "*s* apostrophe" for plural ones. In later exercises, instead of providing the prompt to the entire group, the teacher will monitor the work of individuals and might give the prompt to an individual incorrectly using the "apostrophe *s*" when the plural form is needed. Additionally, in this instance, the teacher may first, before giving the original prompt, ask the student: "Is the possessive word singular or plural? What is the possessive rule for each?" Over trials, the amount of cueing information given to the student is decreased. The steps for guided practice are model, probe, and then check.

Model

The teacher models or demonstrates the correct sequence of behaviors required for successful completion of an academic task. Teachers should select a model based on the needs of the student and the academic task. Typical models could be verbal (*e.g.*, verbally stating each letter of a word in sequential order), written (*e.g.*, steps to complete the problem are written at the top of the page), pictorial (*e.g.*, picture cue demonstrating an action), or a *physical demonstration* (*e.g.*, the teacher demonstrates the physical actions required to complete the appropriate step). Instructional modeling should ensure student responding and be specific to the academic needs of the students. In a scripted verbal presentation, the teacher presents a piece of information and then asks a question derived from the piece of information. This is very different from the way in which most teachers present information in at least two ways. First, the information is delivered to the students in small pieces rather than complete wholes. Second, the information is presented to the students in an answer-and-question format instead of the more traditional question-and-answer form most teachers employ. For example, if you were introducing students to the six levels of the Bloom taxonomy of cognitive objectives, your script might look something like this:

> The Bloom taxonomy has six levels.
> *How many levels does the Bloom taxonomy have?*
> The first level is the knowledge level.
> *Name the first level.*
> The second level is comprehension.
> *Everyone, what's the name of the second level?*
> *Now name the first two levels.*
> The third level is called application.
> *What is the name of the third level?*
> *Everyone, name the first three levels of the taxonomy.*

The piece of information the teacher presents in the script is based on the steps in the objective's task analysis. Typically, the teacher's question is one that the entire group answers rather than being directed to an individual. For example, when teaching students how and when to use the apostrophe, the teacher might first say: "The apostrophe is used to indicate either a contraction or possession." After making the statement, the teacher could ask the following question that the students would answer in unison: "Apostrophes are used to indicate contractions and _____." As soon as the question is delivered to the students, the teacher gives a signal (thumb snap, hand drop, etc.) to cue the group to answer the question as a group.

Probes and Checks

The teacher should informally assess (*i.e.*, these assessments do not affect students' grades) student acquisition of new knowledge and skills. Oral probes requiring choral or individual responses (checks) are done while teaching new content (*i.e.*, during step three of the direct instruction lesson). Written exercises, another type of probe, are usually done after presenting the lesson and help students learn the material and achieve a higher level of fluency (accuracy plus speed). All probes and checks provide the teacher with data that can support whether progress is being made toward achievement of the objectives. If students are not answering probes fluently, the teacher has real-time achievement data suggesting where re-teaching or additional practice is needed, which is one of the characteristics of effective instruction (see Chapter 2 for a discussion of the characteristics of effective instruction). Because instruction is usually presented to the entire group, most oral probes are designed to prompt a choral group response. Written exercises can be done individually or as a group activity. All probes and checks provide the teacher with data that can support whether progress is being made toward achievement of the objectives and where re-teaching may be needed.

Because content and skills are taught in small steps, student responses are almost always correct and can trigger positive feedback from the teacher. Incorrect responses trigger non-punitive corrective feedback and are easier to rectify because the failure invariably is associated with the most recently modeled step. After the choral response, the teacher can either model the next step or ask an individual student a follow-up question related to the step to ensure that all students are engaged with the material. After presenting the first two steps of an objective, the learning process can be facilitated by modeling these steps in sequence. As additional steps are modeled, teachers should precede each new step by demonstrating, probing, and checking the previous steps completed in series. Table 3 presents an example of a scripted lesson for teaching students to add two two-digit numbers together, and Table 4 provides an example of a scripted lesson designed to teach students how to correctly employ the apostrophe when writing. When learning is occurring at the preset mastery level, teachers should transition to providing practice at the independent level.

FORMAL ASSESSMENTS

Steps 5 (independent practice), 6 (exams), and 7 (distributed practice) are all formal assessments. Because performance on these activities affects students'

TABLE 3
A Scripted Lesson for Teaching Two-Digit Addition With and Without Regrouping

Step	Script
1	Up to now we have been adding one number to another. Today we are going to learn how to add two-digit numbers together. Two-digit numbers have two values; a 1's value and a 10's value. In the number 34, the 1's value is 4 and the 10's value is 3. What is the 1's value in the number 47? *(signaled—either by hand or sound—choral response followed by praise)* What is the 10's value? *(choral response)* Good!
	The first thing we have to do when adding two two-digit number together is to make sure that the two numbers are arranged so that the 1's value of the first number is right above the 1's value of the second number, and the 10's value of the first is also right above the 10's value of the second. When we copy a problem, where should the 1's values of the two numbers be? *(choral response)* Yes, the 1's place for both numbers should be one above the other. Where should the 10's place values be? *(choral response)* Good!
	After we write the two numbers to be added we draw a horizontal line under the bottom number. Where does the horizontal line for each addition problem go? *(choral response)* That's right, under the bottom number. Copy this problem so the numbers are positioned for us to add them together: 16 + 22 (Check each student's work.)
2	When we have copied the problem, we first add the two 1's value numbers. What do we add together first, the 1's value numbers or the 10's value numbers? *(choral response)* Right! We add the 1's values first.
	If the sum of the 1's values is 9 or less, we write the sum under the 1's place below the horizontal line. The sum of 6 plus 2 is? *(choral response)* Correct, it is 8. Write the number 8 below the horizontal line under the 6 and 2. (Model the step and check each student's work.)
2a	If the sum of the 1's value numbers is more than 9, we have to write the 1's value sum below the horizontal line and write the 10's value above the 10's value numbers that are above the horizontal line. If the sum of the 1's values is more than 9, what do we do? *(choral response)* Yes, we write the 1's value of the sum below the horizontal line, and carry the 10's value to the 10's column.
3	When we have added both the 1's values together and written their sum below the horizontal line, we add the two 10's value numbers together and write their sum below the horizontal line. What is the sum of 1 and 2? *(choral response)* Right! It is 3. Watch where I write the sum of the 10's values. (Teacher models) Now you write the sum on your paper. (Check each student's work, then perform several other examples for them.)
	Now I am going to write another problem on the board. Copy it, and add the values together. (Give several problems without regrouping; after checking them, give several that require regrouping.)

grades, teachers should not schedule these events until the probes and checks (especially individually completed written exercises) indicate that students have learned the content.

TABLE 4
A Scripted Lesson for Teaching How To Use the Apostrophe

Step	Script
1	The apostrophe is a type of punctuation. The apostrophe, like commas and periods, is a type of what? (After each question, give a hand or audible signal for the students to respond chorally.) Yes, an apostrophe is a type of punctuation.
2	The apostrophe looks like a comma but instead of being at the bottom of a word where commas go, it is at the top of the word. What type of punctuation does an apostrophe look like? *(choral response)* Yes, a comma. (On the board, illustrate and label a comma and an apostrophe.)
3	Like all punctuation, it is understood when we speak, but we have to write it out when we are writing. In which type of communication do we actually use the apostrophe? *(choral response)* Yes, when we write; it is understood when we are talking.
4	The apostrophe is used in two situations when we write. How many ways are apostrophes used? *(choral response)* That's right, two ways.
5	The first way we use apostrophes in our writing is when we put two words together to form a single word called a contraction. When you make a single word from two words what is it called? *(choral response)* Yes, it is called a contraction.
6	When we combine two words into a single word, we typically drop a letter (sometimes two or three letters) from the second word and substitute the apostrophe sign. What does an apostrophe replace in a contraction? *(choral response)* Good! The contraction of the two words is written as a single word that contains an apostrophe.
7	Here are some common examples of words that we can make into contractions by: (1) dropping a letter or letters, or (2) writing the words as a single word with an apostrophe in place of the dropped letters (write list on board): *I am = I'm* *do not = don't* *she is = she's* *they will = they'll* *let us = let's* *I would = I'd* *we have = we've* *should not = shouldn't*
8	Using these examples, change each of the following sets of words into contractions (write list on board): *I will* *can not* *we have* *it is* *you are* Now, let's check your work. Watch as I write the correct contraction next to each set of words. Good job, everyone!

continues

continued

9	(Call on a student.) I want you to tell me where the apostrophes go in this sentence: "The leaves wouldnt burn because they werent dry." *(student's response)* Yes, the sentence needs an apostrophe in the words wouldn't and weren't. Good job!
10	Remember that apostrophes are used in two situations. We've just illustrated the first situation. When we make a contraction we use the apostrophe to replace what? *(choral response)* Yes, the missing or dropped letters from the second word. We also use apostrophes to show ownership or possession. Words that demonstrate ownership are in the possessive case. Words that show ownership are in what case? *(choral response)* Yes, possessive case.

Let's start with nouns. Nouns are names for people, places, ideas/concepts, and things. Nouns are names for what? *(choral response)* Good!

When you have a singular noun, such as girl, man, Ms. Smith, or car, to show ownership you add an apostrophe s ('s) after the last letter of the word. In this list, the noun owns the word that follows it (write sentence on board):

a girl's hairstyle
the man's wallet
Ms. Smith's dress
the car's window

11	If the noun is singular, such as one person, place, or thing, use the apostrophe s form. For example, suppose I want to say something about the performance of Bill on a test. To show that this performance is owned by Bill (and not Margaret), after his name I use an apostrophe s:

What was Bill's test score?

Now, I want each of you to rewrite the following sentences using the apostrophe s correctly (write sentences on board):

Standardized tests measure a persons aptitude or ability.
The cost of freedom is respect for everyones rights, even those we dislike.

12	If the noun is plural you generally use the s apostrophe form. For example, suppose I want to know where I have put your test papers (write on board):

Has anyone seen my students' tests?

Now, I want each of you to rewrite the following sentence using the s apostrophe correctly (write sentence on board):

The students performance on the homework assignment was better today.

(Check each student's answer.)

13	If the conversion of the noun to the plural form is not an instance where you simply add an s, convert the noun to its plural form followed by the apostrophe. For example, country is singular so its possessive form is country's, as in:

my country's educational system.

If we were referring to an educational system possessed by several countries (the plural form of country), we would use the possessive plural in this way (write sentence on board):

These countries' educational systems are computer intensive.

Rewrite the following sentence to show plural possession for the following concept (write sentence on board):

The babies crying was heart wrenching.

Independent Practice

After modeling, probing, and checking during steps 3 and 4 of the direct instruction lesson, the teacher should provide independent practice (also called *seatwork*) on the material (Heward *et al.*, 1990). Independent practice opportunities should be done individually because the work is assigned a grade. The teacher should monitor the students' work as it is being done in order to provide prompts/scaffolding (cues to guide the students) to ensure success. Teachers must understand that the formal assessment steps may occur a number of days after the initial introduction of new information and that not every lesson will include all three formal assessment steps.

Exams

Step 6 of the direct instruction lesson requires the students to take an exam or quiz over the content. While exams can take a variety of forms (*e.g.*, essays, multiple choice), several points need to be kept in mind. First, it is prudent to test only the objectives that have been directly taught. This sounds simple, but this principle of effective testing is frequently violated by teachers. Second, test at the appropriate levels of the Bloom taxonomy. Hummel and Huitt (1994) found that over 80% of teacher assessments only require students to perform at the knowledge and comprehension levels, rather than the higher levels of the Bloom taxonomy. Students will not necessarily learn content at the higher levels of the taxonomy unless teachers require them to perform at the higher levels on informal and formal assessments. For example, a teacher might ask students to list and describe the six levels of the Bloom taxonomy, which would only require students to perform at the knowledge or comprehension level. Had the teacher given the students a set of objectives or test items and required the students to explain which level of the taxonomy each item required the student to perform at, the students would be required to perform at the higher levels of the taxonomy. Obviously, students being able to correctly pinpoint which level of the taxonomy requires more time and effort than simply listing the levels in sequence. Last, more frequent assessments over small pieces of content lead to higher levels of student achievement (Gronlund, 1998).

Distributed Practice

Step 7 of the direct instruction lesson is usually thought of as homework but also includes any work students must complete outside of class, such as reports and projects. There are two central points to focus on when making such assignments. First, the assignment is additional practice for content and skills already learned in class. Too many teachers assign homework on new content that requires students to demonstrate skills and knowledge that they have not yet learned. Second, distributed practice assignments should not only involve practice over new content, but should also help the students to integrate it with content from previous lessons. Frequently, new content is related to, or builds on, information students have already learned. Distributed practice assignments should be designed to connect the new with the old while providing practice over both. For example, in a chronologically based American history class, students may have learned a list of causes that historians believe resulted in World War I. If today's topic in the class deals with the causes of World War II, a distributed practice assignment might require students to describe similarities and differences between the causes of WWI and WWII.

POSITIVE OUTCOMES OF SCRIPTED LESSONS

Research shows that when teachers systematically develop and use scripted direct instruction lessons, several encouraging outcomes can occur. First, students spend more time actively engaged with their subject matter, thereby increasing their achievement (Rieth & Evertson, 1988). Second, students respond correctly at levels more in line with the recommendations for effective instruction such as those provided by the Council for Exceptional Children (1987). In fact, some scripted lessons allow for 4 to 6 responses per minute during instruction and 9 to 12 per minute during practice, demonstrating that effective instruction produces high levels of fluency. Finally, because students respond successfully at such high levels, there are more frequent opportunities for their teachers to attend positively to their correct academic and social responses.

In addition to the benefits previously noted, systematic use of effective instructional practices such as scripted lessons also can decrease misbehavior problems in the classroom. In their review of the literature, Gunter *et al.* (1998) found that much of the misbehavior exhibited by students may be controlled by negative reinforcement. Specifically, when a lesson is beyond the skill level of students or is presented in a boring or passive way, many students act out (which effectively stops the lesson, at least for a while) to escape the tedium or frustration at not being able to follow the presentation. In numerous studies, when teachers employed effective instructional tactics, the students' rate of misbehavior decreased even though such responses were not directly targeted. Thus, it may be concluded that when instruction is structured so that students respond correctly at high rates, not only will students' achievement increase, but also those misbehaviors that are maintained by negative reinforcement will decrease measurably. When it is important to improve achievement and reduce poor behavior, scripted lessons can be of significant help. (What might help improve achievement and reduce poor behavior? Yes! Scripted lessons can lead to lower levels of misbehavior and higher levels of achievement!)

One criticism of teacher-made scripted lessons that is often also directed to commercially available Direct Instruction materials is that scripts based on complete task analyses of learning objectives are too inflexible. Faster students are viewed as being held back, and slower students may be left behind because the pace is too quick. While either could occur, neither needs to occur.

One of the reasons we first do a task analysis on the learning outcomes is to objectively determine a starting point for the lesson. The starting point should be a skill everyone in the class can do without instruction. The script, then, is simply the pedagogical device of choice that feeds new skills and knowledge piece by piece so the students have enough active participation to thoroughly master the complex behavior specified in the lesson's objectives.

During a scripted presentation, based on the students' fluency, teachers can stop at just about any point to provide additional examples and demonstrations, or to discuss specific or extant points possibly requiring greater clarification (based on the students' responding). Scripts should be designed in enough detail so no student is left behind.

References

Bloom, B. S., Englehart, M. D., Furst, E. J., Hill, W. H., & Krathwohl, D. R. (1956). *Taxonomy of educational objectives: The classification of educational goals*. Handbook 1. *The Cognitive Domain*. New York: Longman.

Clarke, S., Dunlap, G., Foster-Johnson, L., Childs, K. E., Wilson, D., White, R. *et al*. (1995). Improving the conduct of students with behavioral disorders by incorporating student interests into curricular activities. *Behavioral Disorders*, 20, 221–237.

Council for Exceptional Children. (1987). *Academy for effective instruction: Working with mildly handicapped students*. Reston, VA: The Council for Exceptional Children.

Davis, C. A., Brady, M. P., Hamilton, R., McEvoy, M. A., & Williams, R. E. (1994). Effects of high-probability requests on the social interactions of young children with severe disabilities. *Journal of Applied Behavior Analysis*, 27, 619–637.

Dunlap, G., Kern, L., dePerczel, M., Clarke, S., Wilson, D., Childs, K. E., et al. (1993). Functional analysis of classroom variables for students with emotional and behavioral disorders. *Behavioral Disorders*, 18, 275–291.

Gagne, R. M. (1962). The acquisition of knowledge. *Psychology Review*, 69, 355–365.

Gagne, R. M. (1977). *The conditions of learning*, 3rd ed. New York: Holt, Rinehart, & Winston.

Gronlund, N. E. (1998). *Assessment of student achievement*, 6th ed. Boston: Allyn & Bacon.

Gunter, P. L., Hummel, J. H., & Conroy, M. A. (1998). Increasing correct academic responding: an effective intervention strategy to decrease behavior problems. *Effective School Practices*, 17(2), 55–62.

Gunter, P. L., & Reed, T. M. (1997). Academic instruction of children with emotional and behavioral disorders using scripted lessons. *Preventing School Failure*, 42, 33–37.

Gunter, P. L., Shores, R. E., Jack, S. L., Denny, R. K., & DePaepe, P. (1994). A case study of the effects of altering instructional interactions on the disruptive behavior of a child with severe behavior disorders. *Education and Treatment of Children*, 17, 435–444.

Heward, W., Courson, F. H., & Marayan, J. (1990). Using choral responding to increase active student responses. *Direct Instruction News*, 9(2), 30–33.

Hummel, J. H. & Huitt, W. G. (1994). What you measure is what you get. *GaASCD Newsletter: The Reporter*, Winter, 10–11.

Kauffman, J. M. (1997). *Characteristics of emotionally and behavioral disorders of children and youth*, 6th ed. Columbus, OH: Merrill.

Martella, R. C., and Nelson, J. R. (2003). Managing classroom behavior. *Journal of Direct Instruction, 3*, 139–165.

Rieth, H. & Evertson, C. (1988). Variables related to the effective instruction of difficult-to-teach children. *Focus on Exceptional Children*, 20(5), 1–7.

Rosenshine, B. & Stevens, R. (1986) Teaching functions, in Wittrock, M. (Ed.), *Handbook of research on teaching*, 3rd ed. New York: Macmillan, pp. 376–391.

Saxon, J. H. (1990). *Algebra1/2: An incremental development*, 2nd ed. Norman, OK: Saxon Publishers.

Slavin, R. E. (2000). *Educational psychology*, 6th ed. Needham Heights, MA: Allyn & Bacon.

CHAPTER

8

The Competent Learner Model: A Merging of Applied Behavior Analysis, Direct Instruction, and Precision Teaching

VICCI TUCCI
Tucci Learning Solutions, Inc.

DANIEL E. HURSH
West Virginia University

RICHARD E. LAITINEN
Tucci Learning Solutions, Inc.

INTRODUCTION

Applied Behavior Analysis (ABA), Direct Instruction (DI), and Precision Teaching (PT) practices are commonly considered the best practices to serve a variety of learners in special and regular education settings. These fields of study have generated an impressive and substantial list of empirically validated best-practice instructional indicators and procedures utilizing the premises and principles of a natural science approach to understanding and analyzing human learning and teaching (Baer, Wolf, & Risley, 1968, 1987). The *Journal of Applied Behavior Analysis, Journal of Direct Instruction*, and *Journal of Precision Teaching*, among many other special and regular education journals, provide ample evidence of this. Despite numerous demonstrations of the validity of these indicators and procedures, most educators do *not* utilize the curricular design or instructional practices suggested by ABA, DI, or PT (Latham, 1997).

One of the reasons these practices have not been readily adopted and utilized by the broader educational system is that ABA, DI, and PT practitioners and researchers have not developed a sufficient technology of persuasion (marketing) and dissemination (training and support) (Bailey, 1991). With this in mind, the Competent Learner Model (CLM) was designed as a teacher-friendly approach for the comprehensive transfer and utilization of the principles and procedures of ABA, DI, and PT (Tucci, 1986; Tucci & Hursh, 1991). The intent behind the design of the CLM was to (1) get educators to master the implementation of ABA, DI, and PT best practices, and (2) motivate them to use these practices in their classroom on a daily basis.

The intended outcome of the Competent Learner Model is the development of Competent Learner Repertoires, which allow learning to occur in everyday circumstances within and across school, home, and community settings. For example, a child who asks a store clerk how to find an item is showing herself to be a competent "problem solver" by the fact that she is asking for the information needed to solve a current problem (finding an item). She subsequently shows that she has become a competent listener if she follows the clerk's directions to the requested item. Basically, a Competent Learner is an individual who can act effectively under novel circumstances—that is, a person who is a capable observer, listener, talker, reader, writer, problem solver, and participator. In learning to implement the CLM, educators master how to arrange instructional conditions that result in the development of repertoires that produce a Competent Learner. In contrast to teaching isolated skills such as color names or shape names, CLM teachers develop learning-to-learn competencies.

Skinner (1953, 1968) has suggested that one of the greatest contributions behavior analysts can make to a person is to set up and manage contingencies that develop repertoires of effective responding. This raises the question, "What repertoires do Competent Learners need when faced with a situation or problem which they have not been explicitly taught to resolve?" When we observe Competent Learners under such situations, we see that they might (1) observe how others respond, (2) listen to suggestions, (3) talk with others, (4) read instructions, (5) write notes, (6) ask for help to solve the problem, and (7) participate until things work out. These are the seven fundamental repertoires utilized by a Competent Learner.

An overview of the CLM (see Fig. 1) shows the connections between these seven repertoires, four key and pervasive instructional conditions, and the possible ways in which the parts of these conditions may be arranged and rearranged to effect learning. As part of its built-in training and support technology, the CLM takes educators through an organized course of study within a personalized system of instruction (see Chapters 12 and 13). As they progress through this curriculum, participants learn about the model's premises and how to carry out its practices. CLM coaches support participants as they progress through the course of study. Coaching continues until each educator has mastered both content and implementation of the model's premises and practices. In addition to the coaches, the CLM employs behavior analysts who collaboratively consult with and support educators as they

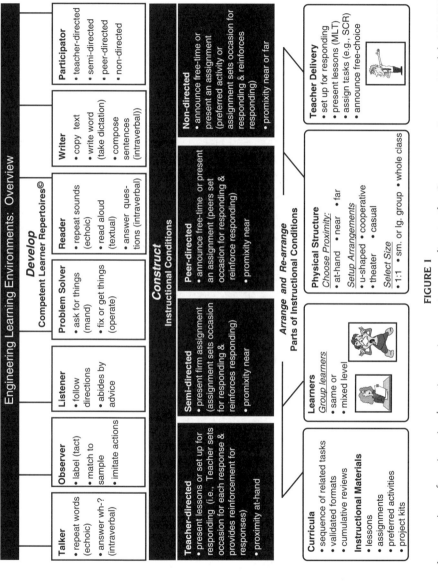

FIGURE 1

An overview of engineering learning environments according to the Competent Learner Model. (©1997 Tucci Learning Solutions, Inc.)

implement the model's practices within their classrooms. Over the years, we have seen that this type of training and support, once faded, helps create a community of educators who support each other to continue the practices. We have also observed that the integration of ABA, DI, and PT technologies is critical to the success of the CLM.

APPLIED BEHAVIOR ANALYSIS
AND THE COMPETENT LEARNER MODEL

The Competent Learner Model utilizes best practice recommendations supported by experimental, conceptual, and applied research from Applied Behavior Analysis, Direct Instruction, and Precision Teaching (Tucci, 2003). The structure of the model provides answers to four questions to guide the design of educational programs. These four questions are derived from Skinner's *The Technology of Teaching* (1968).

What repertoires need to be developed
or weakened?

The obvious starting point in any educational endeavor is to assess what outcomes are needed or desired. The Competent Learner Model does this by assessing the status of each learner's Competent Learner Repertoires (CLRs). Currently, five levels make up the Competent Learner Repertoire assessment (CLRA). Each of these levels assesses various aspects of the seven Competent Learner Repertoires (problem solver, talker, listener, etc.) in terms specific to Skinner's analysis of human verbal (1957) and non-verbal (1953) behaviors. All five CLRAs are designed so they can be completed by anyone who is familiar with the learner. The items of the CLRAs assess (1) whether an aspect of a repertoire is established; (2) if it is established, whether it is exhibited as an approximation or is fully developed; and (3) if it is fully developed, whether it occurs only rarely, frequently, or across all situations where it is appropriate. Example items from the CLRA for naïve learners call for educators or parents to observe whether the learner (1) asks for what he or she wants in an acceptable way throughout the day (a part of the Problem Solver Repertoire), (2) responds correctly when asked questions (a part of the Talker Repertoire), and (3) follows instructions (a part of the Listener Repertoire). Other such questions are answered until a relatively complete profile of the strengths and weaknesses of all of the learner's CLRs is developed. Each item is constructed to assess how the learner performs during various activities typical of most classrooms or homes. The CLRA profile summarizes the learner's CLRs and is used to place the learner in the appropriate level and lesson of the CLM curricula and/or other curricula that provide a clear scope and sequence for the outcomes they are designed to produce.

What stimuli are available to effect change in behavior?

Once it is known which repertoires need to be developed, educators need to know what instructional and reinforcing stimuli (actions or objects) are available to develop or weaken the learner's repertoires. These include stimuli that the learner will work to (1) gain access to, (2) escape from, or (3) avoid. Knowing which actions or objects already serve as reinforcers or aversives for the learner allows the educator to determine whether there are sufficient stimuli to develop the competent learner repertoires.

What contingencies are required to develop or weaken the repertoires?

Through the "arrangement of supplemental contingencies" (Skinner, 1968), the CLM teaches educators to employ available or potentially available instructional and reinforcing stimuli to effect change when the usual curricula and instructional formats are not sufficient to develop a learner's repertoires. These supplemental contingencies are used *only* when needed, moving to the support of more natural contingencies as soon as possible. The arrangement and rearrangement of supplemental contingencies assists us in developing the Competent Learner repertoires. The simplest form of a contingency is the relationship between an Antecedent, a Behavior, and a Consequence. This ABC contingency describes the teaching event (Antecedent) intended to cue or precede a specified Behavior, and the events (Consequences) that will follow correct and incorrect responses. For example, a teacher pointing to one of an array of three or more pictures placed on a table in front of a learner constitutes an Antecedent that cues the learner to label (the Behavior) that picture. Teacher praise for correct labeling behavior constitutes a potentially reinforcing Consequence. Within the CLM, this type of a contingency is used to establish and strengthen labeling behavior in the development of the Observer Repertoire. In addition to the ABC contingency, arranging supplemental contingencies involves employing means to establish or enhance the effectiveness of Reinforcers. These types of contingencies are referred to as Establishing Operations (Michael, 1982) and they are used to influence the learner's motivation to become a Competent Learner. One type of Establishing Operation (EO) is to temporarily limit access to preferred activities or materials which results in those activities or materials becoming more valuable as reinforcers. Another type of Establishing Operation is to allow students to have access to materials or activities for an extended period of time and typically results in those materials and activities becoming less valuable to the learner.

How can the parts of instructional conditions be arranged and rearranged to develop the competent learner repertoires?

The CLM assists educators in doing this by providing them with the knowledge of what repertoires need to be developed, what stimuli serve as potential reinforcers and aversives, and what contingencies are needed to effectively develop or weaken repertoires. This knowledge can then be combined with the skills needed to effectively arrange and rearrange the parts of instructional conditions, thus arranging and rearranging contingencies that can develop or weaken repertoires. For example, the CLM curriculum for naïve learners includes an instructional format in one of the lessons that describes providing the learner with a task they can reliably do while the educator stays nearby to provide help as needed. This format helps to develop the learner's Participator Repertoire in semi-directed (*e.g.*, practice or application) instructional conditions.

DIRECT INSTRUCTION AND THE COMPETENT LEARNER MODEL

The CLM curricula are designed to serve naïve learners, particularly those with special needs and learning histories that have made learning in typical learning environments very challenging. The CLM curricula are designed in accordance with the principles that have been the basis for the highly effective DI curricula (Engelmann & Carnine, 1982; Kame'enui & Simmons, 1990). These principles have been distilled within the CLM to guide teachers in their application and to develop the instructional formats that make up the CLM Curricula (Fig. 2).

All levels of the CLM curricula are compatible with most other curricula and instructional practices because CLM curricula focus on the development of the learning-to-learn repertoires applicable to all learning. The CLM curricula enhance the delivery of other curricula by making conspicuous the contingencies that develop the learner repertoires with any given curriculum content. For example, over the course of many lessons, one of the CLM formats builds a repertoire from having the learner respond to a few teacher instructions in a one-to-one context to having the learner respond to three sets of 10 such instructions in a small group context. This sequence of formats has been designed to establish and strengthen the learner's Participator Repertoire under teacher-directed instructional conditions, something that is incorporated in many, if not all, other curricula. The tracking sheet for the first 16 lessons of the CLM curricula is provided here to show the kinds of outcomes

DESIGNING LESSONS: Summary of Teacher Tasks

Design tasks (formats)	Sequence tasks	Schedule time for each task	Specify correction procedures	Design practice tasks (formats)
Identify Knowledge Form • Verbal associations • Rules • Concepts • Cognitive strategies	Do not sequence a series of difficult tasks back to back. An example of a possible sequence: easy (firm), easy, hard (new), easy. That is, sequence tasks so that the required schedule of reinforcement is ensured.	Determine the approximate time requirements to teach each task to ensure sufficient time to deal with difficult tasks	Prepare or study correction procedures to respond to learner errors	Design expansion activities so learners can use newly acquired knowledge and skills across instructional conditions (e.g., semi-directed and peer-directed)
Select Range of Examples • Limited • Expanded (varied)				
Place Examples in Proper Sequence • Similar (e.g., form or sound of letters) • Dissimilar	Tasks with highly similar response requirements may cause confusion			Response requirements should be maintained across all instructional conditions
Select & Sequence Test Examples • Acquisition • Discrimination • Retention • Generalization				
Select & Sequence Practice Examples • Amount of practice • Structure of practice • Schedule of practice • Student response form	Review new tasks within the same lesson, i.e., establish a firming cycle			

FIGURE 2

Direct Instruction design principles distilled for use within the Competent Learner model. (Adapted from Engelmann & Carnine, 1982; Kame'enui & Simmons, 1990. © 1995 Tucci Learning Solutions, Inc.)

achieved in the development of various CLRs. In addition, it illustrates how the scope and sequence ensure that learners develop more elaborate and complete CLRs as they progress through the curriculum (Fig. 3).

CLM Curricula's Scope & Sequence : pre-1 & 1

| LESSONS: | 1 | 2 | 3 | 4 | 5 | 6 | 7 | 8 | 9 | 10 | 11 | 12 | 13 | 14 | 15 | 16 |

Participator
- 0.505 Selects, USES a variety of objects, & puts objects away in non-directed conditions within 2 minutes without annoying or injurious behaviors with T's help (1 - 16)
- 0.503 Completes one assigned task in semi-directed conditions w/T near; upto 20 parts / task (2-10)
- 1.503 Completes 2 consecutive tasks (tasks @ 5 min / task) in s-d (11-22)
- 0.501 Performs 3 consecutive sets of 10 responses in t-d, 1:2 (314)
- 0.504 Accepts/Gives objects to peers w/Tprompts (8-12)
- 1.504 Takes turns w / Pref item w / in 1 min (13-33)
- 0502. In Td, Answers on signal with FIRM items for 3 consec. sets of 10 (15-16)

Problem Solver
- 0.201 Spontaneously asks for preferred items or T actions using motor beh minimum of 12 per hr. & waits @ 10 secs for item / action (1-9)
- 1.201 Spontaneously asks for missing item or T actions using phrases; waits 60 secs. (10-29)
- 0.801 Manipulates an object to place it or remove it from its location; @ 10 parts / problem (4-9)
- 0.203 Uses motor behavior to say "no" to an offer of a non-preferred item; tolterates 10 sec. delay of removing it (12-14)

Listener
- 0.601 Follows series of 5-7 FIRM single-step directions across variety of situations with T near, 1-5 feet away (3-12)
- 1.601 Performs series of 7-10 FIRM two-step directions, 5-10ft(13-29)
- 0.602 In display of 8, L touches pictures at a set fluency rate when pictures named (9-16)

Observer
- 0.701 Imitates the modeled single-step action performed by T (4-9)
- 0.701 Imitates the modeled two-step actions performed by Peers (10-33)
- 0.702 Finds ea. matching pix & places it below matching pix in 2-3 pix display (13-16)
- 0.102 Labels each picture in a field of 8-10 common items when T touches one (12-16)
- 0.703 Sorts 3 FIRM sets of similar pictures into separate piles and puts 1-2 distractors aside (4-13)

Talker
- 0.002 Repeats sounds related to preferred activities (5-8)
- 0.001 Repeats @ 20 common words w / out item displayed for preferred or non-pref nouns, verbs, attributes (8-14)

Reader
- 0.301 Repeats sounds or words when T is 'playfully' reading a familiar story or T says, "Say, dog" (13-16)

Writer
- 0.401 Imitates direction or shape of the line once it is drawn by T on large paper w/markers... (4-12)
- 1.401 Copies 5-10 pre-drawn lines/shape on unlined paper...(12-29)

revised: 2/16/04

FIGURE 3

The scope and sequence of the outcomes accomplished across all the Competent Learner repertoires for the first 16 lessons of the Competent Learner model curricula. (©2004 Tucci Learning Systems, Inc.)

PRECISION TEACHING AND THE COMPETENT LEARNER MODEL

Once something is learned, it is often important to have the learner practice it until the response is fluent (Binder Haughton, Van Eyck, 1990). The measurement process in Precision Teaching (PT) (Lindsley, 1992) is designed to focus educators' attention precisely on changing the frequency/rate of behavior. This changing frequency/rate is referred to as *celeration*. Programming for celeration integrates nicely with programming to achieve general case mastery learning because something learned fluently is resistant to being interrupted by distractions or lost by lack of practice. Many of us have not roller skated since we were children; yet, because we became fluent roller skaters then, we will usually do well as a model when our own children convince us to teach them how to roller skate. The CLM incorporates PT practices by integrating fluency practice into the outcomes specified in the CLM curricula and the CLRAs where appropriate. For example, one aspect of the Problem Solver Repertoire for naïve learners is to develop their asking (mand) for something they want so that it is occurring at least 12 times per hour throughout the instructional day. It has been our experience that most naïve learners begin to independently ask for what they want as this frequency/rate of asking is reached. Thus, the fluency aim of 12 per hour for asking is incorporated to ensure that asking is developed as a permanent part of the learner's Problem Solver Repertoire.

THE COMPONENTS OF THE COMPETENT LEARNER MODEL

We consider the components required for full implementation of the CLM to be (1) a course of study for educators and parents; (2) coaching for educators and parents; (3) a systematic and organized curriculum for learners; (4) performance assessments for educators, parents, and learners, and (5) collaborative consultations.

The CLM Course of Study

Educators who complete the CLM course of study are coached to master the ABA, DI, and PT aspects of the model and to demonstrate their mastery during performance checkouts following their completion of each of the units in the course. Most of the performance checkouts require the educator to apply what has been learned to one or more of their students in their classrooms. Mastery with respect to each aspect is gained by repeated practice of the skills required to formulate, deliver, and monitor instructional programming for their students. This practice helps to make conspicuous the contingencies that can establish, strengthen, maintain, or weaken the behaviors that comprise the

CLRs. For example, the first three units require educators to accurately assess examples of aspects of the CLRs, set up and deliver an instructional format designed to strengthen one aspect of a CLR, and factually report what they see and hear happening in an instructional interaction. The scope and sequence of the units of phase one of the CLM course of study illustrate how the competencies developed are an integration of the ABA, DI, and PT practices that have been so well supported by applied research over the past 50 years (see Fig. 4).

Each CLM unit has been written by Tucci and associates using the design principles of programmed instruction (Skinner, 1968) and Direct Instruction. Educators read text, view video clips, and answer questions regarding what they have read as a means to evaluate their mastery of the competencies needed to arrange and rearrange parts of instructional conditions so that their learners' CLRs are developed. The range and limits of each tactic are illustrated across successive screens on the CD-ROM. For example, participants see what happens when a rich schedule of reinforcement that has been maintaining a student's participation under teacher-directed instructional conditions is too quickly shifted to a leaner schedule. They are asked to describe what happened, why, and what can be done to improve the situation.

Coaching

Coaching is a critical component of the CLM course of study to ensure that each educator is guided as needed to mastery and practices what is learned to fluency. A CLM coaches course has been developed so that those educators who complete the CLM course of study and want to become coaches may do so. The coaches course focuses on those skills necessary for the coach to establish a collaborative relationship with the educators completing the course of study, maintain a positive rapport with them, and provide the coaching necessary for them to function independently of the coach. Having coaches come from among the educators completing the CLM course of study helps to establish a community of educators supporting each other's efforts to apply what they have learned in their own classrooms. It also makes it feasible for that community to grow as school districts then have a corps of coaches to extend the CLM course of study to many classrooms throughout the district.

Collaborative Consultation

The core of application of the CLM by behavior analysts is collaborative consultation. The educators who operate the classrooms every day have the experience with their students necessary to identify much of the information needed to answer the four questions that guide educational programming. The CLM provides a framework that assists the behavior analyst in forming a collaborative relationship with the educators. It is within the context of this collaborative relationship that information from the educators' experience

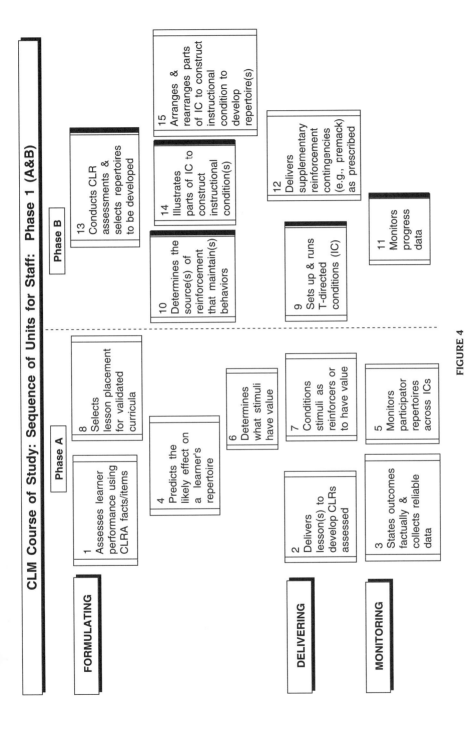

FIGURE 4

The scope and sequence of tasks mastered in phase 1 of the Competent Learner Model course of study.

(© 1997 Tucci Learning Solutions, Inc.)

can emerge and make conspicuous the contingencies operating in the classroom that both support and hinder the development of the CLRs. For example, a behavior analyst who is invited by an educator to assist with a student who consistently disrupts all attempts at establishing teacher-directed instructional conditions can study the case with the educator to determine under what conditions the learner will participate.

Studying the case can mean that the behavior analyst becomes a participant observer in the classroom by recording the ABCs of interactions with the student across instructional conditions and even participates in delivering some of the instructional conditions as they become an accepted part of the environment. In doing so, the behavior analyst can reveal the contingencies in two potentially helpful ways. The ABCs allow the patterns that have been established to emerge while the delivery of some of the instructional conditions allows the educators to see the patterns in action by observing the interactions between the behavior analyst and the student. A behavior analyst who participates in the setting in these ways can consistently call attention to effective practices already in place and make suggestions for practices that are within the educator's repertoire and have a high probability of providing some immediate relief from some aspect of the problem. Thus, the CLM collaborative consultation process is an ongoing functional assessment. The educator, with support from the behavior analyst, assesses the contingencies that are in place, rearranges the contingencies to develop the repertoires, observes the effects, and further rearranges the contingencies as needed.

In this example, the behavior analyst may observe that the student reliably participates in non-directed instructional conditions and that the educator is skilled at offering choices to the students. These two observations can lead to the suggestion that the educator temporarily replace all or almost all teacher-directed instructional conditions with non-directed instructional conditions involving choices for the student among objects or activities that observations have shown are preferred by the student. This is something the educator is likely to be able to do, based on the observations, and it sets up the instructional conditions where the student has been observed to reliably participate. As the educator and student experience success in these arrangements, the Behavior Analyst can suggest that the educator build in short delays between offering choices and the student receiving what was chosen. Eventually, simple teacher-directed tasks can be incorporated within the short delays. This process has some probability of success as it sets up the conditions for the educator to gain value (being useful) with the student, and the behavior analyst to gain value with the educator. Building value among all participants within any setting increases the likelihood of success for any endeavor in that setting. This is the essence of the collaborative consultation process.

EVIDENCE OF THE IMPACT OF THE COMPETENT LEARNER MODEL

The CLM targets development of individual CLRs. Children who undergo programming within the model each have their own program books, which track their progress throughout the curriculum. The Competent Learner Repertoire Assessment is used as both a placement and summary tool within the model. For example, in Fig. 5, a CLRA chart shows the initial and subsequent evaluations of a learner who entered the CLM at 2 years of age. The solid black bars show the learner's profile when he entered the curriculum, and the striped, white bars show his progress over an 8-month period. This profile clearly shows this learner's strengths and challenges and the wide variance of development of his CLRs. As discussed earlier, this interplay of strengths and challenges is

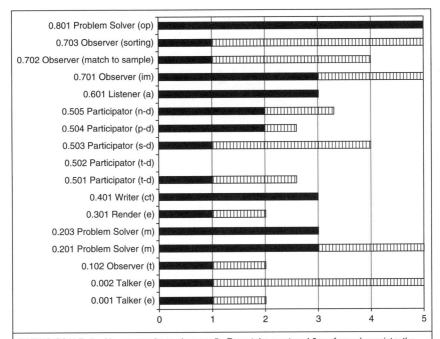

RATING SCALE: 0 = No opportunity to observe; 5 =Repertoire mastered & performed consistently;
4 = Repertoire established but requires further development across people, places, and items;
3 = Repertoire established BUT rarely performed across people, places, and items; 2 =Repertoire is
established but response form is ONLY approximated; 1=Repertoire is NOT established.

FIGURE 5

Example Competent Learner Repertoire assessments from entry to 8 months later for a naïve 2-year-old learner with autism (©2003 Tucci Learning Solutions, Inc.).

used to develop an effective learner profile that organizes what is taught, by whom, where, and when. Again, the goal of this organization is to positively affect the value of teaching and learning for the student by managing that student's moment-to-moment experience with response effort, response pay-off (reinforcement), fatigue, boredom, and motivation.

The learner in Fig. 5 started out with absolutely no motivation to interact with adults (other than his parents and close relatives), a very low tolerance for delayed gratification, no emergent speech, and very little sustained attention. At the time of this writing, he is willing to interact with a much broader range of adults, tolerate delays in gratification, produces recognizable one-word and two-word sentences to ask for and describe items (*e.g.*, says, "green" when asked the color of an object), and will participate in extended circle times and other teacher-directed activities.

The CLM assumes as a premise that the CLRs are the core of all learning (Tucci, 1986; Tucci, 2003; Tucci & Hursh, 1994). The development of CLRs may have an augmentative effect on the mastery of subject matter and possibly an exponential effect on day-to-day functioning. The evidence for the impact of the CLM comes from a variety of sources in addition to the extensive support for the ABA, DI, and PT practices that are integrated within the CLM. Implementation of the CLM results in developing learners' CLRs (Hursh, Tucci, Rentschler, Buzzee, Quimet, 1995). The CLRA produces results that have high inter-observer agreement, are sensitive to change in learners' behavior, and are significantly and positively correlated with measures of day-to-day functional actions (Deem, Hursh, Tucci, 2003). The computer-video interactive format of the CLM course of study is an efficient means to deliver instruction and ensure mastery of the performance outcomes (Hursh, Katayama, Shambaugh, Laitenen, 2001).

Most importantly, the educators served by the CLM have repeatedly succeeded in arranging and rearranging the parts of instructional conditions so that the learners participate in those instructional conditions and progress through their education and often move to less restrictive learning environments at school and in their communities. These successes have been experienced by dozens of teachers and hundreds of learners in regular and special education classrooms serving students with many different diagnoses. It does not matter what the diagnosis, arranging and rearranging the parts of instructional conditions can develop CLRs, and developing CLRs results in learners who function more effectively in everyday situations. The interested reader is encouraged to visit TucciOnline.com for current information and examples of the CLM.

References

Baer, D. M., Wolf, M. M., & Risley, T. R. (1968). Some current dimensions of applied behavior analysis. *Journal of Applied Behavior Analysis*, 1, 91–97.

Baer, D. M., Wolf, M. M., & Risley, T. R. (1987). Some still-current dimensions of applied behavior analysis. *Journal of Applied Behavior Analysis*, 20, 313–327.

Baily, J. S. (1991). Marketing behavior analysis requires different talk. *Journal of Applied Behavior Analysis*, 24, 445–448.

Binder, C. V., Haughton, E., & Van Eyk, D. (1990). Increasing endurance by building fluency: Precision teaching attention span. *Teaching Exceptional Children*, 22, 24–27.

Deem, J., Hursh, D. E., & Tucci, V. (2003) Inter-rater reliability and concurrent validity of the Competent Learner Repertoire Assessment (submitted for publication).

Engelmann, S. & Carnine, D. (1982). *Theory of instruction: Principles and application*. New York: Irvington Press.

Hursh, D., Tucci, V., Rentschler, B., Buzzee, S., & Quimet, D. (1995). *A Replication of the Competent Learner Model*. Paper presented at the convention of the Association for Behavior Analysis, Washington, D.C.

Hursh, D., Katayama, A., Shambaugh, N., & Laitinen, R. (2001). *Efficiencies of computer-video interactive training*. Paper presented at the convention of the Association for Behavior Analysis, New Orleans, LA.

Kame'enui, E. J. & Simmons, D. C. (1990). *Designing instructional strategies: The prevention of academic learning problems*. Columbus, OH: Merrill.

Latham, G. (1997). *Behind the schoolhouse door: Eight skills every teacher should have*. ERIC Document Reproduction Service No. ED408735.

Lindsley, O. R. (1992). Precision Teaching: Discoveries and effects. *Journal of Applied Behavior Analysis*, 25, 51–57.

Michael, J. (1982). Distinguishing between discriminative and motivational functions of stimuli. *Journal of the Experimental Analysis of Behavior*, 37, 149–155.

Skinner, B. F. (1953). *Science and human behavior*. New York: The Free Press.

Skinner, B. F. (1957). *Verbal behavior*. Englewood Cliffs, NJ: Prentice Hall.

Skinner, B. F. (1968). *The technology of teaching*. New York: Appleton-Century-Crofts.

Tucci, V. (1986). *An analysis of a competent learner*, Paper presented at the annual convention of the Northern California Association for Behavior Analysis, February, San Mateo, CA.

Tucci, V. (2003). *The competent learner model: An Introduction*. Aptos, CA: Tucci Learning Solutions, Inc.

Tucci, V. & Hursh, D. (1991). Competent Learner Model: Instructional programming for teachers and learners. *Education and Treatment of Children*, 14, 394–360.

Tucci, V. & Hursh, D. (1994). Developing competent learners by arranging effective learning environments, in Gardner, R., Sainato, D. M., Cooper, J. O., Heron, T. E., Heward, W. L., Eshleman, J., & Grossi, T. A. (Eds.), *Behavior analysis in education: Focus on measurably superior instruction*. Pacific Grove, CA: Brooks/Cole, pp. 257–264.

Computers and Teaching Machines

Effective Use of Computers in Instruction

MARCIE N. DESROCHERS and G. DAVID GENTRY

College of Charleston

The most important method of education always consisted of that in which the pupil was urged to actual performance.—Albert Einstein

INTRODUCTION

Effective instruction is a multifaceted process, whether the instructor is a human or a computer. First, it is important to assess the learner's skills so that instructional material can be presented at an appropriate level and the pace of instructional delivery does not proceed too quickly before learning earlier content, nor too slowly so progress to the next level is impeded (Skinner, 1968). The sequencing of material difficulty and the number of examples and non-examples of each concept can affect the learner's performance. The student must be engaged and attentive. Finally, frequent opportunities to respond to relevant questions with rapid feedback must be available throughout the learning experience (Vargas, 1986).

Having an instructor continuously available to assess each student's performance and to tailor the pace and content to the student's learning situation is not possible in a typical classroom. Instruction from a computer can provide these essential components for each individual student effectively and affordably (Skinner, 1963). In this chapter, we explore the types of instructional software, discuss the characteristics of effective programming of instruction, present evidence for the effectiveness of computer-based instruction, and explain how you can evaluate the software that you plan to use.

But, what exactly is "computer instruction" and how is it delivered? Benjamin (1988) writes that, "A teaching machine is an automatic or self-controlling device that (a) presents a unit of information, (b) provides some means for the learner to respond to the information, and (c) provides feedback about the correctness of the learner's responses" (p. 704). Today's desktop computer equipped with instructional software is ideally suited to serve as a "teaching machine."

WHAT ARE THE TYPES OF INSTRUCTIONAL SOFTWARE?

The three main types of instructional software are *tutorial*, *drill-and-practice*, and *simulation*. Each of these types is well suited for attaining a particular kind of learning objective. The learning objectives can focus on declarative knowledge ("knowing that") or procedural knowledge ("knowing how"). Declarative knowledge includes learning facts (*e.g.*, "whales are mammals") while procedural knowledge includes motor skills (*e.g.*, typing), problem-solving techniques (*e.g.*, solving differential equations), and procedures (*e.g.*, learning to use a word processor). The instructor should select the type of instructional software that corresponds with the instructional objectives.

Tutorial

Tutorial programs are commonly used types of software. Tutorials present the learner with new instructional material, test the learner's knowledge of that material, and provide feedback for responses (*e.g.*, Harrington & Walker, 2002; Jenny & Fai, 2001). Thus, tutorials are ideally suited for teaching declarative knowledge but can also be used for procedural knowledge. For instance, Grant *et al.* (1982) developed a tutorial, which is available on the Internet (see http://psych.athabascau.ca/html/prtut/reinpair.htm), to teach the concept of positive reinforcement. A recent empirical evaluation of Grant's tutorial found that students' performance improved compared to that of a control group (Grant, 2004). Tutorials may also supplement regular instruction to facilitate learning. Flora and Logan (1996) evaluated the effectiveness of computerized study guides with a general psychology class and found an increase in exam scores when they were used.

Drill-and-Practice

Fluency, one characteristic of expertise in an area, is measured by accuracy and speed of responding (Yaber & Malott, 1993). Drill-and-practice programs focus on building fluency with the learning material. Questions concerning some topic are presented, and the speed of the student's responses and the number of questions successfully answered within a set time period are measured. Yaber and Malott (1993) empirically evaluated the effectiveness of drill-and-practice software (*ThinkFast*) to teach fluency with behavioral concepts and terms. Student performance on quizzes was enhanced when using the *ThinkFast* software that contained fill-in-the-blank questions. In another example of drill-and-practice, Washburn (1999) described software wherein students were presented with research reports and were required to discriminate facts from interpretations with simple correct or incorrect statements given as feedback. Initial evaluations of 100 students' performance revealed improvement in scores.

Simulations

A simulation program is a model of a realistic situation in which the learner can respond and receive feedback. Lee (1999) classified simulations according to *practice, presentation*, or *presentation hybrid* functions. Practice simulations are those that follow other instruction and allow students to apply what they have learned. Presentation simulations teach new material through interaction with the program only. This type of simulation teaches through learning by discovery. The hybrid is a combination of instruction and simulation in which the program provides instruction followed by practice. Lee (1999) found that practice simulations are especially effective and that pure presentation simulations may not be effective. Thus, simulations are best suited for teaching or reinforcing procedural knowledge. Simulations may also provide integration of existing skills in lifelike contexts with the ultimate purpose of promoting generalization of learning to natural situations (Thomas & Hooper, 1991).

There are several possible advantages to using simulations. In learning conditions that are difficult to construct, expensive, or unsafe, instructors may favor use of a simulation approach. Moreover, simulation software may deliver more naturally occurring consequences for the behavior (*e.g.*, graphed data of simulated client behaviors) than can be given with traditional instruction.

Desrochers and Hile (1993) describe the *Simulation in Developmental Disabilities: SIDD* multimedia software in which the clinical decision-making skills required to treat individuals with severe problem behaviors and mental retardation/developmental disabilities are practiced. Both formative evaluations (Desrochers & Hile, 1993) and experimental studies (Desrochers, Clemmons, Grady, Justice, 2000, 2001) suggest that SIDD can be an effective method of providing students with practice in behavioral principles and procedures. Moreover, SIDD can serve as a useful addition to the standard lecture format to present information regarding functional assessment (Desrochers, House, & Seth 2001).

Gorrell and Downing (1989) conducted an experiment to evaluate the effectiveness of computer simulations representing realistic classroom situations with undergraduate educational psychology students. The computer simulation group performed better on an application test compared to control, extended lecture, and problem-solving groups. There was no difference in performance on a general knowledge test among these groups, which supports the idea that simulation software might be more effective at teaching procedural knowledge than declarative knowledge.

Computer simulations can also decrease the amount of time spent learning to respond in the actual situation of interest. For instance, Taylor et al. (1999) measured the transfer savings (amount of time needed for learning to criterion for control versus simulation conditions) with aviation software. The researchers found substantial savings in course completion time for the computer-based instruction group who received a comprehensive flight-training program compared to a control group wherein training was provided in an airplane.

WHAT ARE THE FEATURES OF EFFECTIVE INSTRUCTIONAL SOFTWARE?

Key design features of effective instructional software include: (1) use of effective antecedents, information given before the student's response; (2) opportunities for active and frequent student responding; and (3) delivery of feedback regarding student answers. Each of these areas is addressed separately.

Antecedents for Desired Behavior

A variety of antecedents may influence learning. Use of instructions, presenting information to prompt the desired behavior, and adaptive instruction have been studied in computer-based instruction research.

Instructions

Are instructions necessary for learning to occur? It depends on the instructional situation. Learning can occur with or without the use of words as antecedents (Baum, 1994; Skinner, 1969). Usually the antecedent will be a verbal or textual instruction, which basically specifies a "rule" regarding the correct behavior and its consequences. People follow rules due to past rule-following behavior producing favorable results. Behavior can also gradually develop from being influenced by its consequences. Such behavior is said to be *contingency shaped*. Declarative knowledge is easily acquired through the use of rules, which drill-and-practice and tutorial software approaches can help develop. Procedural knowledge may be developed through rules or by contingency shaping, which simulations may foster. Moreover, learning may occur more quickly when rules are presented as compared to being contingency shaped. Learning may be enhanced when instructional objectives, which may serve as a prompt or rule for further learning, are presented to the learner. For example, organization of material has been shown to facilitate verbal learning, and learners may impose their own structure (subjective organization) when it is absent (Sternberg, 1996). Structured overviews may also result in students spending more time with instructional software and having more positive attitudes toward it (Brinkerhoff, Klein, & Koroghlanian, 2001).

Prompting and Fading

To facilitate new behaviors, prompting and fading of prompts can be embedded in instructional programs. Skinner (1961) described this procedure as a "vanishing" technique, whereby critical information is presented and then gradually removed as the learner performs the desired behavior. Examples of prompts include highlighted text, additional information presented on the screen, or "hint" information. It is important that these features added to the learning situation (*e.g.*, highlighted text) be removed so that interference with later occurrence of the behavior learned does not take place. Research has suggested that prompting may be effective for initial learning (Bannert, 2000; Hall & Borman, 1973), and some research suggests that the more prompts that are embedded in computer-assisted instruction to teach math skills to second-grade students, the better the outcome (Noell, Gresham, & Ganze, 2002).

Adaptive Instruction

Can learning be enhanced by tailoring instruction to the student's response? Using this approach to automated instruction, repeated assessments of the student's knowledge is required to determine the content of instruction. Several studies have shown that adaptive instruction does not seem to affect student learning or test scores but does decrease time it takes to learn the material (Litchfield, Driscoll, & Dempsey, 1990; Murphy & Davidson, 1991).

Behavior: Active and Frequent Student Responding

How can students be involved in the learning situation? A main advantage of computer-aided instruction over traditional methods of instruction is that students can be individually engaged with and actively responding to the learning material (Vargas, 1986). Furthermore, using response rate as the objective of instruction, as in the case of drill-and-practice software, may promote response maintenance, resistance to distraction, and generalization (Binder, 1993). Student performance is facilitated when computer-based instruction is interspersed with open-answer or fill-in-the-blank questions (*i.e.*, a constructed response) (Kritch, Bostow, & Dedrick 1995; Thomas & Bostow, 1991). Given the apparent beneficial effects of using a constructed-response format during automated instruction, an important question is whether learning is enhanced by computer-based instruction that includes multiple-choice questions alone or constructed-response questions intermixed in the learning material. A recent study compared the effectiveness of multiple-choice versus constructed-response versus a combined-question format when used to teach a computer-based vocabulary lesson. The results suggested a combination of multiple-choice questions along with the constructed-response method was most effective (Clariana & Lee, 2001). It may be that a multiple-choice format provides a prompt for selection of the correct response, which is further solidified by requiring the student to subsequently type the correct answer.

Consequences: Feedback for Student Responses

How can consequences for student responses facilitate learning? A major advantage associated with computer-aided instruction is that feedback can be presented immediately after the student's response (Anderson Kulhavy, & Andre, 1971; Kulhavy, 1977). This feedback may serve an instructive function or present a rule to the student, both of which affect future responding to similar questions. Researchers have examined various feedback procedures for multiple-choice questions used in computer-based tutorial software. In general, effective procedures include the computer giving the correct answer after one attempt at answering a question or reviewing questions and answers at the end of the unit. Less effective procedures are when no feedback is given or "No, try again" is presented until a correct response occurs (Clariana, 1990; Clariana, Ross, & Morrison 1991).

WHAT MAKES SOFTWARE DESIGN EFFECTIVE?

Consideration of design is critical for instructional software as it provides the context in which learning takes place (Park & Hannafin, 1993). Hannafin and Hooper (1989) note that the purposes of screen design (also known as graphical user interface, or GUI) are to stimulate interest, facilitate responding to the instructional material, and promote navigation through the software. Proper GUI also promotes acquisition, retention, and generalization of learning material. Software features that may influence these functions include: (1) navigational aids; (2) presentation style and organizational structure; (3) distinctiveness of information; and (4) text characteristics.

Navigational Aids

A major difficulty learners can have is navigating through the computer-based material (Kinzie & Berdel, 1990). To reduce this difficulty, online or supplemental written, audio, or visual materials can be used to indicate where the user is in the software program. Navigation aides can include highlighting or checkmarks beside completed items to signify what path has been previously selected or providing a flow-chart depiction of the structure of the software. Another method is to provide an initial orientation to navigation in the software and how information is to be presented (*e.g.*, where the Help option is, how to move forward or go back, or what to consult for assistance with the material).

Presentation Style and Organization Structure

The presentation format for screen design should be clear and complete enough such that the user is not bogged down with learning how to use the software and can focus on learning the material (Lohr, 2000). Particularly because use of educational software often occurs during one session, it is essential that learning to use the software occur as quickly as possible to maximize lesson time. Consistent presentation of information and readily identifiable cues that signal particular information help the user attend to the relevant information and may facilitate learning the instructional material (Lohr, 2000). Grabinger (1993) examined the readability and "studyability" of screens. He found that organization (*e.g.*, specific areas related to certain functions, use of spacing between paragraphs, single-spaced and double-column text) and stimulation of visual interest (*e.g.*, use of lines, boxes, and illustrations and placement of white space along the margins of the screen) were important criteria for positive judgments by users. Orientation to material can also be achieved by manipulating placement, color, and style of information presented on the screen (Aspillaga, 1996). For instance, to enable quick discrimination, similar information can be grouped together on the screen and separated from other categories (namely, use of Gestalt principles of similarity and proximity) (Szabo & Kanuka, 1998).

Distinctiveness of Information

Although important information should be distinctive (*e.g.*, color, size, separation from other information, location) for optimal user responding (Bravo & Blake, 1990), this tactic should be used sparingly so that habituation does not occur (Aspillaga, 1996).

Text Characteristics

A general rule of thumb is that the less text on the screen, the better in terms of speed and user satisfaction (Morrison, Ross, & O'Dell, 1988); however, students may also prefer high-density of text on screens due to the increased contextual support it provides (Morrison, Ross, O'Dell, Schultz, & Higginbotham-Wheat, 1989). One solution is to have both high versus low-text options available and let the user select which is preferred. Other general text characteristics are that the text should be (1) presented in upper and lower case rather than just uppercase letters; (2) a large font, especially if older users are involved; (3) set in contrasting colors (*e.g.*, black on white); and (4) designed to have the focus of information in the center line of vision where visual acuity is sharpest. There is also research to suggest that hypertexted information (highlighted terms that, when selected, provide additional information) neither facilitates nor hampers learning of material (Brown, 1998). Additionally, research has found that accuracy in learner responding increases when navigation information is placed at the top and left of the screen compared to the right and bottom positions (van Schaik & Ling, 2001).

In summary, an effective computer screen design will result in the learner moving easily through the software and being provided with cues to respond quickly to, and should assist in the attainment of educational goals (Lohr, 2000). Whether screen design is effective can be measured by observing users interacting with the software, surveying users' preferences for software features, and administrating objective performance tests with outcomes compared before and after learning or between users and non-users.

WHAT IS THE EVIDENCE FOR THE EFFECTIVENESS OF AUTOMATED INSTRUCTION?

The use of computers in instruction has been evaluated in hundreds of individual studies. The typical procedure for evaluating automated instruction has the following features: A number of students *at some level* would be assigned to one of two groups to learn *some new content* and would receive *feedback in some manner*. Each group *might have a different teacher*, but one would use computers *in some manner* (experimental group) and the other would not (control group). After *some period of instruction*, the students would be evaluated on *some test of knowledge* (perhaps a standardized test). If the experimental group with computers scored significantly higher than the control group without computers, then the use of the computers would be deemed possibly beneficial. Due to the difficulties of doing research in the real world of education, stronger conclusions are usually avoided. The results would then be published *in some publicly available source*.

While such studies have consistently shown that computers improve learning to some extent, there are considerable differences in the outcomes due to the many differences in the methods among these studies. Some of these important procedural differences were italicized in the previous paragraph. Simply put, some procedures reliably produce larger improvements due to computer use than others.

It is important to understand the magnitude of improvements due to computerized instruction that can be expected and the educational significance of those improvements. Meta-analysis, a statistical technique for combining the results of many studies, has been used by several researchers to estimate the effectiveness of using computers in instruction (Khalili & Shashaani, 1994; Kulik, 1994; Kulik & Kulik, 1987, 1991; Lee 1999). The power of meta-analysis is that it can determine not only an average effectiveness but also provide a basis for finding which type of software is better and how much better.

The basic datum for a meta-analysis is the "effect size" found in an individual study. Effect size* is a measure of the improvement in test scores produced by using computer-based instruction compared to not using it. The major benefit of expressing outcomes in effect sizes is that results of all studies are comparable. Thus, the average effect size can be determined from a large number of studies with very different procedures. Furthermore, by selecting only studies with a particular procedure (*e.g.*, drill and practice), the average effectiveness of that procedure can be determined and then compared to the effectiveness of other procedures (*e.g.*, simulations).

A key consideration when performing a meta-analysis is determining which studies will be included in the analysis. Some criteria for inclusion are established and then the studies are collected. For example, the use of a search phrase such as "computer-based instruction" is entered in a database. All retrieved articles are then screened further for inclusion. An obvious criterion for including an article is the availability of proper data for calculating effect size. Other criteria might focus on academic level of students (*e.g.*, only college students) or content area (*e.g.*, only science instruction). As a result of these selection criteria, different meta-analyses will produce different average effect sizes.

Meta-Analytic General Results

Kulik (1994) summarized the findings of 12 published meta-analyses of computer-based instruction. The average effect size of all meta-analyses was 0.35 with a low value of 0.22 and a high value of 0.57. Thus, average effect size has been consistently positive among all of these meta-analyses. The average effect size of 0.35 might seem to be a modest gain, but two points must be considered. First, an effect size of 0.35 might be educationally and socially important. When interpreting this effect size, over 13% of the students who exhibit below-average achievement without computer-based instruction would achieve above-average scores with computer-based instruction. When you consider the large number of students that could be involved in just one school

---

* Effect size is the difference in the means between the experimental and control groups divided by the standard deviation. For example, suppose two groups are formed and one uses computer simulations to supplement the lecture and the other group does not. They are then tested with a standardized test as a criterion measure. If the control group averages 50 and the experimental group averages 53.5 with a standard deviation of 10, then the effect size is $(53.5-50)/10 = 0.35$. Or, saying it another way, the experimental group scored 0.35 standard deviations above the control group.

system, a shift of 13% in the population toward higher scores could mean hundreds or even thousands of additional students scoring above average *due to the addition of computers in instruction*. If begun early enough, such improvements could result in dramatically lower dropout rates and overall greater success in education. In college courses, it could mean more than one letter grade in a course. Second, some of the studies that were selected may have used computers inappropriately or with an ineffective software design; however, if the study met the criteria for inclusion, it would be averaged in regardless. This point will be explored more in the next sections, where more specific criteria for inclusion are used. Some of the differences among studies relate to instructional considerations, such as type of computer application, duration of instruction, student level, feedback, and subject area.

Specific Meta-Analytic Findings

Some of the various types of computer applications have been discussed above. The meta-analyses have found that some applications produce bigger effects sizes than others, but these values depend upon which studies are included. For example, Khalili and Shashaani (1994) found that the average effect sizes were 0.11 for drill and practice, 0.26 for tutorial, and 0.79 for simulation. Kulik and Kulik (1991) found 0.31 for computer-aided instruction, 0.37 for computer-managed instruction (used for testing, recordkeeping, and guidance to material), and 0.26 for computer-enriched instruction (presents exercises, demonstration, etc., to motivate students). Kulik (1994) found 0.38 for tutorial (which included drill-and-practice this time), 0.14 for computer-managed instruction, 0.10 for simulation, and 0.14 for computer-enriched instruction. These results show that the type of application must moderate a general statement about effectiveness.

Lee (1999) explored meta-analyses for simulations in much more detail and found the following effect sizes: 0.54 for practice, −0.01 for presentation, and 0.48 for the hybrid. Thus, even within a type of application, such as simulation, there can be tremendous variability in effect sizes that can be isolated by more refined meta-analyses. Azevedo and Bernard (1995) performed a meta-analysis on the effects of feedback. They found that with immediate testing, feedback produced an effect size average of 0.80 compared to no feedback; with delayed testing, feedback had an average effect size of 0.35.

How do these effect sizes compare with other teaching techniques? Educators have many innovative techniques available to improve learning in their students. A decision on the use of computers should be compared to the other techniques. Kulik (1994) gathered results from various meta-analyses on other innovations in education so that direct comparisons could be made. He further statistically corrected for differences that can obscure outcomes. For comparison purposes computer tutorials had effect size of 0.48, accelerated classes were 0.93, classes for gifted were 0.50, and peer-tutoring procedures were 0.38. These results indicate that computer tutorials are relatively effective while not being limited to a select student population.

HOW SHOULD PARTICULAR INSTRUCTIONAL SOFTWARE BE EVALUATED?

It is essential that pedagogical validity be considered when designing and evaluating automated instructional software. Pedagogical validity is the extent to which an instructional procedure leads students to achieve the instructional objectives. Applied to computer-based instruction, pedagogical validity is the extent to which (1) the intended instructional content is included, (2) desired performance outcomes are attained, and (3) learning generalizes. Instructional software should be developed with a clear definition of instructional content, learning outcomes, and methods to enhance generalization. The decision to use a particular software package should ultimately be based on the software's pedagogical validity and a match between the software design and the instructional requirement.

Content

The instructional content could be as sweeping as a stand-alone course or as limited as a brief demonstration to supplement other teaching methods. Some methods used to determine whether instructional goals are adequately met include expert evaluation of the software domain (Desrochers & Hile, 1993) and comparison of the instructional material with standard knowledge in that area (Desrochers, Hile, Williams-Moseley, 1997).

Outcomes

As previously discussed, the learning outcomes may be declarative knowledge, procedural knowledge, or fluency. The type of student outcome that is desired will influence the design and selection of the software. For declarative knowledge, tutorials would be the preferred type. For procedural knowledge, a practice or hybrid type of simulation would be appropriate. For building fluency, drill and practice would be the preferred option.

Generalization

When a student can perform learned responses in new situations, we can say the behavior has generalized. Stimulus generalization may involve examining whether the correct response occurs to different teachers, materials, or test questions (for example, whether the student engages in the problem-solving procedures taught when presented with a new problem). Behavior generalization refers to whether the student emits a new behavior, other than that taught by the instructional device. For instance, behavioral generalization would occur if teaching students to produce examples of concepts results in them producing new variations along that theme. Moreover, it is important to ensure that information is retained or that student gains persist long after training has ended.

CONCLUSIONS

Automated instruction has come a long way since Pressey (1926) and Skinner (1958) first introduced their teaching machines. Much research has been conducted to elucidate the critical features of effective teaching machines. We have learned that computer-based instruction can be generally effective; however, to ensure that the particular instructional software is having its intended effect, assessment of pedagogical validity is essential. Providing the student with instructions and prompts, requiring frequent and active responding, and delivering immediate feedback are major factors contributing to effective automated instruction (Vargas, 1986). Additionally, research has shown that screen design can directly and indirectly (*e.g.*, through attitudes) impact learning. See Table 1 for a list of considerations to guide selection of automated instructional software.

The future bodes well for automated instruction. Technology is advancing at a tremendous pace providing the exciting possibility for new methods of automated instruction. For instance, computers that accurately recognize

TABLE 1
A Checklist of Considerations for Selection of Instructional Software

✓ Is assessment of student behavior frequent and used to guide instruction?
✓ Are the instructional procedures effective?
- Are antecedents effectively used to promote learning?
  - Are effective instructional objectives presented?
  - Are navigation aides provided?
  - Is assistance or prompts for the desired behavior given? Are prompts gradually faded?
  - Is instruction adaptive or geared to the individual student?
- Is frequent and active student responding required?
- Is immediate feedback delivered?
✓ Is pedagogical validity adequately addressed?
- Do the goals of the software match the instructional purpose?
  - Is new material taught through tutorial method?
  - Is fluency tied to drill–and–practice?
  - Is practice in application of concepts or behaviors taught through use of simulations?
- Does the student learn the desired skills or knowledge?
- Do the learning gains occur across stimuli, behaviors, and time?

speech are on the horizon. Speech recognition teaching machines may be used to develop desired verbal behaviors that are found in the student's natural environment, and this development should lessen generalization concerns. Similarly, use of virtual reality environments with three-dimensional representation of images may also facilitate learning gains. The closer the appearance of training materials to those found in the natural environment, the more likely generalization of responding will occur. No matter the technology employed, it is essential that empirical evaluations of the instructional software provide the foundation for decisions regarding its use.

References

Anderson, R. C., Kulhavy, R. W., & Andre, T. (1971). Feedback procedures in programmed instruction. *Journal of Educational Psychology*, 62, 148–156.

Aspillaga, M. (1996). Perceptual foundations in the design of visual displays. *Computers in Human Behavior*, 12, 587–600.

Azevedo, R. & Bernard, R. M. (1995). A meta-analysis of the effects of feedback in computer-based instruction. *Journal of Educational Computing Research*, 13, 111–127.

Bannert, M. (2000). The effects of training wheels and self-learning in software training. *Journal of Computer Assisted Learning*, 16, 336–346.

Baum, W. M. (1994). *Understanding behaviorism*. New York: Harper Collins.

Benjamin, L. T. (1988). A history of teaching machines. *American Psychologist*, 43, 703–713.

Binder, C. (1993). Behavioral fluency: a new paradigm. *Educational Technology*, October, 8–14.

Bravo, M. & Blake, R. (1990). Preattentive vision and perceptual groups. *Perception*, 18, 515–522.

Brinkerhoff, J. D., Klein, J. D., & Koroghlanian, C. M. (2001). Effects of overviews and computer experience on learning from hypertext. *Journal of Educational Computing Research*, 25, 427–440.

Brown, I. (1998). The effect of WWW document structure on students' information retrieval. *Journal of Interactive Media in Education*, 98, 1–17.

Clariana, R. B. (1990). A comparison of answer until correct feedback and knowledge of correct response feedback under two conditions of contextualization. *Journal of Computer-Based Instruction*, 17, 125–129.

Clariana, R. B. & Lee, D. (2001). The effects of recognition and recall study tasks with feedback in a computer-based vocabulary lesson. *Educational Technology Research and Development*, 49, 23–36.

Clariana, R. B., Ross, S. M., & Morrison, G. R. (1991). The effects of different feedback strategies using computer-administered multiple-choice questions as instruction. *Educational Technology Research and Development*, 39, 5–17.

Desrochers, M. N. & Hile, M. G. (1993). SIDDS: Simulations in Developmental Disabilities. *Behavior, Research Methods, Instruments, & Computers*, 25, 308–313.

Desrochers, M. N., Hile, M. G., & Williams–Moseley, T. (1997). A survey of functional assessment procedures used with individuals with severe problem behaviors and mental retardation. *American Journal on Mental Retardation*, 101, 535–546.

Desrochers, M. N., Clemmons, T., Grady, M., and Justice, B. (2000). An evaluation of Simulations in Developmental Disabilities (SIDD): instructional software that provides practice in behavioral assessment and treatment decisions. *Journal of Technology in Human Services*, 17, 15–27.

Desrochers, M. N., House, A. M., & Seth, P. (2001). Supplementing lecture with Simulations in Developmental Disabilities: SIDD software. *Teaching of Psychology*, 28, 227–230.

Flora, S. R., & Logan, R. E. (1996). Using computerized study guides to increase performance on general psychology examinations: an experimental analysis. *Psychological Reports*, 79, 235–241.

Gorrell, J. & Downing, H. (1989). Effects of computer-simulated behavior analysis on pre-service teachers' problem solving. *Journal of Educational Computing Research*, 5, 335–347.

Grabinger, R. S. (1993). Computer screen designs: viewer judgments. *Educational Technology Research and Development*, 41, 35–73.

Grant, L. (2004). Teaching positive reinforcement on the internet. *Teaching of Psychology*, 31, 69–71.

Grant, L., McAvoy, R., & Keenan, K. (1982). Prompting and feedback variables in concept programming. *Teaching of Psychology*, 9, 173–177.

Hall, K. & Borman, K. G. (1973). Prompting and confirmation as instructional strategies with computer-assisted instruction. *The Journal of Educational Research*, 66, 279–285.

Hannafin, M. J. & Hooper, S. (1989). An integrated framework for CBI screen design and layout. *Computers in Human Behavior*, 5, 155–165.

Harrington, S. S. & Walker, B. L. (2002). A comparison of computer-based and instructor-led training for long-term care staff. *The Journal of Continuing Education in Nursing*, 33, 39–45.

Jenny, N. Y. & Fai, T. S. (2001). Evaluating the effectiveness of an interactive multimedia computer-based patient education program in cardiac rehabilitation. *The Occupational Therapy Journal of Research*, 21, 260–275.

Khalili, A. & Shashaani, L. (1994). The effectiveness of computer applications: a meta–analysis. *Journal of Research on Computing in Education*, 27(1), 48–61.

Kinzie, M. B. & Berdel, R. L. (1990). Design and use of hypermedia systems. *Educational Technology: Research and Development*, 38, 61–68.

Kritch, K. M., Bostow, D. E., & Dedrick, R. F. (1995). Level of interactivity of videodisc instruction on college students' recall of aids information. *Journal of Applied Behavior Analysis*, 28, 85–86.

Kulhavy, R. W. (1977). Feedback in written instruction. *Review of Educational Research*, 47, 211–232.

Kulik, C.-L. C. & Kulik, J. A. (1991). Effectiveness of computer-based instruction: An updated analysis. *Computers in Human Behavior*, 7, 75–94.

Kulik, J. A. (1994). Meta-analytic studies of findings on computer-based instruction, in Baker, E. L. and O'Neil, H. F. (Eds.), *Technology Assessment in Education and Training*. Hillsdale, NJ: Erlbaum, pp. 9–33.

Kulik, J. A. & Kulik, C.-L. C. (1987). Review of recent research literature on computer-based instruction. *Contemporary Educational Psychology*, 12, 222–230.

Lee, J. (1999). Effectiveness of computer-based instructional simulation: A meta-analysis. *International Journal of Instructional Media*, 25(1), 71–85.

Litchfield, B. C., Driscoll, M. P., & Dempsey, J. V. (1990). Presentation sequence and example difficulty: their effect on concept and rule learning in computer-based instruction. *Journal of Computer-Based Instruction*, 17, 35–40.

Lohr, L. L. (2000). Designing the instructional interface. *Computers in Human Behavior*, 6, 161–182.

Morrison, G. R., Ross, S. M., & O'Dell, J. K. (1988). Text density level as a design variable in instructional displays. *Educational Communication and Technology Journal*, 36, 103–115.

Morrison, G. R., Ross, S. M., O'Dell, J. K. Schultz, C. W., & Higginbotham-Wheat, N. (1989). Implications for the design of computer-based instruction screens. *Computers in Human Behavior*, 5, 167–173.

Murphy, M. A. & Davidson, G. V. (1991). Computer-based adaptive instruction: effects of learner control on concept learning. *Journal of Computer-Based Instruction*, 18, 51–56.

Noell, G. H., Gresham, F. M., & Gansle, K. A. (2002). Does treatment integrity matter? A preliminary investigation of instructional implementation and mathematics performance. *Journal of Behavioral Education*, 11, 51–67.

Park, I. & Hannafin, M. (1993). Empirically based guidelines for the design of interactive multimedia. *Educational Technology: Research and Development*, 41, 63–85.

Pressey, S. L. (1926). A simple apparatus which gives tests and scores and teaches. *School and Society*, 23, 373–376.

Skinner, B. F. (1958). Teaching machines. *Science*, 128, 969–977.

Skinner, B. F. (1961). Teaching machines. *Scientific American*, 205, 90–102.

Skinner, B. F. (1963). Reflections on a decade of teaching machines. *Teachers College*, 65, 168–177

Skinner, B. F. (1968). *The technology of teaching*. Englewood Cliffs, NJ: Prentice Hall.

Skinner, B. F. (1969). *Contingencies of reinforcement*. New York: Appleton-Century-Crofts.

Sternberg, R. J. (1996) *Cognitive Psychology*. Fort Worth, TX: Harcourt Brace.

Szabo, M. & Kanuka, H. (1998). Effects of violating screen design principles of balance, unity, and focus on recall learning, study time, and completion rates. *Journal of Educational Multimedia and Hypermedia*, 8, 23–42.

Taylor, H. L., Lintern, G., Hulin, C. L., Talleur, D. A., Emanuel, T. W., & Phillips, S. I. (1999). Transfer of training effectiveness of a personal computer aviation training device. *The International Journal of Aviation Psychology*, 9, 319–335.

Thomas, D. L. & Bostow, D. E. (1991). Evaluation of pre-therapy computer-interactive instruction. *Journal of Computer-Based Instruction*, 18, 66–70.

Thomas, R. & Hooper, E. (1991). Simulations: an opportunity we are missing. *Journal of Research on Computing in Education*, 23, 497–513.

van Schaik, P. & Ling, J. (2001). The effects of frame layout and differential background contrast on visual search performance in web pages. *Interacting with Computers*, 13, 513–525.

Vargas, J. S. (1986). Instructional design flaws in computer-assisted instruction. *Phi Delta Kappan*, 67, 738–744.

Washburn, D. A. (1999). Distinguishing interpretation from fact (DIFF): A computerized drill for methodology courses. *Behavior Research Methods, Instruments, and Computers*, 31, 3–6.

Yaber, G. E. & Malott, R. W. (1993). Computer-based fluency training: a resource for higher education. *Education and Treatment of Children*, 16(3), 306–315.

CHAPTER

10

Adaptive Computerized Educational Systems: A Case Study

ROGER D. RAY

Rollins College

UNDERGRADUATE TEACHING IN THE MODERN UNIVERSITY

Consider a very typical teaching and learning scenario in higher education today. The instructor for a large-enrollment Introductory Psychology (substitute any other scientific discipline you would like) university course begins the first day of classes by distributing a syllabus with textbook reading assignments spread across the semester. Other assignments may also be included, such as research projects or practical volunteer credits, but foremost are the textbook assignments. After all, the textbook has 300+ pages and cost the student more than any other course resource; thus, the textbook plays the most important role in the course outside of the instructor's classes themselves. But, it is interesting to note which assignments gain the students points for grading. The textbook readings almost never generate points directly, while other forms of activities do. How is an instructor expected to track and give credit to 200 or more individuals per class for completing each chapter assigned? Certainly, no partial credits are given for gradations of understanding the readings. Instead students are duly warned that readings will be covered by in-class tests (but typically not

Evidence-Based Educational Methods
Copyright © 2004 by Elsevier Inc. All rights reserved.

more than two to three such exams plus a final are given within a semester). Tests are few in number because they are likely to take the whole class period, and class time typically is precious to lecturers. So in-class exams must also cover lecture materials to make sure students attend class, listen, and learn from what the instructor has to say. But, if 10 to 15 chapters are covered in the semester, then 5 to 8 chapters are covered by each in-class test composed of approximately 60 to 80 items total. That is about 5 questions per chapter, with 5 questions for lectures on the same chapter materials. This means the density of any specific content's sampling is typically quite small, at least bringing into question the reliability of such sparse sampling. No wonder students complain that, despite their feeling that they have substantial knowledge, few of the right questions are ever asked to prove their mastery of the material!

Add to this scenario the actual lecture activities. Instructors hope, with little realistic expectation, that students have read the material in time for the in-class explanations, supplementations, or expansions of the readings assigned. Thus, for example, today's lecture starts coverage of the physiological foundations of behavior with the instructor in high hopes that students have read all about neurons, nerves, and their composite construction of a nervous system, including both peripheral and central components. Given such high expectations, the lecture starts by focusing on one specific central component of significant practical interest—the hypothalamus as a specialized body of neurons and its role in the fundamentals of food intake, body weight maintenance, and sexual behaviors. Just as the instructor is about to transit from neural to hormonal control, some student sheepishly asks if the instructor could please restate what a "neural" is . . . .

It probably is not presumptuous to think that instructors reading this might have had more than one carefully prepared lecture doomed by the sudden realization that few, if any, in the class actually read the assignment prior to class. Students may have been assigned to read and study the material as foundations for today's planned lecture, but it is perhaps one of the few ubiquitous experiences shared by all instructors of introductory courses to find such assignments largely ignored. Consider just one published example to highlight this point.

Because I personally have over 35 years of classroom experience, the following example from the recent literature did not surprise me in the slightest. Sikorski et al. (2002) reported on a two-university survey of student use of introductory texts that found as high as 91%, *but as few as 31%*, of students in introductory psychology classes actually even *purchased* the required text, much less read it or studied it. In fact, the majority of students at both universities surveyed reported " . . . that taking notes and studying them (without reading the text) was the single most important contributor to doing well" (p. 313). So much for lecturing to prepared learners!

UNDERGRADUATE TEACHING IN SMALL LIBERAL ARTS COLLEGES

Most instructors in today's large universities have no direct experience with the existence of educational institutions that pretty much ensure that their students in introductory courses learn through preparatory reading. Instructors with doctorate degrees actually teach individual students, at least as a class supplement and commonly as independent studies, in the rarified atmosphere called the small liberal arts college. Small classes foster early identification of ill-prepared students, and instructors often make individualized help readily available for those having difficulty with class preparations. For example, the last introductory psychology class I personally taught had nine students enrolled. I will admit that this is not typical even for offerings of Introductory Psychology in my school, although an enrollment limit of 25 to 30 is standard. It does, however, stand as an illustrative example of the educational environment being discussed. Thus, the relatively few instructors teaching in the smaller liberal arts colleges across the United States will easily recognize this scenario and find it quite familiar.

Of course students in this environment may still attempt to avoid buying or reading assigned text materials, but class activities tend to focus more on didactic exchanges that make faulty preparations by students more apparent and even personally embarrassing. So many students tend to read assignments, if for no other reason than fear they will be called upon to expound upon this material in class. Or at least they *try* to read assignments. Which brings me to the second element of my small college scenario. This second element is a problem that exists in most of higher education, although it is not as serious at elite institutions that screen applicants with highly selective criteria for admission. The problem? Students are more and more frequently coming to college with poorly developed skills for reading and comprehending textbooks, even if they try. Thus, it is not uncommon to have students who attempt to prepare for class, but who also find that if they are required to discuss or explain the material in class, it is highly difficult for them. When a student has a problem understanding the textbook in my course, either the student seeks me out or I ask that student to seek me out to obtain help. When asked to do so, that student is likely to come to my office for that help. And, because my own efforts to help such students follow many well-known and highly sound behavioral principles, it may be instructive to review these principles.

I assign readings in my introductory class with the goal of establishing a common working vocabulary of the principles, variables, and conceptual foundations for the discipline, and that is where I typically focus my first probes when I work with a problem student. That is, I will ask the student a few questions to get some idea of where to start in remediation (what behavior analysts call "establishing a baseline"). If I determine the student truly has had significant problems getting these fundamentals from reading the chapter, I will ask the student to show me how he or she reads the material and what kinds of note taking and rehearsal activities the student does after reading the material.

If the student demonstrates serious reading skill deficiencies, I start remediation by having the student first read a selected paragraph aloud to me. Then I have the student point out the central concept being introduced or elaborated in that paragraph, sentence by sentence. If the concept cannot be correctly identified, we will spend review time on what a concept is and how to recognize one when it is presented by textual discussion. After the student has successfully identified the primary concept, I will further ask the student to point to the attending or defining properties in the paragraph that elaborate that concept. If the student cannot do this readily, I will have the student re-read the paragraph aloud, and together we will attempt to isolate the sentence that contains the most primary or important concept.

We will then consider what in that sentence and subsequent sentences elaborates on that concept. This continues perhaps by my reading one of the sentences but leaving blank one property so the student can practice filling in the missing words as properties of the concept. For example, I might ask a question to verify that the student understands how the concept and properties relate in a form such as: "*Neurons* (main concept) taken as a collective make up a _____." (*Nerve* would be the desired answer.) Then, I might follow with: "All *nerves* [note the shift to a related concept] considered as an integrated whole makeup the entire _____." (*Nervous system* would be the desired answer). We will typically do this until the student can fill in at least three to four such properties.

Once we have moved through a few paragraphs at this level and the student has shown mastery of this lower skill, we typically move on to consider how the multiples of paragraphs we have covered relate to each other. For example, how do the concepts of synapse and neuron contrast or compare to each other? What is the relation of one to the other? Do drugs tend to influence synapses or neurons?

It is perhaps time to reflect on the behavioral principles being followed here. Cognitive psychologists would likely say that I am working to find what Vygotsky (Berk & Winsler, 1995) called the "zone of proximal development." Having found this zone where the student can work successfully only if I help, I then begin to scaffold the student's learning by focusing on concept and property identification. This is an interesting restatement (apparently unknowingly so) of principles articulated a bit differently by B. F. Skinner (1968) that considered the shaping of behavior through use of a series of "successive behavioral approximations" for making the transition from what a student can already do (*baseline*) to what the teacher aspires for the student to be able to do (the *teaching objective* or *target behaviors*). I believe the behavior analytic articulation afforded by Skinner is more complete because it tells us precisely what we should do and when we should do it to move the student progressively through this process. Thus, how one scaffolds is less clear to me in regard to precise variables, behaviors, and timing than is the articulation of successive approximation strategies.

For example, behavioral principles articulate three concurrent efforts that one should make that could be described as successive approximations during the shaping process. These emphasize what is done regarding (1) behavioral *antecedents* in the environment, (2) stages of *behavioral development* themselves (what is sometimes called a *task analysis*), and (3) stages of how behavioral consequences, in the form of *reinforcement densities*, are managed. I will briefly elaborate on each component of this antecedent–behavior–consequence analysis.

First, the behavior analytic model points to the significant contributions of attendant antecedent stimuli that precede the behavior. These include instructions, the way text is broken down into segments, and many other forms of what may be described as *prompts* to help generate, guide, and sustain desired behaviors. Of course, one does not want to have to use antecedent prompts forever, so one gradually (step by step through a series of successive approximations from high-density prompting to no prompting at all) *fades* the use or presence of such antecedents.

The second use of successive approximation is called *response shaping*, and it focuses not on the antecedents to behavior but rather directly on the behavior being taught. Skills are learned not as full-blown activities but in gradual stages of development, as when a baby learns to crawl through a series of various activities that are foundational components of crawling. Walking likewise starts with standing, then shuffling while holding onto something (an antecedent prompt), then gradually taking what looks more and more like steps, with stepping relying on less and less support until full-fledged walking is occurring. This is sometimes referred to as taking "baby steps" to go from standing to full-scale walking. In any case, the effort is to change behavior in successive and sufficiently small stages from what exists prior to shaping to the desired goal behavior that will terminate shaping.

The third successive approximation procedure focuses on reinforcing consequences in the environment and how frequently they are used. The goal is to decrease the density of reinforcements through a process that might be called *leaning*. Think of this as a metaphor for rich versus lean meats or diets. It all has to do with density of some element (*e.g.*, fat) in the meat or diet. Behavior analytic principles stress, beyond almost anything else, the important role of reinforcing consequences in determining whether behavior will increase or decrease in likelihood.

E. L. Thorndike (1898) discovered the importance of behavioral consequences and formally articulated how he felt they worked in his Law of Effect. But B. F. Skinner made an even more important discovery while working with reinforcements (Skinner, 1956; Ferster & Skinner, 1957). He discovered that one could move, in graded (successive) steps, from high-density use of reinforcement (*i.e.*, reinforcing *every* response occurrence) to extremely low-density reinforcement (lean or intermittent schedules where a very small proportion of responses are reinforced) and thereby actually increase the likelihood of the behavior! Of course if one attempts to "lean" reinforcement density too quickly, disuse of the behavior is most likely because of the process of extinction (Skinner, 1956). So another successive approximation from rich (high density) to lean (low density) delivery of behavioral consequences is also desirable. Thus, we have initial prompting and the gradual fading of these environmental antecedents to behavior, a gradual shaping of the form and function of the behavior itself, and continuous reinforcement being gradually leaned even to rare occurrences as highly specific recipes of variable manipulation. I find this more precise a specification than the usually vague suggestions offered in most discussions of scaffolding the learning process.

Teaching content conveyed by text through successive approximation techniques was partly "automated" very early in the development of scientifically inspired approaches to improved teaching (Skinner, 1968). The technique was then (and still is) called *programmed* instruction (Vargas & Vargas, 1992). In this approach, the tutor is removed from the process by breaking down the text into small units (called a *frame*) to be read and mastered before going to the next frame. Each frame of material presented stays relatively constant in size and complexity so even those with the poorest of reading skills can learn without experiencing failure. One problem with traditional programmed instruction is that it uses no form of successive approximation, except in its formation of the learner's facility with the *content* being taught. It does nothing to fade a student's reliance on programmed forms of text materials, to lean the density of reinforcing feedback, nor to shape better reading skills.

With my side review of behavioral principles complete, let me return to my tutorial scenario where we last left the student as having only succeeded in learning how to read for, and to verbalize, the critical concepts and concept properties paragraph by paragraph. It certainly is not my intent as a teacher to have to do supportive tutoring with the same student for every chapter throughout the course. So, I quickly establish a set of step-wise goals (successive approximations) for shaping the student's reading comprehension and study skills beyond this early stage of development, while also fading my own prompting and questioning as a part of the student's study activity. I also want to get much larger units of behavior from the student before I give reinforcing feedback (that is, I want to lean reliance on high-density reinforcement). To accomplish this, I gradually begin working with larger and larger units of the text, begin to fade my use of the author's own language in favor of a more abbreviated and paraphrased use of terms and properties being presented, and begin to probe more for the student's understanding of what goes with what—eventually asking for the student to verbally outline what is covered in major sections of the chapter without assistance.

This multiple successive approximations of prompting then fading, shaping of concept/term and association selection ability, and leaning out the density of my consequential feedback for accuracy and even fluency (speed of responding) is what most effective tutors would likely do. And, the results are such that before long tutorial help is less frequently needed, can be focused on larger and larger units of study, and can be assessed more and more abstractly by asking who, what, where, when, and why questions regarding major concepts. Eventually the student starts reading and taking notes and rehearsing this material independently.

It is very important to note that in the above scenario I end up teaching two different things simultaneously: one is the teaching of content, which is why the student came to me in the first place; the other is the acquisition of skills required to read with accuracy and fluency regarding the student's reflection of the content being read (what most educators would call *reading comprehension skills*). This process of dynamic and multidomain successive approximation is the epitome of what I will refer to hereafter as *adaptive instruction*. Unfortunately, such effective tutorials must be individually and adaptively focused and thereby can be afforded only to students in the most expensive educational institutions or most highly funded programs (such as remedial tutoring programs for university football and basketball players). The alternative to tutoring the less skilled students in low-tuition and high-enrollment environments is failing students out of the institution altogether, but technology may change that.

COMPUTERS AND ADAPTIVE INSTRUCTION

Efforts in programmed text instruction were quickly translated into mechanized forms for automated delivery via Skinner's elaboration of the "teaching machine" (Skinner, 1963; Vargas & Vargas, 1992) in the 1950s and 1960s. But, by the late 1980s, apparent potentials for a convergence with several additional technologies (behavioral/educational, artificial intelligence, and digital communications/computing) prompted the author to begin exploring ways of addressing shortcomings in this traditional approach. Computer programming was seen as one potential means for creating not only automated but intelligent delivery of the *entire* process summarized in the small college tutorial scenario, not just its first stage. Software programs written from the perspective of artificial intelligence and expert knowledge systems allow one to build a more dynamic and adaptive responsiveness to learner actions which automates many of those same stages of successive approximations to expert reading skills described. The phenomenal explosion of Internet connectivity now allows such computer programs to communicate with more centralized sources of content, so that these expert systems and personalized mirrorings of learning histories may be accessed by students from almost any physical location at any time.

But, why are such adaptive programs required? Well, even though I understand the power and empirical successes of both programmed instruction (Vargas & Vargas, 1992) and personalized systems of instruction (Keller, 1968), I have sufficient reservations about each, as typically practiced, to prompt me to attempt to improve upon both. Programmed instruction tends to present material only in micro-frames that can be mastered by even the slowest learner. Pity the poor student who can read large units of text and quickly assimilate the important concepts and properties being articulated but who now has to read only small units at a time before even being presented the next frame. Thus, relatively skilled learners often find themselves constantly frustrated by the unnaturally slow pace of material presentation.

Also, of course, pity the poor student who has learned to rely exclusively on the small frames as prompts for acquiring verbal facility with the material but who now has to read from a textbook that has not been programmed with lots of framing and other prompts! What are learners who have come to rely upon programmed instruction to do if they have to master material that has never been programmed for their pace of learning? I find traditional programmed instruction is designed almost to enable a dependency on poor reading comprehension skills much like families who unwittingly support a loved one enable a drug dependency! Until the advent of more adaptive computer-based programming, the only alternative seemed to be the "tough love" of the more traditional textbook. There was nothing in between to help those who originally needed programmed instruction to gradually wean them from such programming. Programmed instruction eventually should be faded as the primary prompt for successful learning.

Alternatively, personalized systems of instruction appear to me as favoring only the well-skilled reader and as failing to help readers with poor reading or study skills. True personalized instruction incorporates peer tutors to help students practice their poor reading skills over and over because such tutors typically are not trained to work on comprehension skill building. Thus, students typically end up "discussing" the material with their peer tutor until pure repetition finally allows them to pass a mastery test. It seems to me that these strategies do not address the root causes of not having mastered the material on first testing, if that was what occurred (as it most frequently does).

Prior work by my laboratory on the convergence of control systems and complex behavioral analysis (Ray & Delprato, 1989) inspired a new strategy for addressing this problem. I agreed with Kantor's (1970) assessment of the Experimental Analysis of Behavior movement, in that it was too singularly focused on only one element of a student's development—especially as it was expressed through the mechanics of programmed instructional design. Especially relevant, I believe, are dynamics modeled by adaptive control systems and their implications for computerized educational processes that allow computers to aid in the development not only of a student's facility with the content being presented but also skills that eventually transcend the need for supportive tutorial help in learning such content. These processes are best described as being guided by adaptive educational programming, or simply *adaptive instruction*.

ADAPTIVE CONTROL, TEACHING, AND LEARNING

The computers-in-education literature already reflects at least two quite distinct uses of the term *adaptive instruction*. Both uses of the term *adaptive instruction* include fluctuating goals, processes, and/or strategies that adapt to individual learner differences. However, in some of the literature, adaptive instruction describes mostly mechanical accommodations made only for individuals with physical or mental challenges and includes such solutions as alternative input or output devices for the blind or paralyzed users of computers. Alternatively, adaptive instruction describes how traditional content-oriented education is adjusted to address normal individual differences in learning styles, skills, or rates. My work focuses exclusively on this latter meaning and intent of the term *adaptive instruction*.

As the term is used currently, *adaptive instruction* describes adjustments typical of one-on-one tutoring as discussed in the college tutorial scenario. So computerized adaptive instruction refers to the use of computer software— almost always incorporating artificially intelligent services—which has been designed to adjust both the presentation of information and the form of questioning to meet the current needs of an individual learner in a fashion similar to how I would adjust both of these in direct personal tutorials. Traditional information adjustment ranges from simple, such as online help or navigational guidance systems, to more complex, such as intelligent agents or "find" systems for collecting and delivering pre-selected types of information or highly sophisticated tutoring systems designed to adjust such things as content presentation complexity or even appropriately difficult assessment materials to meet the needs of a given individual learner. I will focus almost exclusively on this latter use where adaptive tutorial and testing services are rendered. To help the reader understand how such a system works, a brief description follows concerning how adaptive instruction and adaptive testing differ and what they have in common.

ADAPTIVE INSTRUCTION

Adaptive instruction focuses on textual presentation and support (prompting) services that adapt to meet the needs of the user in the best way possible; however, even within this meaning the term often describes at least two different instructional service strategies: strategies that are *homeostatic* (Brusilovsky, Schwarz, & Weber, 1996) and those that are truly *adaptive* in the same sense that control systems engineers use the term (Jagacinski & Flach, 2003). General systems theory, cybernetics, and especially adaptive control systems theory views the world as being composed of hierarchically arranged systems (Powers, 1973). These hierarchical systems are defined by unique organizational and operational/process characteristics. Thus, cybernetic systems are those that incorporate feedback in the control and maintenance of a system's structure and/or operational dynamics. Understanding the role of cybernetic feedback helps to differentiate, for example, between homeostatic systems vs. truly adaptive control systems.

Homeostatic characteristics common to home air-conditioning systems serve as a model for almost all modern "adaptive" instructional software systems. Air-conditioning systems incorporate inputs (filtration of outside heat into a room), feedback (current air temperature), a goal (thermostatic setting for desired room temperature), a sensor (thermostat element which is sensitive to the feedback), a comparator (the thermostatic dynamic which allows for differencing between goal setting and current temperature), and a processor (air compressor) controlled by the comparator (thermostat). In this example, the adaptivity is seen when outside temperatures overheat the room, thus causing the current room temperature to exceed the desired setting sufficiently to cause the controller (thermostatic mechanism) to turn the cooling compressor on (and eventually back off), thereby causing a new supply of cooled air to circulate into the room. That is, the air conditioner adapts to the heat by cooling the room, thereby maintaining a homeostatic balance in temperature. Like this example, most so-called "adaptive education systems" are designed to adapt to errors made by a student (analogous to a room being hotter than desired) by helping the student meet the static instructional goal (analogous to the thermostat setting) that has been predetermined by the instructional designer.

Just as a thermostat monitors the room air temperature, such adaptive instruction systems are designed to mirror the current knowledge of the learner—usually through the application of an "automatic knowledge generation" engine—but only to adjust for student failings by adjusting services (analogous to turning a compressor on and off) to meet a singular and pre-established educational content mastery goal (again, analogous to reaching the desired thermostat setting). It is this ability to adjust services that prompts most designers to refer to such instructional design elements as *adaptive*.

Upon closer inspection, this is a somewhat misguided use of the term *adaptive*. It is certainly not consistent with how cybernetic and systems researchers would describe the feedback-driven, disturbance-control dynamics for maintaining stability in homeostatic systems like our air-conditioning example. Systems researchers reserve the term *adaptive* to describe quite a different type of control system—a system that incorporates the capability of adjusting its own homeostatic goals when needed. Purely homeostatic systems incorporate only the previously mentioned metaphorical capabilities of sensing current states, of comparing those states to desired or goal settings via feedback, and then controlling adjustments in the operations of the system to decrease discrepancies between desired and current states. Truly adaptive systems also include the metaphorical ability to learn or *adjust* (another word for adapting) by self-modifying the goal or desired state. This increases dramatically the long-term maintenance or even enhanced development of the system's integrity.

Darwin saw such mechanics of adaptation at work in processes that expanded the variability in existing genetic pools (such as mutations), thereby allowing for evolutionary transformation of the structural and functional capacities and characteristics of entire existing species when changes in environments occurred. But, applying such distinctions and definitions to instructional software systems requires that we understand the limitations of most educational goals as they are built into typical adaptive instruction systems.

As noted, typical "adaptive" educational systems almost always include static goals with dynamic adjustments designed to accomplish those goals. But, to be truly adaptive, educational systems need to incorporate the ability to adaptively teach a student the immediate content as well as the ability to teach higher-level skills that transform the learner in fundamental ways. Learners need to develop reading, listening, and viewing comprehension skills. Better yet, we should add the goal of establishing or improving the student's ability to create self-reflective "mappings" or diagrams of the semantic networks that reflect true understanding (Novak & Gowin, 1984). Eventually, we also need to work on advanced problem-solving or generative behaviors (Epstein, 1993).

Such a system should not only adjust to the momentary (homeostatic) needs of the learner but should also recognize when that learner is becoming more adept at learning the material and should respond by challenging the learner to more advanced forms or levels of learning. That is, adaptive instructional systems should not only improve the students' knowledge base but also their learning skills. To do so requires that such a system be capable of shifting its educational goals as well as its services for helping a student accomplish those goals.

ADAPTIVE TESTING

Many readers will already be familiar with at least one definition of adaptive testing (van der Linden & Glas, 2000; Wainter et al., 2000) as it has already been incorporated into many standardized assessment instruments such as those offered by the Educational Testing Services. Again, I use the term a little differently from the traditional literature. It is not just the content focus, but also the *format* of a question that should change in order for a question not only to assess but also to shape comprehension skills via its role in the tutorial process. Questions offer the reinforcing feedback that reflects successful progress of the student, but questions also help to establish for the artificial intelligence engine which kinds of services (as well as which specific content) are needed to help the student progress. Because this is not intended to be a treatise on adaptive testing, perhaps the best way to convey the subtleties is by concrete illustration.

MEDIAMATRIX AND ITS CURRENT USE IN HIGHER EDUCATION

As an attempt to integrate the various elements presented thus far, let me briefly overview the design and function of a software system called *MediaMatrix*. MediaMatrix was expressly designed to deliver highly integrative adaptive instructional and adaptive testing services, and early versions have been described in detail in prior publications (Ray, 1995a,b; Ray, Gogoberidze, Begiashvilli, 1995). It may thus suffice to give only a cursory summary of the various levels of service and how they manifest themselves to the student user to aid in learning new content while attempting also to improve comprehension skills.

As we have already seen, *prompting/fading*, *shaping*, and *leaning* principles tell us that good teaching is an *adaptive* affair. It requires active and sensitive adjustments as we move a student through the various and concurrent successive approximations that lead to the goal of an effective, independent, and knowledgeable learner. The concept of managing the learning process suggests that we need to be sensitive to where the student is at all times in terms of the student's need for prompting, segmenting content, and reinforcing through testing results. Such principles guide us to begin with the size of content segment best suited to the individual student. *And, that segment may, in fact, vary as a function of the character of the content.* Simple *concepts* built around commonsense terms that denote objects—technically known as *tacts* and *notates* (Skinner, 1957)—will be learned in large segments by most students. *Abstractions* require a much smaller segmenting if the terms are new and somewhat conceptual. Nevertheless, better educated students will find even difficult *abstractions* easy to acquire if their learning history has grounded them in the underlying *concepts* (Catania, 1998).

Thus, what is required is a software system that begins with highly prompted presentations, then follows the learner's responses to questions and, based on a running diagnostic history, has enough intelligence to adapt the programmed instructional material to individual needs. Such adaptations present text in larger or smaller *segments*, *fade* or return concept-related *prompting* as needed, and alter the *questions* between more or less highly *prompted* formats. In addition, gradually shaped responses from the student need to be developed to move the student from simple *recognition/selection* levels of competence to the less prompted and more *generatively* demanding conditions of *full recall* or *response production* and eventually to demonstrations of *problem-solving* and *generative* skills (Epstein, 1993). MediaMatrix was designed to allow such adaptive content presentation and interactivity.

MediaMatrix begins simply with the presentation of a standard textbook that is published electronically via the Internet through a custom browser interface designed to place all the artificial intelligence programming on client computers and all content distributed from remote server databases. Content includes text, graphics, questions, and student history, as well as data for supplemental tools such as a personal notebook system with printable notes. Free, full-service evaluation copies of the Introductory Psychology textbook and tutoring system, as well as a completely illustrated user's guide showing all features, are available on the Internet (http://www.psychi-ai.com), so no graphic illustrations will be provided here.

The MediaMatrix browser has several alternative presentation modes that alter the user's experience of the content and tutorial services. The simplest of these presentations is the Browse mode for reading with all tutoring services turned off. In this mode, the reader has access to full electronic text and graphics topically organized for unit-based reading where such units are defined by typically outlined topics of the textbook's chapters. The alternative to this simple Browse mode is Tutor mode, which turns on the system to offer adaptive instructional/tutorial services that dynamically adjust through two to five alternatives.

MediaMatrix encourages content programmers to design programmed instruction at a minimum of four concurrent levels, although the number of levels is adjustable by the developer as well as by the instructor. Most levels of Tutor mode function somewhat like any other level from the software's point of view, so each level is managed as an alternative software object. It is through content segmenting (how much prompting is given and the varying formats of probe questions) that levels become functionally distinct. This means, of course, that MediaMatrix can make good content programming possible, but certainly does not guarantee it in and of itself. Effective content programming requires a very deliberate effort to incorporate sound behavioral systems and operant learning principles, and poor adherence to those principles should not lay blame to the principles themselves as too often occurs (Erlwanger, 1973).

Tutor Level One: Fully Supported Shaping of Reading Comprehension Skills

In the Tutor Level One mode of studying textual resources, the text that was previously available for unaided reading in Browse mode is now presented in small successive segments by keeping the target segment in full black text, but dimming out all other surrounding text via use of a light gray font. The size of each targeted segment is determined by content developers according to their anticipation of the comprehension level of the lowest portion of the student population likely to study this material. It represents the segment size students will read before being asked a question on its content and meaning and is usually only one paragraph of text.

In addition to segmenting the text into small units and thereby affording the student an opportunity to learn in small steps through frequent testing, Level One mode aids the student even further by incorporating *stimulus prompts* that assist in determining which words within the text serve as the key *associated terms*, as *defining relations* among terms (intraverbals/notants), and as *concept presentations*. Such prompts are presented through underlining the respective words or phrases, which causes them to stand out within the context of all other words. As within the unprompted Browse mode, many of these under-lined terms or phrases may be mouse-clicked to find their definition in a glossary of such terms.

To pass beyond any given segment of presented text, the student must click a Continue Tutor button and is then presented with an appropriately formatted (for that level) question on that segment's content. In addition to the Level One mode being designed for presenting small segments of highly prompted con-tent, it is also designed for the use of highly prompted formats of question-ing—in this case, multiple-choice questions that target primary-concept and single-property association development. This level is for the learner who needs a lot of *prompting* and *shaping* to learn the content, and astute readers will have already noted the high-density use of reinforcing feedback by having question-answering results available for every paragraph read. If a question is answered incorrectly, the student is shown the correct answer and is also prompted to reread the segment again. The student is subsequently presented with alternative questions (usually there are 4 to 12 alternative questions for every one-paragraph segment throughout the entire textbook) until a question is successfully answered and the student is moved to the next subsequent text segment.

Tutor Level Two: Successive Approximations to Less Prompted Learning

At the second level of tutoring, text segments typically involve two paragraphs of content rather than one. To move beyond this segment of text the student must answer correctly a fill-blank form of question that mirrors the question items existing in the multiple-choice format. By moving to the fill-blank format, the same concept or property probe is made but without the prompt of having the correct answer available. On all levels, if the student answers a question incorrectly, alternative questions appear for that segment of text until the student answers a question correctly. In eventual certification testing to demonstrate mastery of an entire chapter, the student is given a test con-structed of a mixture of previously missed questions (to assess for error corrections), previously unasked questions (to improve assessment reliability), and some questions the student has answered correctly during tutoring (to assure some degree of progress reinforcement).

MediaMatrix incorporates an artificially intelligent inference engine that gives the system its ability to acquire data on the concepts, their associates, and the strength of the associate connection based on the developing history of the individual student's performance. Thus, a mirroring of each student's developing verbal associate network is created from the knowledge engine's data on the responses that a student gives to all tutorial and assessment questions on all levels. Such a system also incorporates an expert's image, or *concept map*, of all primary concepts and their verbal associates for comparative purposes. Overlapping areas between the student's and the expert's maps are reinforced while mismatches are used to select corrective questions.

Tutor Level Three: Further Development of Verbal Associate Networks

Tutor Level Three mode really begins advanced utilization of the special system of artificial intelligence that allows for adaptive test construction, as well as individually targeted advising as supplemental feedback. Prior levels have been presenting the student with questions written with specific associations in mind—associations between primary concept terms and elaborative property terms. In Tutor Level Three mode, this system is able to use the accumulated model-of-the-student information to construct exactly the paired-associate practice questions a given individual student needs on any given topic. Such questions may take the form of a single paired-associate item, or a *word associates recognition* testing form as illustrated:

Is *Thorndike* associated with the *Law of Effect*?

Other terms one might offer as potential associates to Thorndike include the following:

Cats
Puzzle boxes
Operant conditioning chambers
Trial and error
Respondent behaviors
Shaping
Law of Effect
Successive approximations

Students knowledgeable about the differences between the work of B. F. Skinner and E. L. Thorndike will quickly isolate cats, puzzle boxes, trial and error (procedures), and Law of Effect as associated with Thorndike, while operant conditioning chambers, respondent behaviors, shaping, and successive approximations originate with Skinner's work. The student's progress in revising misconstrued connections or strengthening weak associations can also be used as a diagnostic for advising the student about what areas require further study or how to better use the system or even to suggest that the student explore undiscovered areas of relevance.

The text a student reads prior to this type of question will by now include four to six paragraphs (thereby shaping advanced approximations to full-text reading and leaned reinforcement, as feedback has moved from one question per paragraph, a 1:1 ratio, to one question per four to six paragraphs, a 4–6:1 ratio). Further, the previous underlining as prompts will have been replaced and now the student will see only primary concepts and their verbal associates as a notes version of terms and properties. This *terms and properties* list appears much like the list in the above illustration of Thorndike as a paired associate question but is now organized correctly with, for example, Skinner and his associated contributions being one group while Thorndike and his associated contributions form another grouping. These prompts disappear, of course, when questions are presented.

Tutor Level Four: Full Development of Verbal Associate Networks

Tutor Level Four mode presents text in the same form and amount as if the student were in Browse mode, and thus is analogous to any printed textbook. Only the primary concept terms appear in the prompting notes area to help the student identify what this text is attempting to teach, and questions presented for tutoring assessment are in the form of multiple-fill blank associates questions, as pioneered by Verplanck (1992a,b). Such a question presents, for example, the name "E. L. Thorndike" with four subsequent blank field areas where a student is expected to supply associated terms that illustrate the student's familiarity with Thorndike's work (terms or phrases like those presented above in the paired-association item illustration).

By now the student has been shaped to read large units of text with minimal prompts, has acquired the skill to isolate the primary concepts being taught by that text, and has learned to identify (and remember) several appropriate descriptive terms or properties associated with those primary concepts. Note that reinforcing feedback has been leaned to where it now only appears after having read and mastered large amounts of material. Prompts have been almost totally faded away, and if the student cannot maintain this level of behavioral study skill and answers a series of questions incorrectly, the system will quickly move that student back down the tutor-level scale until successful performance is once again established. Establishing successful performance at any level only moves the student to a more challenging level for more practice there, just as if a human tutor were tracking progress and determining what current support needs and challenges should be presented. Success at Level

Four mode moves the student into a fifth and final tutorial mode known internally within the system as the Probe mode.

How the Probe Mode Works

In the Probe mode, students are left to read totally unprompted text very much on their own as they do in Browse mode or when reading any other standard textbook; however, in Probe mode, a variable schedule is at work for presenting the student questions. The question bank used in this mode is a collection of all questions improperly answered during study at all lower tutor levels. Any question answered appropriately is removed from the dynamic Probe Test Bank until the student has exhausted all possible questions, whereupon the student is praised for having graduated to unassisted learning levels and is offered the alternative of continuing to work in Browse mode or going directly to Assess mode for certification.

MORE ON ADAPTIVE PROGRAMMED INSTRUCTION: PARAMETRICS OF HOW MEDIAMATRIX WORKS

As noted, students actually begin by default at tutorial Level One, which incorporates smaller chunks of information and the more highly prompted selection/recognition form of question. As a student succeeds with Level One, Level Two is introduced. But, a student who begins either to falter or to excel at Level Two is automatically moved to either Level One or to Level Three, respectively, by the artificially intelligent inference engine of MediaMatrix. The definitions of *excel* and *falter* are *algorithmic*, and the parameters are fully adjustable by instructional designers to be either more or less sensitive. The system defaults to a combination of passing a series of questions with a specified average *accuracy* score plus a minimal *fluency* rate (Binder, 1993). A running average for six successive questions that falls above 90% accuracy and less than the maximum (30 seconds) time allotted to answer a question *(fluency)* moves the student to the next higher level. Alternatively, a running average for six successive questions that falls below 60% accuracy and 125% fluency moves the student to the next lower level. Again, these parameters (including the number of successive questions used as criteria) are fully adjustable to allow for system adaptation to alternative student populations or content difficulty.

ASSESS AND CERTIFICATION MODES

At any time a student may self-assess by directly choosing the user-mode selection button to access an Assess panel that allows students to construct their own (not-for-credit) quiz made up of any number and any types of questions on a given topic of text. Unlike tutorial questions that supply a lot of feedback and allow reviews of the related material for each question, the Assess mode questions give no immediate feedback. Only when the test has been completed is a summary of the test performance and a question-by-question diagnostic offered to the student. Finally, a student who feels sufficiently confident of progress in studying all topics within a chapter of the text may select the Certification mode. This screen is included as a part of the textbook application and offers the student a list of all chapters (with associated completion deadlines) currently still available for "mastery certification" testing. Such tests are adaptively composed for each individual student and graded for accuracy. Accuracy scores are submitted to the server for instructor use in determining course grades. Typically, such adaptively constructed, and thus unique, tests may be retaken any number of times prior to each chapter's deadline to encourage student mastery.

INSTRUCTOR OPTIONS FOR MANAGING STUDENT CONTACT WITH THE TUTORING SYSTEM

MediaMatrix was designed around a server-residing relational database. This database incorporates records for each individual instructor using MediaMatrix-based textbooks with one record for each separate course and, in the case of multiple sections, each section of that course. Student records also are created which relate each student to the appropriate instructor, course, and section. From the student perspective, the primary portal designed for use of this database is the metaphorical electronic textbook with its various modes of text presentation, including tutorials, self-assessments, and mastery certification testing. The mastery certification testing interface allows the student to take tests (supervised or unsupervised, depending on instructor strategies of use) on each full chapter of the text.

Instructors have their own portal into the database that allows them both to set various parameters and requirements of student use and to view both individual and class progress in certification testing. Thus, instructors have control over how many questions will be used in certification testing, what types of question formats should be used, and how long the student has to answer each question. Optionally, the entire test may be timed rather than just the individual questions. The instructor also has control over deadlines for taking chapter certification tests via this administrative system.

Typical use of a MediaMatrix textbook includes allowing students to retake alternative (adaptively constructed) chapter certification tests as many times as necessary for each student to reach a performance level with which that student is satisfied. In such cases, only the highest grade is typically counted, with all chapter grades being combined to account for, say, 50% of the final course grade. The remaining percentage typically comes from in-class testing and projects.

Among the important parameters an instructor may manage are the offerings of gradient-based *bonus* points for tutoring and self-assessing on topics within a chapter *prior to* certification testing on that chapter. Further, the instructor may implement a policy of allowing students to demonstrate that they can achieve satisfactory scores on certification testing (where "satisfactory" is defined by the instructor setting a minimum percent correct, such as 80) merely by reading printed versions of the text (which are made available as downloadable pdf files) and studying on their own. An instructor might allow any number of such diagnostic demonstrations but will typically limit them to two or three tests (via an optional setting) before having the system require a student to tutor on all topics the system has diagnosed as giving that student problems. Such requirements are expressed by showing the student a list of topics that must be successfully tutored to reopen certification. When all topics in the list have been eliminated, the certification testing is again available for the specified number of attempts to exceed the minimum requirement. Both the "bonus" and the "required tutoring after diagnostics" features were designed to encourage students to use the tutorial system to its full advantage.

Finally, an instructor has the option of actively tracking (for research purposes) all interactions students have with the systems assessment activities. There is a research software system that can query the database and offers summaries of how much time students use tutorial services and assessment services, student successes and failures with various levels of tutoring and types of questions, etc. And, while such research has only begun quite recently, it is already illustrating some interesting aspects of this adaptive tutorial and mastery testing/certification system. So, let me conclude with a very brief summary of some of these very early research efforts regarding the system's use and effectiveness.

EMPIRICAL RESEARCH ON MEDIAMATRIX DELIVERED ADAPTIVE INSTRUCTION

It is truly interesting to observe how students use, fail to use, and abuse systems designed to help them improve their learning skills and knowledge of a given academic subject. MediaMatrix was designed primarily as an electronic replacement for textbooks, not as a replacement of instructors. Of course, MediaMatrix *may* be used as an alternative to web-browser distribution of educational content in distance-based educational settings which minimize instructors in the educational process. My personal views of current Internet-delivered instruction typical of most schools is that the Internet has given us an interesting alternative form for delivering *information*, but it has yet to really accomplish much in the area of delivering alternative forms of *education* (*i.e.*, highly interactive and personally adapted services that teach, not just inform). But, getting students in contact with electronic forms of education (where they actually exist) is, itself, turning out to be an interesting challenge.

It is often informally reported among those who implement personalized systems of instruction that student drop rates are typically higher than in traditionally managed classes. In some cases, this is attributed to the loss of contact with scheduled classes, but it may also be largely due to the implicitly increased work loads involved in having to master material at a high level prior to moving forward in the course. Students also frequently find early and frequent testing is highly informative about their probable lack of success without putting in far more effort, and they use that feedback for electing early withdrawal rather than eventual failure in the course.

Like personalized instruction, a MediaMatrix delivered textbook is designed not only to tutor but also to certify mastery of materials published through that system. This mixture of education versus certification makes the electronic system a two-edged sword for students. It both helps them learn and shows them the degree to which they are failing or succeeding in that process. Students who are attempting simply to skim the text before testing find through early feedback that this strategy will not suffice for the course. When such students discover that an instructor expects them to tutor paragraph-by-paragraph and to acquire some mastery level—that often includes actually remembering how terms are used relative to one another—many are dismayed by the implicit expectations. Thus, some students will drop the course quite early, finding it too much work to actually master all the material. Others will complain about the required "memorization" in the course. We have not yet established relative percentages for this, but informally shared experiences find these to be common themes among instructors using the system.

A recent symposium at the meetings of the Association for Behavior Analysis (ABA) included two reports that were data-based evaluations of student use and subsequent performance in courses using a MediaMatrix-delivered textbook on Introductory Psychology (Kasschau, 2000). One study reported by Belden, Miraglia, and Ray (2003) investigated alternative contingency settings regarding (1) the use of bonus point offerings for self-quizzing and tutoring, as well as (2) whether tutoring was required following limited numbers of unsuccessful certification tests. Five different instructors were involved in the comparative study, each with different use settings, as illustrated in Table 1. Table rows may be viewed as qualitatively ranked in terms of what might be considered the most stringent use contingencies and requirements (instructor A) to the least stringent (instructor E). Figure 1 illustrates the corresponding average amount of time students in these respective instructors' courses spent tutoring.

Clearly, the amount of tutor time systematically follows the stringency of the contingency settings for student use. Belden, Miraglia, and Ray (2003). reported that all of these differences, except those between instructor D and E, were statistically significant (with $P<.01$). The authors then compared the

TABLE 1
Listing of Instructors and Their Parametric Settings for the Use of MediaMatrix Based Introduction to Psychology

Instructor	Tutoring levels/types of questions	Required tutoring settings	Bonus status
A	Tutoring: 2 levels Certification: MC/FB	Two attempts to reach 80%	Tutor bonus: on Quiz bonus: on
B	Tutoring: 4 levels Certification: MC/FB	Two attempts to reach 60%	Tutor bonus: on Quiz bonus: off
C	Tutoring: 2 levels Certification: MC/FB	Required tutoring off, PSI format	Tutor bonus: on Quiz bonus: on
D	Tutoring: 2 levels Certification: MC/FB	Required tutoring off, lecture format	Tutor bonus: on Quiz bonus: on
E	Tutoring: 3 levels Certification: MC/FB	Required tutoring off, lecture format	Tutor bonus: on Quiz bonus: on

Note: MC = multiple choice; FB = fill in the blanks; PSI = Personalized System of Instruction.

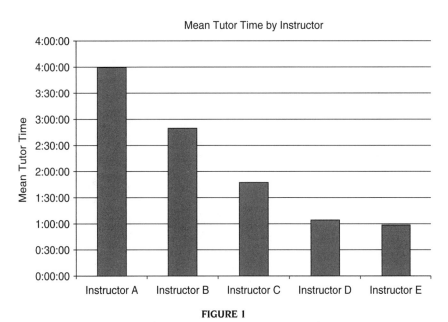

FIGURE 1

Mean tutor time for each of five instructors, using MediaMatrix Courses to deliver Kasschan's (2000) textbook content for introductory psychology.

average certification mastery scores for these same instructors and found that each class was approximately the same, ranging from 80% to approximately 83% accuracy in certification testing (this range is noteworthy in and of itself, as this entire range of scores is within a B grade for all five instructors). However, the instructor with the most stringent criteria (instructor A) had students achieving this maximum score within an average of only two attempts, while other instructors' students on average required from four to five attempts.

When the distribution for total student tutor time for all students across all instructors was separated into quartile groupings, there was a systematic and significant increase in maximum certification mastery scores, quartile by quartile. The lowest quartile achieved an average maximum test score of 78% and grades increased systematically quartile by quartile, with 84% as the mean certification score for the highest quartile grouping. Shifting from statistical to practical significance, these results represent just slightly over half a grade-range improvement in test scores for those who tutored most versus those who tutored least. This suggests that getting students in contact with the tutoring system plays a significant role both in the grade they ultimately achieve and how quickly they reach that grade level with respect to retakes of tests. Regardless, instructors found themselves lecturing and/or leading discussions in classes in which the average student preparation level prior to attending that class was within the course's B grading range. That also has practical significance.

Finally, a second study reported in the ABA symposium by Butterfield and Houmanfar (2003) compared the use of the Kasschau (2000) text delivered via the MediaMatrix adaptive instructional system to the use of a commercially popular printed textbook. Both types of textbooks were used in a Personalized System of Instruction (PSI) environment in which mastery certification testing within MediaMatrix was time limited for each question but not supervised. Certification testing for the printed text was taken via a WebCT based computerized administration of tests supervised by course tutors. Students in both sections also took the same pre- and post-tests covering psychological content common to both textbooks.

Butterfield and Houmanfar reported on a sample of 41 students as representative of their large introductory classes (from 200 to 600 students in each condition) across two different semesters (Spring and Fall of 2002), with their MediaMatrix user settings being those described for instructor C in Table 1. In both semesters studied, the adaptive instruction group had higher increases in average pre-post test scores than the traditional-text/WebCT sections. Almost no students were within the highest performance range (*i.e.*, answering in excess of 21 questions correctly of the 40 questions asked in the pre- and post-testing) for either group during the Spring or Fall term pre-test. But, approximately twice as many adaptive instruction students ended up in this category on post-testing than students from the WebCT group for Spring, and the Fall term had nearly 30% more adaptive instruction students in the high-performance range than students from WebCT. The Fall semester also had approximately twice as many adaptive instruction students both in the A and the B grade range for the final exam compared to the WebCT group. Although not as dramatic in size, a similar difference was reported for the Spring groups as well (*i.e.*, more adaptive instruction students had As and Bs, respectively, on the final exam than the WebCT group). Final course grades earned were more mixed in comparison because they also included points earned from assignments, discussion group attendance, etc.

In fact, truly comparative research on such systems is very difficult to design and even harder to execute. This type of research often comes much closer to representing program evaluation research than controlled experimentation. Over 3000 students were involved in the Belden, Miraglia, and Ray (2003) study, and this makes statistical differences easy to obtain. More important is to consider the practical significance. Their report of over half a grade range difference between those with the least time tutoring vs. those with the most time tutoring is probably much more important to a student than a statistically significant difference between final grades that are all in the B range. Likewise, an instructor is much more likely to be satisfied with a B average for the students' preparation for the lecture, should that instructor still decide to give lectures! It *does* seem that technology *can* address the problem of not having prepared learners for even our largest of university classes. But, there is a downside to this story as well as this obvious upside. It is to this somewhat more cautious element that I now turn.

HIGHER EDUCATION'S FOUR HORSEMEN OF ITS APOCALYPSE

The title of this section says it all. There are four major and significant impediments to accomplishing long-term improvements in our higher education system, and, unlike most pundits, a lack of funds is not really on the list. As is often the case, these four obstacles are often interconnected but are nevertheless worthy of independent as well as interdependent identification and consideration. The four include: (1) limits imposed by current hardware and software technologies; (2) difficulties in changing instructor behaviors (teaching); (3) difficulties in changing student behaviors (learning); and, finally, (4) limits imposed by how little we yet know about the intraverbal dynamics of an expert's verbal associate networks and their effective representation as artificial intelligence.

Let me consider hardware and software first. The system for Internet-delivered adaptive instruction described in this chapter took well over 10 years and in excess of $1 million to develop, debug, and bring to market. Because it is an integrated software and hardware system, it suffers from the current shortcomings of both of these technologies combined. Hardware (servers, Internet backbones, etc.) is still limited and not quite perfected. This translates into occasional server failures, dropped connections, lost data during transmission, and thus frustrations on the part of students, instructors, and technical support personnel alike. But, with the rapid evolution in hardware, this is changing—and that would appear to be a positive. However, hardware evolves so quickly that it also requires a full-time software maintenance program to stay compatible and, thus, to stay in the market. This means development of software is never complete. Worse yet, in systems this complex, the continuity of personnel sufficiently trained to continue software upgrades and to progress to new desirable features is difficult without significant scaling to larger and larger organizations with sustainable financial foundations (translate: larger companies). For such large companies to become involved, the numbers (both in terms of adoptions and its direct associate, revenues) would have to increase substantially. Adoptions and revenues segue into the problem of changing instructor and student behaviors.

Changing instructor behaviors is a first step in changing student behaviors, for instructors set the environmental conditions that shape and maintain not only how students study but also how students establish their expectations for what will be required of them for course credits. It is common that students in a university course expect to do little more than merely race through a long list of multiple-choice questions attempting to recognize answers they have mostly heard before. Remember the Sikorski et al. (2002) report that students felt the most important contributor to doing well in courses was to take notes without reading the text? Such students will almost never spend the time required for developing verbal reproductive fluencies sufficient for sustaining an educated conversation with anyone on the topic or for summarizing major concepts covered in a course along with the properties that make such concepts what they are.

Why? Well, what university instructor has the time, resources, or even the inclination to attempt to develop such behavioral repertoires, as verification typically means grading essay tests or something akin to them? To get instructors to change both their educational goals and their teaching behaviors by changing the form of their assignments, their testing formats, or their adoption of new technologies is difficult. I have demonstrated and explained the adaptive educational system described above to a great many instructors, and few have been sufficiently interested to attempt its use. And, even when instructors adopt it as an alternative to their traditional textbooks, they rarely set it for more than two levels of tutorial services or two alternative forms of certification questions. Explorations of why this is so is another essay altogether, but it is demonstrated in Table 1 when the reader explores the column "Tutoring Levels/Types of Questions" (used in certification testing).

From my own experience in using all tutorial levels and thereby asserting very high-performance expectations, students are very quick to attempt to reciprocally manage my expectations by drawing comparisons between my own requirements and those of my colleagues teaching the same numbered and titled course for the same number of credits. Thus, changing student behaviors also turns out to be very difficult because they are given lower-expectation alternatives and have histories of finding paths of least resistance to their own certification (read: "degree") with the minimum of education (read: "knowledge").

This is an institutional weakness emphasized by administrative efforts to meet consumer demands and thus to populate classrooms with more people, not higher-quality learning processes. So, I personally find limited promise for many adoptions of such technologically enabled tutoring systems that require significantly increased student effort, despite measurably superior outcomes. I am afraid that superior outcome measures are almost at the bottom of many instructors' or administrators' list of concerns in today's institutions of higher education.

Finally, let me offer a parting note on what I have learned about the frontiers of behavioral technologies. Beginning with Skinner's treatise on verbal behavior (Skinner, 1957) and continuing with Kantor's linguistics alternative (Kantor, 1977), the field of behavioral analysis has seemingly assumed far more than it has proven relative to human use of language—especially as this activity is related to educational objectives. Few instructors have attempted to specify for students how their course objectives relate to changing the student's working conversational and written vocabulary. Neither do course objectives attempt to specify the range of circumstances in which this vocabulary might be tested or even used. But, even if we wanted to specify such objectives, our collective failure in understanding how an "educated" student might converse with us is substantial. We know a student educated by our course when we experience one, but we have a very difficult time giving a detailed operational definition of our criteria for one! To specify the requirements for knowing one would be to specify how an expert uses our technical vocabularies.

One of my favorite examples learned from experience illustrates the feebleness of our efforts to build representations of the associations such experts make among concepts. Somewhere in the chapter on psychophysiology in most Introductory Psychology textbooks, a student is most likely to read about rapid eye movements (REM) and stages of sleeping as reflected in the scoring of electroencephalogram (EEG) records, and common is the establishment of a direct association between REM sleep and a sleeper's verbal report of concurrent dreaming upon being awakened from such a state. Further elaboration of this REM stage often reflects on the associated paralysis-like state of the muscles, ensuring that vivid dreams of, say, running, do not find us leaving our beds. So, let us assume you were concept mapping (Novak & Gowin, 1984) this paragraph.

To test a student's own efforts to concept map the paragraph in question, you select to ask a verbal associate question based on *dreaming* as the prompting term. You might well expect the student to respond with *REM, stages of sleep, EEG recordings*, and *paralysis-like muscle states*. But, how would you grade a student who also answered to the term *dreaming* with the associated response *Sigmund Freud*? Suddenly, you find a student who is actually better educated than your educational goals (and its related expert system) anticipated. This student just made a totally appropriate, albeit unanticipated, connection between one chapter's discussion of dreaming and another chapter's discussion of the same topic, but from a totally different contextual perspective.

This "contextualistic" interpretation and modification of the associated properties of a term goes on almost infinitely. And, despite contemporary attempts to deal with such phenomena as relational frames of what is technically referred to as *higher-order stimulus equivalences* (Hayes, Barnes-Holmes, Roche, 2001), the practical translation of such efforts is far from sufficient for allowing us to map all potential associations represented in an introductory psychology course. Students quickly discover just how artificial the embedded "intelligence" of an expert mapping system really is, and I have serious doubts that behavioral principles will be up to this task within my own lifetime. So, the best alternatives will likely remain as "what is good enough" for keeping a student contextually focused and limited, but this is not always convincing for students. As such, even the best of artificially intelligent tutoring systems designed to teach conceptual materials and associated vocabulary are likely to garner a lot of student complaints about how "dumb" (and thus unfair) such systems are in grading student test responses.

CONCLUSION

I have attempted to demonstrate a sharp difference between the teaching that takes place outside of the classroom in universities and the kind that is at least afforded, if not taken advantage of by many, students in a more personalized educational setting such as those in the small liberal arts colleges. I have also described a computer-based technology that allows us to bridge that gap with the advantage of at least having more highly prepared learners sitting in our classrooms. I have cited a limited range of emerging research that supports that proposition as well.

Unfortunately, my enthusiasm for the very technology I have spent over a decade developing and testing is damped somewhat by practical factors limiting the likelihood that instructors will widely adopt it, as well as factors leading to student resistance to using it. Our own surveys on this count find variations in responses among students. When asked if they like the electronic testing outside of class, approximately 50% of students in a large class like it moderately or strongly, about 32% like it somewhat, and the remaining 18% dislike it moderately or strongly. Most (90%) like the opportunity to repeatedly test. A different survey was cited recently in the Butterfield and Houmanfar (2003) presentation at the ABA symposium discussed above. These authors reported that 68% (Spring 2002) and 60% (Fall 2002) of the class surveyed would recommend the traditional-text/WebCT version of the course to a friend versus 41% (Spring) and 45% (Fall) of the adaptive class making the same recommendation to a friend, despite the fact that the adaptive class had higher achievement.

Of course, some instructors value MediaMatrix's adaptive system, continue to use it, and even recommend its use to other instructors. We continue to pursue both software and content improvements just as the capability and reliability of the Internet also improves. Student computer literacy may also improve as more and more primary and secondary systems incorporate technology, and this may ultimately have a positive impact on how students view the system as well as serving to decrease the technical support required of instructors who adopt the system. Time will tell as to whether such electronic innovations that improve education will actually be adopted by a critical mass of instructors and whether this will be tolerated by administrators who seem more sensitive to public relations issues than educational ones. One always hopes . . . .

References

Belden, N., Miraglia, K., & Ray, R. D. (2003). *Getting students to use adaptive TUTORIAL services: Strategies, issues and outcomes.* Paper presented at the meeting of the Association for Behavior Analysis, San Francisco, CA.

Berk L. E. & Winsler, A. (1995). *Scaffolding children's learning: Vygotsky and early childhood education.* Washington, D.C.: National Association for the Education of Young Children.

Binder, C. (1993). Behavioral fluency: a new paradigm. *Educational technology*, XXXIII(10), 8–14.

Brusilovsky, P., Schwarz, E., & Weber, G. (1996). A tool for developing adaptive electronic textbooks on WWW, in *Proceedings of webNet '96: World Conference of the Web Society*. San Francisco, CA: Association for the Advancement of Computers in Education, pp. 64–69.

Butterfield, S. & Houmanfar, R. (2003). *Self-paced interactive system of instruction (SPIN) and Psych-ai Adaptive Instruction: A Systematic Comparison.* Paper presented at the meeting of the Association for Behavior Analysis, San Francisco, CA.

Catania, A. C. (1998). *Learning*, 4th ed. Upper Saddle River, NJ: Prentice Hall.

Epstein, R. (1993). Generative theory and education. *Educational Technology*, XXXIII(10), 40–45.

Erlwanger, S. H. (1973). Benny's conception of rules and answers in IPI mathematics. *JCMB*, 1(2), 7–26.

Ferster, C. B. & Skinner, B. F. (1957). *Schedules of reinforcement*. New York: Appleton-Century-Crofts.

Hayes, S. C., Barnes-Holmes, D., & Roche, B. (2001). *Relational frame theory: A post-skinnerian account of human language and cognition*. New York: Kluwer Academic/Plenum Publishers.

Jagacinski, R. J. & Flach, J. M. (2003). *Control theory for humans: Quantitative approaches to modeling performance*. Mahwah, NJ: Erlbaum.

Kantor, J. R. (1970). An analysis of the experimental analysis of behavior (TEAB). *Journal of the Experimental Analysis of Behavior*, 13, 101–108.

Kantor, J. R. (1977). *Psychological linguistics*. Chicago: Principia Press.

Kasschau, R. A. (2000). *Psychology: Exploring behavior*. Winter Park, FL: (AI)^2, Inc.

Keller, F. S. (1968). "Goodbye, teacher . . .". *Journal of Applied Behavior Analysis*, 1(1), 79–89.

Novak, J. D. & Gowin, D. B. (1984). *Learning how To learn*. New York: Cambridge University.

Powers, W. S. (1973). *Behavior: The control of perception*. Hawthorne, NY: Aldine DeGruyter.

Ray, R. D. (1995a). MediaMatrix: An authoring system for adaptive hypermedia teaching–learning resource libraries. *Journal of Computing in Higher Education*, 7(1), 44–68.

Ray, R. D. (1995b). A behavioral systems approach to adaptive computerized instructional design. *Behavior Research Methods, Instruments, and Computers*, 27(2), 293–296.

Ray, R. D. & Delprato, D. J. (1989). Behavioral systems analysis: Methodological strategies and tactics. *Behavioral Science*, 34, 81–27.

Ray, R. D., Gogoberidze, T., & Begiashvili, V. (1995) Adaptive computerized instruction. *Journal of Instruction Delivery Systems*, Summer, 28–31.

Sikorski, J. F., Rich, K., Saville, B. K., Buskist, W., Drogan, O., & Davis, S. F. (2002). Student use of introductory texts: comparative survey findings from two universities. *Teaching of Psychology*, 29(4), 312–313.

Skinner, B. F. (1956). A case history in scientific method. *American Psychologist*, 11, 221–233.

Skinner, B. F. (1957). *Verbal behavior*. New York: Appleton-Century-Crofts.

Skinner, B. F. (1963). Reflections on a decade of teaching machines. *Teachers College Record*, 65, 168–177.

Skinner, B. F. (1968). *The technology of teaching*. New York: Macmillan.

Thorndike, E. L. (1898). Animal intelligence: an experimental study of the associative processes in animals. *Psychological Review Monograph Supplements*, 2(4).

van der Linden, W. J. & Glas, C. A. W. (2000). *Computerized adaptive testing: Theory and practice*. St. Paul, MN: Assessment Systems Corporation.

Vargas, E. A. & Vargas, J. S. (1992). Programmed instruction and teaching machines, in West, R. P. & Hamerlynch, L. (Eds.), *Designs for excellence in education: The legacy of B. F. Skinner*. Longmont, CO: Sopris, pp. 33–69.

Verplanck, W. S. (1992a). Verbal concept "mediators" as simple operants. *The Analysis of Verbal Behavior*, 10, 45–68

Verplanck, W. S. (1992b). A brief introduction to the Word Associate Test. *The Analysis of Verbal Behavior*, 10, 97–123.

Wainter, H., Dorans, N. J., Eignor, D., Flaugher, R., Green, B. F., Mislevy, R. J., Seinberg, L., & Thissen, D. (2000). *Computerized adaptive testing: A primer*, 2nd ed. St. Paul, MN: Assessment Systems Corporation.

CHAPTER

11

Selected for Success: How *Headsprout Reading Basics*™ Teaches Beginning Reading

T. V. JOE LAYNG, JANET S. TWYMAN, and GREG STIKELEATHER
Headsprout

INTRODUCTION

Reading proficiency provides a crucial foundation for success in all academic areas, yet we are a nation faced with a reading crisis. Four in ten children have literacy problems, and nearly 40% of our nation's fourth graders score below basic reading levels (National Center for Learning Disabilities, 2001). Learning to read is a formidable challenge for more than 50% of our nation's school children (Lyon, 1998), and parents spend billions of dollars each year on extracurricular books, software, tutors, and other reading aids. Teachers and schools face the challenges of finding the best teaching method, implementing these methods in large classrooms, and accommodating students' widely varying abilities and readiness. Despite the time and money spent on solving the reading difficulties of our nation's children, the problems are not disappearing. Headsprout, a Seattle-based applied learning sciences company, has been working on a solution that bridges the efforts of parents, schools, and agencies with the goal of preparing children for success in any core reading program chosen by a teacher, school, or school district.

Headsprout spent nearly 3 years and $5 million in a major research and development effort to build a beginning reading program that incorporates principles derived from the scientific investigation of early reading with principles derived from the experimental and applied analysis of behavior. The result of this effort is Headsprout Reading Basics™, a highly-effective, balanced, phonics-based reading program that teaches the skills and strategies necessary to sound out and read words. Delivered over the Internet, children learn essential reading skills through multiple interactions with engaging, cartoon-based episodes set in the entertaining environs of Space World, Dinosaur World, Undersea World, and Jungle World. Kids, parents, teachers, and learning scientists alike verify the effectiveness of Headsprout's methods in providing children with the skills they need to succeed in classroom reading instruction.

KEY READING SKILLS AND STRATEGIES: STUDENTS AND TEACHERS' BEST FRIENDS

Although phonics instruction has drifted in and out of favor in the educational establishment, a large body of research points to its essential role in the process of teaching children to read. In April 2000, the Congressionally mandated National Reading Panel reported that early systematic phonics instruction improves children's reading and spelling abilities (National Institute of Child Health and Human Development, 2000). Research also suggests that the absence of explicit instruction in phonemic awareness and phonics can cause learning problems that put learners at a permanent educational disadvantage unless they are corrected by the end of the third grade (National Institute of Child Health and Human Development, 2000).

The Public Library Association (n.d.) points out that, "Research has shown that there is nearly a 90% probability that a child will remain a poor reader at the end of the fourth grade if the child is a poor reader at the end of first grade." The research suggests that Headsprout's approach of explicit instruction in phonemic awareness, phonics, and a strategy for sounding out words can prevent many children from developing learning problems and can give almost all children an equal opportunity to become good readers. When Headsprout children arrive at school, they will be prepared no matter how large or small the role phonics plays in their classroom. Headsprout Reading Basics is a teacher's ally (not a teacher's replacement), giving students a boost in essential skills and raising the likelihood of reading success in a busy classroom or even before formal classroom instruction begins.

Research has identified five basic, interconnected sub-skills that all children must master if they are to become proficient readers (National Right to Read Foundation, n.d.), all integral to Headsprout Reading Basics. First, beginning readers must develop what is called phonemic awareness—the recognition that all words are made of separate sounds, called *phonemes*. Second, beginning readers also need to learn phonics, which is the ability to link these sounds to the specific letters or combinations of letters representing them in written language. This association between letters and sounds must become fluent so that learners can decode words almost instantly. Beginning readers must learn a strategy to sound out the sequence of phonemes in a word and blend the sounds back together to read whole words. Third, a learner's spoken vocabulary must be extended to become a reading vocabulary. They must understand that the words they read have meaning just as do the words they say. Further, they should come to understand that words they read have meaning even if they have not yet encountered that meaning. Fourth, reading fluency is important to reading success. Fifth, comprehension of what is read is essential. The process of seeing and saying words, although essential, is not sufficient to create a good reader. Children must understand what they read and be able to act on that understanding.

Headsprout Reading Basics tackles these five important features in the following way:

- *Phonemic Awareness*—Phonemic Awareness instruction is integrated throughout many of Headsprout Reading Basics' teaching routines. Learners hear letter sounds in order to select visual stimuli and then hear them again as confirmation of selections. Learners are asked to say the sounds, listen to cartoon characters say sounds, and then select the character that said the sound just like the child did. Learners put the sounds together, hear them slowly blended, say them slowly blended, then hear the sounds said fast as whole words, and eventually say the words fast. They learn not only to identify and say the sounds that letters make, both independently and as blended units, but also to listen to and identify the sounds they say, a critical step in developing a self-listening and self-editing repetoire.

- *Phonics*—In Headsprout Reading Basics, children learn 34 carefully chosen phonetic elements that maintain a consistent pronunciation in over 85% of the words in which they appear. This early consistency is extremely important to ensuring the transfer of segmenting and blending skills learned in the program, to words encountered outside the program. This allows the natural outcome of reading in a social environment to become the critical consequence for reading. By using one, two, and three letter combinations, learners find that sounds can be combined to make meaningful units of phonemic information. Further, learners quickly discover that some sounds can have other sounds inside them and that sound units can be combined to make new sounds. Headsprout Reading Basics' instructional strategies result in learners reliably "adducing" these insights in a discovery/learning environment rather than having to be directly taught. They learn to use their phonics knowledge for sounding out words in isolation, as parts of sentences, and when reading stories with words they have not been directly taught.

- *Vocabulary Development*—Headsprout Reading Basics provides a critical foundation for early vocabulary building, particularly as it affects reading. An essential component of vocabulary growth is the concept that words are made of sounds that, when put together, have meaning. Headsprout Reading Basics teaches that words have meaning, and that they make sentences that, in turn, make stories. Learners begin to add words that are likely to be in their spoken vocabulary to their reading vocabulary. Through the use of character names, they learn that words they may have never before encountered have meaning as well. More phonetic elements are added as the initial sounding-out strategies are learned; the words made from the elements are practiced to ensure that they become a permanent part of the learner's vocabulary. Once the sounding-out skills are firmed and all 34 sound elements taught, a typical learner would, in less than 15 hours of instruction, have a reading vocabulary of over 500 words. Throughout the program, exercises are provided that have learners match sentences made from their newly learned words to pictures of objects and actions to ensure that learners have a basic understanding of the words they are reading.

- *Reading Fluency, Including Oral Reading Skills*—Fluency is a critical element to all Headsprout Reading Basics activities. Often, fluency work is left to end of the reading process, when a learner practices reading sentences. Headsprout understands that fluency at the component skill level is critical to fluency at the composite skill level (Johnson & Layng, 1992; LaBerge & Samuels, 1974; Samuels & Flor, 1997). From as early as lesson 1, learners engage in fluency-building activities for finding sounds in words. By lesson 4, learners are building fluency on words made up of the sounds they have learned in the previous lessons, and, in lesson 5, learners read their first story. In the 40 lessons that comprise Headsprout Reading Basics, 38 fluency-building opportunities have been specifically designed to build a strong reading repertoire. In fewer than 15 hours of instruction, a learner will have read 23 separate stories. Most of the stories are designed for learners to read independently; however, others are to be read with someone else, such as a parent. These stories are more complicated but include a number of sentences that learners can easily read; thus, learners are exposed to fluent reading at a higher level than they can currently handle and must pay close attention so they can read their sentences when it is their turn.

- *Reading Comprehension Strategies*—An article about beginning reading began with the following observation (paraphrased): Suppose "Look at the ceiling" is written on a blackboard. When a person responds by saying, "Look at the ceiling," the person is decoding; if the person's head tilts back and a glance upward is observed, the person is comprehending (Goldiamond & Dyrud, 1966). Though overly simplified, it emphasizes the important point that the evaluation of comprehension requires indicator responses that are separate from simply seeing and saying words or sentences. These indicator responses are key to teaching and evaluating comprehension. Accordingly, Headsprout Reading Basics employs frequent use of comprehension indicators to test whether what is being decoded is also being understood. Carefully designed indicators are used to teach self-observation as well as sentence and story comprehension. After each reading exercise, learners must choose one of three pictures that go with the sentence. The pictures vary in such a way as to ensure that the words in the sentences have been read and are understood. From as early as lesson five, learners understand that the sentences they read are not simply lists of words, but units of meaning.

Headsprout Reading Basics offers a truly balanced approach to beginning reading instruction that shrinks the chasm between phonics traditionalists and advocates of whole language reading instruction (see Rayner, Foorm, Perfetti, Pesetsky, & Seidenburg, 2002). While it has its foundation in teaching learners to identify letter–sound combinations and combine them with other letter–sound combinations, it incorporates elements that do not appear in many phonics programs. For example, Headsprout Reading Basics teaches children to read full sentences and stories and comprehend their meaning. Moreover, Headsprout has addressed learner and teacher concerns about the rule-filled, exception-filled English language. Too often, learners are expected to begin reading by memorizing rules that dictate sound/letter associations, only to have to memorize further exceptions to those rules. The English language uses the 26 letters of the alphabet to represent 44 sounds—sounds that can be written in over 400 different ways. To untangle this confusing web for the beginning reader, Headsprout Reading Basics begins with very consistent letters and sounds, such as *ee*, *v*, *cl*, and *an*. As noted earlier, the sounds in Headsprout Reading Basics are stable (read the same way) in over 85% of their occurrences, greatly increasing the likelihood of learners reading the word correctly. For example, a child who learns to pronounce *ing* as it is in "sing" will be correct when using that pronunciation in 99% of its other occurrences. With Headsprout Reading Basics, learners gain confidence early in their ability to sound out without being distracted by the challenge of memorizing the English language's many vagaries.

LEARNING METHODOLOGIES: FOUNDATIONAL AND FLEXIBLE

Headsprout also derives its success from a methodology that incorporates four key pedagogical frameworks:

- *Reduced errors*—Headsprout's carefully designed instructional sequence allows learners to start with things they know or can easily do and builds instruction from there. This enables learners to make fewer mistakes and reduces the frustration of trial- and-error learning. Errors that are made are used as teaching opportunities, and the learner is always provided the opportunity to retry and succeed at the task.

- *Mastery criteria*—Headsprout Reading Basics allows children to practice and learn until they have mastered the skill. The program ensures that a learner does not exit an instructional segment without achieving the specific learning goal. For example, a learner may be asked to make five consecutive correct letter–sound discriminations. This might take one learner just five responses. Another may give some wrong answers, be diverted into a brief tutorial session, and then return to the initial task where five consecutive correct answers is still required for exit. Learners who may have required more instruction or practice opportunities still exit meeting the mastery criteria.

- *Guided practice*—Headsprout wants every learner to achieve fluency. For example, in a letter–sound discrimination task, fluency may be defined as the ability to consistently, quickly, and accurately identify sound and letter combinations. Fluency improves the retention of new skills, enhances the comprehension of new material, and facilitates the recognition of new words. This builds confidence and accelerates reading as a whole. When learners read words, time criteria are introduced such that word reading becomes more automatic. This is extended to sentence and story reading as well. Fluent oral-reading examples are provided as models and confirmation that emphasize both rate and prosody.

- *Cumulative review and application*—Headsprout further improves the retention of fresh reading skills with its process of cumulative review. Skills, not pieces of information, are revisited, reused, and extended. Children are not merely memorizing information; they're learning the "hows" of reading which stick with them (just like riding a bicycle), even when there has been a significant period of no or little practice.

Headsprout's multifaceted methodology thus gives rise to instruction that is tailored to meet the needs of each learner and ensures that those needs are met before the lesson comes to an end. The idea of continual adaptation—and evolution—influences Headsprout Reading Basics in many ways. Headsprout supports its reduced error program with moment-to-moment adaptation based on each learner response. According to a learner's frequency and ratio of corrects and errors, click rate, or error patterns, the program immediately adjusts to offer the most beneficial lesson for that learner. Although the core of instruction is the same for everyone, some quick detours—reminders and review sessions (subroutines in the program)—are downloaded in the background, ready to pop up and provide extra skill building and reinforcement if needed. Headsprout is thus predicated upon a flexible constant: learners' overall experiences and session lengths can vary as their successes and errors vary, but all of them emerge from each episode having shown their acquisition of the same target skills. No one moves onto the next episode until successfully completing the one at hand.

In another example of adaptation, new approaches to teaching are continually tested against existing approaches. Methods that produce the greatest learner success are selected, while those methods that are less successful drop out. This commitment to learner testing helps ensure a continuous evolution of the program governed by learner success.

Nine teaching routines comprise the core of Headsprout Reading Basics. An overview of the instructional design process may be found elsewhere (Twyman, Layng, Stikeleather, Hobbins, 2004), and greater elaboration and developmental data for each routine are being prepared for future publication. The nine routines may be summarized as follows:

- *Establishing routines* rapidly teach a learner the initial phonetic and other sound/symbol components of reading. These routines establish sound/ symbol guidance over a young speaker's verbal behavior and transfer that control to textual stimuli, the decoding basis of reading. The careful sequence of specific component skills promotes the rapid acquisition of basic reading strategies. The establishing routine is unique in the way visual and auditory stimuli are presented and sequenced and in the way learner behavior is confirmed or corrected. The establishing routine is also used to teach whole word reading when that is required.

- *Adduction routines* are a special subset of establishing routines that promote the rapid acquisition of new skills with little or no direct learner instruction (Andronis, Layng, Goldiamond, 1997). Discovery learning environments are created that recruit elements of previously learned skills into new skill sets, obviating the need to build these new elements independently. Adduction routines have uniquely designed presentation, confirmation, and correction subroutines.

- *Vocal potentiation routines* (Goldiamond & Dyrud, 1967) encourage learner-spoken behavior in the absence of an independent listener or voice recognition capabilities. The potentiating routine has uniquely designed presentation, confirmation, and correction subroutines that bring learner spoken behavior under the guidance of textual stimuli and their own discriminative repertoire.

- *Blending and segmenting* routines teach the learner a strategy for using sound elements to decode a word. The strategy ultimately requires the learner to hold each sound in a word until the next sound is vocalized. Ultimately, the learner must say the "stretched" word quickly, as one would normally say the word. While this routine is similar to a strategy some other reading programs employ, Headsprout's specific, four-step sequence for teaching each part of the strategy and linking the steps together (particularly in the absence of an independent listener) is unique.

- *Sentence and story routines* are used to establish meaningful reading. Learners learn word order and sentence sense by first hearing and clicking the words as a narrator reads them, then the learner reads the words as highlighted by the software. Finally, the learner reads the sentence and clicks on a picture indicating what the sentence was about. Stories are then introduced in which the learner is released to read independently, applying previously learned skills in a story context. Both comprehension indicators and story indicators are used for these exercises.
- *Fluency routines* are timed, guided-practice exercises that assure retention of newly acquired reading skills after significant periods of no practice and make application of those skills much more likely (Anderson, Fincham, Doughas, 1999a; Johnson & Layng, 1996). Each routine has carefully constructed practice aims, confirmation routines, and correction routines that are unique to the practice environment. Fluency routines are also designed to adapt to the learners practice history and automatically set practice goals based on that history.
- *Motivation routines* define the contexts in which the previously described routines are embedded and applied. These contexts provide for both program-extrinsic consequences, such as vocal praise, fun sounds, and short cartoon movies, and program-specific consequences that occur directly as a function of reading in a social environment (Goldiamond, 1974).
- *Application routines* include graphic-intensive activities that allow learners to demonstrate their reading skills in real-world contexts, such as inter-acting with cartoon characters, reading stories in duets with a parent or guardian, and playing mystery or travel games. Application routines also include reading new words and sentences previously untaught and selecting pictures that illustrate the meaning of the word or sentence.
- *Overall sequencing* of routines is also critical to the program's success. Teaching objectives are achieved by the specific mixed and interlocking sequences of the routines described above. Although currently imple-mented to teach reading, these nine routines may be employed to teach any type of paired associate, multiple discrimination, algorithmic, con-cept, principle, or strategy learning objective.

EMBRACING THE BURDEN OF PROOF: HEADSPROUT'S UNPARALLELED LEARNER TESTING

Just as Headsprout Reading Basics adjusts to the needs of learners, Head-sprout learning scientists have built flexibility into the program itself to ensure that those needs are met as effectively and certainly as possible. When

Headsprout assures parents that their children will depart each episode with a new skill in hand, it does so with the confidence that comes from unparalleled user testing. Headsprout Reading Basics, which has been developed and shaped by the behavior of actual children, may be the only product of its kind to have undergone such rigorous testing and revision cycles.

Whereas any reading program may undergo scientific evaluation (as recently mandated by Congress in the No Child Left Behind Act of 2001), this does not mean the program was developed scientifically. Indeed, such programs may not have even been based upon principles derived from scientific research. Accordingly, there are three possible development or formative evaluation approaches and three outcome or summative evaluation approaches. The design approach may be one of writing a program based on a philosophy of teaching or personal experience, it can be writing a program based on scientific research and principles (Anderson, Greeno, Reder, Simon, 2000) or it may be one of painstaking developing a program in accord with rigorous control/analysis scientific procedures (Markle, 1967; Sidman, 1960). The latter approach does not simply incorporate past scientific research, but it employs a scientific approach throughout the development cycle. Once produced, each approach's program can be evaluated in accord with the three summative evaluation approaches described in Table 1.

Headsprout has chosen to develop its program according to a strict scientific protocol from the beginning. Every portion of Headsprout Reading Basics has been measured and evaluated, from the most basic level of instruction through the complete interlocking sets of skills and strategies. Three phases of empirical testing were used: developmental testing (developing a workable instructional program), validation testing (verifying that the instruction reliably produces its intended results), and field testing (maintaining effectiveness across larger and more diverse groups).

Learning scientists, educators, and instructional designers observed more than 250 children interacting with the program in Headsprout's learning laboratory. Under scrutiny were the basic instructional components, the appeal of the cartoon characters and various program activities, the learners' comprehension of instructions, and their willingness to interact vocally with the program (a factor that precludes the need for voice recognition software).

Above all, Headsprout measured the effectiveness of the lessons for teaching fundamental reading skills. Pre-tests and post-tests of essential skills helped learning scientists and instructional designers measure the acquisition, application, and, just as importantly, the retention of skills from episode to episode. Headsprout then made the required adjustments to ensure instructional reliability and effectiveness. This process was repeated until learners were completely successful with the lesson. Over 10 million interactions have been recorded and analyzed to modify, test, and retest each learning routine used in the program until that routine proved effective. Over the course of development, Headsprout made over 10,000 data based program revisions. No

TABLE 1
The Relation Between Formative and Summative Evaluation in Program Design and Assessment

		1. Experiential: Correspondence to a point of view (philosophy or personal experience); evaluation is based on anecdotal evidence, look and feel, personal satisfaction, testimonials.	2. Evidence Based: Pre-test versus post-test measures, meta-analysis, simple comparison studies, not employing random assignment or other controls.	3. Scientific – Group Research: Controlled group studies; measured against other programs, a standard, or placebo.
A. Experiential: Derived from philosophy or personal experience	(i) Consensus of best practices, experience, point of view; little or no testing during developmental process itself. (ii) Design revisions based on consistency of content with prevailing point of view. (iii) May employ limited tryouts that result in some program revisions; clarity of communication typically the issue.	Works or not with groups or individuals; purely subjective, a matter of opinion that can be argued on point of view—a matter of social agreement.	Provides some indication that the program may be effective with a group.	Can confidently predict group performance.
B. Evidence Based: Derived from scientific principles	Points (i), (ii), and (iii), plus: (iv) Design largely based on previous research, which may come from a variety of disciplines; research may be on elements found in program content and not program itself. (v) Design revisions often based on consistency of content with prevailing point of view; may employ checks for adherence to research.	Cannot confidently predict group or individual performance, but has some validity by relation to past research and perhaps limited tryouts.	Provides some indication that the program may be effective with a group.	Can confidently predict group performance.

continues

continued

C. Scientifically Designed and Validated Individual Research: Content may not be, but typically is, derived from scientific principles and developed according to scientific control/analysis procedures (Headsprout Approach)	Points (i), (ii), and (iv), plus: (vi) All elements of program tested for effectiveness; if it fails criteria, an alternative is built and tested and processes iterated until criteria are met. Performance is always measured against a set of criteria. (vii) Sequence of program steps and the relation of behavior to the sequence are explicitly identified, thereby generating new knowledge; process continues and is aggregated as response requirements and "chunks" of the program units change in size (*i.e.*, a segment of a lesson, a lesson, groups of lessons, the program). (viii) Research based on, and systematically replicated with, individuals; can generalize to individuals (Neuman and McCormick, 2002; Sidman, 1960).	Can confidently predict individual's performance; because program is able to predict an individual's performance, some prediction of group performance is implied; may have some validity by relation to past research.	Can confidently predict individual's performance. Evidence from group performance combined with individual data provides much greater confidence.	Can confidently predict group performance; can confidently predict individual's performance.

3 × 3 matrix: The level of rigor for each type of evaluation is indicated by the letters A, B, and C for formative evaluation, with row C representing the most rigorous; the numbers 1, 2, and 3 indicate the level of rigor for each type of summative evaluation, with column 3 representing the most rigorous. Cell C3 represents the most rigorous intersection of formative and summative evaluation.

change, no matter how seemingly insignificant, has made it into the final product without having been empirically tested and demonstrated effective.

Headsprout designed the program as one might design a new airplane or space vehicle. We did not write it and then test it out to see if it worked. That is, to carry our airplane analogy a step further, we did not build it and then see if more of our airplanes got off the ground and stayed aloft longer than a control group flapping their arms. Instead, we did careful wind tunnel experiments on the design, tested how the bolts were applied and the materials were used, evaluated how the overall aerodynamics was implemented, and finally answered the question, "Did it fly?" Like an airplane, we felt that a reading program should work on its first test flight, and that changes that came from test flights serve to improve stability and reliability even more. It is not acceptable that the "mean" Headsprout child perform better than the "mean" control group child, just as we would not get in a "mean" airplane. The program must fly with individual children, one at a time. And, as a result of our Internet deployment strategy, Headsprout continues to collect data on every child, which allows the learning scientists and instructional designers to continually improve the product. As more data are gathered, improvements are designed, tested, and immediately deployed over the Internet—something even the aerospace industry cannot do.

ENABLING EVOLUTION: HEADSPROUT'S RECOMBINANT TEACHING AND ENGINEERING MODELS

Interestingly, the development and evolution of the product itself mirrors the development and evolution of the teaching process within the product. Headsprout uses a recombinant model (Johnson & Layng, 1992; Lee & Anderson, 2001) in which component letters and sounds are taught and then combined to form a composite, which then becomes a component of a word. Words then become components of sentences and sentences of stories. This unique model is also applied to the instructional framework of Headsprout Reading Basics' episode sequence. Instructional techniques (components) are recombined (into composites) to form the pedagogical foundation of each episode. This entire process is analogous to chemistry: atoms of various elements (always themselves the same) come together in various combinations to yield different molecules. This model also extends to the engineering process. Because the modular computer code underlying component instructional techniques can be reused with different content or with different graphics, Headsprout achieves great efficiencies in product development. The modular structure also enables Headsprout to promptly take advantage of the observations and data gleaned from user testing; if necessary, changes can be incorporated across several episodes with relatively little effort.

In all of these cases, some of the instructional components are no longer used over the course of the program because learners learn how to learn. In other words, they become more efficient in acquiring new knowledge and can learn new things in different, more sophisticated ways. This is yet another instance of Headsprout's ability to evolve along with the learner. These early skills will, of course, continue to be practiced and applied as implicit aspects of other activities. For example, practice with letter/sound combinations is reinforced as learners move on to deciphering whole words and sentences.

HEADSPROUT'S INTERNET ADVANTAGE: BROAD AVAILABILITY AND CONTINUOUS IMPROVEMENT

One of the crucial ingredients in Headsprout's success—perhaps transcending the pedagogical, developmental, and technological innovations described above—is delivery over the Internet. Although the Internet is Headsprout's distribution system and not its defining technology, it is central to the effectiveness of the product. The Internet model enables Headsprout to make changes and improvements to the product at any time, without forcing expensive and/or inconvenient updates on consumers. The program can adapt to every learner's behavior because all learning data are uploaded to Headsprout servers for analysis. More importantly, the Internet makes every non-reading, Internet-connected child in the world (*i.e.*, millions of kids) a potential Headsprout beneficiary.

The end-user experience is uniformly smooth, which is especially crucial when the user is a young child. Headsprout's code is engineered for streaming, allowing Headsprout Reading Basics to run seamlessly, even over 56K modems. Learners spend very little time waiting for program segments to begin because successive segments are downloading in the background as they work. In the event that they do have to wait, any one of 30 interactive screens appears to help pass the time; they can scroll or click to make entertaining changes in the graphics. Also important are the Macromedia Flash animations that drive the entire program and entertain and motivate children as they learn. There are dozens of cute characters featured in Headsprout's episodes; all of them have been created and animated in-house, drawing upon Headsprout staffers' graphical, vocal, and instrumental talents to enliven them with motion and sound. In marrying "state of the science" learning theory, Hollywood entertainment, and Silicon Valley technology, Headsprout has created an Internet technology that seamlessly provides effective reading instruction.

HEADSPROUT READING BASICS: EMPIRICAL DATA

The scientific basis for our claims comes first from a thorough grounding in measurement. We measure all opportunities to interact with our program and all learner interactions on a real-time basis for all learners via the Internet. For each individual learner, we know:

- How many responses were made (in the program, in an episode, or in a segment), information that is used to determine the rate of responding within and between episodes and segments
- How many of these responses were correct and how many were errors, information that is used to determine correct and error rates (ratios of corrects to totals and corrects to errors)

- The error response made, if any, which is used to determine error patterns or potential discrimination problems and what skills are not firm
- The latency (time between opportunity and response) of all responses, which is used to determine the strength of response, or the amount of think time a child may require
- The screen position of all responses, which is used to determine and counteract any position biases or inadvertent clues
- The amount of time the learner spent in each interaction, segment, and episode, which is used to determine skill, strategy and episode sequences

INSTRUCTIONAL ADAPTABILITY

Because Headsprout Reading is broken down into tactics and strategies targeting specific skills, our data inform us about the effectiveness of each instructional strategy across all children and for every individual learner. The data are used to modify the instructional sequence to meet the individual needs of our learners, as well as to continually shape and redesign the overall efficacy of the program. Headsprout knows immediately what works and what does not and can continually make revisions and test them against the established procedure, selecting the procedure that produces the best result.

LEARNER PERFORMANCE DATA

All learner performance data are automatically collected and entered into a database that allows us to look at individual performance as well conglomerates of these data. For example, we analyze the number and rate of opportunities to interact, responses and corrects per episode, response fluency, episode and segment durations, and errors patterns to evaluate learner outcomes. We measure accuracy on literal comprehension tasks and the recombination of taught skills into new skills to obtain indicators of more generative reading skills. Each activity or teaching routine in the program has a designated mastery criterion, which, with exception of the practice exercises, is always 100% accuracy over a consecutive sequence of trials. Failure to reach mastery results in the learner being provided a corrective teaching sequence specific to the particular error pattern. The student is then returned to the mastery sequence and must demonstrate mastery prior to exiting the activity. Learners are required to meet more challenging mastery criteria as they progress through the program. The program is designed to maintain a high level of correct performance as these criteria progressively change during the program.

An additional source of data comes from the videos made of each learner in our laboratory interacting with the program. By way of a split screen, these tapes show both the learner and the display screen as seen by the learner. These allow us to measure and evaluate both learner affect and specifics regarding eye gaze, attention, and reactions to the cartoon sequences.

Figure 1 depicts the growth of fundamental reading skills as a function of progress through Headsprout Reading Basics. Headsprout administers computer-based pre-tests and post-tests with our on-site user test children for each episode presented. These pre-tests and post-tests assess the specific skills targeted for each episode. We have consistently found steady increases in letter–sound reading ability where previously there was little or none.

Figure 2 depicts the ratio of correct to total interactions for over 1000 beta (field-testing) participants. The relatively high correct percentages demonstrate the error reduction and cumulative shaping nature of our program—where new skills are built upon previous skills and there is not an abrupt learning curve for our learners. Correct responding criteria are maintained even as the program requirements become more demanding. The high percentages also reflect our rigorous accuracy criterion that is met on each segment before a learner completes an episode. Each episode reinforces some prior learning and introduces new sounds, skills, or strategies necessary for ultimate reading success.

Figure 3 shows the amount of time it takes our learners, on average, to complete an episode and meet the instructional criteria for exiting segments and episodes. These data assist in arranging the logical flow of instructional sequences while not taxing our learner's ability to be motivated and successful. On average, episodes take 20 minutes to complete and range from just under 10 minutes to slightly over 30 minutes. The data were collected from over 1000 beta test learners.

Opportunities, responses, and corrects are also monitored. Figure 4 displays the ratios between opportunities (each time a learner interaction is available), responses (actual learner interactions, where the child is making a response), and corrects which allow us to evaluate the effectiveness of episodes and segments on a response-by-response basis. It is this fine-grained analysis of individual learner performance (from which this graph is compiled) that has given us confidence in replicating these outcomes for over 1000 learners.

READING OUTCOMES

Figure 5 depicts measures of individual performance on specific word and sentence reading skills and provides additional verification of outcomes. Well over 90% of children tested have demonstrated substantial improvement in their ability to read words, sentences and short stories. The outcomes represented in Fig. 5 show words read correctly in printed Headsprout Readers. These data show reliability of effects (accurate story reading) during systematic replication for initially non-reading preschoolers during developmental testing. A minimum of 15 children were tested in each phase to ensure a reliable

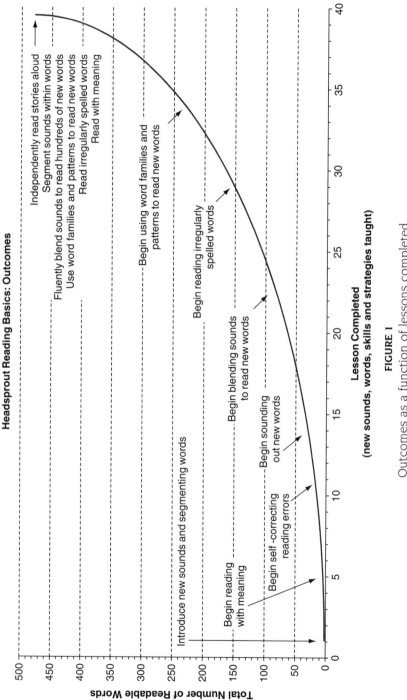

FIGURE 1

Outcomes as a function of lessons completed.

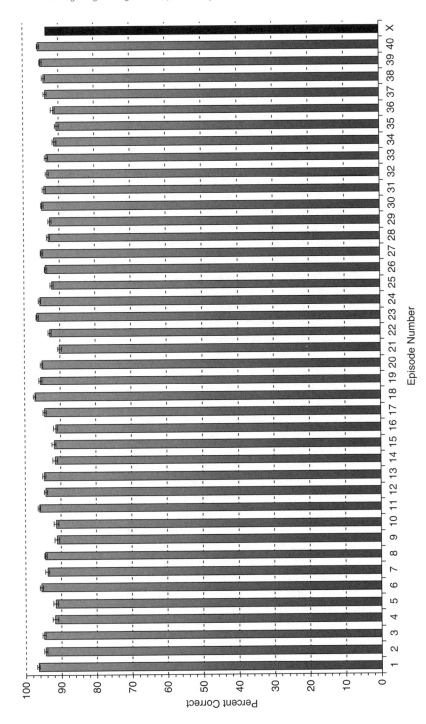

FIGURE 2

Average percent correct per Headsprout Readings Basics episode. Data are for over 1000 learners.

T. V. Joe Layng, Janet S. Twyman, and Greg Stikeleather

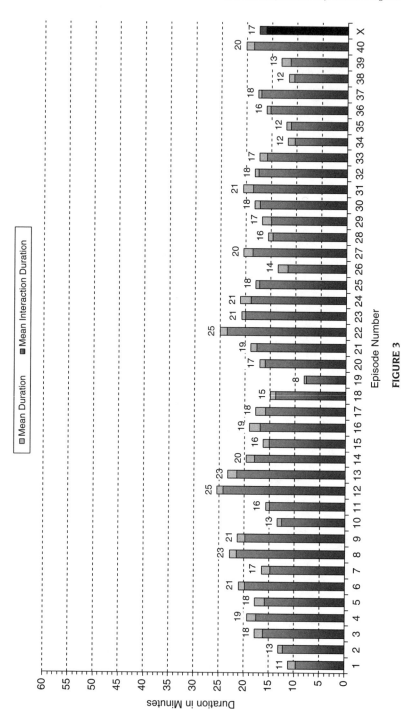

FIGURE 3

Average duration per Headsprout Reading Basics episode. Data are for over 1000 learners.

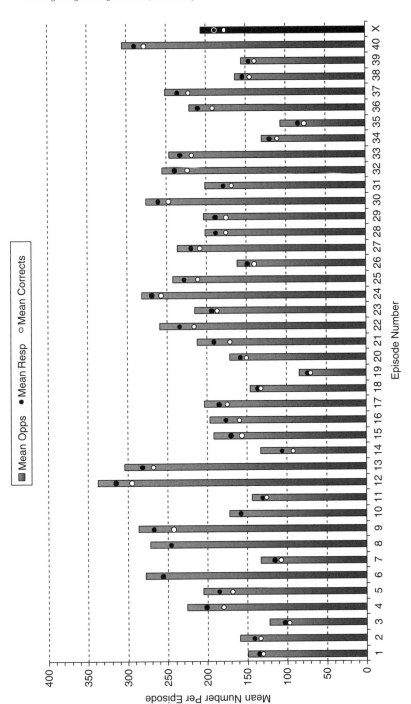

FIGURE 4

Mean number of response opportunities (bars), total responses (filled circles), and correct responses (open circles) per *Headsprout Reading Basics* episode. Data are for over 1000 learners.

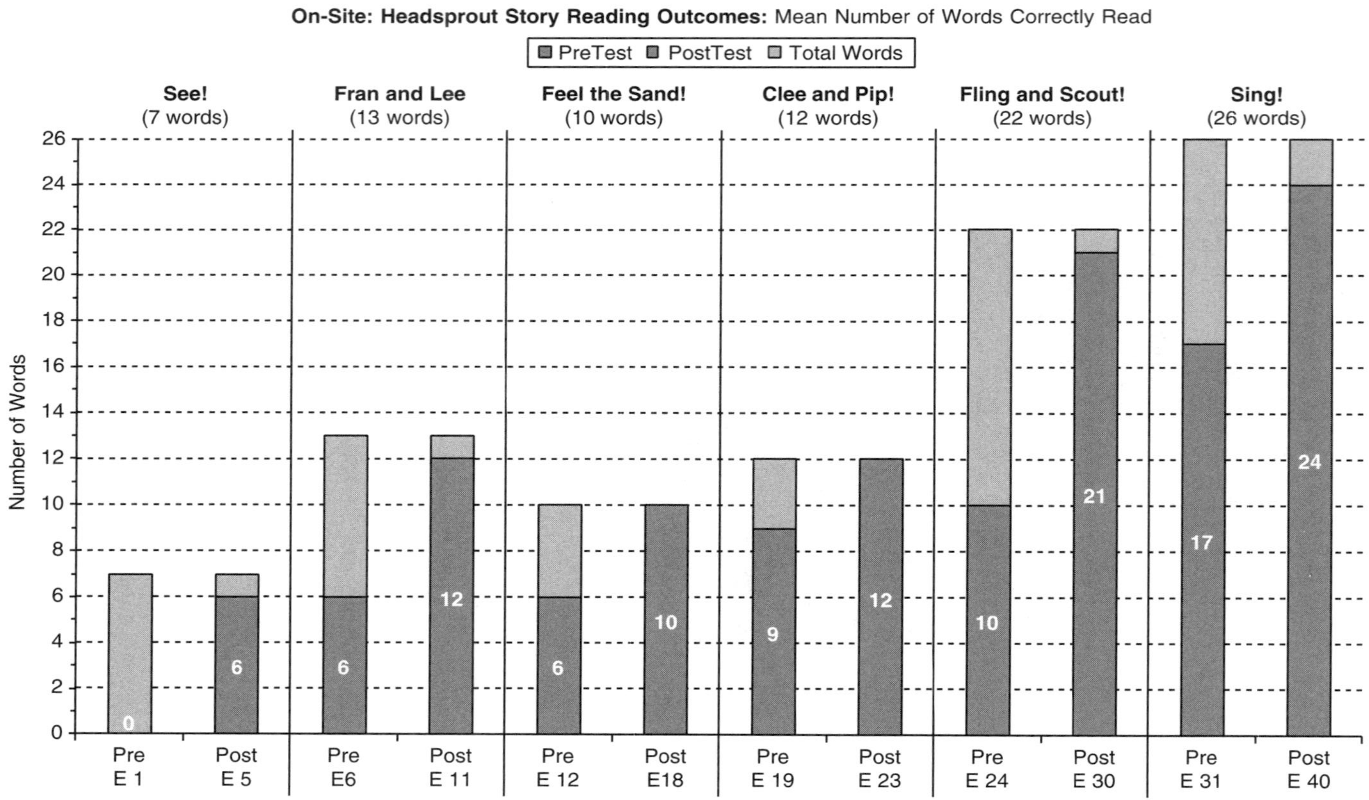

On-Site: Headsprout Story Reading Outcomes: Mean Number of Words Correctly Read

FIGURE 5

Systematic replication depicting the reliability of effects (accurate story reading) for initially non-reading preschoolers during developmental testing. Data are for a minimum of 15 individual learners per testing phase (increasingly complex reading passages). Pre-test corrects in post Phase 1 (See!) indicate carryover of words learned in previous passages that were reused in later stories. Figure shows the number of words read correctly (dark area) on first try on pre-tests and post-tests using Headsprout Reading Basics storybooks.

systematic replication. Each pair of bars represents the pre-test and post-test number of words read correctly in each storybook. Prolonged hesitations and self-corrections were scored as errors, along with word substitution and failure to read a word. There are six Headsprout full-color story books in the program. Increased accuracy in pre-test scores across episodes was a function of words learned in previous phases occurring in later storybooks.

Figure 6 indicates how carefully designed instructional sequences provide a stability of effect across numerous learners. Over 90% of our learners average over 90% correct responding in the program, and complete several learning objectives within each approximately 20-minute lesson. Learners engage in approximately 190 individual interactions (or learn units; Greer, 1994), with each interaction being comprised of a presentation, a response, and a consequence, and give an average of over 180 correct responses per lesson. The program is highly interactive—learners engage in over 9 responses per minute across all 40 episodes.

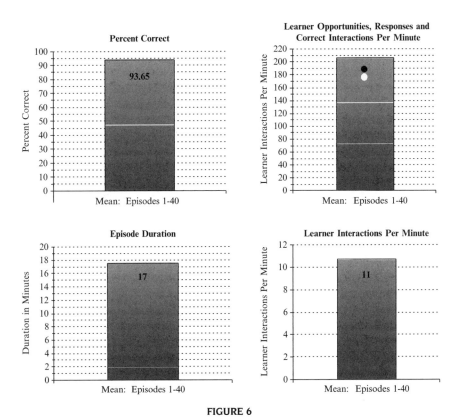

FIGURE 6

Summary of program outcomes for Headsprout Reading Basics. Means are calculated for over 1000 learners.

DEMONSTRATED EFFECTIVE

The Woodcock–Johnson Letter–Word Identification subtest (Woodcock, McGrew, Mather, 2001), was administered to 20 primarily pre-kindergarten children after the completion of 40 20-minute lessons (less than 15 hours of instruction) as part of in-house developmental testing. Figure 7 shows a mean gain for the 20 children of one year, moving from 0.5 to 1.5. Early field-testing standardized test scores for 30 kindergarten students from Thurgood Marshall Elementary School in Seattle, WA, support the data derived from criterion-referenced tests and standardized tests administered during developmental testing for individual students (Fig. 8). The school demographics were:

American Indian	1%
Asian	13%
African-American	63%
Latino	17%
Caucasian	6%
Total (309 students)	100%

Twenty-three students were tested on the Diagnostic Reading Assessment (DRA) test (scheduling conflicts accounted for the difference in test participants). On the DRA, 100% of the students scored at or above their grade level, with 82% of the kindergarten students scoring from early to mid-first grade. In prior years, no more than 50% of students scored above grade level (see Fig. 8).

EDUCATOR FEEDBACK

In addition to the preceding quantitative data, we have received a great deal of qualitative feedback from teachers and administrators who have used Headsprout Reading Basics. They have found Headsprout easy to implement, extremely effective, and fun and engaging for their students. Following is a sample of some comments received from educators:

"All of our kindergarten students finished Headsprout and many of them are able to read non-Headsprout texts. It's very exciting. I'm looking forward to next fall when we should have a bunch of students entering first grade who already know how to read . . . Thanks."
—Ms. Emily Severance, Reading Specialist, St. Paul's School

"The kids love Headsprout. I thought my lower readers would be the only ones to really benefit from this endeavor but all of my students have improved from the extra practice! It is an excellent program. Once the children begin a lesson they are very independent. The children enjoy the program . . . they ask to go to the computer at free play time!"
—Ms. Erica Ernest, 1st Grade Teacher, Central Lutheran Elementary School

"Everyone loves the program. I had a teacher in grade K tell me that she has noticed a difference in the kids on the program. I really like the report format."—Mr. Eric Demeter, Teacher, Clark Elementary School

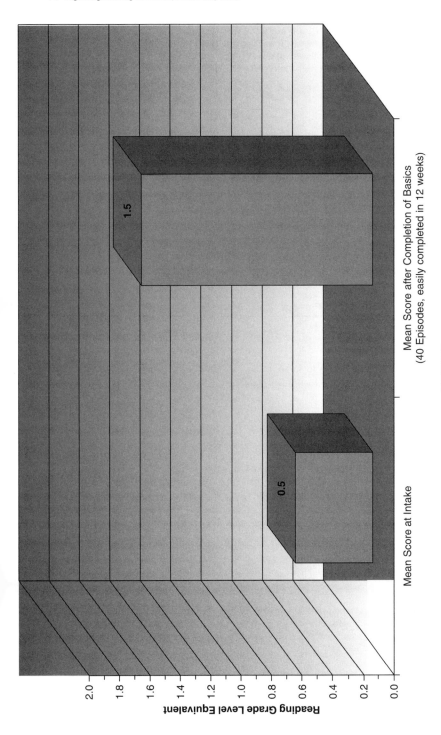

FIGURE 7

Mean grade-level scores for 20 initial developmental testing completers on the Woodcock Johnson Letter–Word Identification Subtest prior to and after finishing Headsprout Reading Basics.

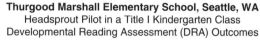

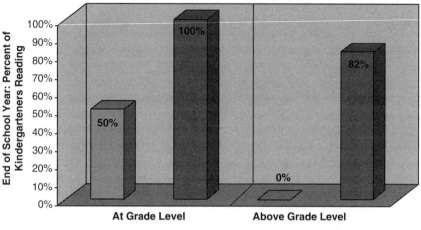

FIGURE 8

Effects on DRA outcomes of supplementing an existing kindergarten curriculum with Headsprout Reading Basics. Previous years (light bars) are compared to 2001–2002 (dark bars) kindergarten student scores.

"Headsprout excites my students about reading and gives them confidence. They're so proud to read me their books . . . It's excellent!"—*Ms. Christine Narayan, Teacher, Branson School*

"One of my first grade groups chose to go to the computer lab to work on Headsprout instead of staying in their classroom for their holiday party. The class was getting ready to exchange gifts, but 5 out of 6 of the students wanted to postpone their present exchange so that they could use Headsprout. I think that's a pretty good testimonial to how engaging your lessons are."—*Elementary School Reading Specialist, Harlem, New York*

"I have to write and say that I am quite impressed. Your program does all you say it does and makes it very easy to introduce a child to reading. As a certified elementary school teacher, I am amazed at the efficiency and effectiveness of the program. I especially enjoy that it is individualized . . . Great program!"—*Elementary School Teacher, Washington*

"The kindergarten children love Headsprout. They really get excited while learning and love the animated 'breaks' with the songs and music. It is exciting for me to watch kids learn to read with Headsprout and have fun doing it."—*Mr. John Humphrey, Education Consultant, Cedar Rapids, Iowa*

"Thank you so much for designing a truly workable program for typical children and special needs children alike. Thank you also for being so attentive to questions and the needs of special kids."—*Behavior Specialist, Salinas, California*

"I just want to tell you how pleased we are with this program. It is remarkable, and well worth the money. Congratulations on a fine contribution to education."—*Dr. Chris McDonough, Principal, Hawthorne Country Day School*

"I just wanted to take this opportunity to tell you how much we have enjoyed working with Headsprout and with the customer support we have experienced. Our students are thoroughly enjoying the program! It is well organized instructionally and has students excited about their learning process."—*Dr. J. Aufderheide, Superintendent, Branson School*

CONCLUSION

Headsprout Reading Basics is the culmination of a major research and development effort that finds its roots not only in the content required for successful reading instruction, but also in the strategies for teaching that are the outgrowth of years of work provided by many dedicated behavioral and learning scientists. It is constructional in its design (Anderson, Reder, Simon, 1999b; Goldiamond, 1974; Skinner, 1968), comprehensive in its development (Holland *et al.*, 1976; Johnson & Layng, 1992; Lindsley, 1997; Markle, 1969, 1990; Skinner, 1957; Tiemann & Markle, 1990), and rigorous in its evaluation (Markle, 1967; Sidman, 1960; Sidman & Stoddard, 1966). In summary:

- Each lesson appears as an interactive, animated web episode and takes about 20 minutes to complete. At 3 to 5 episodes a week, a child will be able to complete the entire program in less than 12 weeks.
- Through highly interactive, positive experiences, a child learns that letters and sounds make words, words make sentences, and sentences make stories.
- Headsprout automatically adapts to a child's pace as it teaches. A child leaves each lesson feeling successful.
- Books are an essential part of the program—every few lessons a child receives a Headsprout Reader booklet, to encourage independent reading. Plus, a variety of other printable stories are available on the Headsprout web site.
- In less than 15 hours of instruction (40 20-minute lessons), a child will read over 20 Headsprout stories, many with words sounded out and read for the first time.
- Children track their progress with colorful Headsprout Progress Maps. Detailed progress reports for each child are available online.

When learning to read is fun, children want to learn. This is fundamental to Reading Basics and the reason Headsprout designed the program as a series of engaging, Internet-based, animated lessons that teach basic skills for reading. But, the real motivation, reflected by their joy, pride, confidence, and enthusiasm, comes from the social reinforcement that being able to read brings to each child.

References

Anderson, J. R., Fincham, J. M., & Douglass, S. (1999a). Practice and retention: a unifying analysis. *Journal of Experimental Psychology: Learning, Memory, and Cognition*, 25, 1120–1136.

Anderson, J. R., Reder, L. M., & Simon, H. A. (1999b). *Applications and Misapplications of Cognitive Psychology to Mathematics Education* (http://act.psy.cmu.edu/personal/ja/misapplied.html).

Anderson, J. R., Greeno, J. G., Reder, L. M., & Simon, H. A. (2000). Perspectives on learning, thinking, and activity. *Educational Researcher*, 29, 11–13.

Andronis, P. T., Layng, T. V. J., & Goldiamond, I. (1997). Contingency adduction of "symbolic aggression" by pigeons. *The Analysis of Verbal Behavior*, 14, 5–17.

Goldiamond, I. (1974). Toward a constructional approach to social problems: ethical and constitutional issues raised by applied behavior analysis. *Behaviorism*, 2, 1–84.

Goldiamond, I. & Dyrud, J. E. (1966). Reading as operant behavior, in Money, J. (Ed.) *The disabled reader: Education of the dyslexic child*. Baltimore, MD: The Johns Hopkins Press.

Goldiamond, I. & Dyrud, J. E. (1967). Some applications and implications of behavioral analysis for psychotherapy, in Schlien, J. (Ed.), *Research in psychotherapy*, Vol. III. Washington, D.C.: American Psychological Association, pp. 54–89.

Greer, R. D. (1994). The measure of a teacher, in Gardner III, R. *et al.* (Eds.), *Behavior analysis in education: Focus on measurably superior instruction*, Pacific Grove; CA: Brooks/Cole, pp. 161–170.

Holland, J. G., Solomon, C., Doran, J., & Frezza, D. (1976). *The analysis of behavior in planning instruction*. Reading, MA: Addison-Wesley.

Johnson, K. R. & Layng, T. V. J. (1992). Breaking the structuralist barrier: literacy and numeracy with fluency. *American Psychologist*, 47, 1475–1490.

Johnson, K. R. & Layng, T. V. J. (1996). On terms and procedures: fluency. *The Behavior Analyst*, 19, 281–288.

LaBerge, D. & Samuels, S. J. (1974). Toward a theory of automatic information processing in reading. *Cognitive Psychology*, 6, 293–323.

Lee, F. J. & Anderson, J. R. (2001). Does learning of a complex task have to be complex? A study in learning decomposition. *Cognitive Psychology*, 42, 267–316.

Lindsley, O. R. (1997). Precise instructional design: guidelines from Precision Teaching, in Dills, C. R. & Romiszowski, A. J. (Eds.), *Instructional development paradigms*, Englewood Cliffs, NJ: Educational Technology Publications, pp. 537–554.

Lyon, G. R. (1998). Statement of Dr. G. Reid Lyon: *Read by grade 3* (http://www.readbygrade3.com/lyon.htm).

Markle, S. M. (1967). Empirical testing of programs. In *Sixty-Sixth yearbook of the National Society for the Study of Education*. Part II. *Programmed instruction*, Chicago, IL: The University of Chicago Press.

Markle, S. M. (1969). *Good frames and bad: A grammar of frame writing*, 2nd ed. New York: John Wiley & Sons.

Markle, S. M. (1990). *Designs for instructional designers*. Champaign, IL: Stipes.

National Center for Learning Disabilities. (2001). Legislative update, 107th Session of Congress (http://www.ncld.org/advocacy/update.cfm).

National Institute of Child Health and Human Development (2000). *Report of the National Reading Panel: Teaching children to read: An evidence-based assessment of the scientific research literature on reading and its implications for reading instruction: Reports of the subgroups*, NIH Publ. No. 00-4754. Washington, D.C.: U.S. Government Printing Office.

National Right to Read Foundation. (n.d.). http://www.nrrf.org/nichd.htm.

Neuman, S. B. & McCormick, S. (2002). A case for single subject experiments in literacy research, in Kamil, M. L., Mosenthal, P .B., Pearson, P. D., & Barr R. (Eds.), *Methods of literacy research*, Mahwah, NJ: Erlbaum, pp. 105–118.

No Child Left Behind Act of 2001 (2002). Public Law 107-110, 107th Congress of the United States of America (http://www.ed.gov/legislation/ESEA02/107-110.pdf).

Public Library Association (n.d.). http://www.read+lang.sbs.sunsb.edu/pla2/research.htm.

Rayner, K., Foorm, B. R., Perfetti, C. A., Pesetsky, D., & Seidenberg, M. S. (2002). How should reading be taught? *Scientific American*, 85–91.

Samuels, S. J. & Flor, R. (1997). The importance of automaticity for developing expertise in reading. *Reading and Writing Quarterly*, 13, 107–122.

Sidman, M. (1960). *Tactics of scientific research: Evaluating experimental data in psychology*. Boston, MA: Authors Cooperative.

Sidman, M. & Stoddard, L. (1966). Programming perception and learning for retarded children, in *International review of research in mental retardation*, Vol. 2, New York: Academic Press.

Skinner, B. F. (1957). *Verbal behavior*. New York: Appleton-Century-Crofts.

Skinner, B. F. (1968). *The technology of teaching*. New York: Appleton-Century-Crofts.

Tiemann, P. W. & Markle, S. M. (1990). *Analyzing Instructional Content: A Guide to Instruction and Evaluation*. Champaign, IL: Stipes.

Twyman, J. S., Layng, T. V. J., Stikeleather, G., & Hobbins, K. A. (2004). A non-linear approach to curriculum design: the role of behavior analysis in building an effective reading program, in Heward, W. L. *et al.* (Eds.), *Focus on behavior analysis in education*, Vol. 3. Upper Saddle River, NJ: Merrill/Prentice Hall.

Woodcock, R. W., McGrew, K. S., & Mather, N. (2001). *Woodcock–Johnson III battery*. Itasca, IL: Riverside Publishing.

Personalized System of Instruction

chapter 12

The Personalized System of Instruction: A Flexible and Effective Approach to Mastery Learning

ERIC J. FOX

Arizona State University

INTRODUCTION

Most educators devote a considerable amount of time and effort to deciding exactly what it is they would like their students to learn. The scope and sequence of the curriculum is carefully determined, specific learning objectives are constructed for each unit or lesson, instructional activities are designed to support the objectives, and assessments are created to measure whether students have gained the desired skills and knowledge. Unfortunately, in most educational settings this thoughtful attention to the purpose and nature of our instruction is often accompanied by the dangerous underlying assumption that relatively few students will (or can) actually meet the course objectives. We accept that final scores will be more or less normally distributed in the shape of the familiar bell curve, and "the instructor expects a third of his [or her] pupils to learn well what is taught, a third to learn less well, and a third to fail or just 'get by'" (Bloom, 1971, p. 47). Such a set of expectations certainly does not seem to promote educational excellence or a positive learning experience for many students, yet it has become practically a defining characteristic of American education.

Some instructional methods, however, are based on a rather different set of assumptions about learning. These methods, often organized under the rubric of "mastery learning," recognize the importance of building basic component skills and competencies to mastery before teaching more complex or composite material and assume that most students *can* master a particular topic if given enough time, attention, and instruction to do so (Ormrod, 2000). The challenge, of course, is that in most classrooms it can be very difficult to provide each student with enough time, attention, and instruction to ensure mastery. Since at least the 1920s, a variety of mastery learning strategies have been developed to address such challenges (Block, 1971). From Washburne's Winnetka Plan (1922) to Morrison's approach at the University of Chicago's laboratory school (1926) to Carroll's model of school learning (1963) to Bloom's Learning for Mastery (1968) to many of the systems described in this volume, each is designed to maximize the proportion of students who attain our educational goals and to make certain that no student is left behind. One of the most prominent examples of mastery-based teaching is the Personalized System of Instruction (PSI) (Keller, 1968).

Developed and introduced in the 1960s as an alternative to the dominant lecture-based method of college teaching, PSI shares several features in common with other approaches to mastery learning. Yet PSI is distinguished by the considerable flexibility with which the details of the system can be implemented and, more importantly, by the remarkable amount of research demonstrating its effectiveness in a variety of settings. Few educational innovations have been subjected to the empirical scrutiny PSI has, and fewer still have emerged so unscathed. Although interest in PSI peaked in the 1970s and has decreased sharply in the decades since (Buskist, Cush, & De Grandpre, 1991), it remains an attractive model for educators concerned with improving the quality of their instruction. Further, advances in information technology and telecommunications have the potential to greatly improve certain aspects of PSI courses and alleviate some of the factors that have contributed to its decline.

HISTORY AND OVERVIEW

Fred Keller, Gil Sherman, Rodolpho Azzi, and Carolina Martuscelli Bori initially developed PSI in 1963 while founding the department of psychology at the new University of Brasilia (Keller, 1968, 1982a). Keller became the most ardent advocate of PSI, and the system is sometimes called the *Keller Plan* or the *Keller Method* in his honor. Dissatisfied with conventional teaching methods and well-trained in learning theory, the designers sought to create a system that rewarded students more than it penalized them, promoted mastery of the content, and increased the amount of interpersonal communication within the classroom. The result was a general course model first piloted by Keller in a small, short-term laboratory course at Columbia University in 1963 and later implemented on a larger scale by Azzi and Bori at the University of Brasilia in 1964 and by Keller and Sherman at Arizona State University in 1965 (Keller, 1968).

Key Features of PSI

The distinguishing features of PSI have been described as self-pacing, unit mastery (requiring the demonstration of mastery of each unit before proceeding to the next), the use of lectures and demonstrations for motivational purposes (rather than delivery of course content), an emphasis on the written word and textual materials (for delivery of course content), and the use of proctors for individual tutoring and assessment (Keller, 1968; see Table 1). Courses based on PSI are also characterized by their use of specified instructional objectives, small-step sequenced materials, repeated testing, immediate feedback, and credit for success rather than penalty for errors (Sherman, 1992). Note that virtually all of these features, in some combination or another, can be found in the other empirically supported teaching methods appearing in this volume and in other mastery learning programs. Indeed, as Keller once commented, "There is probably no single aspect of our system that is really new" (1982a, p. 10). What *was* new about PSI was the way it explicitly linked each of these components to learning and reinforcement theory, emphasized the use of student proctors to personalize instruction, and combined the features into a general model for teaching that quickly gained widespread appeal (Keller & Sherman, 1982a).

All of the key components of PSI were derived from the overall goal of promoting mastery of the course content (Sherman, 1982a). Mastery of each unit is required because a full understanding of material appearing later in a course is usually dependent upon mastery of the concepts, principles, facts, and/or skills appearing earlier in the course. Some degree of self-pacing is required for any mastery-based teaching method because students learn at different rates, and there will be considerable variability in the amount of time it takes each student to master a unit. Lecturing, as a live performance designed

TABLE 1
Key Features of PSI

Component	Description
Unit mastery	Students are required to demonstrate mastery of each unit before proceeding to the next.
Self-pacing	Students proceed through the course at their own pace.
Lectures for motivational purposes	Lectures are used for demonstrations and motivational purposes, rather than for primary delivery of course content.
Emphasis on written word	Textual materials are used for primary delivery of course content.
Proctoring	Proctors are used to administer and score exams, deliver feedback, and provide tutoring.

to convey critical content, is impractical in such a course because it prevents the students from progressing through the material at their own pace (or would require that each unit lecture be delivered multiple times). This leads to a reliance on textual materials, which can be accessed at the student's convenience, as the primary vehicle for delivering the course content. Finally, proctoring was deemed necessary for PSI courses in order to administer the many assessments and, more importantly, to provide students with immediate feedback, additional tutoring or instruction, and some degree of social reinforcement for their performance.

In the prototypical PSI course, students use a study guide and text book to individually work through small units of material. When the student is ready, he or she will then complete an assessment, or test, based on the unit. The assessment often takes the form of a brief multiple-choice test, but virtually any format can be—and has been—used, including short-answer items, essay exams, interviews/oral assessments, problem-solving tasks, or a demonstration of skills. Upon completing the assessment, the student immediately meets with a proctor for grading and feedback, discussion, and/or tutoring. If the student meets the mastery criterion for the assessment, he or she is free to continue on to the next unit; if not, then the assessment (or, more frequently, a parallel version thereof) must be taken again later until mastery is achieved. Students are allowed to retake the test as many times as necessary without penalty until their performance indicates sufficient mastery of the material. This cycle is repeated for each unit of material, with the student progressing through the course at his or her own pace. Lectures, demonstrations, laboratory exercises, and review assignments may also be incorporated throughout the course. The course is completed when the student meets the mastery criteria for all of the units.

Many PSI courses implement one or more of the key components somewhat differently (see Kulik, Jaska, & Kulik, 1978). Common variations include the use of deadlines to reduce student procrastination and ensure timely completion of the course, the complete elimination of lectures, adjusting the criteria for mastery, modifying the size of the instructional units, using different student populations to serve as proctors, limiting the number of times a test can be retaken, altering the role of the proctor, eliminating proctoring, and using computers to deliver content, administer tests, and/or provide feedback. Determining exactly which features must be implemented—and how—in order for a course to be deemed a PSI course can be a troubling issue (Sherman, 1992). Guidance can be found in the empirical literature, however, and this is a topic to which we shall return later.

The Rise of PSI

Shortly after PSI was described in Keller's seminal 1968 article "Goodbye, Teacher . . ." and at various professional conferences, others began using the system and reporting their experiences. Sherman (1982b) provides an excellent account of the dramatic expansion of PSI research and application, and some of the more revealing details are summarized below. By 1973—only 10 years after a prototype PSI course was first tried at Columbia University and only 5 years after most people had even heard of PSI—over 300 papers, articles, and research reports on PSI had been published, and by 1979 there were close to 3000 such publications. Most of the earliest implementations of PSI were for college-level courses in psychology, physics, and engineering, but this quickly changed as a series of PSI workshops and conferences in the early 1970s, along with the remarkable success of PSI reported in the literature, drew the interest of educators from a wide range of disciplines at all levels of education. Before long, PSI was being used to teach many different subjects to many different populations in elementary and secondary schools, community colleges, four-year colleges and universities, hospitals, businesses, prisons, and the military. Even though it has always been used predominantly with college students, PSI was proving to be flexible enough to work in a variety of settings, and in 1979 there were over 5000 PSI courses known to be in existence.

From 1971 to 1979, the *PSI Newsletter* served as a communication forum for PSI teachers and researchers, and from 1973 to 1979 the Center for Personalized Instruction at Georgetown University "served an information clearinghouse function, surveying PSI courses in different disciplines and at all educational levels throughout the country" (Sherman, 1982b, p. 74). The Center also sponsored PSI workshops and conferences, assumed publication of the *PSI Newsletter*, and began publication of an academic journal entitled the *Journal of Personalized Instruction*. Within a short period of time, PSI had emerged as a powerful educational movement that was inspiring countless research studies, garnering extensive support and interest, and encouraging many teachers to rethink the purpose and process of education.

The Fall of PSI

After the Center for Personalized Instruction became defunct in 1979, it became much more difficult to characterize the PSI landscape. It is unclear, for example, whether the number of PSI courses being taught continued to increase, stabilized, or decreased in the years immediately following the Center's closure. It *is* clear, however, that there are far fewer PSI courses in existence today than there were in 1979 (Lloyd & Lloyd, 1986) and that the number of research articles pertaining to PSI has decreased dramatically since the 1970s (Buskist et al., 1991; Lamal, 1984). Although PSI continues to be used in a variety of contexts (Conard, 1997; Hambleton, Foster, & Richardson, 1998; Hansen, Brothen, & Wanbach, 2002; Houmanfar et al., 2000; Koen, 2002; Pear & Crone-Todd, 2002; Price, 1999), it was never able to firmly entrench itself in the educational mainstream.

The reasons for PSI's fall from favor are varied, but the most significant likely include the greater amount of initial development time required for PSI courses, the difficulty in adapting a self-paced and mastery-based model to the traditional academic calendar, the hesitation of instructors to transition from a teacher-centered approach to a learner-centered approach, the tendency of educational administrators to value novelty over efficacy (and PSI is no longer novel), and the general inertia of lecture-based teaching (Buskist *et al.*, 1991; Sherman, 1982b, 1992). In many ways, the truly personalized, self-paced, and mastery-based instruction offered by PSI simply does not mesh well with established educational practices. It changes the role of the teacher in important ways (from a "performer" to a "manager" of learning), requires more planning and organization, and demands that academic progress and advancement be governed by student performance rather than a calendar. Further, the widespread use of PSI might have rather striking implications for education: "Imagine what would happen if the entire educational system were PSI-based: huge numbers of peoples, most still in the throes of puberty, might be graduating from college—an unsettling thought for many educators" (Buskist *et al.*, 1991, p. 231). Whatever factors may have contributed to the decrease of interest in PSI, failure to improve student learning and performance was certainly not one of them.

EFFECTIVENESS

Many movements in education are emphatically touted by their advocates but plagued by a lack of supportive empirical data. Constructivism, for example, has gained many adherents in the field of education recently, but as one commentator notes, "At this point, (constructivist) theory and conjecture far outstrip empirical findings" [Driscoll, 2000, p. 395]. This is not the case with PSI. It has been estimated that over 2000 PSI research studies have been conducted (Sherman, 1992), and the vast majority of these have shown that students in PSI courses learn the course content better, remember it longer, and like the experience more than students in traditional classes.

Given the tremendous amount of PSI research that has been conducted, it may be useful to summarize the findings of several published reviews of this literature. One of the earliest reviews was by Taveggia (1976), in which the results of 14 studies of courses from introductory psychology, learning, cultural anthropology, chemistry, electrical engineering, mechanical engineering, and nuclear engineering were analyzed. He found that "when evaluated by average student performance on course content examinations, the Personalized System of Instruction has proven superior to the conventional teaching methods with which it has been compared" (p. 1032). One of the progenitors of PSI found Taveggia's conclusion to be particularly exciting because "it came from a critic of educational research, unassociated with PSI, who was best known for articles demonstrating that nothing one does in the classroom makes any difference (*e.g.*, Dubin & Taveggia, 1968)" (Sherman, 1992, p. 59).

A more extensive review (Kulik, 1976) looked at over 400 PSI articles and found only two that favored traditional course formats over PSI. Moreover, 31 of these studies provided systematic and methodologically sound comparisons of PSI to other methods, and in 25 of these final exam scores were significantly higher for the PSI students (the remaining six studies found no statistically significant difference between the scores of students in PSI courses and those of students in traditional courses). Support for PSI was found in studies that reported measures other than final exam performance, as well. In these studies, PSI was found to produce superior outcomes in all six studies focusing on retention scores, all four studies focusing on transfer effects, and in six of the seven studies focusing on student attitudes about the course.

Kulik *et al.* (1979) conducted a meta-analysis of 72 studies that compared PSI to conventional instruction for a total of 75 different courses. A meta-analysis is a statistical method for integrating the findings from a large set of individual research studies and is used to provide a general account of empirical knowledge in a particular domain (Glass, McGaw, & Smith, 1981). The meta-analysis conducted by Kulik *et al.* used only studies that did not have "crippling" methodological or design flaws and focused on the five types of outcome measures reported in the studies: final exam scores, final course grades, student satisfaction, course completion/withdrawal rates, and student study time. PSI courses produced outstanding results in each of these areas. Final exam scores of students in PSI courses were found to be, on average, about 8 percentage points higher than those of students in lecture-based classes (indicating an average effect size of .5), and this difference increased to 14 percentage points for retention exams administered several months after the end of a course. Likewise, final course grades in PSI courses averaged nearly a full letter grade higher (.8 using a traditional 4.0 grading scale) than final grades in other courses. Measures of student satisfaction also favored PSI, with PSI receiving higher ratings in most studies for overall quality, learning, overall enjoyment, and work load. The authors relate that "students rate PSI classes as more enjoyable, more demanding, and higher in overall quality and contribution to student learning than conventional classes" (p. 317). Finally, course completion rates and estimates of student work load were found to be similar in PSI and conventional classes.

A meta-analysis of mastery learning programs (Kulik, Kulik, & Bangert-Downs, 1990), including courses based on PSI and Bloom's Learning for Mastery (1968), provides further support for PSI's effectiveness. Of the 108 mastery learning studies included in the analysis, 72 used PSI in college-level courses. Although several different outcome measures were examined, effects specific to the PSI studies were reported only for final exam scores and course completion rate. With regard to exam performance, 62 of 67 PSI studies reported higher final exam scores for PSI students, and 69% of these results were statistically significant. On average, the effect of PSI was to improve exam scores by .48 standard deviations. It is noted that this is a relatively strong effect in educational research, as a review of meta-analyses in education (Kulik & Kulik, 1989) indicates that "few educational treatments of any sort were consistently associated with achievement effects as large as those produced by mastery teaching" (Kulik et al., 1990, p. 292). Unlike their previous meta-analysis of PSI research (Kulik, Kulik, & Cohen, 1979), this review indicated a slightly lower completion rate for PSI classes. However, an analysis of the 29 studies in which data on both course completion and examination performance are reported did not indicate that examination effects were related to course completion. The lower course completion rate found in some PSI courses is probably related to the difficulty some students have completing self-paced courses on time, and various strategies have proven effective at rectifying this problem (see Implementing PSI in the 21st Century section).

FLEXIBILITY

It is likely that much of PSI's popularity has been due to the inherent flexibility of the system. From its inception, PSI was designed to provide a general framework for effective teaching that would allow the instructor the option of using a variety of instructional materials or techniques within individual course lessons. The core unit of instruction in PSI is "more like the conventional home-work assignment or laboratory exercise" and "the use of a programmed text, a teaching machine, or some sort of computer aid within such a [PSI] course is entirely possible and may be quite desirable, but it is not to be equated with the course itself" (Keller, 1968, p. 84). By employing this larger and more general unit of instruction and analysis, PSI grants the instructor considerable flexibility in utilizing other pedagogical tools within the course, and makes the system easier to implement with conventional instructional materials (such as textbooks and study guides). Evidence suggests that instructors can improve the quality of their courses by "simply" adopting the core elements of PSI, while still being able to incorporate whatever types of activities, assignments, assessments, and/or experiences they may value. This makes the model exceptionally accessible to a wide range of instructors, as its implementation requires neither an advanced degree in instructional design nor the use of a prescribed set of instructional materials.

The flexibility of PSI is most apparent in at least two respects. First, PSI has been effectively combined with numerous other instructional technologies. For instance, several of the other methods described in this volume, including the Morningside Model of Generative Instruction (Johnson & Layng, 1994) and the Comprehensive Application of Behavior Analysis to Schooling (CABAS; Greer, 2002), incorporate PSI into their systems. The Computer-Aided Personalized System of Instruction (CAPSI; Kinsner & Pear, 1988; Pear & Kinsner, 1988) outlined in the next chapter combines PSI with computer-based instruction, as have others (Conard, 1997; Crosbie & Kelly, 1993). Jacksonville State University's

TABLE 2
Tips for Implementing a PSI

1 Choose quality instructional materials that are appropriate for your students' comprehension level; empirically verified materials are preferable.

2 Make the first units easy (and perhaps smaller) to build confidence; increase difficulty gradually.

3 Avoid including too much material in each unit; the units have to appear manageable to the students.

4 When possible, include review material in assignments, assessments, and other instructional activities.

5 Make assessments as comprehensive and consistent with unit objectives as possible, but also as brief as possible (some students will be taking them multiple times!).

6 Make use of faster students within the class to tutor slower ones.

7 Encourage frequent feedback from students so that instructional materials and assessments can be revised and made more effective for future students.

8 Provide students with easy access to their course records; using a web-based course management system, such as Blackboard or WebCT, may be a good solution.

9 Choose tutors carefully and reward them appropriately; explore different tutoring options and arrangements until you find one that works for your course.

10 Start small, and be prepared for a large initial expenditure of time developing assignments and assessments; as with any course, future implementations should require less time.

Source: Adapted from Lewis and Wolf (1973).

devote sufficient resources are unlikely to be successful (Green, 1982). Keller (1982c) adds that PSI should not be adopted by teachers hoping to alleviate their teaching responsibilities, for "the role of the teacher is not lessened under PSI; it has only been given a different form" (p. 56). Educators who cannot secure the support of their administration for a course that has few lectures and awards many A's and incompletes (depending on how one arranges the grading contingencies) may wish to avoid PSI, as well (Green, 1982; Keller, 1982c). Depending on the nature of the instructional materials employed, courses in which the students have poor reading or independent learning skills may also not be good candidates for PSI (Green, 1982; Roberts Suderman, Suderman, & Semb, 1990).

Key Features of PSI: Updated and Revised

As mentioned previously, the many different permutations of PSI can lead to some difficulty in accurately defining and identifying what PSI is. The inherent flexibility of PSI is one of its primary strengths as a general model for course development, but it can also create problems. These difficulties are illustrated in this warning by Sherman (1992): "A rigid definition [of PSI] can freeze the method into a numbing formula and limit the audience . . . on the other hand, a very broad definition makes PSI so inclusive as to be meaningless" (p. 62). Fortunately, the extensive research on the various components of PSI can be used to develop a list of empirically derived core features that succinctly outlines the basic parameters of PSI but also permits flexibility in their implementation when appropriate.

While some might find it objectionable to alter the "classic" listing of PSI components, it seems worthwhile for several reasons. First, the empirical literature clearly reveals that not all of the features originally identified as critical are necessary for the system to work. The use of lectures for "motivational purposes," for example, does not appear to have any discernible effect on either student achievement or motivation (Calhoun, 1976; Lloyd et al., 1972; Phillips & Semb, 1976; Roberts et al., 1990). It seems counterproductive and needlessly inflexible to continue insisting on the inclusion of components that do not seem to contribute to the improvement of student learning. Also, some of the features (or at least their basic descriptions) could be refined to reflect our current knowledge about the most effective way to execute them. Finally, other characteristics should be modified in light of recent advances in information technology. As noted earlier, for instance, the reliance on textual materials is no longer an absolute necessity given the range of media now readily available for instructional purposes. For these reasons, the features and guidelines described below and summarized in Table 3 are proposed for use in the definition and implementation of PSI.

Unit Mastery

The mastery requirement of PSI appears to be one of the most significant factors in determining student achievement (Caldwell et al., 1978; Hursh, 1976; Kulik et al., 1978; Robin, 1976). This finding is corroborated by reviews of the research on mastery learning programs in general (Kulik et al., 1990). Thus, requiring students to master each unit before advancing to the next should remain a key component of PSI. Research suggests that mastery criteria set at a

TABLE 3
Key Features of PSI: Updated and Revised

Component	Description
Unit mastery	Students are required to demonstrate mastery of each unit before proceeding to the next.
Flexible pacing	Students proceed through the course at their own pace, but strategies to reduce procrastination are recommended.
On-demand course content	Primary delivery of course content is via instructional materials that are available to students whenever needed.
Immediate feedback	Students receive immediate feedback on educational assessments which can be delivered via humans or computers.
Peer tutoring	Peer tutors are available to discuss material and provide tutoring (as well as administer assessments and provide feedback, if necessary).

high level (such as requiring 100% accuracy) may improve student learning (Kulik et al., 1990), but it seems this finding would be relative to the instructional objectives and nature of the assessment used. Recent theoretical and empirical advances related to the notion of mastery, such as work in the area of behavioral fluency (Binder, 1996, 2003; Johnson & Layng, 1992, 1996; Kubina & Morrison, 2000), could also be incorporated into PSI courses. Additional research in this area might be useful for specifying the parameters under which "mastery" could or should be defined, but simply requiring unit mastery—however it is defined—seems to be sufficient for improving student learning. A related point is that the setting of mastery criteria for units requires the specification of instructional objectives, another characteristic of PSI that must endure. Mager (1997) provides superb guidelines for developing quality instructional objectives.

Several investigators have examined the relative merit of using either small or large units in PSI courses (Calhoun, 1976; Semb, 1974), and "evidence tends to show that small units and frequent quizzes are more effective in stimulating student achievement than large units and less frequent quizzes" (Kulik *et al.*, 1978, p. 6). Unit size is a relative matter, of course, so additional guidance is useful. A unit usually covers about a week of work, and a course offered during a 15-week semester typically includes about 15 to 20 units (Keller & Sherman, 1982b). Each unit or module of instruction should consist of the presentation of the course material, an assessment, and feedback. Assessments should be consistent with the unit objectives, and as comprehensive of the unit material as possible. To provide for the mastery requirement, parallel versions of the assessment instrument for each unit may need to be developed (although this depends on the nature of the instrument). It is also recommended that some systematic review be incorporated throughout the course, either through review units or review items on unit quizzes (Keller & Sherman, 1982b). Research suggests that review procedures in PSI courses enhance student learning and retention (Kulik et al., 1978).

Flexible Pacing

The self-pacing aspect of PSI can prove somewhat troubling and controversial (Ainsworth, 1979; Born & Moore, 1978). A certain degree of self-pacing is necessary in order to allow students of varying abilities to each achieve mastery of the material, but research on the issue indicates that self-pacing in and of itself does not impact student learning (Kulik et al., 1978). In fact, there is some evidence that mastery programs that limit self-pacing may produce superior achievement (Kulik et al., 1990).

Of course, the primary problem associated with total self-pacing is that of student procrastination. When a student has complete control over when they study and take quizzes for a course, it is not difficult to understand how competing obligations with fixed deadlines can quickly take priority.

Procrastinators can create logistical problems for themselves, their instructors, and their institution's administration (Born & Moore, 1978), as well as get so far behind that they "despair of catching up, and drop out, frustrated and demoralized" (Kulik et al., 1978, p. 9). Indeed, the self-paced nature of PSI is likely the primary reason some PSI courses have lower completion rates than conventional courses (Kulik et al., 1990).

Several methods for preventing procrastination and promoting timely completion of PSI courses have been offered. Incentive systems which provide students with bonus points or other rewards for meeting various course deadlines can be effective (Riedel, Harney, LaFief, & Finch 1976; Semb Conyers, Spencer, & Sanchez-Sosa, 1975), as can teaching students time-management skills (Glick & Semb, 1978; Keenan et al., 1978). Contingency contracting, in which students who fail to meet instructor-imposed deadlines are required to establish contracts with the instructor for new deadlines, can also improve student progress and reduce the number of student withdrawals (Lamwers & Jazwinski, 1989). Having students establish self-imposed deadlines can also positively impact student pacing and performance (Lloyd and Zylla, 1981; Roberts, Fulton, Semb, 1988; Roberts & Semb, 1989). It is recommended that PSI instructors utilize techniques such as these to avoid the negative effects student procrastination may have, and this is why self-pacing has been renamed *flexible pacing* here. Courses that are entirely teacher paced and do not even allow for advanced students to progress through the course at an accelerated pace should not be identified as PSI.

On-Demand Course Content

Previous listings of the distinguishing properties of PSI included the reduced use of lectures and an emphasis on textual materials (Keller, 1968). Lectures were discouraged as the primary vehicle for delivering course content because they are ephemeral events that students cannot access whenever needed, impose a teacher-determined schedule of learning on all students, and force students to begin attending to new material regardless of whether they had mastered the previous information. Printed material does not have these limitations, and PSI courses thus became heavily reliant on textbooks and study guides.

The true issue, however, is not a matter of the form or medium of the instruction—it is a matter of accessibility. For a self-paced (or flexibly paced) and individualized mastery program such as PSI, it is imperative that students have access to instruction whenever needed in order to accommodate individual learning rates. At the time that PSI was initially developed, textbooks, study guides, and other printed matter were the most common and cost-effective way to accomplish this. Sherman (1982d) noted that in PSI "written materials (or audiovisual media where available and economically justifiable) must become the major informational source" (p. 23). In the modern Information Age, the multimedia instruction to which Sherman referred is both readily available and affordable, and there is no need to restrict PSI to written or textual materials. Rather than listing "an emphasis on the written word" as a core component of PSI, it seems both more accurate and prudent to simply list "on-demand course content" as a defining feature. The quality of such content—whether it is in print or electronic format—can vary widely, of course, and its careful selection or production will have a considerable impact on the quality of the course.

Immediate Feedback

Immediate feedback on academic performance has always been an important characteristic of PSI. Typically, this function has been served by proctors, who would grade student quizzes immediately upon completion and provide written or oral feedback. In fact, the literature suggests that the provision of immediate feedback is the proctor function that has the most significant impact on student learning (Kulik et al., 1978). Because feedback can also be delivered effectively via computerized means (Crosbie & Kelly, 1993), however, it seems useful to separate this component from other proctor functions. While proctors or other people can certainly still be used to provide feedback, using computers to do so can relieve some of the administrative stress associated with PSI and allow course personnel more time to engage in tutoring and discussion with the students. Of course, some forms of assessment (such as those requiring the written composition of answers) may still require a human to evaluate and provide feedback. No matter what method is used to deliver the feedback, though, immediacy is important: research shows that "delaying feedback in PSI courses interferes with student retention of course material" (Kulik et al., 1978, p. 135).

Peer Tutoring

As originally conceived, proctors in a PSI course served to administer and score quizzes, provide feedback on student performance, and discuss the material with the student or provide tutoring. Even though some of these functions, such as quiz administration and the provision of feedback, can now be performed by computers, proctors still play an important in personalizing the student's learning experience. Proctors can be key to improving the individualization of instruction, increasing student motivation, and enhancing the "personal-social aspect of the educational process" (Keller, 1968, p. 83). There is some evidence that interaction with proctors for the purposes of discussion or tutoring may not improve student learning in PSI courses (Caldwell et al., 1978; Fernald, Chiseri, Lawson, Scroggs, & Riddell, 1975; Hindman, 1974), but there is a larger body of research on tutoring in general that suggests the process can have beneficial effects for both the tutor and the tutee (Cohen & Kulik, 1981; Cohen, Kulik, & Kulik, 1982; Hedin, 1987). Determining exactly how (or even whether) proctors should be used, trained, and rewarded has been the subject of much research (Conard & Semb, 1977; Croft, Johnson, Berger, & Zlotlow, 1976; Crosbie & Kelly, 1993; Johnson & Sulzer-Azaroff, 1978; Robin, 1977; Robin & Cook, 1978), but there do not seem to be many clear answers.

Proctoring is renamed *peer tutoring* here for two reasons. The first is that the term *tutoring* seems to better reflect the most meaningful role of the PSI proctor, as the term *proctoring* typically suggests merely the supervision and/ or administration of exams. When Keller and Sherman (1982a) describe the proctor as the "mediating figure, the bridge that helps to span the student-teacher gap of understanding" (p. 61), they seem to be referring to far more than just the proctor's administrative skills. Further, proctors in PSI courses are usually fellow students who have completed the course already (external proctors) or are currently enrolled in the course (internal proctors), making them true peers. An additional reason for using the term *peer tutoring* is to more directly connect PSI and its users to the substantial amount of educational research that now exists on tutoring and peer tutoring (Cohen & Kulik, 1981; Cohen et al., 1982; Hedin, 1987). This literature is certain to hold valuable guidance on how PSI teachers can best incorporate this important yet complex feature into their own courses (Sherman, 1992, p. 63). Refer to Chapter 17 for further information on this topic.

CONCLUSION

When PSI was introduced four decades ago, few could have imagined the attention it would receive or the impact it would have. And, while the number of PSI courses and research studies has certainly decreased since its heyday in the 1970s, PSI endures. Other instructional innovations and technologies, including those presented in this volume, have surfaced and competed with PSI, but none have fully supplanted it. Perhaps this is because many of these methods complement PSI more than truly compete with it: Where PSI is general, they are specific; where PSI focuses on large units of instruction and responding, they focus on smaller ones. This generality and flexibility has served PSI well, as the widespread use of the system and its integration with other instructional strategies over the years serves testament.

At its core, PSI is a general model for course development that is relatively easy to understand and applicable to many settings, learners, and subjects. The basic components of PSI ensure that whoever uses the model will attend to certain key features of quality instruction, such as clear instructional object-ives, active and frequent student responding, careful sequencing of materials, and immediate feedback. It is not surprising that these same characteristics can be found in most other empirically supported educational methods. It is also not surprising that this constellation of features resulted in a system that has proven remarkably effective at improving student learning and achievement for so many years and that continues to serve as an exceptional model for individualizing and strengthening the educational experience.

References

Ainsworth, L. L. (1979). Self-paced instruction: an innovation that failed. *Teaching of Psychology*, 6, 42–46.

Binder, C. (1996). Behavioral fluency: evolution of a new paradigm. *The Behavior Analyst*, 19, 163–197.

Binder, C. (2003). Doesn't everybody need fluency? *Performance Improvement*, 42(3), 14–20.

Block, J. H. (1971). Introduction to mastery learning: theory and practice, in Block, J. H. (Ed.), *Mastery Learning: Theory and Practice*. New York: Holt, Rinehart & Winston, pp. 2–12.

Bloom, B. S. (1968). Learning for mastery. *Evaluation Comment*, 1(2), 1–12.

Bloom, B. S. (1971). Mastery learning, in Block, J. H. (Ed.), *Mastery Learning: Theory and Practice*. New York: Holt, Rinehart & Winston, pp. 47–63.

Born, D. G. & Moore, M. C. (1978). Some belated thoughts on pacing. *Journal of Personalized Instruction*, 3(1), 33–36.

Boylan, H. R. (1980). PSI: a survey of users and their implementation practices. *Journal of Personalized Instruction*, 4(1), 82–85.

Buskist, W., Cush, D., & DeGrandpre, R. J. (1991). The life and times of PSI. *Journal of Behavioral Education*, 1(2), 215–234.

Caldwell, E. C., Bissonnettee, K., Klishis, M. J., Ripley, M., Farudi, P. P., Hochstetter, G. T., & Radiker, J. E. (1978). Mastery: the essential essential in PSI. *Teaching of Psychology*, 5, 59–65.

Calhoun, J. F. (1976). The combination of elements in the Personalized System of Instruction. *Teaching of Psychology*, 3(2), 73–76.

Carroll, J. B. (1963). A model of school learning. *Teachers College Record*, 64, 723–733.

Cohen, P. A. & Kulik, J. A. (1981). Synthesis of research on the effects of tutoring. *Educational Leadership*, 39(3), 226–227.

Cohen, P. A., Kulik, J. A., & Kulik, C. C. (1982). Educational outcomes of tutoring: a meta-analysis of findings. *American Educational Research Journal*, 19(2), 237–248.

Conard, C. J. (1997). Fairbanks system of instruction at Fairbanks Country Day. *Behavior and Social Issues*, 7(1), 25–29.

Conard, C. J. & Semb, G. (1977). Proctor selection, training, and quality control: a longitudinal case study. *Journal of Personalized Instruction*, 2(4), 238–240.

Croft, R. G. F., Johnson, W. G., Berger, J., & Zlotlow, S. F. (1976). The influence of monitoring on PSI performance. *Journal of Personalized Instruction*, 1(1), 28–31.

Crosbie, J. & Kelly, G. (1993). A computer-based Personalized System of Instruction course in applied behavior analysis. *Behavior Research Methods, Instruments, and Computers*, 25(3), 366–370.

Dineen, J. P., Clark, H. B., & Risley, T. R. (1977). Peer tutoring among elementary students: educational benefits to the proctor. *Journal of Applied Behavior Analysis*, 10(2), 231–238.

Driscoll, M. P. (2000). *Psychology of Learning for Instruction*, 2nd ed. Needham Heights, MA: Allyn & Bacon.

Dubin, R. & Taveggia, T. C. (1968). *The teaching-learning paradox: A comparative analysis of college teaching methods*. Eugene, OR: Center for the Advanced Study of Educational Administration.

Fawcett, S. B., Mathews, R. M., Fletcher, R. K., Morrow, R., & Stokes, T. F. (1976). Personalized instruction in the community: teaching helping skills to low-income neighborhood residents. *Journal of Personalized Instruction*, 1(2), 86–90.

Fernald, P. S., Chiseri, M. J., Lawson, D. W., Scroggs, G. F., & Riddell, J. C. (1975). Systematic manipulation of student pacing, the perfection requirement, and contact with a teaching assistant in an introductory psychology course. *Teaching of Psychology*, 2, 147–151.

Glass, G. V., McGaw, B., & Smith, M. L. (1981). *Meta-analysis in social research*. Beverly Hills, CA: Sage.

Glick, D. M. & Semb, G. (1978). Effects of pacing contingencies in personalized instruction: a review of the evidence. *Journal of Personalized Instruction*, 3(1), 36–42.

Green, B. A. (1982). Fifteen reasons not to use the Keller Plan, in Sherman, J. G., Ruskin, R. S., & Semb, G. B. (Eds.), *The Personalized System of Instruction: 48 seminal papers*. Lawrence, KS: TRI Publications, pp. 15–17.

Greer, R. D. (2002). *Designing teaching strategies: An Applied Behavior Analysis Systems Approach*. San Diego: Academic Press.

Hambleton, I. R., Foster, W. H., & Richardson, J. T. (1998). Improving student learning using the personalized system of instruction. *Higher Education*, 35, 187–203.

Hansen, G., Brothen, T., & Wambach, C. (2002). An evaluation of early alerts in a PSI general psychology course. *Learning Assistance Review*, 7(1), 14–21.

Hedin, D. (1987). Students as teachers: a tool for improving school. *Social Policy*, 17(3), 42–47.

Herring, M. & Smaldino, S. (1997). *Planning for Interactive Distance Education: A Handbook*. Washington, D.C.: AECT Publications.

Hindman, C. D. (1974). Evaluation of three programming techniques in introductory psychology courses, in Ruskin, R. S. & Bono, S. F. (Eds.), *Personalized Instruction in Higher Education: Proceedings of the First National Conference)*. Washington, D.C.: Georgetown University, Center for Personalized Instruction, pp. 38–42.

Houmanfar, R., Fox, E. J., Boyce, T. E., Roman, H., Mintz, C. M., & Garlock, M. G. (2000). *A New SPIN on the Personalized System of Instruction*. Poster presented at the annual meeting of the Association for Behavior Analysis, Washington, D.C.

Hursh, D. E. (1976). Personalized systems of instruction: what do the data indicate? *Journal of Personalized Instruction*, 1(2), 91–105.

Johnson, K. R. & Layng, T. V. J. (1994). The Morningside Model of Generative Instruction, in Gardner, R., Sainato, D. M., Cooper, J. O., Heron, T. E., Heward, W. L., Eshleman, J., & Grossi, T. A. (Eds.), *Behavior analysis in education: Focus on measurably superior instruction*, Belmont, CA: Wadsworth, pp. 173–197.

Johnson, K. R. & Layng, T. V. J. (1996). On terms and procedures: fluency. *The Behavior Analyst*, 19, 281–288.

Johnson, K. R. & Sulzer-Azaroff, B. (1978). An experimental analysis of proctor prompting behavior in a personalized instruction course. *Journal of Personalized Instruction*, 3(3), 122–130.

Keenan, J. B., Bono, S. F., & Hursh, D. E. (1978). Shaping time-management skills: two examples in PSI. *Journal of Personalized Instruction*, 3(1), 46–49.

Keller, F. S. (1968). "Goodbye teacher . . .". *Journal of Applied Behavior Analysis*, 1, 79–89.

Keller, F. S. (1982a). The history of PSI, in Keller, F. S. & Sherman, J. G. (Eds.), *The PSI Handbook: Essays on Personalized Instruction*. Lawrence, KS: TRI Publications, pp. 6–12.

Keller, F. S. (1982b). PSI and reinforcement theory, in Keller, F. S. & Sherman, J. G. (Eds.), *The PSI Handbook: Essays on Personalized Instruction*. Lawrence, KS: TRI Publications, pp. 46–53.

Keller, F. S. (1982c). PSI is not for everyone, in Keller, F. S. & Sherman, J. G. (Eds.), *The PSI Handbook: Essays on Personalized Instruction*. Lawrence, KS: TRI Publications, pp. 54–57.

Keller, F. S. and Sherman, J. G. (1982a). Afterthoughts and leftovers, in Keller, F. S. & Sherman, J. G. (Eds.), *The PSI Handbook: Essays on Personalized Instruction*. Lawrence, KS: TRI Publications, pp. 58–71.

Keller, F. S. & Sherman, J. G. (Eds.) (1982b). *The PSI Handbook: Essays on Personalized Instruction*. Lawrence, KS: TRI Publications.

Kinsner, W. & Pear, J. J. (1988). Computer-aided personalized system of instruction for the virtual classroom. *Canadian Journal of Educational Communication*, 17, 21–36.

Klishis, M. J., Hursh, D. E., & Klishis, L. A. (1980). Individualized spelling: an application and evaluation of PSI in the elementary school. *Journal of Personalized Instruction*, 4(3), 148–156.

Koen, B. V. (2002). *Web-based implementation of the Personalized System of Instruction (PSI) in a mechanical engineering required freshman computer course*. New York: American Society of Mechanical Engineers (http://www.asme.org/education/enged/awards/cia01/utexas.pdf).

Koen, B. V., Wissler, E. H., Lamb, J. P., & Hoberock, L. L. (1975). PSI management: down the administrative chain. *Engineering Education*, Nov., 165–168.

Kubina, R. M. & Morrison, R. S. (2000). Fluency in education. *Behavior and Social Issues*, 10, 83–99.

Kulik, C. C., Kulik, J. A., & Bangert-Drowns, R. L. (1990). Effectiveness of mastery learning programs: a meta-analysis. *Review of Educational Research*, 60, 265–299.

Kulik, J. A. (1976). PSI: a formative evaluation, in Green, B. A., Jr. (Ed.), *Personalized instruction in higher education: Proceedings of the second National Conference*. Washington, D.C.: Center for Personalized Instruction.

Kulik, J. A. & Kulik, C. C. (1989). Meta-analysis in education. *International Journal of Educational Research*, 13, 221–340.

Kulik, J. A., Jaksa, P., & Kulik, C. C. (1978). Research on component features of Keller's Personalized System of Instruction. *Journal of Personalized Instruction*, 3(1), 2–14.

Kulik, J. A., Kulik, C. C., & Cohen, P. A. (1979). A meta-analysis of outcome studies of Keller's personalized system of instruction, *American Psychologist*, 34(4), 307–318.

Lamal, P. A. (1984). Interest in PSI across sixteen years. *Teaching of Psychology*, 11, 237–238.

Lamwers, L. L. & Jazwinski, C. H. (1989). A comparison of three strategies to reduce student procrastination in PSI. *Teaching of Psychology*, 16, 8–12.

Lewis, D. K. & Wolf, W. A. (1973). Implementation of self-paced learning (Keller Method) in a first-year course. *Journal of Chemical Education*, 50(1), 51–56.

Lloyd, K. E. (1978). Behavior analysis and technology in higher education, in Catania, A. C. & Brigham, T. A. (Eds.), *Handbook of Applied Behavior Analysis: Social and Instructional Processes*. New York: Irvington Press, pp. 482–521.

Lloyd, K. E. & Lloyd, M. E. (1992). Behavior analysis and technology in higher education, in West, R. P. & Hamerlynck, L. A. (Eds.), *Designs for Excellence in Education: The Legacy of B. F. Skinner*. Longmont, CO: Sopris West, pp. 147–160.

Lloyd, K. E., Garlington, W. K., Lowry, D., Burgess, H., Euler, H. A., & Knowlton, W. R. (1972). A note on some reinforcing properties of university lectures. *Journal of Applied Behavior Analysis*, 5, 151–155.

Lloyd, M. E. & Lloyd, K .E. (1986). Has lightning struck twice? Use of PSI in college classrooms. *Teaching of Psychology*, 13, 149–151.

Lloyd, M. E. & Zylla, T. (1981). Self-pacing: helping students establish and fulfill individualized plans for pacing unit tests. *Teaching of Psychology*, 3, 100–103.

Mager, R. F. (1997). *Preparing instructional objectives: A critical tool in the development of effective instruction*, 3rd ed. Atlanta, CA: CEP Press.

McDade, C. E. & Goggans, L. A. (1993). Computer-based precision learning: achieving fluency with college students. *Education and Treatment of Children*, 16(3), 290–305.

McLaughlin, T. F. (1991). Use of a personalized system of instruction with and without a same-day retake contingency on spelling performance of behaviorally disordered children. *Behavioral Disorders*, 16(2), 127–132.

McLaughlin, T. F. & Malaby, J. E. (1975). Elementary school children as behavioral engineers, in Ramp, E. A. & Semb, G. (Eds.), *Behavior analysis in education: Areas of research and application*. Englewood Cliffs, NJ: Prentice Hall, pp. 329–328.

McMichael, J. S., Brock, J. F., & Delong, J. (1976). Job-relevant Navy training and Keller's personalized system of instruction: reduced attrition. *Journal of Personalized Instruction*, 1(1), 41–44.

Morrison, H. C. (1926). *The practice of teaching in the secondary school*. Chicago: University of Chicago Press.

Ormrod, J. E. (2000). *Educational psychology: Developing learners*, 3rd ed. Upper Saddle River, NJ: Merrill.

Pear, J. J. & Crone-Todd, D. E. (2002). A social constructivist approach to computer-mediated instruction. *Computers and Education*, 38, 221–231.

Pear, J. J. & Kinsner, W. (1988). Computer-aided Personalized System of Instruction: an effective and economical method for short- and long-distance education. *Machine-Mediated Learning*, 2, 213–237.

Pear, J. J. & Novak, M. (1996). Computer-aided Personalized System of Instruction: a program evaluation. *Teaching of Psychology*, 23(2), 119–123.

Pennypacker, H. S. (1978). The computer as a management tool in systems of personalized instruction. *Journal of Personalized Instruction*, 3(3), 304–307.

Phillips, T. W. & Semb, G. (1976). Quizzes, lecture attendance, and remediation procedures in a contingency-managed university course, in Fraley, L. E. & Vargas, E. A. (Eds.), *Behavior research and technology in higher education*. Gainesville, FL: Society for Behavioral Technology and Engineering, pp. 23–34.

Price, R. V. (1999). Designing a college web-based course using a modified Personalized System of Instruction (PSI) model. *TechTrends*, 43(5), 23–28.

Reid, H. P., Archer, M. B., & Friedman, R. M. (1977). Using the personalized system of instruction with low-reading-ability middle school students: Problems and results. *Journal of Personalized Instruction*, 2(4), 199–203.

Riedel, R., Harney, B., LaFief, W., & Finch, M. (1976). The effect of time as a contingency on student performance in an individualized course, in Green, B. A., Jr. (Ed.), *Personalized instruction in higher education: proceedings of the second National Conference*. Washington, D.C.: Georgetown University, Center for Personalized Instruction, pp. 128–130.

Roberts, M. S. & Semb, G. (1989). Student selection of deadline conditions in a personalized psychology course. *Teaching of Psychology*, 16, 128–130.

Roberts, M. S., Fulton, M., & Semb, G. (1988). Self-pacing in a personalized psychology course: letting students set the deadlines. *Teaching of Psychology*, 15, 89–92.

Roberts, M. S., Suderman, L, Suderman, R., & Semb, G. (1990). Reading ability as a predictor in a behaviorally based psychology course. *Teaching of Psychology*, 17, 173–175.

Robin, A. L. (1976). Behavioral instruction in the college classroom. *Review of Educational Research*, 46, 313–354.

Robin, A. L. (1977). Proctor training: snapshots, reflections, and suggestions. *Journal of Personalized Instruction*, 2(4), 216–221.

Robin, A. L. & Cook, D. A. (1978). Training proctors for personalized instruction. *Teaching of Psychology*, 5, 9–13.

Semb, G. (1974). Personalized instruction: The effects of grading criteria and assignment length on college student test performance. *Journal of Applied Behavior Analysis*, 7, 61–69.

Semb, G. (1976). Building an empirical base for instruction. *Journal of Personalized Instruction*, 1(1), 11–22.

Semb, G., Conyers, D., Spencer, R., & Sanchez-Sosa, J. J. (1975). An experimental comparison of four pacing contingencies, in Johnston, J. M. (Ed.), *Behavior Research and Technology in Higher Education*. Springfield, IL: Charles C Thomas, pp. 348–368.

Sherman, J. G. (1982a). The theory behind PSI, in Sherman, J. G., Ruskin, R. S., & Semb, G. B. (Eds.), *The Personalized System of Instruction: 48 seminal papers*. Lawrence, KS: TRI Publications, pp. 12–14.

Sherman, J. G. (1982b). PSI today, in Keller, F. S. and Sherman, J. G. (Eds.), *The PSI Handbook: Essays on Personalized Instruction*. Lawrence, KS: TRI Publications, pp. 72–78.

Sherman, J. G. (1982c). Applications in diverse settings: introduction, In Sherman, J. G., Ruskin, R. S., & Semb, G. B. (Eds.), *The Personalized System of Instruction: 48 seminal papers*. Lawrence, KS: TRI Publications, p. 266.

Sherman, J. G. (1982d). Logistics, in Keller, F. S. & Sherman, J. G. (Eds.), *The PSI handbook: Essays on personalized instruction*. Lawrence, KS: TRI Publications, pp. 22–45.

Sherman, J. G. (1992). Reflections on PSI: good news and bad. *Journal of Applied Behavior Analysis*, 25(1), 59–64.

Sherman, J. G., Ruskin, R. S., & Semb, G. B. (Eds.) (1982). *The Personalized System of Instruction: 48 seminal papers*. Lawrence, KS: TRI Publications.

Simonson, M., Smaldino, S., Albright, M., & Zvacek, S. (2003). Research and distance education, in Simonson, M., Smaldino, S., Albright, M., & Zvacek, S. (Eds.) *Teaching and learning at a distance: Foundations of distance education*, 2nd ed. Upper Saddle River, NJ: Merrill/ Prentice Hall, pp. 61–84.

Taveggia, T. C. (1976). Personalized instruction: a summary of comparative research, 1967–1975. *American Journal of Physics*, 44, 1028–1033.

Tosti, D. & Jackson, S. M. (1980). A personalized system of instruction in bank training. *Journal of Personalized Instruction*, 4(2): 109–111.

Washburne, C. W. (1922). Educational measurements as a key to individualizing instruction and promotions. *Journal of Educational Research*, 5, 195–206.

Zencius, A. H., Davis, P. K., & Cuvo, A. J. (1990). A personalized system of instruction for teaching checking account skills to adults with mild disabilities. *Journal of Applied Behavior Analysis*, 23(2), 245–252.

CHAPTER 13

Making the Most of PSI with Computer Technology

JOSEPH J. PEAR and TOBY L. MARTIN

University of Manitoba

INTRODUCTION

Personalized System of Instruction (PSI) was developed prior to the widespread availability of computers, and numerous assistants were required to help administer the system. Traditionally, most of these individuals were students in more advanced courses who received some credit in their course for helping with the PSI procedure in a less advanced course. The amount of administrative work required is likely the main reason for the decline of interest in PSI. Another obstacle may have been the difficulty of obtaining a more advanced course from which to draw students. In addition, students in another course are unpaid labor, which violates contracts that some universities and colleges have with campus unions. The enormous processing capacity of modern computers provides technological solutions to these problems, as well as a means to enhance PSI. We believe that all effective courses include methods for: (1) presenting specific study objectives, (2) providing contingencies that result in verbal activity relating to the objectives, and (3) monitoring this activity and providing the students with feedback. PSI is a highly systematic method for doing each of these things and thus is well suited to computer-aided delivery. This chapter describes Computer-Aided Personalized System of Instruction (CAPSI), an approach to higher education that grew out of this line of reasoning.

COMPUTERS IN HIGHER EDUCATION

Many resources have been invested in generating computer programs that develop a variety of the skills needed to interact with complex phenomena, but higher education consists of more than just learning such skills; it is typically seen primarily as developing the complex verbal abilities that we call knowledge, comprehension, critical thinking, and higher-order thinking. This presumably is the purpose of activities such as listening to lectures, participating in discussions, reading texts, and writing papers, tests, and examinations. In the large majority of classes, computer technology has not had a major impact on these activities. The most dramatic change computer technology has brought to college and university teaching has been in the use of e-mail. On the whole, computers have served in this regard simply as a messaging system—an extremely convenient one both for instructors and students—but not in itself a primary teaching tool. Computer technology in higher education also provides access to online catalogues of library material, databases of literature citations, and articles and other information posted on websites. Direct applications of computer technology in higher education have largely been devoted to an attempt to import standard classroom activities into a web environment. These applications, however, do little to address problems that exist in many standard classroom activities.

If recreating standard course procedures on the Internet is not an efficient use of computer technology in higher education, what is required? We believe that contingencies resulting in course-related verbal activity must be combined with methods for presenting specific study objectives, monitoring the activities of students, and providing them with feedback. PSI is a highly systematic method for doing this and thus should be well suited to computer-aided delivery. PSI and computers appear to be a natural match, and it seems to follow that computerizing PSI is an efficient way to use computers in higher education.

A BRIEF HISTORY OF CAPSI

The first version of CAPSI was implemented in the 1983/84 academic year as a computerization of a PSI method that the senior author used to teach his undergraduate psychology courses at the University of Manitoba (Kinsner & Pear, 1988; Pear & Kinsner, 1988). Rather than using student assistants from another course, this method used students from the same class who had passed a given unit as peer reviewers. To pass a given unit, a student was required to demonstrate mastery on each question assigned on a test for that unit. If a student's test did not demonstrate mastery, a "restudy" result was assigned—meaning that after a period of time allotted for restudying the unit, the student could take another test on that unit. The instructor monitored the peer reviewers' work and they received a small amount of course credit for each unit test they reviewed.

All questions were of the short-answer or short-essay type. When the computer was introduced, its main function was to randomly select question numbers indicating which study questions a student was to answer and to select the instructor or teaching assistant to evaluate the test or two peers to review it. Both peer reviewers had to independently agree that the student had demonstrated mastery in order for the computer to credit the student with a pass. Students worked at a teletypewriter terminal called a DecWriter; this was connected to the university's mainframe computer by telephone. There were often long lines at the terminal, which were alleviated to some extent by increasing the time that the classroom was available. A second terminal was introduced in the 1984/85 academic year. When e-mail came into effect in the 1986/87 academic year, students who had access to terminals and modems were allowed to write tests outside of the classroom and e-mail their answers to the instructor for marking. In the 1987/88 academic year, the program was integrated with e-mail so that the computer automatically mailed tests to students requesting them and mailed the completed tests to two peer reviewers, a teaching assistant, or the instructor.

In the 1994/95 academic year, a DOS version was implemented on a LAN server in the psychology department of the University of Manitoba. With a few minor upgrades, this is the version currently in use (Pear & Crone-Todd, 1999). Students access the program either from campus labs or off campus via a telnet connection. In a course taught using CAPSI, students complete study questions selected by the program from a bank of essay-type questions on the material they have just learned. Students proceed at their own pace through the study units. Students who demonstrate mastery of a unit (defined as correctly answering all questions on the unit assignment or test) may serve as peer reviewers for that unit (Figs. 1 and 2). The program is applicable to any course topic and any set of questions or problems. It is currently being used successfully in a number of undergraduate psychology courses taught at the University of Manitoba, and it has been used to teach distance education courses as well as on-campus courses. In addition, a collaboration with another university merged two courses on the same topic at the two institutions.

HOW CAPSI UTILIZES COMPUTER CAPABILITIES

A course taught by CAPSI starts out in design like a traditional PSI course. A text covering the course material is chosen, the course material is broken down into study units, and study questions are written that define what the student is expected to have learned as a result of reading the text. After this, however, the method takes full advantage of the computer's information-processing, data-storage, and communications capabilities. We consider each of these in turn.

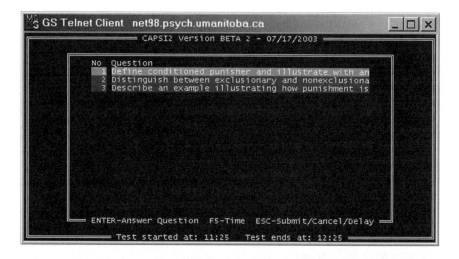

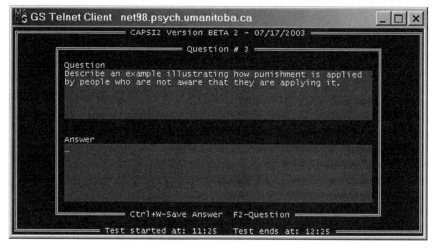

FIGURE 1

(Top) Computer screen as viewed by a student receiving a unit test consisting of three short-essay questions. (Bottom) Upon opening one of the questions, the student sees the entire question field and a field for typing the answer. The student can scroll in the windows if necessary.

Information-Processing Capabilities

Despite the immense information-processing capabilities of computers, their linguistic abilities at present fall far short of those of humans. This might seem to limit the use of computers in PSI to restricted-answer questions (*e.g.*, true/false, multiple-choice, fill-in-the-blank) or, at best, questions requiring just a

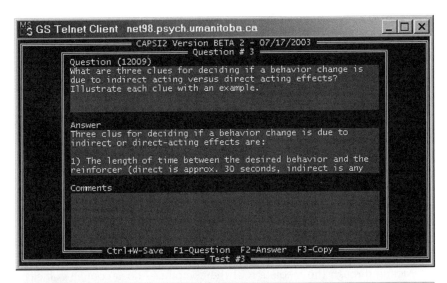

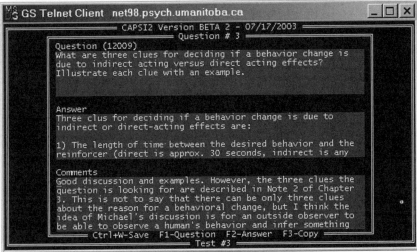

FIGURE 2

(Top) The student's answer, as seen by a peer reviewer, to the question shown in Figure 1. (Bottom) The peer reviewer comments on the answer. The reviewer can scroll in the windows if necessary.

few words. There are computerized PSI programs that take this approach. We believe, however, that unless restricted-answer questions are simply being used for screening purposes, this is a step in the wrong direction. The power of PSI, in our view, lies in the large amount of verbal behavior and large number of interactions between learners that it has the potential to generate. It is true that restricted-answer questions are sometimes used in traditional PSI courses; however, in these cases, the student assistants ideally provide oral feedback so that there is opportunity for discussion of the material. The generation of expository verbal behavior, not the mere choosing of a provided option, is essential to effective learning. Such behavior is not likely to occur when the answer is constrained by a few choices that are generally provided on the test; or, if it does occur, will be limited to the private level. Moreover, we cannot assume that a correct response on a restricted-answer test necessarily implies that the appropriate private behavior (*i.e.*, thinking) has occurred.

When a student produces expository verbal behavior, however, his or her thinking is in plain view to be reinforced with positive comments if it meets the criterion for reinforcement or changed with corrective feedback if it does not. Despite the computational capabilities of modern computers, they are not yet at the level at which they can, in general, respond to expository verbal behavior with sufficient understanding to reinforce it appropriately. With CAPSI, however, the system as a whole—which is the collection of individuals who are interacting through the mediation of the computer—does contain sufficient understanding. In fact, the system generates understanding of the material at an exponential rate. Although the computer itself as one component of the system may not be able to provide adequate feedback, it can locate the requisite knowledge and understanding within the system as a whole. Less abstractly, the computer knows each student's level of mastery in the course at any given instant. Thus, in addition to being able to assign the instructor or teaching assistant to provide feedback on a given answer, the computer can assign this task to a student in the course—a peer reviewer—who has mastered the unit of the test. All that is needed is an algorithm for assigning tests to qualified peer reviewers. In passing, it might be noted that the system as a whole, consisting of complexly interacting parts resulting in states that are not totally predictable from earlier states, is an example of what is termed a *dynamical system* (Kinsner & Pear, 1990).

Personalized System of Instruction reorganizes the transfer of expertise that occurs in more traditional classrooms. Instead of a single teacher dispensing knowledge to a large number of students, students in PSI respond to the subject matter throughout the course and receive frequent guidance. The computer's selection of peer reviewers from within a CAPSI-taught course further transforms these relationships, in that students learn directly from each other as well as from the instructor and teaching assistants. The system is also highly scalable within limits—as class size increases, the pool of available peer reviewers keeps pace. In large classes, students continue to receive rapid and frequent feedback in quantities well beyond what a single instructor could provide. There is, of course, an upper limit to the number of students that can be handled by a single instructor who must oversee the whole course; however, class size could potentially be quite large if there is a commensurate increase in number of paid teaching assistants.

Data Storage Capabilities

The computer's vast capacity for storing and accessing data means that every interaction in the course is available for scrutiny by the instructor or by a researcher. Throughout a course, students request tests and answer questions, indicate their availability to review the tests of other students, write comments as feedback to answers on other students' tests, make judgments about the overall mastery shown in those tests, and (sometimes) appeal the results of their tests. The program stores the date and time of all these events, enabling the instructor to evaluate student progress in the course at any time; however, CAPSI provides not merely a transaction record, but a true relational database of course activity. That is, an instructor or researcher can make queries that efficiently reorganize the data into nearly any useful form. It is as easy to generate a longitudinal record of test writing by a single student as to examine all the answers given by a class to a particular study unit or even a single study question. This latter function permits rapid identification of course topics and objectives to which students are not responding effectively. In such a case, the objectives can be restructured or supplemented, and the results of these changes can be assessed with equal rapidity. The activity of peer reviewers can also be related to study units and objectives, which can help to identify objectives that are especially difficult to assess. This information can be used to locate and reduce vagueness in the objectives or to identify skill deficiencies in the peer reviewers. Queries can also be made to monitor the work done by individual peer reviewers, for the important purpose of providing feedback to improve their performance. Ultimately, the data storage capabilities of a computer-aided system should help not only to optimize individual courses but also to discover how course variables affect the learning process.

Communications Capabilities

One of the features of PSI is that the method does not require all students to attend class at the same time. There are, for example, PSI courses in which assistants are available at extended periods throughout the day and students can choose to take tests from a wide range of times. The communication capabilities of the computer extend this convenience without limit. Computers allow access 24 hours a day, 7 days a week, permitting asynchronous testing and feedback. Moreover, students do not have to go to a central location to be tested. This means that CAPSI is employable in a virtual environment, both temporally and spatially. We have used it for both on-campus and distance courses. We have also combined on-campus and distance courses. Students of widely varied backgrounds can interact, even without necessarily realizing that they are interacting with students from other locales. Knowing the background, current location, or situation of the person they are interacting with is not relevant to learning the course material. The heterogeneity thereby introduced may have beneficial learning effects as well as result in more efficient course delivery.

The flexible design of PSI makes it especially suited to accommodating students with disabilities (Brothen, Wam bach, Hansen, 2002). These advantages are accentuated by use of the computer. Students with chronic health difficulties do not need to worry about missing test dates in CAPSI-taught courses and do not even need to be physically able to travel to the classroom. Moreover, the instructor can adjust time requirements on an individual basis so that students with learning disabilities can take as much time as needed in reading the text-based materials and composing answers, without feeling pressure to keep up with a lecture or class discussion. Indeed, the computer-mediated nature of CAPSI permits persons with virtually any disability to be readily accommodated with specialized computer programs or equipment.

REFINEMENTS OF CAPSI

The bare outlines of CAPSI have been sketched above; however, further details and additional features that have been or can be incorporated require clarification.

Higher-Order Thinking

Some computer-mediated instruction can be fairly criticized for emphasizing learning by rote or for developing knowledge without providing the kinds of experiences that develop higher-order or critical thinking. PSI, too, has been criticized on these grounds, although the charge has been answered (Reboy & Semb, 1991; Ross & Semb, 1981). CAPSI avoids this pitfall with at least three major features that explicitly require higher-order thinking by students.

The first feature is the systematic incorporation of study objectives that require more than simple knowledge. To teach higher-order thinking, it is necessary to define it precisely enough that it can be recognized when displayed by students. In CAPSI, our approach to operationally defining higher-order thinking is based on Bloom's taxonomy (Bloom, Englehart, Furst, Hill, & Krathwohl, 1956); however, Bloom's definitions were not precise enough to allow us to obtain good reliability using them, so the definitions were modified (Crone-Todd, Pear, & Read, 2000; Pear Crone-Todd, Wirth, & Simister, 2001). Table 1 summarizes the modified definitions, and Figs. 3 and 4 show flow charts for defining question and answer levels, respectively. The reliability of these definitions usually ranges from moderate to good, although more work is needed to improve their reliability.

The peer review system makes the use of the higher-level objectives feasible. It may be possible to compose restricted-answer questions that test the higher levels of thinking, but it is certainly more difficult than it is to compose essay-type questions that do so. This is particularly true at the synthesis and

TABLE 1
Modified Definitions of the Categories in Bloom's Taxonomy

Categories I and II

The answers to these types of questions are in the assigned material (*e.g.*, textbook or lecture) and require no extrapolation.

I. Knowledge	Answers may be memorized or closely paraphrased from the assigned material.
II. Comprehension	Answers must be in the student's own words, while still using terminology appropriate to the course material.

Categories III, IV, V, and VI

These questions go beyond the textual material in that they must be inferred or extrapolated from the information in the assigned material.

III. Application	Requires recognizing, identifying, or applying a concept or principle in a new situation or solving a new problem. Questions in this category may require identifying or generating examples not found in the assigned material.
IV. Analysis	Requires breaking down concepts into their constituents or identifying or explaining the essential components of concepts, principles, or processes. Questions in this category may require the student to compare and contrast or explain how an example illustrates a given concept, principle, or processes.
V. Synthesis	Requires the putting together of parts to form a whole (*i.e.*, the opposite of Level IV). Questions may require generating definitions (*i.e.*, going from specific to general) or combining principles or concepts to produce something new.
VI. Evaluation	Requires the presentation and evaluation of reasons for and against a particular position and (ideally) to come to a conclusion regarding the validity of that position. The most important part of the answer is the justification or rationale for the conclusion, rather than the answer *per se*. A good discussion in this category involves the use of all preceding levels.

Source: Crone-Todd, D. E. *et al.*, *Academic Exchange Quarterly*, 4(3), 99–106, 2000. With permission from *Academic Exchange Quarterly*.

evaluation levels (Bloom's levels V and VI, respectively). Consider, for example, how one might devise a multiple-choice question that would test a student's ability to design a self-modification program for washing the dishes after each meal or a multiple-choice question that would test a student's ability to state and defend a position on the justifiability of a particular war. Creativity, which is required at Bloom's levels V and VI, is particularly difficult (if at all possible) to test with restricted-answer questions, because by definition creative behavior cannot be specified in advance. That is, one can often recognize a creative answer when one sees it but not predict in advance all possible creative solutions to a particular problem; however, individuals who are well

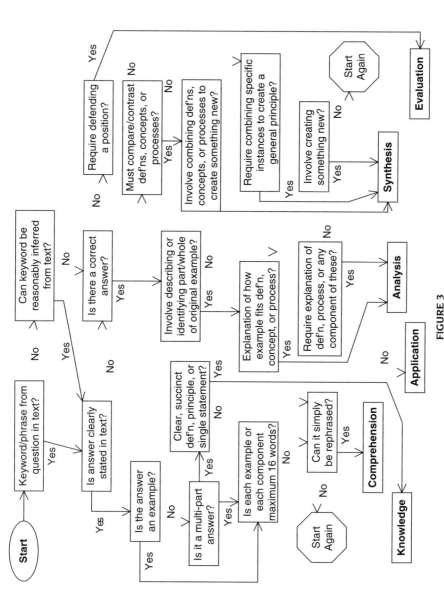

FIGURE 3

Flow chart for determining thinking levels of questions. (From Crone-Todd, D. E. et al., *Academic Exchange Quarterly*, 4(3), 99–106, 2000. With permission from *Academic Exchange Quarterly*.)

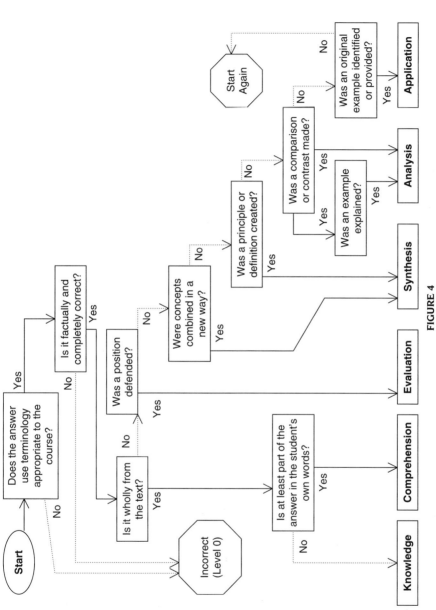

FIGURE 4

Flow chart for determining thinking levels of answers. (From Pear, J. J. *et al., Academic Exchange Quarterly,* 5(4), 94–98, 2001. With permission from *Academic Exchange Quarterly.*)

versed in a particular subject can make judgments regarding the creativity of particular answers to questions in that subject. Automation of these judgments is not technologically possible at the present time, and it may be quite some time (if ever) before it is.

The second feature conducive to higher-order thinking and creativity is CAPSI's peer-review process. Students are instructed to explain the result they assign to each unit test they review. These reviews, therefore, represent activity at Bloom's level VI.

Finally, CAPSI incorporates an appeal process as a check against assignment of "restudy" results when "pass" is warranted. Students are instructed to appeal a restudy result to the instructor if they disagree with it. Making an appeal involves addressing the reviewer's comments in a clear and convincing manner. If the instructor accepts the student's argument, the result of the test is changed. In most cases, arguments provided are above the level of that of the question itself; typically, in fact, arguments of a structured level VI responding are required in order for an appeal to be successful. Feedback on appeals of tests is also provided to the peer reviewers of the appealed tests in the expectation that this will have a positive effect on their thinking levels as well.

Incentives for Student Behavior

It is essential to provide incentives (or reinforcers) for students to engage in the behaviors required by the system. Specifically, students must prepare answers to study questions, write tests, and review other students' answers. A simple point system, translatable into grades at the end of the term, is effective at maintaining these behaviors for most students. Curving of marks is possible but not necessary or recommended; however, it is not enough that students perform certain behaviors—a minimum level of quality is also expected. It is important, for example, that peer reviewers provide feedback promptly. Delays in feedback are alleviated by having students indicate their availability for peer reviewing to the computer, which will then only select students who can respond within a specified time period (*e.g.*, 24 hours). A mild point penalty is levied on a student assigned to review a test if he or she has not done so within a certain specified time after the student has submitted it. The test would also be reassigned to another reviewer or to the instructor or teaching assistant.

Feedback given by peer reviewers should also be accurate. Requiring mastery on a given unit before a student may review tests of that unit is part of the solution to this problem; however, there can be slippage in the system because of its hierarchical nature. Students who are last in finishing a unit may have their tests reviewed by students who were next to last, and so on. Careful spot-checking of peer reviews and providing appropriate feedback can alleviate this problem. The data collection capabilities of computers facilitate this monitoring. Research (Martin *et al.*, 2002a,b) has shown that it is possible to reliably measure feedback accuracy and that a quality control measure of having two (as opposed to just one) peers review each test decreases the number of failures by peer reviewers to detect errors.

Future versions of the system could allow students to rate the peer reviewers who review their tests, in terms of both quality and promptness of feedback. These interlocking social contingencies would mirror those responsible for much of our behavior in everyday life, while maintaining a formal structure amenable to control and record keeping by the computer.

Plagiarism

Administering tests asynchronously at distant locations means that tests are not supervised; hence, answers may be copied from the text or other sources. There are various solutions to this problem: (1) programs can scan for copied or closely paraphrased material that does not credit its source; (2) a time limit, managed by the computer, may be imposed on each test measured from the time it is received to the time it is submitted; (3) heavily weighted supervised exams, separate from the PSI portion of the course, may be given at a centralized location; and (4) test questions should be designed at the higher thinking levels so that answers are not readily available to be copied. While the possibility of plagiarism and cheating is always present, the issue is no more serious for CAPSI than it is in any course that assigns work outside of class. Indeed, the problem may be less for a CAPSI-taught course because the answers to study questions (especially the higher-level questions) may be less readily available than papers on specific topics.

Preventing Mastery-Criterion Circumvention

Computer-Aided Personalized System of Instruction employs a mastery criterion; however, it is not feasible to ask every question in a unit on each test of that unit. Questions must be randomly sampled. We have found a random sample of three questions to be convenient; however, because CAPSI provides a student the option of canceling a test after receiving it, a student might in theory continue requesting tests until one occurs that contains only questions he or she can answer. Informal observations, as well as sampling theory, show that most students quickly discover that a strategy of learning the answers to only a few questions in each unit is ineffective. First, there is a minimum time requirement between successive attempts on a unit; trying to obtain favorable questions on every unit greatly slows a student's progress through the units. Second, the most important concepts in a course typically recur throughout the units; thus, it would be very difficult for students to progress through all the units without learning those concepts.

A procedure that is not present in the current version of CAPSI, but which might well be incorporated into future versions, is stratified sampling of questions rather than strictly random sampling. That is, questions would be randomly sampled from set categories (*e.g.*, the categories in Bloom's hier-archy). Midterm and final examinations integrated with the CAPSI component of a course constitute another check that is used to help ensure that a high grade in the course signifies a high level of mastery of the course content. While we feel that these steps go a long way toward preventing circumvention of the mastery criterion, we acknowledge a need for studies to determine how best to ensure mastery in a CAPSI-taught course.

Training

A variety of skills are required to take a CAPSI-taught course. One needs to know how to study for tests, how to write acceptable answers, and how to evaluate one's own work and review that of others. A variety of skills are also required to be an instructor of a CAPSI taught course. The question, therefore, arises as to how individuals are trained to function in CAPSI-taught courses.

Students

We find that the system works well with no explicit training outside of the system. This is because CAPSI contains built-in training features. First, the program can be used to teach itself. In our CAPSI-taught courses, the first study unit is about the system itself. In that unit, students learn from a manual containing study questions about how to use the technology, how to write unit tests, and how to review their own work and that of others. Second, students receive feedback through the course on how they are performing as test writers and as peer reviewers. Third, the program is highly menu based, and students have a great deal of experience with menu-based programs, as well as experi-ence answering questions in courses. There is, of course, always room to do more with regard to training of peer reviewers. For example, skill deficiencies could be assessed and special tutorials devised. Students could be given practice taking tests and peer-reviewing them prior to beginning to write tests on actual units.

Instructor

Most instructors who use CAPSI have previously been students in CAPSI-taught courses; therefore, it is difficult to say how much training is necessary for instructors who have no familiarity with CAPSI. However, our experience in teaching a new CAPSI instructor suggests that an instructor can be shown how to independently create and administer courses in an hour or two. As with the student portion of the program, the instructor portion is heavily menu based, which is extremely helpful in learning and remembering the functions of the program. Also, like most individuals in our culture, instructors are very familiar with the process of asking and answering questions. Moreover, we hope that our work on thinking levels of questions and answers will be helpful to instructors in their design of questions that help to establish behavior at the desired levels.

Programming CAPSI

A final problem to be mentioned is that there currently is no commercially available CAPSI computer program, and the CAPSI functions (in particular, the peer-review procedure) cannot be incorporated readily into any contemporary commercial online or web-based instructional program. The only existing CAPSI program is the current DOS program, which continues to function well after 9 years of continuous use at the University of Manitoba but which is not readily transferable to other institutions. However, a web-based CAPSI is currently being developed at the University of Manitoba

THE PEER REVIEW SYSTEM AT WORK

Figure 5 shows workload dynamics averaged from 3 successive years of a CAPSI-taught class in behavior modification. It can be seen from the figure that the instructor and teaching assistant marked the majority of unit tests

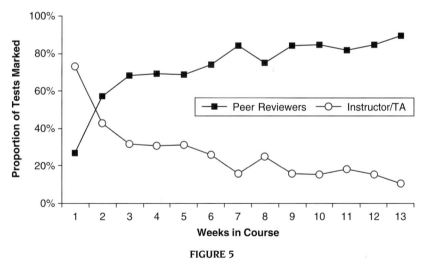

FIGURE 5

Proportion of feedback given by instructor, teaching assistant, and peer reviewers over the 13 weeks of a course. The data are averaged across three successive terms of the same course.

during the first few weeks of a course. As the course progressed, the instructor and teaching assistant continued to mark tests for the first few students completing each unit, but by the end of the course, 90% on average of all unit tests were being peer reviewed.

Table 2 shows data from a single class on the amount of substantive or rich feedback (defined as a comment that is clearly and explicitly related to the question or the student's answer) each student in the class received and provided. Note that students are listed in descending order according to the

TABLE 2
Units of Substantive Feedback Given and Received in the Course

| | | Units of Substantive Feedback | | |
Student	Total	From instructor/ teaching assistant	From other students	To other students
1	36	29	7	32
2	38	27	11	28
3	45	20	25	48
4	46	18	28	68
5	23	15	8	75
6	69	12	57	43
7	40	9	31	40
8	29	7	22	7
9	42	7	35	42
10	28	4	24	28
11	33	3	30	47
12	57	3	54	25
13	56	2	54	23
14	66	2	64	20
15	100	1	99	2
16	19	0	19	1
17	25	0	25	32
18	28	0	28	77
19	30	0	30	31
20	34	0	34	73
21	35	0	35	45
22	35	0	35	4
23	39	0	39	3
Total	953	159	794	794

Source: Pear, J. J. and Crone-Todd, D. E., Computers and Education, 38, 221–231, 2002. With permission from Elsevier.

amount of feedback received from the instructor or teaching assistant. It is apparent that all students in the course received the majority of their substantive feedback from peers. Figure 6, which is based on Table 1, contrasts the amount of substantive feedback received from the instructor or teaching assistant with the amount received from peer reviewers. It is clear that the students provided far more substantive feedback than the instructor. We believe that this amount of feedback cannot be equaled in a traditionally taught course.

Figure 7 shows data from the same 23 students from the class used in Table 2. Each student is plotted according to both the amount of substantive feedback received on unit tests and the amount of substantive feedback given while serving as a peer reviewer. Although all students received considerable feedback, a few students gave very little. Nevertheless, a majority of students were near or above a ratio of 1:1 (shown by the diagonal line) for these measures. In other words, most students received as much or more substantive feedback than they gave. Table 3 shows typical examples of the substantive feedback that the students gave. It seems clear that the feedback students gave is of high quality.

Because students provide so much of the feedback in CAPSI-taught courses, it is important that their comments are accurate. A study of feedback accuracy by Martin, Pear, & Martin, (2002b) provided data on two types of errors in feedback given by peer reviewers. Some changes suggested by reviewers were unnecessary because the student's answer in fact contained the required information. Other suggested changes were unnecessary because,

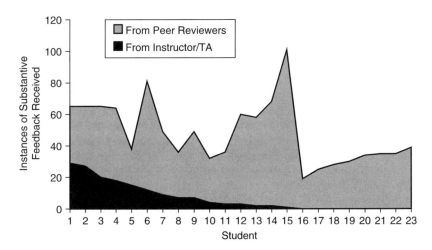

FIGURE 6

Instances of substantive feedback given by the instructor or teaching assistant and by peer reviewers in a typical course.

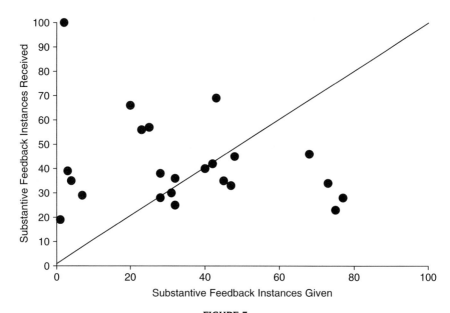

FIGURE 7
Relationship between amount of substantive feedback received and given in a typical course.

TABLE 3
Examples of Substantive Feedback Provided by Students

You are on the right track; however, it is not quite clear if you fully understand the concepts. The examples are not complete; check out page 5. The first example does not show circular reasoning and in the second example, pursue what? Using examples is a great way to convey ideas. Just make sure they are complete and get your message across.

Correct. It may be helpful to follow up your answer with examples.

Check out page 44 in the text again. *Hint:* Reread item 2. I think you misunderstood the identifying clue. Also, explain your examples in more detail; they do not completely illustrate the concepts.

The explanation for FI is incorrect. Refer to pages 76 and 77 in the text book. Reading the example might help clear up things. Also, the question asked for spaced-responding DRL, not DRI.

Some key info in your explanation of what is specifically wrong is missing. Check out pages 109 and 110. *Hint:* Distinguish behavioral and cognitive psychology. Michael makes some interesting points. Be very careful on your spelling; "cure" should be "cue"—two very different meanings; also, "regence" should be "reference."

Good. Not that it is asked for, but you may want to explain what an "unprogrammed reinforcer" is as it is a new term. Just a thought, but no biggie. Your answer is a perfect answer on its own anyway. Excellent!

Good answer, and good suggestion on a treatment.

Good job. Great example. Could have mentioned a few other situations. See pages 51 under #3 setting.

Source: Pear, J. J. & Crone-Todd, D. E., *Computers and Education*, 38, 221–231, 2002. With permission from Elsevier.

although the student's answer did not contain the information specified in the feedback, that information was not required for mastery. Yet, in the course assessed, 87% of all instances of substantive feedback were free from either kind of error. These results indicate that in this teaching method students receive and give large quantities of high-quality substantive feedback.

Data also suggest that this feedback leads to student learning. Martin *et al.* (2002b) examined occasions on which students answered a particular study question, received substantive feedback on the answer, and subsequently had reason to answer that question again (either on a repeated unit test or on an exam). The subsequent answers improved in ways consistent with the specific content of the feedback in 61% of these instances.

COMPARISON WITH TRADITIONAL COURSES

Thus far, we have not compared CAPSI empirically with traditional courses. Such a comparison is important. Because it is based on PSI to a very large degree, we expect that CAPSI will prove superior to the traditional lecture method (see previous chapter). In addition, there is considerable evidence demonstrating the effectiveness of both computer-based instruction (Kulik & Kulik, 1991) and mastery learning programs (Kulik, Kulik, & Bangert-Drowns, 1990). This should not be surprising if we think of learning an academic subject matter as the learning of a set of largely verbal skills. As with any set of skills, practice of those skills is important in the development of mastery. We would not expect someone to become a competent driver, for example, merely by listening to lectures on driving or watching demonstrations of it. Thus, systems that require active learning and mastery typically produce better learning of academic subjects just as they do of other skills. As indicated previously, students in a CAPSI-taught course write much more and receive far more feedback than would typically be possible in a traditional course.

COMPARISON WITH OTHER COMPUTER-MEDIATED COURSES

Most computer-mediated courses attempt to adapt the computer to traditional methods of teaching. Courses taught in this fashion may be highly unsystematic with little assurance—or the means to ensure—that students are learning much of anything relevant to the subject matter. The problem lies with trying to adapt traditional educational methods—which already lack effectiveness—to an environment that is unsuited to them. Because of its highly systematic procedure (almost by definition; note that the middle initial of PSI stands for "system"), PSI adapts naturally to the computer environment.

Many computer-mediated teaching methods fail to take advantage of the tremendous capacity of the computer to provide structure to student–student and student–instructor interactions. The result frequently is a lack of focus on the course topic in discussions, lack of involvement by many students in the process, and a large quantity of verbal material to be evaluated that represents little actual work by many students. Many courses involving computer-mediated communications use the computer primarily for extended commentary by the instructor and students on given course topics (see Pear & Novak, 1996). CAPSI, in contrast, takes full advantage of the ability of the computer to provide structure to the critical interactions that occur in an educational environment (see Kinsner & Pear, 1990).

EXPANDING ON TECHNOLOGY

We have not addressed the more impressive multimedia capabilities of computers, such as presenting realistic images and simulations. There is no reason why these features should not be exploited to the fullest, once the basic aspects of CAPSI are in place. For example, the computer could provide online teaching sequences prior to a given unit and could test students to determine whether they are ready to be tested by the human components of the system. There is no escaping the fact that, for the foreseeable future, judgments regarding the higher thinking levels will have to be done by humans. Indeed, even if computers were able to make these types of judgments, CAPSI would probably still use peer review if for no other reason than students learn to evaluate their own work by reviewing other's work. Nevertheless, CAPSI can only stand to benefit from any advances that may occur in the field of artificial intelligence. These advances could lead to improved methods for developing CAPSI-taught courses, evaluating and providing feedback to learners in these courses, providing tutorials for them, and analyzing the data resulting from the courses (see Kinsner & Pear, 1988, 1990).

RESEARCH STUDIES ON CAPSI

The system we have described provides many areas for scientific study, including the development of higher-order thinking, the optimal operational levels of the parameters of the peer review system, and the provision of effective feedback to students. Although CAPSI differs significantly from traditional courses, the variables in CAPSI are traditional educational variables. Traditional courses contain textual material on which students are tested, and through discussions and other activities students, as well as instructors, provide information and feedback to other students. CAPSI therefore provides a laboratory for the systematic manipulation and study of traditional educational variables.

References

Bloom, B. S., Englehart, M. D., Furst, E. J., Hill, W. H., & Krathwohl, D. R. (1956). *Taxonomy of educational objectives: The classification of educational goals.* Handbook 1. *The Cognitive Domain.* New York: Longman.

Brothen, T., Wambach, C., & Hansen, G. (2002). Accommodating students with disabilities: PSI as an example of universal instructional design. *Teaching of Psychology,* 29(3), 239–240.

Crone-Todd, D. E., Pear, J. J., & Read, C. N. (2000). Operational definitions for higher-order thinking objectives at the post-secondary level. *Academic Exchange Quarterly,* 4(3), 99–106.

Kinsner, W. & Pear, J. J. (1988). Computer-aided personalized system of instruction for the virtual classroom. *Canadian Journal of Educational Communication,* 17, 21–36.

Kinsner, W. & Pear, J. J. (1990). Dynamic educational system for the virtual campus, in Gattiker, U. E. (Ed.), *Studies in technological innovation and human resources.* Vol. 2. *End-User Training.* Berlin: Walter de Gruyter, pp. 201–228.

Kulik, C.-L. & Kulik, J. A. (1991). Effectiveness of computer-based instruction: An updated analysis. *Computers in Human Behavior,* 7, 75–94.

Kulik, C.-L., Kulik, J. A., & Bangert-Drowns, R. L. (1990). Effectiveness of mastery learning programs: A meta-analysis. *Review of Educational Research,* 60, 265–299.

Martin, T. L., Pear, J. J., & Martin, G. L. (2002a). Analysis of proctor marking accuracy in a computer-aided personalized system of instruction course. *Journal of Applied Behavior Analysis,* 35, 309–312.

Martin, T. L., Pear, J. J., & Martin, G. L. (2002b). Feedback and its effectiveness in a computer-aided personalized system of instruction course. *Journal of Applied Behavior Analysis,* 35, 427–430.

Pear, J. J. & Crone-Todd, D. E. (1999). Personalized system of instruction in cyberspace. *Journal of Applied Behavior Analysis,* 32, 205–209.

Pear, J. J. & Crone-Todd, D. E. (2002). A social constructivist approach to computer-mediated instruction. *Computers and Education,* 38, 221–231.

Pear, J. J., Crone-Todd, D.E., Wirth, K., & Simister, H. (2001). Assessment of thinking levels in students' answers. *Academic Exchange Quarterly,* 5(4), 94–98.

Pear, J. J. & Kinsner, W. (1988). Computer-aided personalized system of instruction: An effective and economical method for short- and long-distance education. *Machine-Mediated Learning,* 2, 213–237.

Pear, J. J. & Novak, M. (1996). Computer-aided personalized system of instruction: A program evaluation. *Teaching of Psychology,* 23(2), 119–123.

Reboy, L. M. & Semb, G. B. (1991). PSI and critical thinking: compatibility or irreconcilable differences? *Teaching of Psychology,* 18(4), 212–215.

Ross, G. A. & Semb, G. B. (1981). Philosophy can teach critical thinking skills. *Teaching Philosophy,* 4, 56–63.

Significant Developments in Evidence-Based Education

The Morningside Model of Generative Instruction: An Integration of Research-Based Practices

KENT JOHNSON   ELIZABETH M. STREET

Morningside Academy   *Central Washington University*

ABOUT MORNINGSIDE ACADEMY

In 1980, Kent Johnson founded Morningside Academy in Seattle, Washington, to provide behaviorally designed academic and social programs for children and youth and to prepare teachers and other school personnel. Morningside has grown to be a corporation with distinct programs serving each of the original goals. First, Morningside Academy is a school, operating during the school year and in summer. Second, Morningside Teachers' Academy participates in formal external partnerships with schools and agencies throughout the United States and Canada. It also offers a summer institute for teachers, graduate students, and other professionals. Morningside's programs are continually evolving to better prepare students for successful schooling and citizenry. This chapter provides an update of a previous article and chapter (Johnson & Layng, 1992, 1994) and describes recent program developments in the Morningside Model of Generative Instruction.

CURRENT WORK

Morningside Academy is a school for elementary and middle school students, most of whom have performed poorly in their previous schools, to catch up and get ahead. Entering students typically score in the first and second quartiles on standardized achievement tests in reading, language, and mathematics. Some have diagnosed learning disabilities (LD); others are labeled as having attention deficit disorder (ADD) or attention deficit/hyperactivity disorder (ADHD). Some lag behind their peer group for no diagnosed reason. Students' IQs range from low average to well above average. A small percentage of students have poor relations with family members and friends, but most do not.

Morningside Academy's elementary school students typically enroll for 1 to 3 years to catch up to their grade level. Many middle-school students enroll for all of middle school. Morningside Academy offers a money-back guarantee for making 2 years of progress in 1 school year in the skill of greatest deficit. In 23 years, Morningside Academy has returned less than 1% of school-year tuition.

The academic program focuses upon the three main foundation skills—reading, writing, and mathematics—including language, facts, skills, concepts, principles, problem solving, and organizational aspects. Literature, social studies, and science are the grist for teaching these foundations. Each student participates in extensive entry assessments of academic, learning, and performance skills. Students with similar needs and goals are grouped together for instruction. Groupings change throughout the day and year, depending on subject matter and student progress.

Morningside Academy's teachers coach students to perform their best using clearly defined rules and expectations for performance and productivity, explicit modeling of high performance, and moment-to-moment monitoring and feedback. Students carry a daily report card throughout the day. Points are earned and recorded for meeting specific academic, learning skills, and citizenship aims that the teacher specifies before each class period. Students share their report cards with their families each day. Many students earn home-based rewards such as extra television, computer access, or telephone time for meeting their aims. In addition, classroom wall charts display the points that each student earns.

In the middle school, in addition to the aforementioned Foundation skills, students learn how to study and perform successfully in content classes in the social and natural sciences and the humanities. Each program explicitly teaches textbook reading, note taking, studying, participating in class discussions, test taking, and essay and report writing.

Morningside Academy offers a 5-week summer school program that focuses on reading, language, writing, and mathematics. The summer school program offers a money-back guarantee for progressing 1 year in the skill of greatest deficit. Morningside Academy has returned less than 2% of summer school tuition.

MORNINGSIDE TEACHERS' ACADEMY

External Partnerships

Morningside Teachers' Academy helps public and private schools and agencies implement its programs through formal external partnerships. Our collaboration with each partner is extensive, usually lasting from 3 to 5 years. Four main goals of external partnerships are (1) to help their students achieve grade level performance; (2) to teach their faculty the assessment, teaching, and learning strategies that will serve them throughout their teaching career; (3) to teach their principals how to become instructional leaders and support their faculty's teaching efforts; and (4) to develop implementation, teacher education, and internal coaching systems to maintain our efforts after we leave. To achieve these goals, we provide 40 to 60 hours of workshops and 30 to 50 days of individualized, in-classroom coaching per school year. Morningside also maintains frequent contact with school district personnel, focusing upon problem solving, program expansion, and self-maintenance, including train-the-trainer models that are suited to a school district's ongoing relationship with its schools. As of this writing, 86 schools and agencies throughout the United States and Canada have contracted for partnerships since 1991.

Summer School Institute (SSI)

Morningside Teachers' Academy offers a 4-week intensive summer institute for individual teachers, graduate students, parents, and other professionals who want to learn our programs. Participants can earn graduate credits. Over 300 professionals have attended SSI since its inception in 1991. Individuals may also contract for school-year internships and sabbaticals and experience a customized institute.

MORNINGSIDE TECHNOLOGY TRANSFER

Each Morningside program is competency and mastery based, with a set of procedures and expected outcomes for both learners and teachers. Morningside takes an applied science approach to teaching the competencies to mastery. In the Morningside system, research-based components of curriculum and instruction are combined into a generic model of teaching and learning. The science of human learning informs the generic model, just as engineering is informed by its parent science, physics. We describe the generic model, the Morningside Model of Generative Instruction, later in the chapter. In this section, we describe the origins of the curriculum and instruction components that we draw upon. In a continuing expansion of best practices, Morningside's leadership (1) seeks out research-based, learner-verified materials, methods, and tools to use during instruction, practice, assessment, and measurement of performance; (2) selects certain research-based curricula and instructional methods to user-test at the Academy; (3) adapts materials, methods, and tools to Morningside's behavioral framework for teaching; (4) user-tests the curricula, methods, and tools at the Academy and collects data on student and teacher performance; (5) develops workshops to teach others how to implement programs that offer improvements over current practice; (6) user-tests the workshops and programs with veteran external partner schools; (7) revises the workshops and makes further adaptations to the programs; (8) designates the program a technology, a practice that is replicable and that can be taught to others; and (9) transfers the technologies to others, as part of the Morningside Model of Generative Instruction.

PHILOSOPHICAL AND EMPIRICAL UNDERPINNINGS

In their 1992 article in the *American Psychologist*, Johnson and Layng described the Morningside Model of Generative Instruction. The Morningside model prescribes a stepwise progression through an instructional sequence from entry to true mastery of an objective and aligns classroom practices with each step in the progression. Instruction has three phases: establishing, practicing, and applying. True mastery is defined as performance that is accurate, speedy, durable, smooth, and useful. Underpinning the model is the selectionist approach to understanding human behavior advocated by psychologist B.F. Skinner and the progressive philosophy of John Dewey.

Skinner first advocated a selectionist approach to understanding human behavior in 1969 in *Contingencies of Reinforcement: A Theoretical Analysis*. Compared to a structuralist approach, which emphasizes form and process, the selectionist approach emphasizes the function of particular behaviors in meeting environmental contingencies. Skinner draws a parallel between the emergence of complex behavioral repertoires and the emergence of complex forms in evolutionary biology. The environment selects simple forms, and a more complex entity gradually emerges. In the case of human behavior, reinforcement or success selects the element. In evolutionary biology, reproductive advantage is responsible. The Morningside Model represents a selectionist approach to understanding complex human behavior and designing instructional protocols. The program builds complex intellectual skills from combinations of successful elements. In addition, the model is, itself, evolutionary. It responds to emerging evidence, refining some practices and discarding others that are ineffective in meeting important educational contingencies.

Dewey's American pragmatism and philosophy of education (1900, 1902, 1916, 1938) describes the kind of selectionist process that occurs during the advanced segments of the Morningside continuum of curriculum and instruction. Dewey emphasizes natural influences over learning, taken from the student's current activity, goals, and values systems, rather than arbitrary parcels of subject matter teaching, teacher-initiated research, and teacher-initiated project assignments. For Dewey, this selection process is automatic and evolving, leading different learners down different functional paths in the real world. Morningside's program begins with basic elements and tools and builds repertoires that make possible the kind of naturally reinforced learning that is characteristic of project-based learning and Dewey's progressive education.

The Morningside model builds on five separate but overlapping streams of research: generativity and contingency adduction; instructional design and implementation; critical thinking, reasoning, and self-regulated decision making; program placement and modification based on continuous measurement; and classroom organization and management, Johnson and Layng (1992, 1994) review the work of numerous behavior analysts and educators whose contributions are reflected in the model, only a few of which will be repeated here.

GENERATIVITY AND CONTINGENCY ADDUCTION

The Morningside model is a model of generative instruction. It hinges on evidence that complex behavioral repertoires emerge without explicit instruction when well-selected component repertoires are appropriately sequenced, carefully instructed, and well rehearsed. Ferster (1965) was among the first behavioral psychologists to observe that new learning and novel behavior is a result of a *rearrangement of existing repertoires*. Epstein, a student of Skinner, used the term *generativity* to describe the unprompted interconnection of existing repertoires to solve a problem (Epstein, 1991; Epstein, Krishnit, Lanza, & Rubin, 1984). Andronis, Layng, & Goldiamond, (1997) applied the term *contingency adduction* to a related phenomenon. In their account, new contingencies or performance requirements may recruit performances learned under other contingencies. The new contingency shares common features with the original contingencies that produced the performance.

Alessi's pivotal paper in 1987 discussed the implications of generativity for the design and power of instruction. He reasoned that most curricular strands have an infinite set of relationships, all of which cannot be taught directly. Instead, children learn to respond to a general case; they learn a pattern of responding that produces effective responding to many untrained relations. The elegance of an instructional program depends on the programmer's ability to detect and teach some minimal response or generative set which can combine and recombine into the universal set of possible relationships.

Although the phenomenon of contingency adduction or generativity occurs naturally, the arrangement of events to maximize its occurrence does not. Morningside programs are generative because they focus on specific sequences of skills, teach minimum response repertoires, and establish the general case. Instructional programs are built on a logical and empirical analysis of the knowledge, skills, and relationships in a field of study. Skills are introduced in an order that makes it most likely that previously learned skills will be recruited to meet new performance requirements.

A SYSTEM OF INSTRUCTION

Morningside adopts a scientific approach that builds on a system of instruction first outlined by Markle and Tiemann (1967) at the University of Illinois at Chicago. Instructional protocols are developed according to a set of principles, and programs are tested on naïve learners to ensure they produce intended results. Designers begin with clearly stated goals and *objectives*, conduct *content and task analyses* to identify curricular tasks on which mastery of terminal objectives hinges, construct *criterion tests* that fairly represent the stated outcomes, specify the *entry repertoire* the learner must demonstrate in order to be successful in the program, design an *instructional sequence* using the minimum set of instructional tasks required to achieve the outcome, and adjust the program based on *performance data* from naïve learners.

Central to the system are (1) a thorough analysis of the content area that is the subject for instruction; (2) instructional protocols that match what Robert Gagne (1965) and others have called types of learning, learning typologies, or learning outcomes; (3) ordering of elements in the curriculum to ensure that learners progress through it seamlessly; (4) elegant instructional protocols that achieve outcomes with the minimum amount of instructional intervention; and (5) field-testing and fine-tuning curricular assumptions and instructional programs at every turn. Morningside likes this system because Morningside, too, is an evolutionary system. Programs are evaluated on the basis of their ability to produce happy, competent learners, naturally reinforced by progress. When programs don't, they are changed.

ESTABLISHING OBJECTIVES
AND ANALYZING CONTENT

When Morningside designers develop an interest in a content area, they read research in the field, examine scope and sequence charts from a variety of curricular materials, and review existing instructional protocols. The work of establishing instructional objectives and analyzing content is interdependent rather than linear. Typically, a general goal is established, and the instructional design team begins a dance between understanding the topic of study and setting explicit objectives that derive from it. Content analysis uncovers critical foundational skills that learners must master to meet terminal goals. Content analysis at Morningside is of two primary types: content-dependent and content-independent.

Content-Dependent Analysis

As Morningside's content analysts become familiar with the overall contour of the content area, they identify major skill sets within it. Major skill sets may be thought of as the socially validated goals of instruction within a content area. Once major skills sets are identified, analysts attempt to discover the broad range of sub-skills and knowledge that make up these socially validated outcomes. Fine-grained task analyses reveal tool skills and component skills that constitute the authentic outcomes. Underlying knowledge and skills are organized to discover common foundational skills (*tool skills*) and common second-level skills (*component skills*) that constitute more complex composite or *compound skills*. In essence, the analyst builds, from the various major skill sets, a series of overlapping pyramids that have common foundational building blocks and component skills. This work serves three purposes. It reveals a hierarchy of foundational skills which, when mastered, will aid in acquiring higher-level skills. It also reveals where particular skills should be inserted into the scope and sequence. Last, it clarifies when order of presentation of a skill in the instructional sequence is critical and when it is not.

Content-Independent Analysis

In addition to content-dependent analyses, Morningside designers analyze content according to content-independent typologies. Two primary typologies form the basis of this work: *learning channel analysis* and *learning outcomes analysis*.

Learning Channels

Haughton (1980) applied the term learning channel to a method of describing objectives on the basis of their stimulus and response characteristics. Stimulus characteristics, in this model, are defined in terms of the sense through which the stimulus is experienced. Using everyday language, Haughton referred to them as see, hear, touch, smell, and taste. Later, he added "think" (which now is referred to as "free") to describe stimuli that are not present in the external environment but rather reside in the history of the learner. Response characteristics are described on the basis of common movements (for example, say, write, point, and do). A stimulus–response pair (for example, see–write, hear–point, free–say) is called a *learning channel*. Designation of learning channels allows the instructional programmer to ensure that all combinations required to operate effectively in authentic tasks are included in the instructional regimen.

Learning Outcomes

Morningside analysts rely heavily on Tiemann and Markle's analysis of *learning outcomes* which first appeared in their text, *Analyzing Instructional Content* (1983,

1990). Tiemann and Markle's typology is reminiscent of Gagne's types of learning first described in his seminal work, *The Conditions of Learning* (1965). Tiemann and Markle's account extends Gagne's work, provides a different classification scheme that is somewhat more teacher friendly, and, most important, includes extensive training in how to develop efficient instructional protocols. Nine learning outcomes are proposed: three psychomotor skills, three simple cognitive skills, and three complex cognitive skills. Morningside's programs focus primarily on simple and complex cognitive skills. An instructional protocol is matched to each type and channel of learning and becomes a kind of authoring system into which new content can be entered, producing a more or less explicit script for teachers to follow in facilitating the learner's progress.

Instructional Program Development

We either develop our own instructional materials or select, enhance, and incorporate promising materials into the existing content analysis. When otherwise promising materials fail to use empirically supported protocols for skill acquisition or provide insufficient opportunities to practice, Morningside designers overlay instructional protocols or design additional practice to ensure that the material meets Morningside's standards.

The Morningside design team develops or selects protocols and programs for both well-defined and hard-to-define objectives. Following Markle's (1990) and Engelmann and Carnine's (1982) recommendations, instruction for well-defined objectives minimizes teacher talk in favor of active responding by students. Designers strive for faultless communications in which only one conclusion is possible. Morningside designers also favor lean programs that move students out of instructional routines into practice routines as quickly as possible. Current instructional design efforts attempt to teach the more difficult-to-define strategic objectives as principle applications, a complex cognitive skill in the Tiemann and Markle model, and then support students to add the novel strategies necessary to solve a series of problems without assistance.

Instructional programs are designed to fit the learner. Desired performances are broken down until they link with an individual learner's entering repertoire. There are no assumptions based on age or grade of the learner. Instead, learners are placed into instructional programs that coincide with their individual entering repertoires. Often corrective or remedial learners can skip segments of instruction because their foundation repertoires are spotty. Performance data collected during instruction ensures that students skip segments at appropriate times. Sometimes performance data reveal that additional lessons or program pieces are needed to form a bridge between the learners' current repertoires and the terminal goal.

The instructional block at Morningside is made up of three primary activities: instruction, practice, and application. Each instructional objective or set of objectives is taught in these three phases.

Instruction

Instruction refers to establishing a new repertoire; learners acquire a skill that they could not perform previously. Instructional protocols teach basic academic skills, including associations, sequences, concepts, and principle applications. The specific format of the lesson is a function of the learning channel and learning outcome of the task it is designed to teach.

During instruction to establish acquisition, students engage with a teacher in highly interactive lessons that introduce one skill at a time and combine skills as accuracy emerges. Gilbert's mathetics model (1962a,b) is the primary method for establishing new well-defined skills. Lessons are fairly tightly structured, and their design is intended to produce the speediest possible acquisition of new skills, judged by the degree to which they match an expert's performance—in this case, the teacher's performance or the "answer key." Each instructional lesson is an interchange between the teacher and a single learner, a small group of learners, or an entire class.

When component skills require brief, uniform responses, we employ Engelmann's Direct Instruction (DI) variant of mathetics (Englemann & Carnine, 1982). In DI, teachers present scripted lessons to learners, who answer teacher-initiated questions in unison. Teachers and students move through a series of questions in a predictable way, providing attending cues to ensure that all students are focused on the question and signals to ensure that students respond together. Teacher and students volley many times a minute with their questions and answers. Teachers praise and correct student responses until all students are accurate. Logically and empirically validated sequences lead students through nearly errorless learning in which stimulus discrimination is explicitly taught and response forms are shaped. The explicitness and careful progression of DI lessons ensures that students develop flawless skills very quickly.

The challenge for teachers is to faithfully present the lesson as designed, achieve choral responding among learners, listen carefully to the quality of their responses, provide encouraging feedback following correct responses, and apply error correction procedures that effectively reduce errors. Even though teachers may consult the script during the lesson, they must be conversant enough with its pattern to maintain eye and ear contact with learners. The best results occur when teachers are able to implement programs with a great deal of procedural reliability, although the method is robust enough to accommodate small lapses in procedure.

Throughout instruction, teachers address errors as they arise. Errors provide an opportunity to determine imperfections in the instructional lesson or provide for immediate and error-specific error correction. If it becomes apparent that several elements necessary for correct responding are missing for some or all students, the teacher may conduct a brief review to firm up a tool or component skill or revert to a point in the curriculum where performance stabilizes.

Although they are best known for teaching tool and component skills, Direct Instruction lessons have been designed to teach many complex skills in word problem solving, pre-algebra and algebra, chemistry, earth science, economics, history, logic and argumentation rules, and study skills, to name a few. Once basic foundations skills, including learning skills, are established, teachers can shift instruction from DI to a looser mathetics approach. Thus, we have a continuum of Direct Instruction that starts with Engelmann and Carnine's very formal DI and graduates learners to the more general mathetics case.

Establishing and acquiring are the gateway to mastery and fluency, but they are not synonymous with it. We have found that students who move from skill to skill with halting, if accurate, performance encounter greater and greater difficulty with each subsequent skill. Thus, when prescribed levels of accuracy emerge, students enter the second stage: the practice stage.

Practice

Following successfully completed instructional lessons, students practice their freshly learned skills until they achieve levels of performance characterized by durability and applicability. Practice is timed, highly structured, goal-oriented, and continuously monitored.

Practice sessions apply Precision Teaching (PT) technology, an approach that defines mastery in terms of rate of response. Morningside adopted PT early on and has been a partner in its continued development. The approach was conceived by Lindsley (1972, 1990) at the University of Kansas in his quest for a mechanism that brought continuous measurement and rate data into educational practice. A student and colleague, Haughton (1972) developed the now-standard 1-minute timing to track performance frequencies during practice. Lindsley and Haughton promoted practice regimens that quickly produced high-frequency accuracy rates and low-frequency error rates on well-calibrated curriculum slices.

Morningside recommends optimal performance frequencies that may be characterized as *fluent*. As a metaphor, fluent performance is flowing, flexible, effortless, errorless, automatic, confident, second nature, and masterful. Fluent performance is fun, energetic, naturally reinforced behavior. Binder (1993, 1996) coined the term *fluency building* to refer to practice activities that are designed to achieve these goals. Currently at Morningside, five characteristics of performance determine fluent performance frequencies: retention, endurance, stability, application, and adduction (RESAA). Until a frequency aim has been empirically demonstrated to produce these five characteristics of fluent performance, we use the term *frequency building* instead of fluency building.

Morningside students spend as much as 40% of their school day practicing skills, much of it in the context of our peer coaching technology (Johnson & Layng, 1992, 1994). During peer coaching, pairs of students work together to build skills to achieve frequency aims, although sometimes they practice alone or in threes. During practice, students time themselves on specially designed frequency-building materials until they can perform a certain amount—accurately, smoothly, and without hesitation—in a certain amount of time. Students record their timed performance on specially designed charts, called *Standard Celeration Charts* (Lindsley, 1972, 1990; Graf & Lindsley, 2002; Pennypacker, Gutierrez, Lindsley, 2003).

Teachers set both performance and celeration aims. Performance aims tell the student how many of a skill they should be able to do in the timing period. Celeration is a measure of the change in rate over time and indicates whether the student is reaching a performance aim in a timely manner. A celeration aim is a line of progress drawn on a chart at a certain angle from the learner's first performance frequency to the frequency aim. The celeration line tells how many days it should take for the student to reach the performance aim, thus providing an empirical definition of progress. As students practice, they plot their own frequencies and compare their progress to the celeration aim lines. Their comparisons tell them whether they are making sufficient progress or whether they need to ask the teacher or another student for help.

Timings typically are of 1-minute duration, although students will do several timings in a single practice session. For selected tasks, students who meet their performance aim during a 1-minute timing move into an *endurance phase*. Endurance training ensures that students maintain speed and accuracy for appropriately long periods of time.

Application

Application is the third activity that occurs in a daily class session at Morningside. After instruction and practice, students apply the skills they have learned in the context of compound-composite tasks such as games, simulations, and real-world applications. Effective application activities adduce a combination of key component elements already in the learner's repertoire to achieve a certain outcome or effect. Application activities may involve explicit, direct instruction in the necessary recombination of elements or they may function as probes to assess automatic combinations of elements.

Most classroom schedules today are driven by activities, not instruction. The activities are made up of challenging compounds to stimulate creative principle application and problem solving. Project-based learning is currently in vogue from late elementary school through college. Most project-based learning arrangements are an "upside-down" approach to curriculum planning: They assume that students can perform all the component elements and that the composite, compound tasks will produce the appropriate contingency adduction. Proponents contend that projects are inherently interesting and stimulating and believe these anticipated motivational features outweigh component skill weaknesses. The assumption is that, if the task is sufficiently interesting, learners will employ a battery of skills to figure it out. In the end, some learners do and some learners don't. While we agree that meaningful projects are important educational endeavors, we design Dewey's progressive, real-world applications by introducing compounds later in a "right-side-up" sequence of instruction that teaches from elements to compounds.

We design at least two kinds of application activities. The first kind requires the student to engage in a previously learned performance in a new context. For example, after reading essays in their controlled reading program and engaging in teacher-directed discussions, students may read a newspaper and discuss the articles with their peers or write a letter to the editor of the newspaper about a particular article after learning and practicing the basic rubrics of writing a persuasive essay.

An important reading application activity in our curriculum involves strategically applying comprehension skills during reading. In this application, students, working in groups, take turns reading a selection aloud. At certain points, a teacher stops the reading and engages in "think aloud" monologues that model applications of comprehension skills that students have previously acquired. The teacher may pause the group reading at various points to make a prediction about what will happen next or what a character will do or may make a connection between the plot or a character and the teacher's own life experience. After two or three think-alouds, the teacher uses a *delayed prompting method* to assess and prompt students to apply previously acquired skills. First, the teacher calls on a student at certain points during the group reading to make a prediction or connection that will help to make sense of the reading or help the student relate more closely to it. If the student does not respond competently, the teacher provides very general prompts to adduce the application. If the student's application still does not meet criterion, prompts become increasingly specific and intensive, eventually moving to a full model of the application as needed for the student to achieve a successful response. Thus, the student stays engaged with the teacher until becoming successful, no matter how many volleys are required between them. The teacher provides increasing support until the student is successful. The relevant data to collect are the number and kind of teacher prompts that are provided, not the accuracy of the student's response, as all students stay engaged with the teacher until they are successful. This delayed prompting method is a reverse of mathetics, in which the teacher demonstrates, then prompts, then tests. Here the teacher tests, then prompts, then finally models until student performance meets criterion. Delayed prompting could be used to promote any application.

The second kind of application activity we design requires new combinations of previously learned elements. More advanced operations in arithmetic, such as long multiplication or division of numbers, are combinations of previously taught addition, subtraction, and multiplication elements. More advanced forms of sentences and compositions are combinations of elements learned separately during previous writing instruction. More advanced field sports are combinations of many previously learned motor activities and chains. The compound called debating combines elements such as argumentation rules, oratory style, and quick refutation. The elements in all of these activities can be separately taught; the compound can be taught as an application activity that can recruit the necessary elements.

Both kinds of application activities promote generativity and contingency adduction, helping to evolve creative thinkers and problem solvers over time. Applying generic reasoning and self-regulation skills also greatly improves application performance. Students can learn to monitor their own performance and apply reasoning skills to recruit appropriate component elements they have already mastered.

Instructional Blocks

Morningside devotes 90 minutes daily to the primary academic content areas of reading, mathematics, and writing. Time is allocated to ensure adequate time for instruction, practice, and application of skills. Teachers divide time among building tool skills, building component skills, and building compound skills.

Critical Thinking and Self-Regulation

Morningside directly instructs and monitors improvement in strategic thinking, reasoning, and self-monitoring skills. Strategic thinking is the glue that allows students to employ component skills and strategies in productive problem solving. Typically, problems provide opportunities for learners to combine known associations, algorithms, and concepts in ways that may not be dictated by an existing formula or that may yield more than one answer. Morningside's instructional and practice strategies build tool and component skills that are readily accessible for problem solving, but they do not instill the reflective contingencies that are required to adduce relevant knowledge and skills to solve a particular problem.

In opposition to some contemporary educational practice, we directly teach a productive type of thinking called problem solving through reasoning. It involves a dance between a speaker and a listener residing in the same body. Self, as speaker, constantly provides practical, supplementary verbal stimulation to self, as listener. The speaker constructs responses during a series of private volleys, prompts, and probes of the learner's own behavior. At Morningside, we view the failure to self-monitor and reason during problem solving as a failure of instruction rather than as a failure of the learner. This perspective has provided a challenge to develop instructional strategies that turn learners into productive thinkers and problem solvers.

In response, Morningside turned to an approach developed by Whimbey and Lockhead in the 1970s (Whimbey & Lockhead, 1999). Procedures for thinking-aloud problem solving (TAPS) were developed originally to improve analytical reasoning skills of college students. Whimbey and colleagues, in *Blueprint for Educational Change* (1993), cite five categories of common errors in problem solving: inaccurate reading, inaccurate thinking, weak problem analysis, lack of perseverance, and failure to think aloud. Robbins (Robbins, 1996; Robbins 1995) adapted Whimbey and Lockhead's methodology for younger children and has proceduralized the instructional regimen. She has designed scripted instruction to ensure that elementary school students can engage in the reasoning process. During TAPS instruction, teachers model both speaker/ problem-solver and active listener roles and verify that students can identify the behaviors associated with the characteristics of each role. Teachers model process errors, and learners catch them. Learners then take turns playing each role, making occasional errors that other learners must detect. The TAPS instructional program begins as a training exercise using complex problem-solving and logic exercises, but as learners' skills with both repertoires become firm, teachers integrate the procedure into all academic areas. At Morningside, we employ the Robbins TAPS design in three stages. Students first develop each role—problem solver and active listener—in pairs and then learn to serve both roles simultaneously, moving back and forth between offering solutions and then critiquing and encouraging performance, first publicly, then privately.

Morningside teaches TAPS as an underlying repertoire that structures discovery learning. TAPS routines facilitate the combination of elements that have been learned as well-defined tasks. TAPS also helps to reform the isolated skills and clarify how they interlock or chain together. A delayed prompting method can be used to teach such specific reasoning routines, and students can engage in these strategies during TAPS to combine elements and solve problems successfully. Technically, current problems may occasion certain reasoning routines embedded in a generic TAPS repertoire, which in turn may produce the contingencies that result in the appropriate recombination of already-mastered component elements.

Self-Direction and Independence

When visitors drop by Morningside Academy, they might very well get the best lesson in the Morningside model from one of the students. This is because Morningside teachers constantly and intentionally strive to make the instructional protocols and decision-making process transparent to parents and students. They encourage students to take charge of their own learning. Students chart their own timings and begin to set their own celeration aims—sometimes much more ambitious ones than the teacher would have set for them. Students manage their own practice and recommend program modifications. They know when programs are working and when they are not. Students learn important goal-setting, self-monitoring, self-management, organizational, and cooperative learning skills. They also learn self-management and self-determination through the freedom to take their own performance breaks and still meet their expected goals, skip lessons when they can demonstrate mastery, move through the curriculum at their own pace, select their own arrangement of tasks to accomplish in a class period, choose their own free-time activities, and give themselves report card points, among other opportunities.

PROGRAM PLACEMENT AND MONITORING BASED ON CONTINUOUS MEASUREMENT OF PERFORMANCE

A hallmark of Morningside procedures is the continuous interplay between instruction and assessment. The primary purpose of assessment at Morningside is to ensure that students are correctly placed in an instructional program and that they are making gains that promise long-term academic benefit. Assessment at Morningside consists of five primary elements:

- Standardized norm referenced assessment, typically administered twice yearly, gauges a learner's performance level in relation to peers and gauges growth using socially validated measures of performance.
- Diagnostic/prescriptive testing determines initial placement in an instructional program.
- Weekly standardized performance probes track progress through a curriculum using the curriculum-based measurement (CBM; Knutson & Shinn, 1991) technology developed at the University of Oregon.
- Daily measurement of accuracy and rate of responding on highly calibrated tool and component skills using PT technology dictate progress through a program.
- Portfolios authentically illustrate and provide social validation of students' progress.

The speed with which students can complete a course of study is dependent, at least in part, on the accuracy of their program placement. Morningside uses a variety of diagnostic and placement instruments to determine a student's placement in a program. Some are more formal than others, and it is common for Morningside teachers and administrators to use more than one measure to ensure correct placement. Morningside also tracks progress on important learning outcomes throughout the year, using CBM protocols. The most common CBM measures are in reading, math, spelling, and writing.

Assessments are timed, and performance is scored according to explicit CBM criteria. Because CBM measures are somewhat more molar than the molecular measures charted on a daily basis in classrooms and because they are more explicitly representative of state curriculum standards and standardized achievement test objectives, they provide external validation of the student's growth.

By far the most important tool for the teacher in monitoring the effectiveness of instructional programs is Precision Teaching timing and Standard Celeration Charting. The chart provides a picture of the learner's performance rate, error rate, and growth rate in a standardized format that allows teachers to make decisions at a glance about the learner's progress (Johnson & Layng, 1992, 1994). Teachers and students use these learning pictures to make daily decisions about what would be best for the learner to do next, how to allocate classroom time, when the curriculum step or slice is too large or too small, and when the timing protocol requires modification.

CLASSROOM MANAGEMENT

Morningside classrooms are busy, high-energy classrooms, and teachers manage many instructional activities simultaneously. Morningside's commitment to learning and, in many cases, to making up for lost time means that students need to be academically engaged throughout a class period. There is no time to waste, no time for disruptive behavior. All of this means that teachers need to establish workable classroom routines, and students need to develop a battery of skills that support their learning.

The Daily Report Card has evolved since Morningside's inception (Johnson, 2004) to become the first line of prevention in Morningside teachers' classroom management toolbox. At the beginning of each day, students receive a daily report card on which is listed their classes and expectations for the day. Students earn points for demonstrating four categories of skills: academic, learning, organization, and citizenship. Students receive academic skill points for their ability to meet or exceed performance aims and to demonstrate adduction or generativity. Learning skills points reward "looking like a student," answering on signal, following along with the lesson, and following directions. Organization skill points acknowledge students being on time, having their materials, keeping their work area neat, and charting in pencil. Citizenship points are awarded for using appropriate language, respecting other people's space, using one's voice appropriately, using one's body appropriately, and respecting physical property.

Behavioral expectations are clearly stated and posted on the wall. At the beginning of the school year and when new students enter the program, teachers model and prompt the behaviors that are expected. Teachers distribute points in each category throughout each class period. At the end of the day, students meet individually with their teachers to discuss their academic progress and comportment. The teacher writes summary comments, and students take the report cards to their parents, who in some instances sign and return them. As students transition to project-based learning, daily reports become less structured.

EMPIRICAL DATA SUPPORTING TECHNOLOGY TRANSFER OF THE MORNINGSIDE MODEL OF GENERATIVE INSTRUCTION

Four features of the Morningside Model constitute its core: (1) learner-verified instructional methods, tools, and programs are incorporated for basic academic and learning skill development; (2) a significant amount of school time is allocated to practice, using fluency and celeration; (3) children learn reasoning, thinking, problem-solving, research, and cooperative learning skills; and (4) children are transitioned into more independent learning environments in which they apply their basic academic, reasoning, research, and cooperative skills to learning social studies, science, and literature, according to their interests. Morningside Academy arranges such a learning environment for its children and youth, and they make enormous progress in school.

The remarkable results of Morningside Academy's initial 11-year study of its children's mean standardized test gains in reading, language arts, and mathematics have been reported elsewhere (Johnson & Layng, 1992, 1994). Reading averaged 2.5 years growth per school year. By the end of the study, language arts gains approached an average of 4 grade levels and mathematics gains rose to more than 3 grade levels of improvement per school year. Morningside completed its formal lab school evaluation process in the spring of 1992. Currently, it assesses its students in September and June on a variety of in-house, state, and national measures. Children's median achievement test performance remains above 2 grade levels per year in reading, language arts, and math.

Since 1991, Morningside Teachers' Academy (MTA) has successfully implemented programs with over 17,000 students in Illinois, Washington, Georgia, Pennsylvania, British Columbia, South Dakota, and Oklahoma. Students in the Chicago Public Schools, the Nechako School District in British Columbia, the Seattle Public Schools, DeKalb County (Georgia) Public Schools, and elsewhere have profited from our services. MTA has also contracted with several First Nation and American Indian schools in British Columbia, Washington, South Dakota, and Oklahoma, helping them to develop programs in their schools and adult literacy centers. Adult learners in the City Colleges of Chicago and at Motorola Corporation in Phoenix have also made enormous strides in their reading, writing, reasoning, and math skills. Student achievement test results will be reported in a forthcoming book (Johnson and Street, 2004, in press).

CONCLUSION

Morningside has more than 20 years of commitment to the ideals of educational accountability and empirically verified approaches to instruction, one that places the responsibility for student success squarely on the shoulders of educators. Schools are not to act as mere sorting machines for determining degrees of natural, genetic, or pre-existing talent. Instead they must act so that all children are literate and can function as effective citizens in a democracy. We have inherited children who have been left behind, and we have helped them catch up and move ahead. We have believed that if the child was not learning, we were not teaching. We have included learners in the teaching process, as coaches with each other. We have reformed our practices until the evidence revealed that our practices work for kids. And, we have shared the effective practices with others whose children were left behind. We have stood behind our practices, offering parents money-back learning guarantees. In the end, we believe we have helped define what it *really* means to leave no child behind.

Acknowledgments

This chapter is a short version of a book (Johnson & Street, 2004) that is being published concurrently. Dr. Kent Johnson is the executive director of Morningside Academy and Morningside Teachers' Academy. Dr. Elizabeth Street is a professor of psychology and executive assistant to the president at Central Washington University. She also has been a consultant to Morningside Academy throughout its existence. We are indebted to Drs. Joanne Robbins, T. V. Joe Layng, and Warren Street for their thoughtful comments and editorial assistance during the development of this book chapter. We also are indebted to the many teachers at Morningside and at partner schools and agencies whose feedback and insights have strengthened the Morningside Model, and to the students whose learning has been the most important feedback of all.

References

Alessi, G. (1987). Generative strategies and teaching for generalization. *The Analysis of Verbal Behavior*, 5, 15–27.

Andronis, P. T., Layng, T. V. J., & Goldiamond, I. (1997). Contingency adduction of "symbolic aggression" by pigeons. *The analysis of verbal behavior*, 14, 5–17.

Binder, C. V. (1993). Behavioral fluency: a new paradigm. *Education Technology*, Oct., 8–14.

Binder, C. V. (1996). Behavioral fluency: evolution of a new paradigm. *The Behavior Analyst*, 19, 163–197.

Dewey, J. (1900). *The school and society*. Chicago: University of Chicago Press.

Dewey, J. (1902). *The Child and the Curriculum*. Chicago: University of Chicago Press.

Dewey, J. (1916). *Democracy and education: An introduction to the philosophy of education*. New York: Free Press.

Dewey, J. (1938). *Experience and education*. New York: Collier Books/Macmillan.

Engelmann, S. & Carnine, D. W. (1982). *Theory of instruction: Principles and applications*. New York: Irvington.

Epstein, R. (1991). Skinner, creativity, and the problem of spontaneous behavior. *Psychological Science*, 2, 362–370.

Epstein, R., Kirshnit, R., Lanza, R., & Rubin, R. (1984). "Insight" in the pigeon: antecedents and determinants of an intelligent performance. *Nature*, 308, 61–62.

Ferster, C. (1965). Verbal behavior as magic (paper presented at the 50th anniversary conference of the graduate school of education, The University of Pennsylvania.) in Ferster, C. B., Culbertson, S., & Boren, M. C. P. (Eds.), *Behavior principles*, 2nd ed.(1975) Engelwood Cliffs, NJ: Prentice Hall, pp. 563–568.

Gagne, R. (1965). *The Conditions of learning*. New York: Holt, Rinehart, & Winston.

Gilbert, T. (1962a). Mathetics: The technology of education. *Journal of Mathetics*, 1(1), 7–74.

Gilbert, T. (1962b). Mathetics II: The design of teaching exercises. *Journal of Mathetics*, 1(2), 7–56.

Graf, S. A. & Lindsley, O. R. (2002). *Standard celeration charting 2002*, Preliminary ed. Poland, OH: Graf Implements.

Haughton, E. (1972). Aims: growing and sharing, in Jordan, J. B. & Robbins, L. S. (Eds.), *Let's try doing something else kind of thing*. Arlington, VA: Council for Exceptional Children, pp. 20–39.

Haughton, E. (1980). Practicing practices: learning by activity. *Journal of Precision Teaching*, 1(3), 3–20.

Johnson, K. (2004). *The daily report card*. Seattle, WA: Morningside Press.

Johnson, K. R. & Layng, T. V. J. (1992). Breaking the structuralist barrier: literacy and numeracy with fluency. *American Psychologist*, 47, 1475–1490.

Johnson, K. R. & Layng, T. V. J. (1994). The Morningside model of generative instruction, in Gardner, R., Sainato, D., Cooper, J., Heron, T., Heward, W., Eshleman, J., & Grossi, T. (Eds.), *Behavior analysis in education: focus on measurably superior instruction*. Belmont, CA: Brooks/Cole, pp. 173–197.

Johnson, K. & Street, E. M. (2004). The morning side model of generative instruction. Boston, MA: Cambridge Centre for Behavioral Studies, in Press (www.behavior.org).

Knutson, N. & Shinn, M. R. (1991). Curriculum-based measurement: Conceptual underpinnings and integration into problem-solving assessment. *Journal of School Psychology*, 29, 371–393.

Lindsley, O. R. (1972). From Skinner to precision teaching: the child knows best, in Jordan, J. B. & Robbins, L. S. (Eds.), *Let's try doing something else kind of thing*. Arlington, VA: Council for Exceptional Children, pp. 1–11.

Lindsley, O. R. (1990). Precision teaching: by teachers for children. *Teaching Exceptional Children*, 22(3), 10–15.

Markle, S. M. (1990). *Designs for instructional designers*. Champaign, IL: Stipes.

Markle, S. M. & Tiemann, P. W. (1967). *Programming Is a process* [film]. Chicago: University of Illinois.

Pennypacker, H. S., Gutierrez, A., & Lindsley, O. R. (2003). *Handbook of the standard celeration chart*, Deluxe ed. (www.behavior.org).

Robbins, J. K. (1996). *TAPS for teachers. Seattler, WA: Robbins Layng & Associates.*

Robbins, J. K., Layng, T. V. J., & Jackson, P. J. (1996). *Fluent thinking skills*. Seatler, WA: Robbins Layng & Associate.

Skinner, B. F. (1969). *Contingencies of reinforcement: A theoretical analysis*. New York: Appleton-Century-Crofts.

Tiemann, P. W. & Markle, S. M. (1983, 1990). *Analyzing instructional content: A guide to instruction and evaluation*. Champaign, IL: Stipes.

Whimbey, A. & Lockhead, J. (1999). *Problem solving and comprehension*, 6th ed. Mahwah, NJ: Erlbaum.

Whimbey, A., Johnson, M., Williams, E., & Linden, M. (1993). *Blueprint for educational change: Improving reasoning, literacies, and science achievement with cooperative learning*. Washington, D.C.: The Right Combination, Inc.

Learning Efficiency Goes to College

GUY S. BRUCE

Saint Cloud State University, APEX Consulting

INTRODUCTION

According to the latest government data from the National Center for Educational Statistics, only 36.5% of students with the goal of earning a Bachelor's degree who enrolled in a 4-year institution in 1996 completed that degree within 4 years (Berkner, He, Cataldi, & Knepper, 2002). This figure is troubling for several reasons. Students who do not complete their degrees within 4 years have wasted a large amount of money and time, both theirs and society's. Colleges and universities are heavily subsidized by taxpayers, and the costs of education are justified only if our institutions are producing graduates prepared for employment in their field of study.

What factors predict timely completion of a bachelor's degree? "The characteristics of students who were mostly likely to graduate within four years with a bachelor's degree fit a commonly held perception of what a college student looks like—he or she receives a good academic preparation in high school, enters college immediately after high school, enrolls in college full time, and is continuously enrolled" (Berkner et al., 2002, p. x). Other factors that predict success include type of institution attended, gender, race, and dependent family income.

As a college professor, there is nothing that I can do to change these predictors, except perhaps for one. "Students who entered college with good academic preparation—those who received mostly As in high school took two

267

or more Advanced Placement tests, or had high SAT scores—also had higher completion rates than others. About 80 percent competed a bachelor's degree within 6 years, and more than one-half (55 and 61 percent) graduated within 4 years" (Berkner et al., 2002, p. *vii*). Although it is clear that good academic preparation increases a student's chances of success, what is unclear is how that works. Do students with good academic backgrounds have better study and study management skills? If so, perhaps it is those skills that help them persist. Traditional college courses rely much more heavily on student skills than the typical high school course. Most professors still use the "lecture, assign, and test" method. It is up to the students to design their own study materials and use them effectively to prepare for tests.

When I asked the students in my CPSY 101 course (a freshman Community Psychology course) if they had ever been taught how to study, only one or two raised their hands. I then tested their skill at writing study questions by asking them to prepare a test over an assigned reading. Most wrote very simple, definition-type questions, unlike the type that professors typically ask. Few had ever used flash cards, and none reported keeping track of their progress as they studied for tests. Studying is hard work. If students see little or no progress when they study, they may find it difficult to persist.

So, I decided to teach them two skill sets: (1) how to study for college tests, and (2) how to track their own progress as they studied. I taught them how to write study questions like the kind that a professor might ask and how to use those materials to prepare for college tests. I also taught them how to measure, chart, and evaluate their own progress as they studied for tests. I called this progress measure their *learning efficiency*.

WHAT IS LEARNING EFFICIENCY?

Learning efficiency is a measure of improvement in performance accuracy and speed per amount of learning time. To calculate learning efficiency, we must measure two things: (1) performance improvement, and (2) learning time:

$$\text{Learning Efficiency} \ = \ \text{Performance Improvement} \ \div \ \text{Learning Time}$$

Performance improvement is the improvement in a learner's accuracy and speed as a result of that learner's interaction with a learning program. Suppose two students take their final exams on the first day and the last day of class. The improvement in their test performance is a measure of how much they learned during the course. One student correctly answered 1 question per minute on the pre-test and 10 questions per minute on the post-test, achieving an improvement of 9 correct per minute. The other correctly answered 9 questions per minute on the pre-test and 10 per minute on the post-test, achieving an improvement of 1 correct answer per minute. Which one learned more? The student that made the most improvement learned the most. Performance improvement allows us to assess the effectiveness of a course but not its efficiency. To measure learning efficiency, we need to measure learning time.

Learning time is the amount of time that learners spend interacting with the learning program. Consider two additional students in our course. Both made the same amount of improvement, from correctly answering 5 questions per minute on the pre-test to 10 questions per minute on the post-test, but was the course equally efficient for both? Suppose that we asked both students to record the number of minutes each spent studying for the course. The data revealed something interesting: One student spent twice as much time as the other to get the same improvement. That second student displayed greater learning efficiency by achieving the same performance improvement in one-half the learning time.

Learning efficiency is a measure of academic progress that takes into account both performance improvement *and* the student's learning time. The higher the learning efficiency, the less time it takes for learners to achieve competence. If students were to collect data on their own learning efficiency, such data would provide them with more feedback on their progress as they prepare for tests and could also be used to improve the efficiency of their studying.

THREE POSSIBLE CAUSES OF POOR LEARNING EFFICIENCIES AND THEIR SOLUTIONS

We can group the causes of poor learning efficiency into three categories: (1) students who cannot learn efficiently because professors do not provide the information and tools they need; (2) students who do not want to learn efficiently because the consequences produced by attending class and studying are weaker than the consequences for alternative activities; and (3) students who do not know how to learn efficiently because they have never been taught efficient study and study management techniques. To solve the "can-do" problem, professors can provide students with measurable learning objectives, well-designed instructions, practice, and feedback, peer tutoring, and multiple testing opportunities. When professors adopt this approach, sometimes referred to as the Personalized System of Instruction (PSI) (see Chapter 12), more students achieve mastery; however, the cost can be prohibitive. Professors and student helpers devote many more hours designing instructional and testing materials, tutoring, and grading than is required by the traditional college course. Perhaps for this reason, few professors currently run PSI courses.

To solve the "want-to" problem, professors can design their courses to increase the amount of time students spend attending class and studying. They can do this by giving weekly tests and tying the course grade very tightly to studying for the tests. Some versions of PSI set weekly deadlines for passing tests. Although this approach does get students to spend more time studying, it is also very labor intensive. More frequent testing requires more frequent grading. Professors who use PSI either spend many additional hours grading papers or restrict their tests to machine-graded, multiple-choice formats.

To solve the "know-how" problem, professors can teach their students how to study and how to manage their own studying. One might assume that most students who enter college have already learned these skills, as they have already completed 12 years of schooling; however, as mentioned previously, only one or two students in my CPSY 101 course report being taught how to study. Teaching students how to study and manage their own study is the least expensive solution to the problem of poor learning efficiencies than the other two solutions. If students can be taught how to design and use their own learning materials, professors can continue to teach the traditional way: lecture, assign readings and papers, and occasionally test. For this reason, the author has begun to teach his students how to study for tests in his CPSY 101 course.

CASE STUDY: EVALUATING LEARNING EFFICIENCIES IN A CPSY 101 COURSE

At the beginning of the semester, I announced that the course objectives included learning how to study for college tests and how to evaluate the student's own learning efficiencies while preparing for those tests. Students were given examples of different types of test questions that any professor might ask. These included questions that asked students to compare or contrast problem-solving theories, questions that asked students to distinguish between examples of different types of problems, and questions that asked students to design solutions to those problems. Their weekly assignment was to write questions like those that the professor might ask using the information in the assigned reading and the kind of questions provided by the professor in lecture and handouts. I then asked the students to read their study questions to the class and commented on their quality. Students turned in typed copies of their study questions to earn points for both quantity and quality. See Fig. 1 for examples of study questions from three different students in the CPSY 101 course.

Students were also taught how to use flash cards to practice with their study questions. The professor demonstrated how students could use a variation of delayed prompting by looking at a question on the front of a flashcard and then, if unsure of the correct answer, turning the card over and reading it. Delayed prompting is a procedure that has been demonstrated to increase the learning efficiencies of students with learning difficulties (Godby, Gast, & Wolery, 1987).

Students were required to record their number of correct answers to study questions, number of "not yets" (errors), number of corrects per minute,

Sample of RM's Study Questions for the Final Exam

Card Front: Q: What is pinpointing?
Card Back: Ans: Define behavior and results specifically enough to measure them

Sample of Learner JN's Study Questions for the Final Exam

Front of Card: Pinpoint

Back of Card:

1. Define results objective-nail length of 8-11 mm
2. How will I measure it?-millimeter side of a ruler
3. Compare it to my current results-Nail length of 6 mm
4. Define performance objective-Crochet Afghan 6 rows/week
5. How will I measure it? Count # of rows per week
6. Compare it to my current performance? # of rows per week is 1.5

Sample of Learner RB's Study Questions for the Final Exam

Front of Card	Back of Card
Pinpoint-Define results	I want to lose 4 pounds by the end of the semester
Pinpoint-Measure results	Current Weight: 132 pounds
	I want to weigh: 128 pounds
Pinpoint-Evaluate results	Gap: 4 pounds, 100% gap
Pinpoint-Define performance objective	A-running C-2.5 miles E-on cardio machines at Eastman S-3 times a week
Pinpoint-Measure performance objective	I am going to Eastman 1-2 times per week for 20 minutes Gap of 1-2 time per week of 10 min each
How/What did I pinpoint? (6 steps)	Define results Measure results Evaluate results Define performance objective Measure performance objective Compare current results to performance

FIGURE 1

Samples of study questions for CPSY 101 Final Exam from three different students in the course, RM, JN, and RB.

number of "not yets" per minute, and the total amount of time they spent studying on a special learning efficiency recording sheet. See Fig. 2 for an example of the learning efficiency recording form. The students were then taught how to plot these data on a standard learning efficiency chart, so that they could get feedback on their learning efficiencies for each test.

I have provided examples of learning efficiency charts from three students who prepared study questions and practiced with them for the course final

CSPY 101, Section 02 Learning Efficiency Recording Sheet, Test #7 (Final)

Learner Name: RB Date Started: 4/30/03   Date Completed: 5/6/03

Date	Learning Session Start/Stop Time	Timing Duration	Number Corrects	Number Not Yets	C/Min (Plot)	N/Min (Plot)	LearningTime (Stop–Start)	LT/#Timings (LT Plot)
4/30/03	10:00	2 min	10	10	5	5		4 min
		2 min	10	10	5	5		4 min
	10:12	2 min	11	9	5.5	4.5	12 min	4 min

FIGURE 2

Example of learning efficiency recording sheet from RB.

exam. See Fig. 3 to compare the learning efficiencies of RM, JN, and RB. Each chart shows the improvement in the number of correct responses per minute and the number of "not yets" per minute (errors) per minute of student learning time as a slope that runs from the left to the right side of the chart. A comparison of the slopes of the correct-per-minute lines for each learner reveals that learner RM had the highest learning efficiency (the steepest slope) and learner RB had the lowest learning efficiency (the shallowest slope). The charts also show that RB had much higher corrects and "not yets" per minute at the beginning of practice (on the left side of her chart) than the other two students. However, these practice data do not tell the whole story. Figure 4 shows learning efficiencies plotted from the pre-test score, post-test score, and learning time for each student. In this chart, it is clear that student JN, the student with the second steepest learning efficiency, scored highest on the post-test, because she had a greater improvement from pre- to post-test than RM.

An examination of JN and RM's flash cards in Fig. 1 can account for the discrepancies between their practice learning efficiencies and their scores on the post-test. Because the exam asked the students to describe how they would solve a performance problem, using an example, JN's study materials allowed for more appropriate practice than RM's. JN's answers much more closely approximated the professor's.

WHAT THE DATA CAN TELL US ABOUT HOW TO IMPROVE LEARNING EFFICIENCIES

Collecting data on student learning efficiencies is only the first step in an effort to discover ways to improve learning efficiency. Now that we have a way to measure and evaluate learning efficiency, we can begin our search for those factors that speed or slow learning. What advice could we give to RB, the student with the lowest learning efficiency (the flattest slope in both Figs. 3

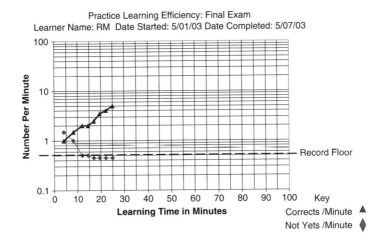

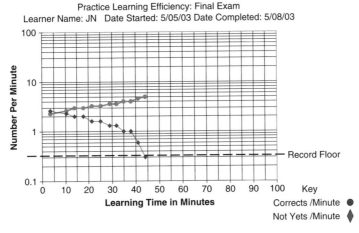

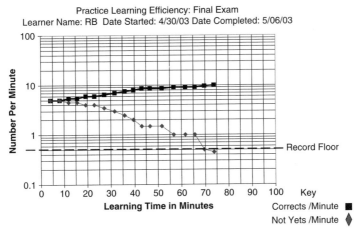

FIGURE 3

Practice learning efficiencies for students RM, JN, and RB.

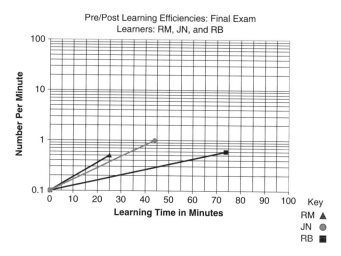

FIGURE 4

From Pre- to post-test learning efficiencies for students JN, RM, and RB.

and 4) and the highest "not yets" per minute at the beginning of practice? Here is what we know based on the handful of studies that have been done so far. Several studies have shown that delayed prompting is more efficient than other types of prompting techniques. Not only is delayed prompting more efficient, but it also tends to produce fewer "not yets" (errors) than other practice methods (Godby et al., 1987). Is RB looking at the question on the front of the study card, then, if she is unable to answer the question correctly after a short delay, is she turning the card over to read the correct answer on the back of the card when she practices? Although the professor demonstrated this technique, there was no guarantee that all students were using it correctly. One way to find out is to ask RB to demonstrate her flashcard technique. At least one study suggests that using an error correction technique (additional practice of missed questions) also improves learning efficiency (Johnson, Schuster, Bell, 1996). Is RB spending additional time practicing with her "not yet" cards? We can check whether RB is using the error correction procedure by asking her to demonstrate it to us.

LEARNING EFFICIENCY GOES TO COLLEGE

So, as a reader what should you conclude from this chapter on learning efficiency? (1) College students can be taught how to study efficiently and to evaluate their own learning efficiency. (2) Many reported that the flashcard method helped them prepare for the tests; some even reported that they had begun to use the same method to study for their other classes. (3) This method of collecting data on learning efficiency is fairly easy to implement, as the students are collecting their own data, but, of course, we cannot be sure that the data are accurate without reliability checks by independent observers. (4) At this point, there is insufficient research on variables that affect learning efficiency to guide our efforts to improve it. I hope I have made a case for the need to conduct such research.

References

Berkner, L., He, S., Cataldi, E., & Knepper, P. (2002). *Descriptive Summary of 1995–96 Beginning Postsecondary Students: Six Years Later*, NCES 2003-151. Washington, D.C.: National Center for Education Statistics, U.S. Department of Education Institute of Education Sciences.

Godby, S., Gast, D., & Wolery, M. (1987). A comparison of time delay and system of least prompts in teaching object identification. *Research in Developmental Disabilities*, 8, 283–306.

Johnson, P., Schuster, J., & Bell, J. (1996). Comparison of simultaneous prompting with and without error correction in teaching science vocabulary words to high school students with mild disabilities. *Journal of Behavioral Education*, 6(4), 437–458.

CHAPTER

16

Teaching the Generic Skills of Language and Cognition: Contributions from Relational Frame Theory

YVONNE BARNES-HOLMES,
DERMOT BARNES-HOLMES, and
CAROL MURPHY
National University of Ireland Maynooth

INTRODUCTION

Language and cognition are important domains in the discipline of psychology and are often the primary focus in the study of psychological development and in the design of programs of remedial education (Lovaas, 1981; Piaget, 1967). The Applied Behavior Analysis (ABA) approach to autism, for example, considers the establishment of language skills a primary treatment goal because these abilities are prerequisites for most other types of learning and are frequently deficient in autistic populations (Sundberg & Michael, 2001).

Most ABA approaches to language training are based in large part on Skinner's (1957) definition of verbal operants, including mands, echoics, textuals, transcription and dictation-taking, intraverbals, tacts, extended tacts, and autoclitics. According to Skinner, verbal operants differ from other operant responses because reinforcement in the former is provided indirectly through a social mediator, rather than directly through environmental contingencies. This approach to verbal behavior is functional in that it does not conceptualize language as a translation of "meaning," and this distinction has important implications for how verbal behavior is established. In contrast, an approach to training language that emphasizes "meaning" (rather than function) rests on the assumption that spontaneous transfer from one verbal operant to another will occur once a child is taught the meaning of a word (Sundberg & Michael, 2001). For example, a semantic theory of language would predict that learning a verbal operant such as a tact (*e.g.*, uttering "juice" in the presence of actual juice) could provide the child with words as tools that can then be applied with other verbal operants such as a mand (*e.g.*, asking for juice). Based on this assumption, training the verbal skill of tacting will likely produce the collateral verbal skill of manding or *vice versa*; however, children with severe language difficulties do not typically utilize words in the manner in which the words-as-tools analogy suggests (although spontaneous transfer from one verbal operant to another may be facilitated by learning in more sophisticated speakers; Sundberg & Michael, 2001). Indeed, Skinner (1957) pointed to the general imbalances found between listening and speaking skills and between reading and writing skills as evidence for distinct verbal functions that do not automatically transfer across behavioral domains. Training regimes based on the establishment of Skinner's verbal operants, therefore, characteristically attempt to establish verbal operants such as mands and tacts as distinct verbal repertoires (Greer, 2002).

Although Skinner's approach to verbal behavior was widely accepted as the first comprehensive account of language based on operant principles and was incorporated into the design of many (if not most) behavioral interventions, it has met with criticism within and beyond the behavioral tradition. Chomsky (1959), for example, argued that Skinner's approach to verbal behavior could not adequately account for the generativity of language found even in young children. More recently, a number of behavioral researchers have suggested that Skinner's account ultimately failed as a basis for an experimental analysis of verbal behavior (Hayes, Barnes-Holmes, Roche, 2001a).

The core argument offered by Hayes et al., (2001a) is that Skinner's definition of verbal behavior was too broad. Specifically, Skinner's definition of verbal operants rests on the mediation of reinforcement of verbal responses by a listener or listeners who have been conditioned to mediate verbal responses in a particular way. This definition turns out to be extremely broad, however. And, indeed, Skinner appears to have been aware of this fact when he argued that the interaction between a human experimenter and a non-human subject constitutes a small verbal community in which the former supplies reinforcement in much the same way as a listener. Although appealing in its simplicity, particularly for a basic science of behavioral psychology that was primarily focused on the behavior of nonhumans, a definition of verbal behavior that effectively includes most human–nonhuman interactions renders superfluous the conceptual class *verbal*.

One solution to this problem is to redefine verbal events in terms of what are called *derived arbitrary stimulus relations* (Barnes-Holmes, Barnes-Holmes, Cullinan, 2000; Chase & Danforth, 1991; Hayes et al., 2001). According to this view, the derivation of *multiple* stimulus relations (explained subsequently) is believed to be the core process involved in human language and cognitive abilities. As well as offering a new functional definition and experimental analysis of verbal behavior, some researchers have suggested that it may be possible to harness these newly defined verbal processes in the development of programs for remediating deficits in language and cognition (Barnes-Holmes, Barnes-Holmes, Cullinan, 2001a). In the first part of this chapter, we outline the basic features of this approach, known as Relational Frame Theory (RFT). We then turn our attention to RFT-driven research that has direct implications for the design of empirically supported educational methods.

RELATIONAL FRAME THEORY

Defining Derived Relational Responding

At its simplest, *relating* may be defined as responding to one event in terms of another and is demonstrated readily by nonhuman and human organisms alike (Reese, 1968). Most living organisms, with a history of appropriate training, are able to respond to the *nonarbitrary* relations among the physical properties of stimuli or events. For example, adult rhesus monkeys can be trained to select the taller of two stimuli (Harmon, Strong, Pasnak, 1982), and this type of behavior may be described as relational responding because it relies upon relative comparisons among the stimuli involving discriminations based on their formal properties (*i.e.*, one stimulus is actually physically taller than the other).

Relational responding, however, becomes more complex when it is brought under the control of contextual features beyond the formal (nonarbitrary) properties of the stimuli. *Arbitrarily applicable* relational responding is the term used to describe relational responses that can be brought to bear on any stimuli presented in an appropriate context. For example, if you are told that "X is taller than Y," you can derive that Y is shorter than X without actually seeing what X and Y refer to. In this way, arbitrarily applicable relational responding may be controlled by contextual cues that are modified entirely by social whim. For instance, in a game, children may be instructed that "Tall means short and short means tall." In this case, the relational functions of tall and short are *applied* in a purely *arbitrary* fashion and are not governed by the actual formal dimensions of the stimuli.

In order for relational responding to come under appropriate forms of contextual control, as would be required for competent performances in the example of the children's game above, children must learn to discriminate between the relevant features of the task (*i.e.*, responding relationally to events in the presence of appropriate contextual cues) and the irrelevant features of the task (*e.g.*, responding to the physical properties of the stimuli). This training history is clearly illustrated in the establishment of the bidirectional stimulus relations that emerge between words and their referents that form a large part of early naturalistic language interactions.

Early experiences of learning to name objects comprise a wealth of name–object and object–name relations across an extensive range of objects and names. That is, young children are trained as follows: Given the name of an object → select the object (the name–object relations are explicitly trained), and given the object → select the name of the object (in this case, the object–name relations are explicitly trained). In essence, reinforcement is being provided for responding in accordance with the bidirectional relations between object names and actual objects and *vice versa*. Reinforcement for such bidirectional responding is rich in early natural language interactions but occurs only in certain contexts, such as in the presence of phrases such as "What's that?" and the juxtaposition of objects and words. According to RFT, this training in bidirectional relations ensures that in certain contexts name–object relations reliably predict object–name relations and *vice versa*, and *generalized* bidirectional responding emerges. For example, explicit training in a new name–object relation (given the name "teddy" → select the teddy) may result in the *derived* or untrained object–name relation (given the actual teddy and asked "What's this?" → say the name "teddy"). This training history is brought to bear on novel stimuli by the presence of specific contextual cues (*e.g.*, "What's this?") that control responding in accordance with the bidirectional stimulus relations. Note that in the example of naming, the stimulus relations are entirely arbitrary because, in practically all cases, the words do not bear any formal resemblance to the actual objects to which they refer (*i.e.*, the word "teddy" looks nothing like an actual teddy).

From the perspective of RFT, arbitrarily applicable relational responding has three defining properties: mutual entailment, combinatorial entailment, and the transformation of stimulus functions. The term *mutual entailment* is used to describe the basic bidirectionality of relational responding outlined previously. Arbitrary stimulus relations are always mutual—if A is related to B, then B is always related to A. That is, if the first relation is specified, the second relation is entailed (hence the term *mutual entailment*). Technically defined, mutual entailment applies when, in a given context, A, for example, is related in a characteristic way to B and, as a result, in that context B is related in another characteristic way to A.

The term *combinatorial entailment* is used to describe a derived stimulus relation in which two or more relations mutually combine. For example, if you are only told that A is more than B and B is more than C, then you can derive that A is more than C and C is less than A. From a developmental or educational perspective, it is likely that combinatorially entailed relations emerge later than mutually entailed relations.

The third defining feature of arbitrarily applicable relational responding is the *transformation of stimulus functions*. This term is employed when the functions of a given stimulus are modified or changed as a result of derived relations with other stimuli. If, for example, an individual is told that B is the opposite of A, and a conditioned *punishing* function is attached to A, the functions of B may be transformed such that it becomes a conditioned *reinforcer* because of its participation in a relation of opposition with A (Roche & Barnes, 1997; Roche, Barnes-Holmes, Smeets, Barnes-Holmes, & McGready, 2000).

Just as the relational response is controlled by context, the transformation of stimulus functions must also come under contextual control. Consider some of the perceptual functions of a lemon, including its bitter taste, its rough texture, and the fact that it is bright yellow in color. When an individual is asked to imagine a lemon, many of these perceptual features become psychologically present. In the technical language of RFT, this psychological event is described as follows. The word "lemon" and actual lemons participate in what is called a relational frame of coordination. In addition, the words "imagine a" function as a context in which some of the perceptual functions (especially visual functions) are elicited based on the relational frame. In another context (*e.g.*, "imagine tasting a . . . "), other functions would be elicited. Contextual cues, therefore, control not only the type of relational frame involved but also the transformation of functions that are enabled by the frame in question.

Relational Framing

Relational Frame Theory employs the generic term *relational frame* to describe particular patterns of arbitrarily applicable relational responding (Hayes & Hayes, 1989). A number of generic relational frames have been discussed in the literature (although others may yet be identified). These include frames of coordination, opposition, distinction, comparison, hierarchy, and deictic frames of perspective-taking (Hayes, Barnes-Holmes & Roche, 2001b). Perhaps the most commonly known pattern of relational responding involves the frame of *coordination*, in which the relations are ones of identity or similarity. The example of naming described previously is an often-cited instance of the frame of coordination, and this frame is probably one of the first to be established.

The relational frame of *opposition* requires the abstraction of a dimension along which stimuli can be ordered and distinguished in equal ways from a reference point. In natural language, *opposite* typically implies the relevant dimension. For example, saying that "fast is the opposite of slow" implies that speed is the dimension along which the related events are to be ordered. Furthermore, RFT suggests that the frame of opposition will emerge later than coordination because the combinatorially entailed relations within frames of opposition are frames of coordination. For example, if fast is the opposite of slow, and slow is the opposite of quick, then fast and quick are the same (*i.e.*, coordinated), not opposite.

Relational frames of *distinction* involve responding to the differences among stimuli or events, typically also along a particular dimension; however, in frames of distinction, the relevant dimension is rarely implied. Consider, for instance, the statement: "This is not a person of average intelligence." Based on only this information, it is not possible to determine whether this person is of extremely high or extremely low intelligence. Furthermore, a combinatorially entailed difference relation is unspecified. For example, if you are told that A is different than B, and B is different than C, then A and C may be the same or different. This type of unspecified relation is a defining property of the frame of distinction.

There are many specific types of frames of *comparison*, including bigger and smaller and faster and slower. These frames involve responding to events in terms of a quantitative or qualitative relation, again along a specified dimension (*e.g.*, speed). If I say that "a lion is faster than a dog and a dog is faster than a mouse," the events can be compared along the dimension of speed, and you can derive that "the lion is faster than the mouse and the mouse is slower than the lion." Furthermore, comparative relations may be made more specific by quantification of the dimension. For example, if you are told that "a lion is twice as fast as a dog and a dog is twice as fast as a mouse," you can now derive that the lion is exactly four times faster than the mouse and the mouse is four times slower than the lion.

The final family of relational frames that we will describe here involves *deictic relations*, which appear to be involved in perspective-taking (Barnes & Roche, 1997; Hayes, 1984). The three key deictic frames seem to be I and YOU, HERE and THERE, and NOW and THEN. Relational Frame Theory argues that taking a perspective involves responding in accordance with these relational frames. In other words, taking a perspective involves responding from I, HERE, and NOW with respect to events located THERE and THEN. For example, saying "I cannot see what you see" requires that the speaker distinguish between I and YOU (*i.e.*, that we do not always see the same things), and that what I am seeing HERE and NOW is not what YOU are seeing THERE and THEN. We will return to this type of relational framing toward the end of the chapter.

There is much more to RFT than has been presented thus far. For example, RFT also describes the relating of relations and the relating of relational networks with other relational networks. These processes are believed to account for competence in verbal skills such as analogy, metaphor, and story telling, but it is beyond the scope of the current chapter for these issues to be described fully (but see Hayes *et al.*, 2001a, for a book-length account). The important point to be gleaned here, however, is that from the RFT perspective *deriving relations underpins developmental or educational achievement, and a small number of psychological processes are sufficient to yield the full gamut of cognitive skills.*

RESEARCH IN RELATIONAL FRAME THEORY
AND ITS IMPLICATIONS FOR EDUCATION

From the perspective of RFT, over-arching relational skills can be taught, and subsequent improvement in relational responding should lead to improved abilities in areas of cognition and language, as well as in intelligence in general (Hayes, 1994). The RFT approach to education has two core assumptions. First, skills in relational responding provide the basis for a wide range of cognitive abilities that correlate with educational achievement. Second, multiple-exemplar training provides an important method for harnessing these cognitive skills and building up flexibility in relational repertoires. This section of the chapter briefly describes a number of RFT studies in which multiple-exemplar training was successfully employed to establish novel relational repertoires. In each study, a relational or cognitive deficit is identified in the behavior of the experimental participants, and then the study seeks to remediate this deficit by reinforcing one or more exemplars of the relevant relational repertoire. These studies thus provide examples of how the RFT approach can inform educational practice. We should add that multiple-exemplar training is not exclusive to RFT and indeed is an inherent feature of traditional educational practice (Englemann & Carnine, 1982). For example, children are often presented with tasks that are grouped by content that establish flexibility in over-arching relational skills (*e.g.*, adding numbers together, filling in missing numbers in a sequence, or identifying the nouns in sentences). However, an approach to education based on RFT seeks to identify tasks that can be grouped according to the relational skills involved rather than according to traditional content areas.

Derived Transformations of Function
in Accordance with Symmetry

One of the first RFT-based studies that attempted to analyze the development of relational framing in young children involved a systematic analysis of the role of multiple-exemplar training in establishing simple derived relations (Barnes-Holmes *et al.*, 2001c). In this study, young, normally developing children between the ages of 4 and 5 years old were selected and a task was designed to investigate the transformation of function in accordance with symmetry. The children were first trained in an action–object conditional discrimination task. During this training, when the experimenter waved, choosing a toy car was reinforced with feedback (*i.e.*, the trained relation was *wave–car*), and, when the experimenter clapped, choosing a doll was reinforced (*i.e.*, the trained relation was *clap–doll*). Following this training, the children were tested without feedback for the derived object–action symmetry relations. That is, when the experimenter now presented a toy car, the child was required to wave (*i.e.*, the tested relation was *car–wave*), and, when the experimenter presented a doll, the child was required to clap (*i.e.*, the tested relation was *doll–clap*). Of the 16 children, 11 failed to show the target derived symmetry performances on the first test. At this point in the study, a multiple-baseline design was used to phase in the introduction of explicit symmetry or object–action training for those children who failed the symmetry test. In other words, after failing to demonstrate symmetry, some children were then re-exposed to the same trials as in the symmetry test, but corrective feedback was provided after each trial. In order to test the effect of this training, the children were thereafter exposed to an entirely new set of actions and objects in the same training and testing format. In simple terms, the children were trained on one exemplar and then tested on another. With the multiple baseline design, some children were exposed to several sessions of training and testing with the novel sets of stimuli prior to receiving the explicit symmetry training in order to determine whether these children would improve in the absence of explicit object–action training across exemplars.

The results of the studies overall showed that for all 11 children who failed the first symmetry test, explicit symmetry training was effective in establishing the derived transformations of function in accordance with symmetry, and that for the majority of children only one exemplar of training was necessary for the derived performance to occur on a novel set of stimuli. As an aside, a number of similar experiments employed an alternative naming intervention commonly used in education and found this to be much less effective than the multiple-exemplar training in establishing the derived test performances (Barnes-Holmes, Barnes Holmes, Roche, Smeets, 2001b).

One issue that arose from this series of studies was the very limited number of exemplars required for the children to demonstrate the target derived performances. This suggested that the exemplar training simply activated a previously established relational repertoire of symmetrical responding, and the age and verbal sophistication of the children supported this conclusion. The obvious limitation of this work, therefore, is that it did not demonstrate the establishment of previously absent repertoires of relational framing, which is often what is required in educational programs. The three studies outlined subsequently address this concern.

Teaching Derived Manding

Establishing a manding repertoire is very important for children with language deficits, because it provides immediate control of the social and non-social environment and facilitates the development of speaker and listener reper-toires (Sundberg & Michael, 2001). It is not surprising, therefore, that mands are typically the first verbal operants humans acquire naturally or are trained to acquire in educational programs (Bijou & Baer, 1965; Skinner, 1957).

One of the most common difficulties in educational programs that attempt to build manding repertoires in individuals for whom they are found to be absent is the identification or establishment of a variety of deprivation states. Although many kinds of deprivation may already be present in a child with autism, for example, these may remain unknown to the instructor who is presented with generic responses such as crying and pulling, but not with specific indicators of deprivation (Sundberg & Michael, 2001). Given that children with autism have successfully demonstrated derived relational responding (Eikeseth & Smith, 1990), a recent study attempted to establish derived manding via relational frames in young normally developing and autistic children (Murphy, Barnes-Holmes, & Barnes-Holmes, 2003).

The experimental sequence employed in this study consisted of three phases: mand training, conditional discrimination training, and testing for a derived transfer of mand functions. During Phase 1, participants were trained to use two stimulus cards, each with an abstract symbol on it, to mand for a pink token and a yellow token, respectively (these two cards will be referred to as A1 and A2). A "state of deprivation" was created by presenting participants with a task that required them to mand for the appropriate number of either pink or yellow tokens. That is, the participant was presented with a token mat that contained a number of pink and/or yellow tokens and, to complete a mand training trial successfully, the participant had to mand for only those pink or yellow tokens that were needed to complete the missing set (i.e., if a participant manded for a token that he or she did not need, the trial was recorded as incorrect).

Participants who successfully completed mand training were trained in two conditional discriminations using a matching-to-sample procedure. During this training, the children were taught to relate the symbol on the A1 stimulus card to a second symbol (B1) and to relate this second symbol to a third symbol (C1). The training also involved teaching the children to relate the A2 symbol to the B2 stimulus and the B2 stimulus to a C2 stimulus. In this way, two relational frames of coordination were established (A1–B1–C1 and A2–B2–C2). The critical test from an RFT perspective involved determining if the children would spontaneously use the two C stimuli to mand for the appropriate colored tokens. In other words, would the yellow manding function of A1 transfer via coordination to C1, and similarly the pink manding function transfer from A2 to C2?

The three normally developing children and two of the autistic children readily demonstrated the predicted derived transfer of mand functions on their first exposures to the test; however, one of the autistic children completely failed the derived transfer test (the data for this child are presented in Fig. 1). Consequently, this child was exposed to exemplar training in the derived transfer of mand functions. That is, when the child failed to show the derived transfer, he was immediately exposed to the derived transfer tasks again, but this time corrective feedback was provided after each response (labeled as "Transfer Training" in Fig. 1). Subsequently, the child was re-exposed to the mand training, conditional discrimination training, and derived

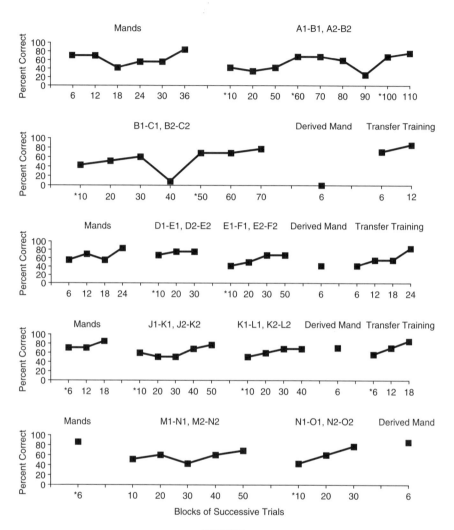

FIGURE 1

Mands: Percent correct across blocks of 6 trials. A1–B1, A2–B2; B1–C1, B2–C2; D1–E1, D2–E2; E1–F1, E2–F2; J1–K1, J2–K2; K1–L1, K2–L2; M1–N1, M2–N2; and N1–O1, N2–O2: Percent correct across blocks of 10 matching–to–sample training trials in each set. *Derived mands:* Test for derived transfer of mand functions A1–C1, A2–C2; D1–F1, D2–F2; J1–L1, J2–L2; and M1–O1, M2–O2. *Transfer training:* Percent correct across blocks of 6 training trials involving direct training of transfer of mand functions. Asterisks indicate break of at least one day between sessions.

mand testing but with a completely novel set of abstract symbols for the A, B, and C stimuli (*e.g.*, Set D, E, and F). In total, the child required five exemplars of explicit derived mand training before successfully demonstrating a derived transfer of mand functions on a novel set of stimuli (Set M, N, and O) in the absence of corrective feedback. As can be seen from Fig. 1, the improvement in derived manding was gradual across exemplars, and this suggests that a genuinely novel relational repertoire was established in the behavior of this child.

This recent research provides a good example of how the relational concepts of RFT, and its emphasis on exemplar training, can be brought to bear on more traditional behavioral approaches to the teaching of verbal behavior. The one child who repeatedly failed the derived transfer of mand functions test clearly demonstrated that directly trained and derived manding may exist as functionally distinct verbal skills and that the latter may require extensive remediation in an educational context to become firmly established in a child's behavioral repertoire. Clearly, much more work remains to be done, but this recent study indicates that the application of RFT methodologies and strategies to educational research and practice may be of considerable value.

Establishing the Relational Frames of More-Than, Less-Than, and Opposite

An important cognitive skill that children are required to master involves relational reasoning, particularly when that reasoning gives rise to conclusions that were not explicitly taught or instructed. The ability to take generic relational skills and apply them to new content across a range of contexts constitutes an important educational goal. A recent RFT study systematically examined how generative relational reasoning might be established when it is found to be absent in the behavior of young children (Barnes-Holmes, 2001). This study used a basic problem-solving task to test and train derived relations in accordance with the relational frames of *more-than, less-than*, and *opposite*. The basic task employed for establishing both frames involved presenting a child with a number of identically sized paper circles (these were referred to as "coins" because the task involved choosing one or more of the circles on the basis of their stated value). On each trial, the experimenter described specific more-than, less-than, or opposite relations among the coins in terms of value (because the coins were actually the same physical size, the comparative values were entirely arbitrary, as is the case with real money). Based on this comparison, the child was then asked to pick the coin that would buy as many sweets as possible. For example, during a more-than trial, the child might be instructed as follows: "If this coin [experimenter points to the first coin designated as coin A] buys more sweets than this coin [experimenter points to coin B], and this coin [experimenter points to coin B again] buys more sweets than this coin [experimenter points to coin C], which would you choose to buy as many sweets as possible?" In this case, a correct response consisted of the child selecting the first coin (A). This was the format employed for all trials, and each training trial provided corrective feedback. Numerous sets of coins were employed to create multiple exemplars for training the more-than, less-than, and opposite relations and testing the appropriate derived relations.

Three normally developing children each required 30 to 40 experimental sessions before demonstrating responding in accordance with the target arbitrary relations of more-than and less-than. After this extensive training and testing, the children also demonstrated flexible relational repertoires in that they could respond appropriately: (1) when the experimenter pointed to the coins in any direction from left to right or *vice versa* and from top to bottom and *vice versa*; (2) when presented with a novel set of three random objects instead of coins (*i.e.*, a different set of objects such as three cups instead of the three coins that had been presented previously; and (3) when asked which coin(s) they would *not* choose in order to buy as many sweets as possible. The issue of establishing flexibility in relational responding is important from the perspective of RFT because of its emphasis on the relational skill *per se* rather than the content involved in the response. For example, if a child has learned to correctly derive opposite relations among three stimuli and the training responsible for establishing this skill was conducted with three coins, the child who has learned the relational skill in question should in principle now be able to demonstrate that type of responding with any three objects (such as three cups) without requiring explicit training with those objects. The presentation of tests involving novel stimuli not presented during explicit training, therefore, is an important feature for RFT in testing the emergence of new skills because this type of performance provides evidence of the child's ability to derive the relations in question.

Although the generative and flexible nature of the performances that were established via exemplar training were impressive, given the complete absence of more-than and less-than relational reasoning skills in the children at the outset of the study, the analysis of opposite relations produced an even greater level of relational complexity. In order to study opposite relations, the task was modified. During the first test for opposite responding, a child may have been presented with four coins and asked: "If this coin [coin A] buys many sweets and is opposite to this coin [coin B], and if this coin [coin B] is opposite to this coin [coin C], and if this coin [coin C] is opposite to this coin [coin D], which would you take to buy as many sweets as possible?" The correct answer on this trial involved selecting coins A and C, because A buys many and is opposite to B (so B buys few), B is the opposite to C (thus C is the same as A and buys many), and C is the opposite to D (thus, if C buys many, D buys few).

Three normally developing children each required extensive exemplar training before demonstrating a complex and flexible repertoire of responding in accordance with the target arbitrary relations of opposite. In the final test phases, the children demonstrated appropriate responding: (1) in the presence of a novel experimenter; (2) when the experimenter pointed to the coins in any direction from left to right or *vice versa*, from top to bottom or *vice versa*, or in a completely random sequence; (3) when presented with a set of novel objects instead of coins; (4) when asked which coin(s) they would *not* choose in order to buy as many sweets as possible; and (5) when presented with various numbers of coins or other items up to and including ten. For example, the children were trained explicitly with three coins, and they were repeatedly tested to determine that they could derive the relevant opposite relations among these items. The children were then presented with four coins, five coins, six coins, and so on up to ten coins. On each number of coins, they were tested first and, if the performances were weak, they were then trained explicitly on the opposite relations among that number of coins (*e.g.*, with four coins). After testing on four coins, for example, they were then presented with five coins and asked to derive the opposite relations among these. This type of testing and training continued until the children had been trained and tested in a series of six coins. After this number, none of the children needed further explicit training. In other words, when they were subsequently presented with a series of seven coins, eight coins, nine coins, and even ten coins, they passed the tests immediately by deriving all of the target opposite relations. After these tests, they were then presented with a sequence of ten alternative objects, such as ten pens, and they were immediately able to derive the correct opposite relations among these items without training. This type of performance clearly indicated the presence of a complex and flexible repertoire of derived relational responding in accordance with the frame of opposite.

The foregoing studies provided evidence that highly complex and flexible repertoires of relational responding in accordance with the relational frames of more-than, less-than, and opposite may be effectively established with very young children by a history of multiple-exemplar training. Although the same basic methodology of training across multiple exemplars was employed to establish these relational repertoires, a number of features specific to the various frames were observed. First, responding arbitrarily in accordance with more-than and less-than appeared easier than responding in accordance with opposite. Second, responding in accordance with nonarbitrary more-than and less-than relations was useful in establishing the more complex arbitrary relations (*e.g.*, different numbers of sweets were placed on top of the coins to create actual comparisons of more-than and less-than in order to facilitate the transition between nonarbitrary and arbitrary responding). Third, many exemplars of training were needed to establish even mutually entailed opposite relations. Fourth, training combinatorially entailed opposite relations was even more difficult than mutually entailed relations. Fifth, explicit instructions with regard to the relation of "same" helped to facilitate combinatorially entailed opposite relations (*i.e.*, if A is opposite to B, and B is opposite to C, then A and C are the same). Sixth, participants required many exemplars of training to derive the opposite relations between two, three, four, and five coins but needed few or no exemplars of training when working with six, seven, eight, nine, or ten coins (*i.e.*, this would suggest that increasing the number of trained coins helped establish opposite responding as a generalized cognitive skill that could be applied arbitrarily, in principle, to any number of stimuli).

The types of studies outlined so far address what appear to be clear examples of generative or novel verbal behavior and relational reasoning. Relational Frame Theory, as an account of human verbal behavior, is directly relevant to these domains; however, RFT also approaches cognitive skills that do not immediately appear to be primarily relational in largely relational terms. Although such an approach may seem counterintuitive, preliminary empirical work in the domain of perspective taking, or what cognitive psychologists call the Theory of Mind (ToM), suggests that there may be some value in adopting a relational interpretation of this phenomenon.

Relational Responding and Perspective Taking

According to RFT, cognitive perspective taking (Howlin *et al.*, 1999) involves increasingly complex forms of contextual control of the perspective-taking relational frames of I–YOU, HERE–THERE, and NOW–THEN. As was the case with the establishment of the frames described previously, RFT would predict that the most effective means of establishing these repertoires would be to target the relational frames or generic relational repertoires directly.

As part of a complex research program on perspective taking in children, Barnes-Holmes (2001) attempted to establish the relational skills that appear to underlie perspective taking in young children. In this study, responding in accordance with the relational frame of I–YOU was the first perspective-taking frame to be targeted directly. For illustrative purposes, consider the following simple scenario. The participant was presented with two colored blocks and asked: "If I [experimenter] have a green block, and YOU have a red block, which block do I have? Which block do you have?" If the child responded incorrectly to either question, corrective feedback was provided until correct responding was established. Once these simple I–YOU relations were established, the I and YOU relations were reversed in order to facilitate flexibility in this type of relational responding. The participant, for example, was asked: "If I was YOU, and YOU were ME, which block would YOU have? Which block would I have?"

Once simple and reversed I–YOU relations were established, responding in accordance with HERE–THERE and its combinations with I–YOU was targeted directly. Consider the following scenario: "If I am sitting HERE on the black chair, and you are sitting THERE on the blue chair, where are YOU sitting? Where am I sitting?" With simple HERE–THERE relations in place, reversed HERE–THERE relations were then targeted. During these trials, for example, the participant may have been asked: "I am sitting HERE on the black chair, and you are sitting THERE on the blue chair. If HERE was THERE, and THERE was HERE, where would YOU be sitting? Where would I be sitting?" In this particular trial type, it is apparent that the HERE–THERE relation is reversed, but the I–YOU relation remains simple. When responding to this type of complex HERE–THERE reversal was established, the task was made even more complex by reversing both I–YOU and HERE–THERE statements simultaneously. Consider the following example of what was called a double reversed I–YOU/HERE–THERE relation: "I am sitting HERE on the blue chair and YOU are sitting THERE on the black chair. If I was YOU and YOU were ME, and if HERE was THERE and THERE was HERE, where would YOU be sitting? Where would I be sitting?"

Once the perspective-taking frames of I–YOU and HERE–THERE were established, the relational frame of NOW–THEN was targeted. One feature of NOW–THEN responding that differed from HERE–THERE responding is that I and YOU could not be presented together in each trial because responding to I–YOU and NOW–THEN simultaneously renders some of the relations unspecified. In order to establish simple patterns of responding in accordance with NOW–THEN, the participant, for example, was presented with the following scenario: "Yesterday I was watching TV, today I am reading. What am I doing NOW? What was I doing THEN?" Once this pattern of simple NOW–THEN responding was established, the relation was reversed as follows: "Yesterday I was watching TV, today I am reading. If NOW was THEN, and THEN was NOW, what would I be doing NOW? What would I be doing THEN?"

With flexible patterns of NOW–THEN responding established, NOW–THEN and HERE–THERE were mixed to produce new types of double-reversed relations. Consider the following example: "Yesterday, I was sitting THERE on the red chair; today I am sitting HERE on the green chair. If HERE was THERE, and THERE was HERE, and if NOW was THEN and THEN was NOW, where would I be sitting NOW? Where would I be sitting THEN?"

In the Barnes-Holmes study, two normally developing children were exposed to these relational perspective-taking procedures. One 7-year-old female mastered the entire training protocol but required training on the reversed and double-reversed relations. A 3.5-year-old boy was also exposed to I–YOU and HERE–THERE trial types and required extensive training across exemplars, particularly on the reversed and double-reversed relations. In a more recent replication of this work, McHugh, Barnes-Holmes, & Barnes-Holmes, (2003) demonstrated that extensive and systematic exemplar training was necessary to establish even simple NOW–THEN relations in a 4-year-old child.

Although these RFT data on the teaching of perspective-taking are preliminary, the protocols that have been developed in this research have been subjected to systematic empirical analysis using cross-sectional developmental methodologies (McHugh, Barnes-Holmes, & Barnes-Holmes, in press). The findings from this research suggest that the relational skills that are involved in the perspective-taking frames are required in order to successfully complete ToM tasks that have typically been used to study and teach perspective taking in educational contexts. Furthermore, additional RFT protocols are currently being developed to study more advanced forms of perspective taking, including false belief and deception (Barnes-Holmes et al., in press). Treating perspective taking as an inherently relational activity, therefore, appears to promise new insights and methodologies for studying and teaching this poorly understood and complex human skill.

SUMMARY AND CONCLUSIONS

Based on a relatively small array of psychological and behavioral processes, Relational Frame Theory allows even complex verbal events, such as cognitive perspective taking, to be approached behaviorally and established systematically. In this chapter, we have outlined preliminary findings from a research agenda in the experimental analysis of human behavior that has clear and widespread implications for empirically validated educational practices. This exciting research initiative consists of studies in which both simple and complex forms of derived relational responding were targeted for assessment and remediation using interventions indicated by RFT. A key theme running throughout the diverse content areas covered in this chapter is the role of a basic understanding of relational responses in teaching important cognitive skills in both children and adults. It is our belief that identifying the core relational units involved in these cognitive skills and targeting their fluid and flexible development with appropriate training will lead to significant improvements in the methods used in many educational settings.

References

Barnes, D. & Roche, B. (1997). A behavior-analytic approach to behavioral reflexivity. *The Psychological Record, 47*, 543–572.

Barnes-Holmes, Y. (2001). Analysing relational frames: Studying language and cognition in young children, unpublished doctoral thesis. Maynooth: National University of Ireland.

Barnes-Holmes, D., Barnes-Holmes, Y., & Cullinan, V. (2000). Relational frame theory and Skinner's *Verbal behavior*: A possible synthesis. *The Behavior Analyst, 23*, 69–84.

Barnes-Holmes, Y., Barnes-Holmes, D., & Cullinan, V. (2001a). Education, in Hayes, S. C., Barnes-Holmes, D., & Roche, B. (Eds.), *Relational frame theory: A post-skinnerian account of human language and cognition*. New York: Plenum.

Barnes-Holmes, Y., Barnes-Holmes, D., Roche, B., & Smeets, P. M. (2001b). Exemplar training and a derived transformation of function in accordance with symmetry: I. *The Psychological Record, 51*, 287–308.

Barnes-Holmes, Y., Barnes-Holmes, D., Roche, B., & Smeets, P. M. (2001c). Exemplar training and a derived transformation of function in accordance with symmetry: II. *The Psychological Record, 51*, 589–604.

Barnes-Holmes, Y., McHugh, L., & Barnes-Holmes, D. (in press). Perspective-taking and theory of mind: A relational frame account. *Behavior Analyst Today*.

Bijou, S. & Baer, D. (1965). *Child development: The universal stage of infancy*, Vol. 2. Englewood Cliffs, NJ: Prentice Hall.

Chase, P. N. & Danforth, J. S. (1991). The role of rules in concept learning, in Hayes, L. J. & Chase, P. N. (Eds.), *Dialogues on verbal behavior*. Reno, NV: Context Press.

Chomsky, N. (1959). A review of B.F. Skinner's *Verbal Behavior. Language*, 35, 26–58.

Eikeseth, S. & Smith, T. (1990). The development of functional and equivalence classes in high-functioning autistic children: the role of naming. *Journal of the Experimental Analysis of Behavior*, 58, 123–133.

Englemann, S. & Carnine, D. (1982). *Theory of instruction: Principles and applications*. New York: Irvington.

Greer, R. D. (2002). *Designing teaching strategies: A behavioral analysis systems approach*. New York: Elsevier Press.

Harmon, K., Strong, R., & Pasnak, R. (1982). Relational responses in tests of transposition with rhesus monkeys. *Learning and Motivation*, 13(4), 495–504.

Hayes, S. C. (1984). Making sense of spirituality. *Behaviorism*, 12, 99–110.

Hayes, S. C. (1994). Relational frame theory: A functional approach to verbal events, in Hayes, S. C., Hayes, L. J., Sato, M., & Ono, K. (Eds.), *Behavior analysis of language and cognition*. Reno, NV: Context Press.

Hayes, S. C. & Hayes, L. J. (1989). The verbal action of the listener as a basis for rule-governance, in Hayes, S. C. (Ed.), *Rule-governed behavior: Cognition, contingencies, and instructional control*. New York: Plenum.

Hayes, S. C., Barnes-Holmes, D., & Roche, B. (2001a). *Relational frame theory: A post-skinnerian account of language and cognition*. New York: Plenum Press.

Hayes, S. C., Barnes-Holmes, D., & Roche, B. (2001b). Relational frame theory: A précis, in Hayes, S. C., Barnes-Holmes, D., & Roche, B. (Eds.), *Relational frame theory: A post-skinnerian account of human language and cognition*. New York: Plenum, pp. 132–142.

Howlin, P., Baron-Cohen, S., & Hadwin, J. (1999). *Teaching children with autism to mind-read: A practical guide*. Chichester: Wiley.

Lovaas, O. I. (1981). *Teaching developmentally disabled children: The ME book*. Austin, TX: PRO-ED, Inc.

McHugh, L., Barnes-Holmes, Y., & Barnes-Holmes, D. (2003). *Training perspective-taking with young children*. Paper presented at the annual convention of the Association for Behavior Analysis, San Francisco, CA.

McHugh, L., Barnes-Holmes, Y., & Barnes-Holmes, D. (in press). Perspective-taking as relational responding: a developmental profile. *The Psychological Record*.

Murphy, C., Barnes-Holmes, D., & Barnes-Holmes, Y. (2003). *Manding and derived transformation of function in children with autistic spectrum disorder*. Paper presented at the annual convention of the Association for Behavior Analysis, San Francisco, CA.

Piaget, J. (1967). *Six psychological studies*. New York: Vintage.

Reese, H. W. (1968). *The perception of stimulus relations: Discrimination learning and transposition*. New York: Academic Press.

Roche, B. & Barnes, D. (1997). A transformation of respondently conditioned function in accordance with arbitrarily applicable relations. *Journal of the Experimental Analysis of Behavior*, 67, 275–301.

Roche, B., Barnes-Holmes, D., Smeets, P. M., Barnes-Holmes, Y., & McGeady, S. (2000). Contextual control over the derived transformation of discriminative and sexual arousal functions. *The Psychological Record*, 50, 267–292.

Skinner, B. F. (1957). *Verbal behavior*. New York: Appleton-Century-Crofts.

Sundberg, M. & Michael, J. (2001). The benefits of Skinner's analysis of verbal behavior for children with autism. *Behavior Modification*, 5, 698–724.

CHAPTER

17

Key Instructional Components of Effective Peer Tutoring for Tutors, Tutees, and Peer Observers

R. DOUGLAS GREER, DOLLEEN-DAY KEOHANE,
KATHERINE MEINCKE, GRANT GAUTREAUX, JO ANN PEREIRA,
MAPY CHAVEZ-BROWN, AND LYNN YUAN
Columbia University Teachers College and Graduate School of Arts and Sciences

INTRODUCTION

We briefly summarize the findings of the major reviews of tutoring research and describe the critical topics that remain to be researched as identified by the last review. Next, we present several new research studies that address the identified needs. The results of this program of research are then discussed in terms of classroom practice and future research.

Tutoring is one of the most researched and effective pedagogical tactics in both the educational and psychological literature. Stephens' (1967) comprehensive review of the educational research prior to the mid-1960s, identified peer tutoring as one of only *two* reliably effective tactics out of all of the interventions tested in hundreds of research studies in the education literature for that period of time (see also Cloward, 1967, for a review of tutoring *per se*). A subsequent review of the tutoring literature (Devin-Sheehan, Feldman, & Allen, 1976) reviewed additional studies in psychology and education to the mid-1970s. This paper divided the findings into effects on tutees (those who were tutored) according to same-age peer tutoring, cross-age peer tutoring, and trained versus untrained peer tutoring. The majority of the studies showed that tutoring was effective across all of the categories identified by the reviewers, in cases in which the tutors were trained in tutoring procedures. The effect of tutoring on tutors' academic or social behaviors was not a topic of investigation. During the 1980s and 1990s, much of the educational research (research not using behavior-analytic procedures or constructs) was associated with students teaching other students and took the form of "cooperative learning." The research on the cooperative learning tactic had mixed findings. Axelrod and Greer (1994) reviewed the cooperative learning literature and argued that, in cases where cooperative learning was effective, the effects appeared to be traceable to peer tutoring components.

During the late 1970s and early 1980s, the brunt of research in tutoring came from the applied behavior analysis literature. This research may be divided into research (1) on the effects of tutoring on the learning of tutees with regard to comparisons of peer tutoring with teacher instruction, (2) the effects of peer tutoring on the tutor's learning that which was tutored, and on the collateral behaviors of tutors. Two studies investigated the effects of peer tutoring on teacher performance as well (Davis, 1972; Polirstok & Greer, 1977). A review of that research and excellent descriptions of the types of tutoring and management of tutoring in applied behavior analysis were provided by Miller *et al.* (1994). Their review represents a statement of the state of the research literature to the mid-1990s. A review by the authors of this chapter of the major journals in behavior analysis revealed that no real change has occurred in the state of our understanding of tutoring as a tactic since the Miller *et al.* review. Moreover, the authors' recommendations for further research have not been addressed in the research to date. Miller *et al.* noted that the strong effects of peer tutoring could not be fully understood without an *identification of the key instructional components of peer tutoring*. The research that we report herein directly addresses the identification of the critical ingredients of effective peer tutoring on both tutee and tutor responding.

Research on the key instructional components, however, must be viewed in the context of the robust mainstream findings in behavior-analytic and educational research on the generic factors present in most effective instruction. These findings are associated with *engaged academic time*, also referred to as *active student responding* (Heward, 1994; Miller, Barbetta, & Heron, 1994); *opportunity to respond* (Greenwood Hart, Walker, Risley, 1994); and *learn units* (Greer, 1994, 2002; Greer & Hogin-McDonough, 1999). The findings associated with these terms actually represent a progression in the identification of key processes in effective instruction incorporating findings from educational research on the distribution of behavior between and within groups and findings in the behavior-analytic research on the components of effective instruction. In the former research, the identification of what works is based on outcomes after a period of time for a group, while in the latter research the identification of what works is based on comparisons of instructional components that led to mastery for each individual. Regardless of the difference in focus, the two literatures came to an unusual consensual dénouement, and such consensus increases the validity of the outcome of this work (Greer, 1983).

RESPONDING, ENGAGEMENT, AND AN EFFECTIVE TEACHER MEASURE

Group research studies over several decades came to identify *engaged academic time* as the single most robust finding in their investigations of gross generic pedagogical practices in classrooms and schools that were found to be more effective when socioeconomic variables were statistically controlled (Berliner, 1980; Stallings, 1980). Classrooms that provided their pupils with more engaged academic time or "active academic responding" produced better outcome. Engaged time simply meant that the teachers spent more actual time having the students respond to academic material. These classrooms had less down time, and the responding was to valid curricula. Students spent more time responding to academic material in written or vocal forms. Indeed, in the educational research literature, it was, and remains, the single, strong finding concerned directly with pedagogy. However, engaged academic time is a measure of topography rather than behavior products, thus educators and researchers needed a better identification of just what was going on.

While the specifics of the components of engaged academic time were not clearly specified in the educational literature, findings from applied behavior analysis by Greenwood (1984) showed that one component was the provision of opportunities for students to respond to academic material. Greenwood *et al.* found that simply providing more academic antecedents and response opportunities doubled learning for students. Later on, Greenwood and his colleagues developed the class-wide, peer-tutoring tactic that multiplied students' response opportunities and consequences to students' responses (Greenwood, Delquadri, & Hall, 1989). In a related finding concerning parents teaching children language, Hart and Risley (1989, 1991, 1996) found that the provision of response opportunities and more positive and elaboration prompts were the key components of mother–child interactions that built effective language in toddlers and preschoolers in homes regardless of a family's socioeconomic status. This body of research coincided with the identification of a measure of teacher effectiveness that incorporated opportunities to respond with instructional antecedents and consequences in teacher–student or computer–student interactions—the learn unit (Emurian, Delquadri, & Hall, 2000; Greer & Hogin-McDonough, 1999).

Teacher–student or computer–student interactions that consisted of learn units represented convergence in the literature on the importance of students' responding and on the antecedents and consequences to responding. The learn unit led to more learning than did interactions that were not learn units; the greater the numbers of learn units received by students, the greater the number of criterion referenced instructional standards achieved by students (Albers & Greer, 1991; Babbit, 1986; Bahadorian, 2000, Emurian, Hu, Wang, Durham 2000; Greer, McCorkler, Williams, 1989; Ingham & Greer, 1992; Lamm & Greer, 1991; Selinske, Greer, & Lodhi, 1991). Learn units are measures of teacher–child or parent–child interactions that meet certain criteria and include the key generic components to effective pedagogy.

First, the teacher must ensure that the student attends to the relevant antecedent instructional component, also known as the target or potential S^d (which stands for discriminative stimulus), before presenting instructions in written or spoken forms (or combinations thereof, such as "read the word" and the printed word) as the student's antecedent to responding (*e.g.*, saying the word or textually responding). Second, the student must respond or have the opportunity to respond (written, vocal, selection, production, or construction responses). Third, the consequence for the student's response or lack of response must be appropriate. The third component has two parts: (1) correct responses must be followed by positive reinforcers (consequences that act to increase antecedent-behavior relationship for the student); and (2) incorrect responses must be followed by a teacher correction that *requires the student to emit the correct response* in the presence of the relevant target antecedent (*i.e.*, word, number problem, or question) before the next presentation of an instructional antecedent or target stimulus. Delayed consequences are equally effective for written responding provided that the student attends to their previously written response and the antecedent or target S^d (Hogin, 1996). That is, the student observes the teacher's mark for an error and hears or sees the teacher's correction. Next, the student writes a corrected response. Thus, work from the previous day can function as learn units.

In addition, the rates of the presentations of learn units are a key variable, with faster rates being more effective generally than slower rates. Moreover, the more learn units the students receive, the better are their instructional outcomes.

What is learned by the student in the learn unit is the target student's antecedent, response, and consequence within the setting of the instruction or the operant and context. As students learn component skills, the initial learn unit, the teacher's learn unit progressively incorporates more and more responses for the student such that learn units are needed only at points in which unlearned components or composite skills are the target of instruction. For example, for solving addition problems, the early learn units involve individual numbers of single-digit combinations; later they involve multiple digit operations in which the single operations are the target until mastered. Next, the entire composite operation of a single problem is the target, followed by completing an entire page or grouping of problems with 100% accuracy. Next, the students need to meet a rate or time constraint in which they must respond to all of the problems on a page quickly and accurately. In the last stage, the accurate completion of an entire page or collection of problems constitutes a single learn unit. This newly fluent component becomes a single component in a larger more complex operation (see Greer, 2002, Chapter 2, for an in-depth treatment). In the behavior-analytic literature, this constitutes something like chaining; however, the learn unit identifies not only how the student's progression through components of a task is consequated but also what the teacher or experimenter must do to make the process likely to work.

Interestingly, the second of two important findings reported by Stephens (1967) in his review of educational research was the strong effects of programmed instruction, which we will show are related to the learn unit. Programmed instruction was developed by B. F. Skinner (1968) as a means of incorporating what was known at the time about learning from basic research in laboratories with nonhuman species such that instruction could occur without the teacher being present. Programmed instruction led to longer maintenance of learning than did teacher-directed study and provided greater short-term mastery across a range of subjects and ages. Programmed instruction was delivered by teaching machines or in a programmed text format but can now be delivered by computers if the instruction is designed as programmed instruction (Emurian et al., 2000; see also Section 4 of this book). The instruction involved *frames*, each of which included instruction (what we call antecedents to the students' responses) and a requirement that the student construct a response (*e.g.*, written) or, in some cases, to choose the correct response from those provided (Vargas & Vargas, 1991). If the response was correct, the student proceeded to the next frame; if not, the student had to perform a correction response. In some cases, the machine delivered edibles or tokens as reinforcement for correct responses, while in other cases simply being permitted to move to the next frame acted as the reinforcement. In short, Skinner's frame was what we have come to identify, albeit belatedly, as the learn unit.

Some have confused the learn unit with the student three-term contingency formation or operant, or what the student learns. Actually, the learn unit is a teaching operation of an automated device (*e.g.*, a computer instructional program) or teacher that occasions or sets the stage for the formation of the operant or the student's learning and includes the student's responses as well as all of the necessary teacher or teaching device responses to the student's responses. Learn units are simply the pedagogical components that are necessary if not sufficient to teach students concepts, skills, and, operations. By *necessary if not sufficient*, we mean that in most cases where the student has the necessary prerequisites, the learn unit alone is sufficient; however, in other cases, additional tactics need to be employed with the learn unit (see Chapter 4 in Greer, 2002). The learn unit is a measure of the teacher, the teaching device, or, indeed, an experimenter's effectiveness in creating conditions that are necessary if the students or subjects in experiments are to learn (Greer, 1994).

The learn unit is one of the most, if not *the* most, robust predictors of teaching effectiveness and thus must be taken into account in any analysis of other tactics and strategies. It is a measure of the effectiveness of the teacher or teaching device and can be systematically observed in any instructional setting (see Chapter 9 in Greer, 2002). We believe that the learn unit is a key factor in the relative success of peer tutoring as well as teacher instruction. The studies reported herein test this assertion.

Most tutoring studies have compared teacher instruction versus peer tutoring, and that research has shown that students learn more under tutoring conditions. Few, if any, of those research studies have controlled for learn units or components of instruction such that both teacher and tutor interactions were constant. Are the benefits of peer tutoring over teacher presentations findings due to a special peer or social effect, or are the results due to differences in types or numbers of teaching interactions? In addition, we address the following related questions associated with tutoring: What are the benefits for tutees and tutors involved in the tutoring process and peers who observed the tutoring process under conditions with and without learn units? Will tutors and tutees learn responses not directly taught as a function of tutoring a subset of material that they could then use to emit untaught novel responses without direct instruction (*e.g.*, pronouncing words they have never seen before)? Can scripts of problem-solving or rule-governed tasks be used to teach both tutors and tutees new conceptual operations?

To answer these questions, we present the following series of studies. All of the experiments involved teaching repertoires that are part of the state and national academic standards that are key to curricular goals associated with academic literacy and problem solving (Greer, 2002). The instructional standards that were taught included those concerned with spelling, social studies, identifying national monuments, selection and production responses for contractions, morpheme textual responses, algebra, rounding numbers, learning conceptual operations, and reading bar graphs. The experiments are presented in a series of brief reports using a standard format followed by a discussion of the findings (the complete papers are available from the senior author). Taken together, the investigations are a programmatic research effort to identify the key instructional components of effective tutoring for tutees and tutors. We have also added a new individual to the mix—the peer who observes tutoring, because other than learn units one of the other means by which students learn in classrooms is by observation.

All of the experiments were conducted in classrooms using the CABAS® (Comprehensive Application of Behavior Analysis to Schooling) instructional model (Greer, 1996, 2002). All of the schools are publicly funded schools for classrooms of children and adolescents with the demographic characteristics of students who are typically left behind in schools that use non-scientifically based approaches to education. The model is described in Chapter 3 in this book. Inter-observer agreement for all of the experiments was measured using the formula of point-to-point agreements between independent observers that summed agreement plus disagreement divided into agreements, thus providing a percentage of agreement index of the accuracy of the data.

NEW EXPERIMENTAL ANALYSES OF COMPONENTS OF EFFECTIVE TUTORING: BRIEF REPORTS OF FIVE STUDIES

Study 1

Researchers and Topic

M. Chavez-Brown, L. Morsillo, and R. D. Greer (2002). Peer versus teacher instruction in controlled learn-unit presentations: tutor and tutee gains in identifying national monuments, social studies, and spelling (Columbia University Teachers College).

Abstract

This study compared instruction delivered by a peer versus instruction delivered by a teacher on mastery of instructional material by tutees, when learn units were present under both teacher and peer tutor conditions. We also investigated the effects on correct responding by the tutors on the material they did not know prior to the functioning as a tutor. All tutees received instruction to a preset mastery criterion for state standards. All participants attended a classroom within a public middle school, located on the outskirts of a major metropolitan area.

Definition of Behaviors

The responses that were taught included taking dictation of spelling words, tacting or vocally identifying pictures of various national monuments, and intraverbal responding to social studies facts (*i.e.*, answering questions about social studies). All instruction was tied to state and national standards (New York State Standards, 1998; English Excellence in Education Standards, 1998). The first standard taught was writing spelling words. A response was considered correct if the participant independently wrote the spelling word correctly within 5 seconds of the vocal antecedent, which was the word to be spelled. A response was considered incorrect if the participant did not independently write the spelling word correctly within 5 seconds of the vocal antecedent or did not respond within 5 seconds of the vocal antecedent. During each phase, a set of five spelling words was taught.

The second standard taught was tacting and identifying pictures of various national monuments. The participants were required to respond vocally to the presentation of a picture. In some cases, the antecedent was simply the presentation of the picture; in other cases, the antecedent was the presentation of the picture and one of the following vocal antecedents: "What is this?" or "This is the _____." The participants could also respond by pointing to the correct picture when presented with an array of pictures and one of the following the vocal antecedents: "Which one of these is the _____?" or "Point to the _____." During each phase, a set of five national monuments was taught.

The third standard taught was intraverbal responding to social studies facts. The participants were required to vocally respond to a vocal antecedent such as "Who was the first President of the United States?" A response was considered correct if the participant responded with the correct intraverbal to the vocal antecedent independently within 5 seconds. A response was considered incorrect if the student did not respond within 5 seconds of the vocal antecedent or responded with the incorrect intraverbal. During each phase, a set of five social studies facts was taught.

Data Collection

Peer and teacher instruction phases: Data were collected using the same method for both the teacher instruction and peer instruction sessions across behaviors. Data were collected using a paper and pencil format for correct and incorrect responses to learn-unit presentations. A plus (+) was recorded for a correct response, and an incorrect response was recorded as a minus (−). During both peer and teacher instruction phases, a correction was given immediately when the student responded incorrectly. A correction was a model of the correct response. Corrections were considered and recorded as incorrect responses. During the teacher instruction phase, the teacher collected data for each student response. During the peer instruction phase, the tutor as well as the teacher independently collected data. This served as inter-observer agreement. At the end of each session, the total number of correct responses out of 20 presented learn units was calculated and a data point was placed on the graph. The criterion for mastery was preset at two consecutive sessions at 90% or above for all phases. *Pre- and post-treatment probes:* Pre-treatment probes were administered to all participants and were conducted as trials; no reinforcement was delivered for correct responses, and no correction was delivered for incorrect responses. Data were collected and graphed as the number of correct responses to the trial presentations. A total of 20 trials were conducted for each probe. In order to assess tutors' gains during treatment, a post-treatment, the same as the pre-treatment probe, was administered to each tutor at the conclusion of the study.

Design

A multiple-treatment counterbalanced design was used.

Inter-Observer Agreement

The teacher collected data with the tutor in all sessions. Inter-observer agreement for all pre- and post-treatment sessions was 100%. For the spelling instruction, inter-observer agreement for the teacher instruction phase was 100% during the two sessions it was calculated. For the peer instruction phase, inter-observer agreement ranged from 80% to 100%, with a mean of 90%. For the tacting of pictures of national monuments, inter-observer agreement observations were conducted in 57% of the teacher-directed sessions. Inter-observer agreement ranged from 95% to 100%, with a mean of 98.8%. Inter-observer agreement observations during the peer instruction phase were conducted in 100% of the sessions and ranged from 95 to 100%, with a mean of 98.3%. For the social studies facts, inter-observer agreement observations during the teacher instruction phase were conducted in 50% of the sessions. Inter-observer agreement was 100% across all sessions. Inter-observer agreement observations during the peer instruction phase were again conducted in 100% of the sessions and were 100% across all sessions.

Peer and Teacher Instruction Tactics

Tutor training: The tutor had previously been taught to use learn units for tutoring operations; therefore, only one 15-minute session was conducted to review learn-unit presentation such as presenting unambiguous antecedents, reinforcing correct responses with verbal praise and tangible reinforcers (points for back-up reinforcers), providing timely corrections for incorrect responses to ensure that the student emitted the correction, and collecting data accurately. *Peer instruction:* During the peer instruction phase, the tutors delivered learn units in a one-to-one setting; 20 learn units were presented during each session. *Teacher instruction:* During the teacher instruction phase, the teacher delivered learn units in a one-to-one setting; 20 learn units were presented during each session.

Participants

The participants were four male tutees, one female tutor, and one male tutor, and they ranged in age from 12 to 15 years old. All participants were diagnosed with a behavior disorder and had reader/writer levels of verbal behavior, including inappropriate speaker repertoires, and listener repertoires that were not fluent. Their academic repertoires placed them between the second- and fourth-grade levels.

Results

For the instructional objective (Fig. 1) of tacting (identification of pictures of national monuments), participant 1 required 80 learn units during the first teacher instruction phase, 60 learn units during peer instruction, and 80 learn units during the second teacher instruction phase. Participant 2 required 60 learn units during the first peer instruction phase, 60 learn units during teacher instruction, and 60 learn units during the second peer instruction phase to meet criterion for the same behavior. Participant 3 required 60 learn

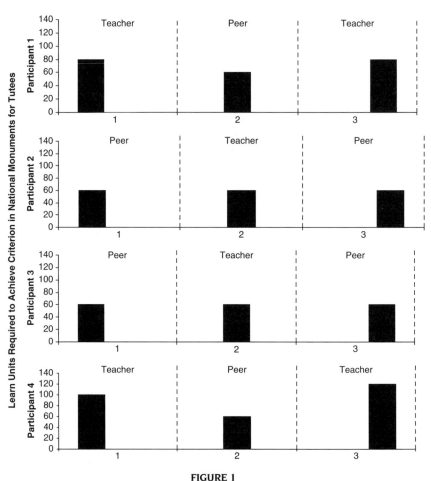

FIGURE 1

Numbers of learn units required to achieve criterion for identifying national monuments during teacher instruction and peer instruction phases for tutees 1, 2, 3, and 4.

units during the first peer instruction phase, 60 learn units during teacher instruction, and 60 learn units during the second peer instruction phase to meet criterion for the same behavior. Participant 4 required 100 learn units during the first teacher instruction phase, 60 learn units during peer instruction, and 120 learn units during the second teacher instruction phase. Two participants required more learn units in the teacher phases, and two participants showed no differences.

For the second instructional objective (Fig. 2) of intraverbal responding to social studies facts, participant 1 required 60 learn units during peer instruction and 100 learn units during teacher instruction. Due to circumstances beyond the teacher's control, participant 1 was not available to participate after reaching criterion for the second phase. Participant 2 required 60 learn units during the first teacher instruction phase, 60 learn units during peer instruction, and 60 learn units during the second teacher instruction phase. Participant 3 required 60 learn units during the first teacher instruction phase, 60 learn units during peer instruction, and 80 learn units during the second teacher instruction phase. participant 4 required 60 learn units during peer instruction and 120 learn units during teacher instruction. Due to circumstances beyond the teacher's control, Participant 4 was not available to participate after reaching criterion for the second phase. For one of the students for whom we had incomplete data, more learn units were required in the teacher phases. There were no real differences in the two tutees for which we had complete data.

For the spelling words (Fig. 3), participant 1 required 100 learn units during the first teacher instruction phase, 60 learn units during peer instruction, and 80 learn units during the second teacher instruction phase. Participant 2 required 40 learn units during the first peer instruction phase, 80 learn units during teacher instruction, and 40 learn units during the second peer instruction phase. Participant 3 required 120 learn units during the first peer instruction phase, 60 learn units during teacher instruction, and 80 learn units during the second peer instruction phase to meet criterion. Participant 4 required 100 learn units during the first teacher instruction phase, 80 learn units during peer instruction, and 60 learn units during the second teacher instruction phase to meet criterion for the same behavior. Only one participant required fewer learn units with the peer tutor across all instructional objectives; for all of the others, there were no clear differences.

During the pre-treatment probe conducted for spelling instruction (no figures are presented), tutor 1 responded correctly to 0 of the 20 probe trials prior to tutoring but responded correctly to all trials following serving as a tutor. During the pre-treatment probe conducted for tacting of national monuments, tutor 2 responded correctly to 2 of the 20 presented items and responded correctly to all presented items following serving as a tutor. During the pre-treatment probe conducted for intraverbal responding of social studies facts, tutor 1 responded correctly to 0 of the 20 probe trials and responded correctly

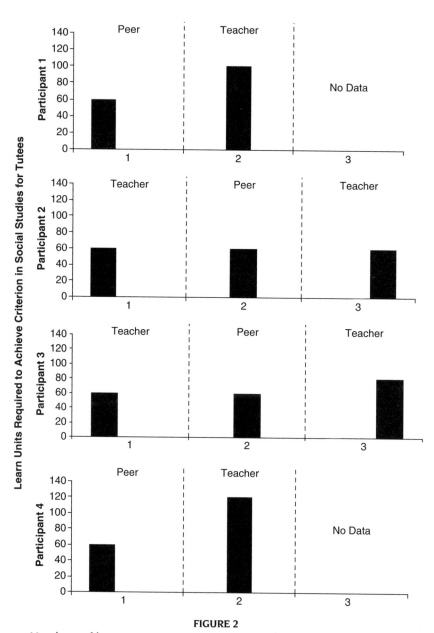

FIGURE 2

Numbers of learn units required to achieve criterion for social studies
facts during peer instruction and teacher instruction phases for
tutees 1, 2, 3, and 4.

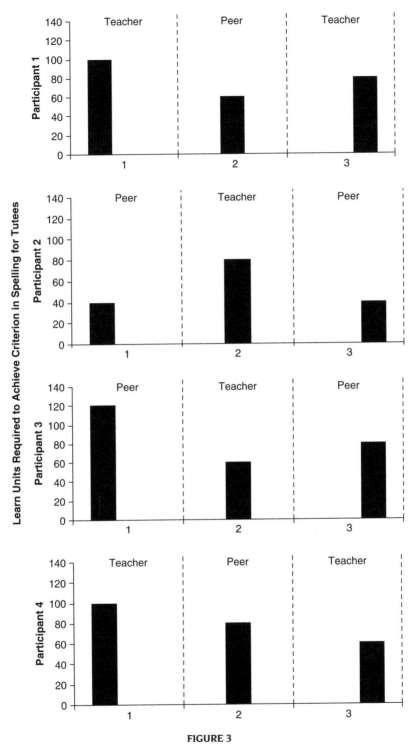

FIGURE 3
Numbers of learn units required to achieve criterion for writing spelling words during teacher instruction and peer instruction phases for tutees 1, 2, 3, and 4.

to 19 of the 20 presented items. After serving as tutors, the two tutors acquired correct responses to probe trials on responses they did not have in their repertoires prior to tutoring.

These results differ from most teacher–tutor comparisons because this study controlled for learn units. Specifically, all instruction was delivered using learn units by both the teacher and the tutors during each session. Only one student benefited from having the peer do the instruction, suggesting that tutoring benefits for tutees, when learn units are used in both teacher and tutor instruction, is a tactic that may be differentially beneficial for certain students only.

Study 2 (Experiments 1 and 2)

In this study, we investigated the effects of peers observing the tutoring process for tutors and tutees under conditions in which the tutors presented tutoring without learn units and conditions in which the tutor used learn units. We also investigated the effects of tutoring and observing tutees responding with and without corrections.

Researchers and Topic

K. Meincke and J. Hong (2002). Effects of peer tutoring with corrections compared to observing tutoring in which the tutees receive all correct responses on foreign language for the tutee, tutor, and an observer (Columbia University Teachers College).

Abstract

We investigated the academic benefits of peer tutoring of foreign language terms for the tutor, tutee, and an observer across two experiments. Pre- and post-tutoring probes were administered to all three participants on the terms that were peer tutored. The results of experiment 1 showed that peer tutoring increased correct responses during the post tutoring probes for all three participants even though it was only the tutee who received direct instruction. The results were consistent with research on peer tutoring, supporting the suggestion that it is an effective and profitable tactic to use in individualizing education. The results of experiment 2 showed a higher number of correct responses during the correction condition compared to the reinforcement condition.

Participants

The participants were three males (ages 12 to 15) diagnosed with emotional and behavioral disorders. The tutor had speaker, reader, and writer levels of verbal behavior with emergent listening and self-editing repertoires. The tutee and the observer had speaker, reader, and writer levels of verbal behavior with emergent listening repertoires. At the time of the study, a formal peer-tutoring program had not been implemented in the classroom. During experiment 2, a teaching assistant participated as a confederate. The teacher assistant had no prior experience in peer tutoring.

Definition of the Behaviors

The behavior taught was translating five printed phonetic Korean terms into English. According to the ninth-grade New York State Standards (1998), students should be able to communicate with the use of another language other than English. The dependent variables were (1) the number of correct responses to probe trials that were not learn units (no consequences) during baseline and (2) correct responses to learn units during tutoring sessions. A trial was defined as a teacher presenting an antecedent and the student responding. No reinforcements or corrections were provided to the student during or after the trial. The independent variable was peer tutoring, which consisted of the learn units presented during the tutoring sessions between the tutor and tutee.

Procedures and Data Collection for Experiment 1

Before any tutoring occurred, a probe was conducted on all three participants for 20 trials on 5 Korean terms. The 5 terms were basic and common terms. Each word was written phonetically on one side of a 3 × 5 index card, and the phonetic equivalent was written on the opposite side. The experimenter prompted the tutor initially to correctly present the vocal antecedent. During tutoring, the tutor phonetically read the terms and the tutee gave a vocal response. The tutor reinforced the tutee by saying "Good job, great!" when the tutee gave a correct response. If the response was incorrect, then the tutor gave a correction, which involved the tutor stating the correct responses and the tutee repeating it. Then, the tutor presented the next vocal antecedent. Both the teaching assistant and the observer recorded the accuracy of the tutor's learn-unit presentations using a modified version of the Teacher Performance Rate and Accuracy Observation (TPRA) during both experiments (Ingham and Greer, 1992; see Chapter 3). During the learn-unit presentations by the peer tutor, data were collected using a paper and pen format. When a correct response was observed, a plus (+) was recorded, and a minus (−) was recorded when an incorrect responses was observed. A correction by the tutor immediately followed the incorrect response and the tutee was required to give the correct response; correct responses were praised. Criterion was set at 90% or above for 2 consecutive sessions for the tutees' mastery of the instruction.

Inter-Observer Agreement for Experiment 1

Inter-observer agreement was conducted throughout this and the second study during pre- and post-intervention probes and during learn-unit presentations. Inter-observer agreement was 100%.

Design of Experiment 1

We used a multiple probe design for this and the second study.

Results of Experiment 1

Tutee, tutor, and observer scored 0 correct responses during the pre-intervention probe. During the post-intervention probe, the tutee scored 19 correct responses, the tutor scored 20 correct responses, and the observer scored 11 correct responses (Fig. 4).

Procedures for Experiment 2

This experiment used the same tutoring procedures with the addition of two conditions. A reinforcement condition and a correction condition were used in this study. In the reinforcement condition, with a new set of Korean terms another pre-intervention probe was given to the tutor and the observer for 20 trials. The tutor presented the vocal antecedent and the tutee gave the correct vocal response. The tutee had previously learned the Korean terms and acted as a confederate in the study such that only reinforcement operations would be given for all 20 learn units for 3 sessions. A post-intervention probe was given to both the tutor and observer. In the correction conditions, 5 more Korean terms were introduced and another pre-intervention probe was conducted. Three tutoring sessions were then conducted and the tutee acted as a confederate in the study; only correction operations were given for all 20 learn units for 3 sessions. A post-intervention probe was given to both the tutor and observer. The observer measured the accuracy of the learn units by using the modified TPRA observation for all sessions as discussed in Experiment 1.

Results for Experiment 2

Tutor and observer scored 0 correct responses during both pre-intervention probes for the reinforcement and correction conditions (Fig. 5). Following the reinforcement condition, the tutor scored 7 correct responses in the post-intervention probe. The observer scored 2 correct responses during the post-intervention probe. In the correction condition (Fig. 6), the tutor and observer scored 0 correct responses during the pre-intervention probe. Following the correction condition, the tutor scored 20 out of 20 correct

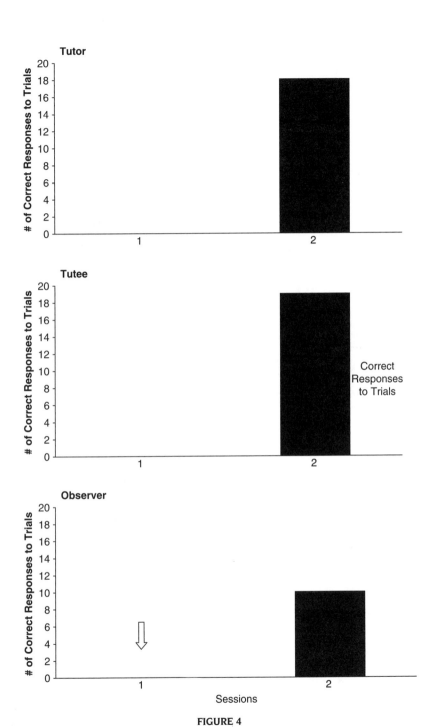

FIGURE 4

Pre- and post-tutoring responses to Korean language words for a tutor, a tutee, and an observer.

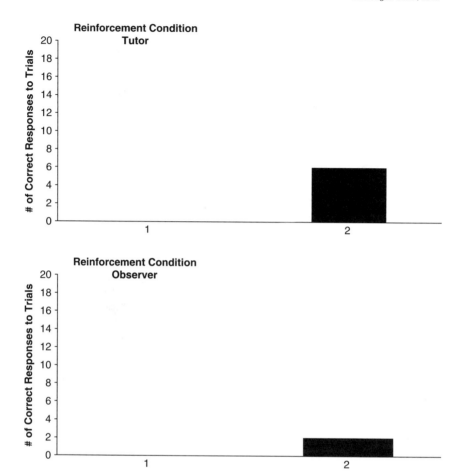

FIGURE 5
Pre- and post-tutoring responses to Korean language terms when the
tutee emitted all correct responses and received reinforcement
operations only.

responses in the post-intervention probe. The observer scored 19 out of
20 correct responses in the post-intervention probe. Thus, in these studies
we found that serving as a tutor or an observer resulted in the tutor and the
observer learning from either acting as a tutor or collecting data on tutoring as
an observer. In the second study, we found that observing corrections or
providing tutoring corrections was the key factor in the tutor or observer
learning. Thus, the operations and experiences involved in the correction
process for the learn unit were the key to success.

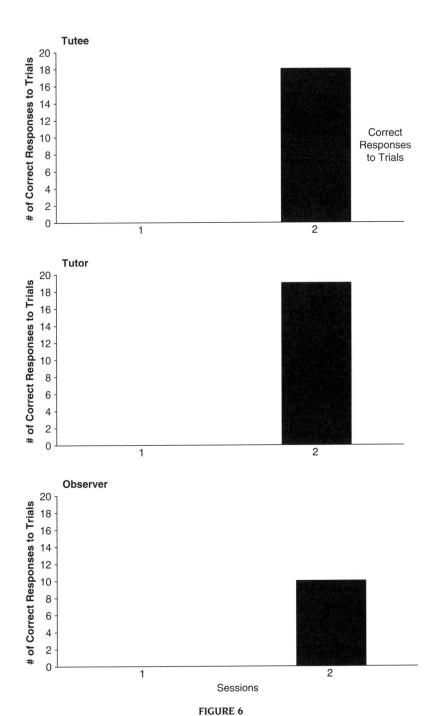

FIGURE 6

Pre- and post-tutoring responses to Korean language terms when the tutee received learn units with corrections and reinforcement operations for correct responses.

Study 3

In this study, we investigated the effects of tutoring on students who were observers to the tutoring process under conditions when the tutors did not provide learn units and under conditions in which the tutors did provide learn units.

Researcher and Topic

G. Gautreaux (2002). The effects of a peer observing the peer tutoring process in the presence and absence of learn units for social studies (Columbia University Teachers College).

Abstract

In the study, five middle school students served as observational learners across six instructional phases in order to test the effect of the presence or absence of learn units on observational learning. The content of the material presented was social studies vocabulary. Pre-experimental and post-treatment probes were conducted in a multiple-probe, counterbalanced ABABAB or BABAB design. The results of the study showed that students who observed learn-unit tutoring sessions had significant gains over sessions that involved tutoring when learn units were not present. These findings showed that peers who were functioning as observers learned as a function of observing learn-unit presentations by tutors to tutees.

Participants

All participants (3 males, 2 females) had diagnoses of behavior disorders and ranged in age from 12 to 14. Three participants were near grade level academically with fluent reader/writer and speaker listener repertoires and emergent self-editing skills. The other remaining participants had significant deficits in their reader/writer repertoires and read at approximately the third-grade level.

Setting

This study was conducted across two classrooms that were located in a suburban middle school serving students with emotional or behavioral disorders. The students in the classroom had been trained in peer tutoring procedures, and peer tutoring was considered part of their daily routine.

Data Collection

Pre-experimental probes: One pre-experimental probe consisting of 30 questions was conducted across each experimental phase for each participant. Each phase contained a different content area (U.S. history, world history, geography). Students were required to textually respond to preprinted index cards on which the definitions of words appeared. They were asked to emit a vocal verbal response to each definition by supplying the word that reflected the definition. No feedback was given during these probe sessions. *Peer tutoring phases:* In each of the experimental phases, a tutor, tutee, and peer who was conducting a TPRA participated in the session. The peer served in the role of an observational learner, as he was simply required to record the behavior of both the tutor and tutee. *Post-tutoring probes:* Upon completion of the peer tutoring sessions of each phase, a post-treatment probe was administered. These probes were conducted in the same manner as the pre-experimental probes and, again, no feedback was given.

Design

This study used a counterbalanced multiple probe design (ABABAB). For each phase, the content area was changed. Also, phases alternated between sessions that included learn units and those that contained non-learn-unit presentations.

Results

The results of this study showed that across all five participants, a significant difference occurred between post-treatment probes that followed learn-unit presentations and those that did not (Figs. 7 to 9). The results showed that when students observed learn units they showed impressive gains compared to when they observed non-learn units.

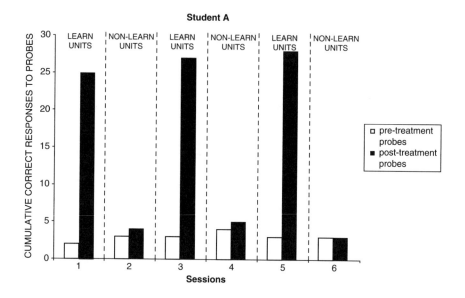

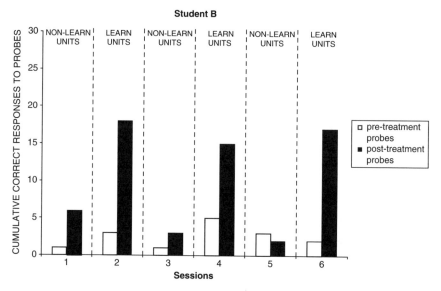

FIGURE 7

Observation by peers of tutoring without learn units (pre-learn-unit probes)
and observation by the peers of peer tutoring done with learn units (post-
learn-unit probes) for students A and B.

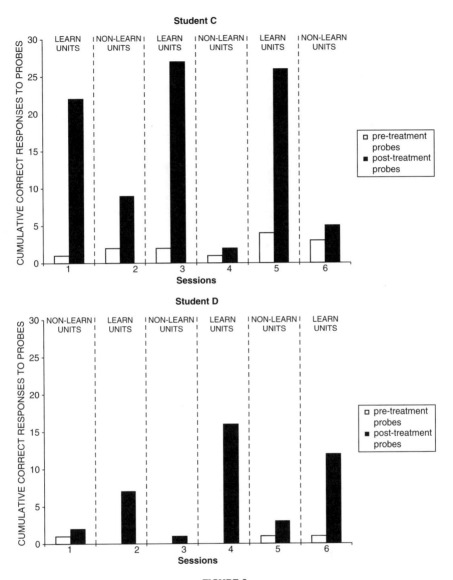

FIGURE 8

Observation by peers of tutoring without learn units (pre-learn-unit probes) and observation by the peers of peer tutoring done with learn units (post-learn-unit probes) for students C and D.

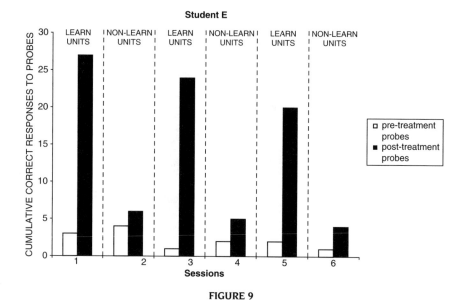

FIGURE 9

Observation by peers of tutoring without learn units (pre-learn-unit probes) and observation by peers of peer tutoring done with learn units (post-learn-unit probes) for student E.

Study 4

This study tested the effect of tutoring that used multiple exemplar instruction on the emergence of responses not directly taught. The tutees were taught a subset of responses such that untaught responses that belonged to the same class emerged without direct instruction (see Chapter 16.)

Researchers and Topic

L. Yuan and R. D. Greer (2003). The effects of multiple exemplar instruction on contractions and morpheme responses not directly taught for tutors and tutees (Columbia University Teachers College).

Abstract

We examined the effect of peer tutoring of multiple exemplar instruction on the use of contractions and morphemes not directly taught for both tutors and tutees. Two participants were paired as a tutor and a tutee for the contraction words program, and two other participants were paired as a tutor and a tutee for the morpheme program. Prior to the experiment, probe sessions were conducted to determine the number of correct responses emitted by the tutor and the tutee on different response forms of contractions and on the morphemes. In the baseline condition, the tutees were taught to master one of the response functions for contractions (selection) and one morpheme set to a mastery criterion, with probe sessions on untaught morpheme responses being conducted following mastery of the single set. The tutors then taught the tutees set 2 contraction words and set 2 morphemes using multiple exemplar training until the students achieved criteria. Multiple exemplar instruction involved alternating the two response functions (selection or production) in the case of contractions or alternating the morphemes across different untaught forms for the set 2 tasks. Probe sessions were conducted for the set 1 untaught responses following the multiple exemplar training on the set 2 tasks. The tutees were then taught to master one of the response forms and one of the morpheme sets with set 3, and the other untaught responses were probed. After multiple exemplar training was taught by the peer tutors, the data showed the emergence of untaught responses for both the tutors and tutees for both programs, indicating that the multiple exemplar training contributed to the transfer of function (from selection to production) and the development of derived relational responding (from a subset of morphemes to untaught morphemes) for the tutees who was receiving the instruction as well as for the tutors who were delivering instruction.

Definition of the Behavior

The dependent variable consisted of the number of correct responses on the students' emission of untaught responses that belonged to the same class as those that were tutored or to a different response function. The dependent variable for participant B, when he functioned as a tutor, was the correct responses on the production responses after tutoring the tutee for set 1, the correct responses on production responses in set 1, and the production responses for set 3 after tutoring the multiple exemplar instruction. The same behavior was measured for tutee T. The dependent variable for participant A, when he functioned as a tutor, was the number of correct responses on the morpheme probe set after set 1 was taught, the number of correct responses on the probe set in set 1, and the probe set in set 3 after tutoring the multiple exemplar instruction. Same behavior was measured for tutee B.

Data Collection

For the dependent measure of the contraction words program, the pre-experimental probes consisted of the tutors and tutees' untaught production responses for set 1 and set 3 contraction words taught as selection responses. For the independent measure of the contraction words program, we taught and collected data on both selection and production responses in alternating fashion (the multiple exemplar training condition) with set 2 contraction words and then taught selection responses only for set 3 contractions. For the morpheme program, the pre-experimental probes consisted of the tutors and tutees' untaught textual responses (or vocal reading responses) to set 1 and set 3 morphemes. For the independent measure of the morpheme program, data were collected on the taught responses in the multiple exemplar training condition with set 2 morphemes (alternating combinations of morphemes) and then taught responses for set 3. Correct responses were recorded using a pen and paper format with a plus (+) and incorrect responses and no responses were recorded with a minus (−). All probe sessions consisted of no reinforcement or correction procedures.

Inter-Observer Agreement

Inter-observer agreement was assessed by having two observers simultaneously but independently collect data on 40% of the instructional sessions across all conditions as well as scoring the permanent product for the contraction words program. The inter-observer agreement for all probe sessions and instructional sessions was 100%.

Design

A multiple baseline probe design across students and programs was used in the study. Prior to the baseline condition, all response topographies in each program and the combination of morphemes were probed in 20 trial sessions for both tutors and tutees. In the baseline condition of the contraction words program, selection response was taught to mastery with 90% correct and two sessions consecutively; in the baseline condition of the morpheme program, one set of morpheme was taught to mastery. As the tutees met criterion, probe sessions were conducted on the correct responding of both tutors and tutees' untaught responses (production for the contraction words program and another set of morphemes for the morpheme program). The multiple exemplar training condition was then introduced, and the selection and production response forms in the contraction words program as well as the combinations of morpheme sets were taught to the tutees in an alternating fashion by the tutors. After the tutees achieved criteria, probe sessions for set 1 morphemes not directly taught were conducted for the tutors and the tutees. Following the probe sessions, set 3 morphemes were presented and taught to the tutees by the tutors. After the criterion was met, another probe session was conducted on the untaught responses for both tutors and the tutees.

Procedures for Tutoring Multiple Exemplars

The independent variable of the study was the tutors' presentations of learn units of the multiple exemplar training to the tutees. As part of the independent variable, the tutor was instructed to record data on the tutee's correct and incorrect responses in addition to consequating the tutee's responses. The teacher also obtained reliability with the tutor's presentation of learn units to ensure that all instruction of the tutor was correctly done. The independent variable also consisted of correct and incorrect responses to learn-unit presentation of the two response topographies in the contraction words program on set 2 contraction words. For the morpheme program, the independent variable consisted of correct and incorrect responses to learn-unit presentations of five combinations of morphemes, each set starting with a vowel (*a, e, i, o, u*), using multiple exemplar training.

Participants

Three of the students were from the same special education, self-contained classes. Participant B (tutor B for the contraction words program and tutee B for the morphemes program) was classified with a language delay. This participant was a 6-year-old, first-grade male who functioned at a listener/speaker and an emerging reader/writer level of verbal behavior. Prior to the study, the student has mastered taking data on another student, and he also had mastered peer tutoring across various academic programs. Participant T (tutee T) was a 6-year-old female who was classified with mental retardation. Participant T functioned at a listener/speaker and emerging reader/writer level of verbal behavior. Participant A was a 6-year-old male who was classified with a language delay and other health impairments. Participant A (tutor A) functioned as a listener/speaker and an emerging reader/writer level of verbal behavior. For the contraction words program, participant B functioned as a tutor and was paired with participant T, who was a tutee; for the morphemes program, participant A functioned as a tutor and was paired with participant B, who functioned as a tutee.

Results

Prior to the experiment for the contraction words program, the participants did not emit any of the correct responses across response forms on the contraction words program. Figure 10 shows the untaught responses prior to and after the multiple exemplar training for both the tutor and the tutee. The results showed that prior to the multiple exemplar training in the contraction program, the tutee emitted 0 (0%) correct production responses, and the tutor also emitted 0 (0%) correct production responses on the set 1 contraction words program. After the multiple exemplars training, the number of correct production responses increased for both participants with Set 1 contraction words; tutee T emitted 12 (60%) correct production responses, and tutor B emitted 7 (35%) correct production responses. Both participants also showed transformation of stimulus function, from selection to production, in set 3 contraction words in the final training phase in which the tutee was taught one response form (selection) and probed on the untaught response form (production). Tutee T emitted 8 (40%) corrects on the untaught production response, and tutor B emitted 3 (15%) corrects on the untaught production response. In the same figure, the data show that in the morpheme program the tutee did not emit any correct responses to the

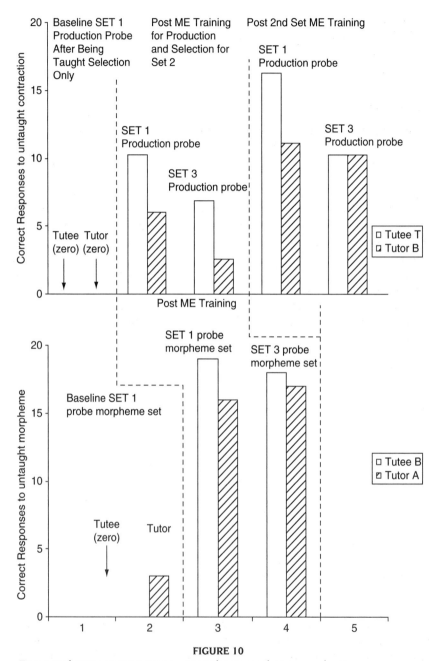

FIGURE 10

Tutor and tutee responses to untaught general case production responses
to contractions (top panel) and untaught morpheme combinations
(bottom panel) before and after tutoring in multiple exemplars.

probe set after the tutor instructional session; however, the tutor emitted 3 (15%) correct responses after tutoring the tutee with set 1 morphemes. Stronger results accrued for the first tutor tutee pair for the third set of contractions.

Study 5

This study addressed the effects of tutors using a script for teaching problem-solving operations across a variety of national and state academic standards. The research represents a test of tutoring benefits for complex problem-solving tasks.

Researchers and Topic

J. Pereira, L. Yuan, and R. D. Greer. The effects of peer tutoring on the tutor and tutee's problem-solving repertoires utilizing a script for tutoring algebra, rounding numbers, and bar graphs (Columbia University Teachers College).

Abstract

We tested the effects of peer tutoring on teaching students to respond accurately to problem-solving tasks utilizing academic scripts (Marsico, 1998). The participants were four students, two males and two females. This study was conducted across school settings. In each setting, one student served as the tutor and the other student served as the tutee. Across both settings, the students completed three problem-solving activities. A multiple probe design was implemented in which a baseline probe demonstrated that the students did not independently respond accurately to the problem-solving tasks without and with the use of a script. In the subsequent phases, peer tutoring was implemented as a tactic in which one student in each setting tutored the tutee utilizing learn units to teach a script of the steps in solving the problems. The results showed that the tutee learned from the tutor across problem-solving tasks. The tutor also responded at a higher level than they had in their pre-tutoring baseline following having served as tutors to teach the tutees to criterion on the problem solving tasks. Furthermore, in some instances, the tutee and tutor met criterion within one session following peer tutoring. This study suggests that peer tutoring is an effective tactic for teaching students to use written rules.

Definition of Behaviors

The dependent variables were correct responses to learn-unit presentation across three problem-solving tasks for the tutee during peer tutoring. In addition, the dependent variables were probes that were conducted with and without a script for the tutee and tutor prior to and following tutee training by the tutor across problem-solving tasks.

Data Collection

The data were collected as responses to learn units by the tutor during training sessions. The pre-experimental and post-experimental probes for the tutor and tutee were administered by the teacher with and without a script. All responses were collected as permanent products. In addition during peer tutoring, the instructor on the tutor conducted TPRA observations across all sessions.

Inter-Observer Agreement

The teacher collected agreement data with the tutor in 100% of the sessions. The inter-observer agreement was 100% across all sessions. The data recorded for correct and incorrect responses across programs and across students were observed during both probe and instructional sessions. Inter-observer agreement was assessed by having two observers independently record the number of correct and incorrect responses on 30% of the students' permanent product across all conditions and classrooms. In addition, inter-scorer agreement was conducted for 100% of the sessions and was calculated at 100% across programs and settings.

Tactics

The independent variable of the study was having the peer tutor teaching the tutee to solve problems using a script (see Chapter 7 for more information). The classroom teacher for each problem-solving program wrote a script providing students with step-by-step instructions that led to the solution to each problem. Prior to the onset of this study, both tutors had been taught to tutor using learn units to a predetermined criterion. As part of the independent variable, the tutor was instructed to present learn units and record data on the tutee's correct and incorrect responses using a pen and paper format. The teacher also consequated the peer tutor for the correct learn-unit presentation and gradually faded her presence once the peer tutor achieved reliability with TPRA observations (Greer, 2002).

Participants

Four students enrolled in a public school located in a suburb of a major city participated in the study. Participants B and T were 5-year-old students diagnosed with developmental disorders. Participant B was a male who was classified with a language delay; he functioned as a listener/speaker and an emerging reader/writer according to the Preschool Inventory of Repertoires for Kindergarten (PIRK). Participant T was a female who was classified with mental retardation and was functioning at a listener, pre-speaker, and emerging reader/writer level of verbal behavior. Participants R and M were 14-year-old students diagnosed with behavior disorders. Participant M was a female who was diagnosed with emotional and a learning disability; she was functioning at a reader, writer, and self-editor level of verbal behavior. Participant R was a male who was classified with an emotional disability and was functioning as a non-listener, reader, writer, and emerging self-editor.

Results for Tutor B and Tutee T

Prior to the experiment, both participants did not emit any correct responses either with or without a script across bar graphs, word puzzles, and word problems, as shown in Figs. 11 and 12. After the tutor presented learn units using a script (data not shown for brevity's sake) across the instructional programs, the tutee quickly learned to solve the problems. A probe session was conducted, and the data showed that the tutor (Fig. 11) also learned to solve the bar graphs with 100% accuracy without a script after teaching tutee T (Fig. 12).

Results for Tutor M and Tutee R

The results for tutor M and tutee R were similar to the previous findings. The baseline probe for the tutee and tutor across the three problem-solving programs—algebra, rounding numbers, and bar graphs—demonstrated a low level of responding with and without a script (Figs. 13 and 14). During tutee training sessions where the tutor tutored the tutee utilizing a script, the tutee met criterion within one session for each program, responding at 18, 20, and 20 correct responses to the problem-solving programs. A post-experimental probe session following tutee training showed that the tutor (Fig. 13) and tutee (Fig. 14) learned to solve each of the problems and responded at a high level without a script.

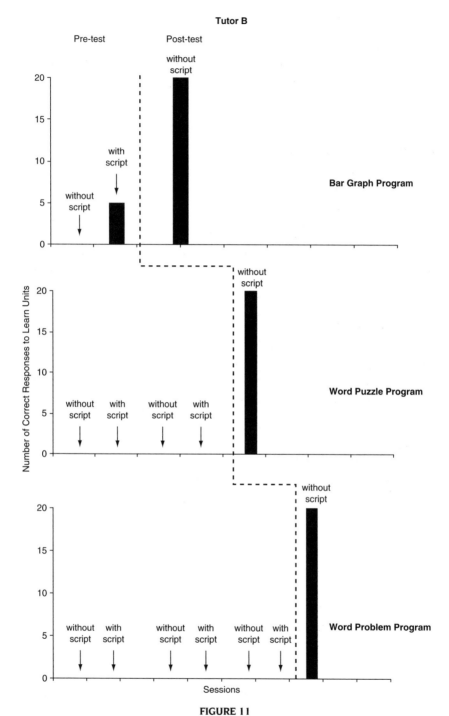

FIGURE 11

Correct responses of tutor B before and after tutoring using scripts for tutoring bar graph problems, word puzzle problems, and word problems.

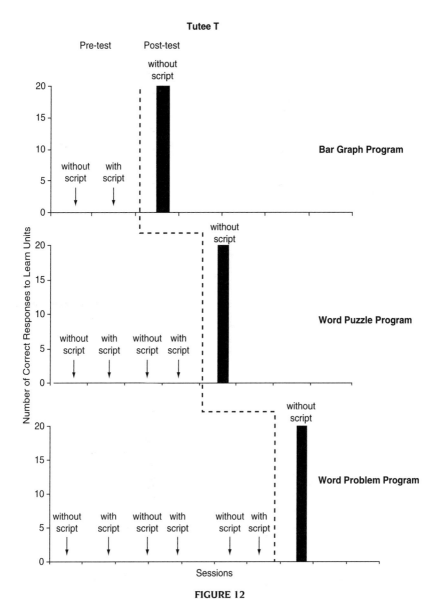

FIGURE 12

Correct responses of tutee T before and after tutoring using scripts for tutoring bar graph problems, word puzzle problems, and word problems.

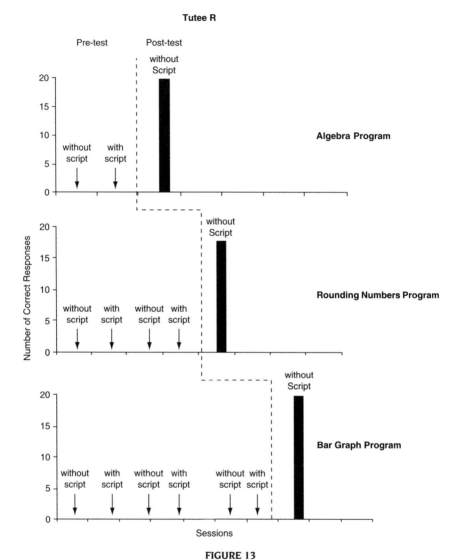

FIGURE 13

Correct responses of tutee R before and after tutoring using scripts for tutoring algebra, rounding numbers, and bar graphs.

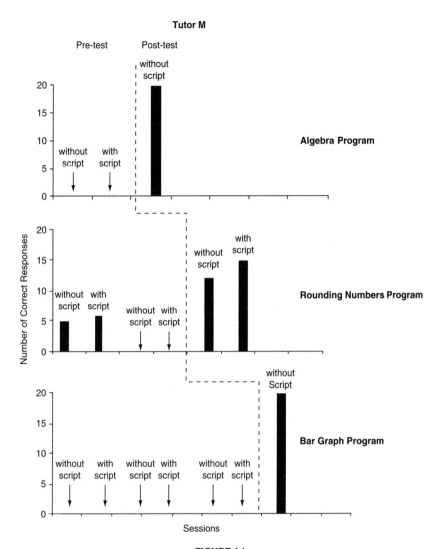

FIGURE 14

Correct responses of tutor M before and after tutoring using scripts tutoring algebra, rounding numbers, and bar graphs.

GENERAL DISCUSSION

These series of experiments provide evidence that the key ingredients for effective tutoring, as in the case of effective teacher presentations, are the presence of the components of learn units. Not only are learn units the key components for tutors and tutees, but they are also necessary for students who are observing tutoring if the observing students are to learn. One student in the teacher versus tutor comparison study, with learn units constant, did learn more across all three tasks when the tutor presented the learn units than when the teacher did so, suggesting that for some students there may be a peer advantage; however, for the most part, the presence of learn units ameliorated any differences between peer tutoring and teacher presentations. Other researchers have shown that the presence of learn units was necessary for criterion-level performance when instruction was delivered in programmed form by computers (Emurian *et al.*, 2000). In summary, the evidence to date shows that learn units should be present when students engage in peer tutoring or when teachers or computers present instruction. These research studies addressed the need identified by Miller, Barbetta, & Heron, (1994) for the identification of key instructional components for successful tutoring. The students who achieved mastery of the standards taught were students who had been left behind in their prior schooling—the very category of students that our educational system does not serve. The evidence from our studies demonstrates that these students can be taught skills with adequate *scientifically based instruction* that they were not able to learn before.

Studies 1, 2, 3, and 5 involved students whose learning deficits were a result of lack of prior learning opportunities and the lack of scientifically derived schooling procedures similar to the students identified by Greenwood et al. (1994) and Hart and Risley (1996). The students in the fourth study were children who had native learning disabilities (*e.g.*, diagnoses of autism or developmental disabilities). In fact, the students with developmental disabilities acquired repertoires associated with learning responses not directly taught, and both the tutor and the tutee learned.

The other tutoring research need that was identified by Miller *et al.* (1994) concerned possible social benefits or effects that might accrue from tutoring or being tutored. We did not address that issue; thus, future research should do so. However, prior research (Greer & Polirstok, 1982; Polirstok & Greer, 1986) did identify changes in collateral behaviors for tutors as a function of serving as tutors with nine different tutors over a 3-year period. That is, these students' academic and social behaviors changed in educational settings and in subject matter areas not related to the areas that they had functioned as a tutor. Those studies identified that the collateral changes were linked to approvals received by tutors from their tutees. We suggest that this is an important line of research concerning possible social benefits for both tutors and tutees. Given the effects of observing tutoring that we found in the studies reported here, a fruitful line of inquiry for investigating the source of collateral behavior change for tutors would seem to be related to the observational learning process.

Clearly tutoring that contains learn units benefits tutors, tutees, and students observing the tutoring. Tutoring that does not include learn units is not as effective. Interestingly, benefits did not result from observing students receiving correct responses alone (*i.e.*, tutees emitted only correct responses, with no correction). That is, observing other students emit the correct answer and receive reinforcement did not lead to observational learning. Thus, learning is occasioned for tutors and peer observers when they observe correction operations done by tutors with tutees. How students benefit from observation in classrooms appears to be critical to a student's success in a mainstream setting. Data from classrooms in which the teachers are not expert in behavioral procedures suggests that relatively few learn units are occurring (Greer, 1994). If few learn units are presented in these classrooms, and if our findings on the necessity for the presence of corrections hold widely, the possibility for students learning by observation is reduced even more dramatically. It would appear that if education is to leave no child behind the first critical step is to train teachers to present instruction using learn units. The process of teaching teachers to present learn units is not difficult and it is a cost-effective and relatively simple procedure. It can be done in the classroom by trained observers who provide consequences and visual displays to teachers, as Ingham and Greer (1992) found.

Tutoring provides one of the most powerful ways for teachers to increase learn units in classrooms. Learn units *are a necessary if not sufficient* component of any teaching effort devoted to leaving no child behind. Moreover, students who teach other students or observe tutoring benefit as much, if not more, than those who are tutored, and they do so across a wide range of curricular goals concerned with academic literacy, problem-solving repertoires, and responses that lead to novel applications of tutored responses. While tutoring is only one of the 200 or so tactics in the educational arsenal of applied behavior analysis (Greer, 2002), it is one that needs to be present in every classroom. Were all teachers to use frequent learn units and multiply the effect of learn units by using peers to present learn units, we would make a significant step toward saving more children.

It is important to note that in these studies the research was conducted by teachers in classrooms where they were responsible for all instruction. Moreover, these teachers use tutoring and many other tactics from applied behavior analysis (see Chapter 3). Thus, the procedures of applied behavior analysis are doable in real-world settings, if teaching is approached as a science rather than an art.

Acknowledgments

We acknowledge the assistance of Lisa Morsillo, now at the Dublin CABAS School, and Susan Mariano-Lapidus, of the Rockland CABAS School, in the collection of data for these experiments and in the pursuit of what was truly a programmatic effort by many CABAS professionals in the United States, Ireland, and England.

References

Albers, A. & Greer, R. D. (1991). Is the three-term contingency trial a predictor of effective instruction? *Journal of Behavioral Education*, 337–354.

Axelrod, S. & Greer, R. D. (1994). A commentary on cooperative learning. *Journal of Behavioral Education*, 4, 41–48.

Babbit, R. (1986). Computerized data management and the time distribution of tasks performed by supervisors in a data based educational organization (doctoral dissertation, Columbia University, 1986). *Dissertation Abstract International*, 47, 3737a.

Bahadorian, A. J (2000). *The effects of learn units on the achievement of students in two university courses*, unpublished doctoral dissertation, Columbia University.

Barbetta, P. M., Heron, T. E., & Heward, W. L. (1993). Effects of active student response during error correction on the acquisition and maintenance of geography facts by elementary students with learning disabilities. *Journal of Behavioral Education*, 3, 217–233.

Berliner. D. C. (1980). The half-full glass: A review of research on teaching, in Hosford, P. L. (Ed.), *Using What We Know About Teaching*. Alexandria VA: Association for Supervision and Instruction, pp. 51–77.

Cloward, R. (1967). Studies in tutoring. *The Journal of Experimental Education*, 36, 14–25.

Davis, M. (1972). Effects of having one remedial student tutor another remedial student, in Semb, G. (Ed.), *Behavior analysis and education*. Lawrence: University of Kansas.

Department of Educational Excellence (1998). *Standards of excellence for English schools*. London: Department of Educational Excellence.

Devin-Sheehan, L., Feldman, R., & Allen, V. L. (1976). Research on children tutoring children: a critical review. *Review of Educational Research*, 46(3), 355–385.

Emurian, H. H., Hu, X., Wang, J., & Durham, D. (2000). Learning JAVA: A programmed instruction approach using applets. *Computers in Human Behavior*, 16, 395–422.

Greenwood, C. R. (1991). Longitudinal analysis of time engagement, and achievement in at-risk versus non-risk students. *Exceptional Children*, 57, 521–535.

Greenwood, C. R., Delquadri, J. C., & Hall, R. V. (1984). Opportunity to respond and student achievement, in Heward, W. L., Heron, T. E., Trapp-Porter, J., & Hill, D. S. (Eds.), *Focus on Behavior Analysis in Education*. Columbus OH: Merrill, pp. 58–88.

Greenwood, C. R., Delquadri, J. C., & Hall, R. V. (1989). Longitudinal effects of classwide peer tutoring. *Journal of Educational Psychology*, 81, 371–383.

Greenwood, C. R., Hart, B., Walker, D. I., & Risley, T. (1994). The opportunity to respond and academic performance revisited: a behavioral theory of developmental retardation, in Gardener III, R. *et al.* (Eds.), *Behavior analysis in education: Focus on measurably superior instruction*. Pacific Groves, CA: Brooks/Cole.

Greer, R. D. (1982). Counter controlling the American Educational Research Association. *The Behavior Analyst*, 5, 65–76.

Greer, R. D. (1983). Straightening the nail: a rejoinder. *Educational Researcher*, Jan., 13–14.

Greer, R. D. (1994). A systems analysis of the behaviors of schooling. *Journal of Behavioral Education*, 4, 255–264.

Greer, R. D. (2002). *Designing teaching strategies: A behavioral systems approach*. New York: Academic Press.

Greer, R. D. & Hogin-McDonough, S. (1999). Is the learn unit the fundamental measure of pedagogy? *The Behavior Analyst*, 20, 5–16.

Greer, R. D. & Polirstok, S. R. (1982). Collateral gains and short-term maintenance in reading and on-task of inner city students as a function of their use of social reinforcement while tutoring. *Journal of Applied Behavior Analysis*, 15, 123–139.

Greer, R.D., McCorkle. N. P., & Williams, G. (1989). A sustained analysis of the behaviors of schooling. *Behavioral Residential Treatment*, 4, 113–141.

Hart, B. & Risley, T. R. (1989). The longitudinal study of interactive systems. *Educational Treatment of Children*, 12, 347–358.

Hart, B. & Risley, T. R. (1991). Variations in American parenting that predict child outcomes at three. *Developmental Psychology*, 28, 1096–1105.

Hart, B. & Risley, T. R. (1996). *Meaningful differences in the everyday life of America's children*. New York: Brookes.

Heward, W. L. (1994). Three "low-tech" strategies for increasing frequency of student of active responses during group instruction, in Gardner III, R., Sainato, D. M., Cooper, J. O., Heward, W. L., Eschelman, J. W., & Grossi, T. A. (Eds.), *Behavior analysis in education: Focus on measurably superior instruction*. Belmont, CA: Brooks/Cole.

Hogin, S. (1996). *Essential contingencies in correction procedures for increased learning in the context of the learn unit*, unpublished doctoral dissertation, Columbia University, New York.

Ingham, P. & Greer, R. D. (1992). Changes in student and teacher responses in observed and generalized settings as a function of supervisor observations. *Journal of Applied Behavior Analysis*, 25, 153–164.

Lamm, N. & Greer, R. D. (1991). A systematic replication of CABAS in Italy. *Journal of Behavioral Education*, 1, 427–444.

Marsico, M.J. (1998). Textual stimulus control of independent math performance and generalization to reading (doctoral dissertation, Columbia University, 1998). Abstract from UMI Proquest Digital Dissertations [on-line], Dissertations Abstracts Item: AAT 9822227.

McGee, C. S., Kaufman, J. M., & Nussen, J. L. (1977). Children as therapeutic change agents: reinforcement intervention paradigms. *Review of Educational Research*, 47, 451–477.

Miller, A. D., Barbetta, P. M, & Heron, T. E. (1994). START tutoring: designing, training, implementing, adapting, and evaluating tutoring programs for school and home programs. *Behavior Analysis in Education: Focus on Measurably Superior Instruction*. Belmont CA: Brooks/Cole.

New York State Department of Education. (1998). *Educational standards: K–12*. Albany: New York State Department of Education. (http://www.hysed.gov/)

Polirstok, S. R. & Greer, R.D. (1977). Remediation of a mutually aversive interaction between a problem student and four teachers by training the student in reinforcement techniques. *Journal of Applied Behavior Analysis*, 10, 707–716.

Polirstok, S. R. & Greer, R.D. (1986). A replication of collateral effects and a component analysis of a successful tutoring package for inner-city children. *Educational Treatment of Children*, 9, 101–121.

Selinske, J., Greer, R. D., & Lodhi, S. (1991). A functional analysis of the comprehensive application of behavior analysis to schooling. *Journal of Applied Behavior Analysis*, 13, 645–654.

Sherman, T. M. and Cormier, W. H. (1974). An investigation of the influence of student behavior on teacher behavior. *Journal of Applied Behavior Analysis*, 7, 11–21.

Skinner, B.F. (1968). *The technology of teaching*. New York: Appleton-Century-Crofts.

Stallings, J. (1980). Allocated academic learning time revisited, or beyond time on task. *Educational Researcher*, 9, 11–16.

Stephens, J. M. (1967). *The process of schooling*. New York: Holt, Rinehart & Winston.

Vargas, E. A. & Vargas, J. S. (1991). Programmed Instruction: what it is and how to do it. *Journal of Behavioral Education*, 1, 235–252.

CHAPTER

18

Training Professionals Using Sequential Behavior Analysis

TOM SHARPE AND DANIEL BALDERSON

University of Nevada, Las Vegas

HOSUNG SO

California State University, San Bernardino

Only about 8% of all psychological research is based on any kind of observation. A fraction of that is programmatic research. And, a fraction of that is sequential in its thinking. This will not do. Those of us who are applying these new methods of observational research are having great success.
—R. Bakeman and J. Gottman (1997, p. 184)

HISTORY AND INTRODUCTION

Behaviorally based feedback strategies designed for undergraduate teacher education activities have been documented as effective in training teachers to use a variety of effective instructional behaviors in a variety of undergraduate practice teaching settings (Cooper, Thomson, & Baer, 1970; Cossairt, Hall, & Hopkins 1973; Hall, Panyon, Rabon, & Broden, 1968; Ingham & Greer, 1992; Kamps, Leonard, Dugan, Boland, & Greenwood, 1991; Page *et al.*, 1982). A consistent finding in the education literature is that direct observation and feedback provision on select target behaviors (*i.e.*, behaviorally based feedback) is effective in altering the classroom behaviors of teachers and, consequently, the behavior of their pupils. Many professional teacher-training programs that have implemented behavior analysis data as an ongoing instructional feedback and goal-setting treatment package are also procedurally available in the literature (Darst, Zakrajsek, & Mancini 1989; Landin, Hawkins, & Wiegand, 1986; Miller, Harris, & Watanabe, 1991; O'Reilly & Renzaglia, 1994; Warger & Aldinger, 1984).

Though documented as effective in the primary training setting, behaviorally based feedback approaches to teacher education are currently the subject of criticism in the mainstream teacher education profession. The main criticism suggests that the criterion-based approaches used in this method are inappropriate. *Criterion-based* is defined in this argument as a procedure in which teacher-trainees are held accountable for the demonstration of a predetermined number or percentage use of a particular behavior or set of behaviors (*e.g.*, verbal instruction, feedback, questioning) that are hypothesized to be effective across a variety of instructional settings. A pupil behavior measure (*e.g.*, activity engagement, on-task behavior, or ratio of correct to total skill trials) has traditionally been used to determine the relative effectiveness of a teacher's instructional activities when using traditional behavior feedback strategies. (For examples of criterion-based behavior feedback techniques, refer to Carnine and Fink, 1978; Greer, 1985; Ingham and Greer, 1992; Kamps et al., 1991.) Doyle (1990) states that this criterion-based approach to teacher training provides a simplistic and inappropriately generic characterization of teaching. He concluded that it does so by stripping an analysis of complex interactive settings (such as those that teaching exemplifies) of all setting context and curriculum content through the fragmentation of the interactive process into discrete elements that are oftentimes wrongly assumed to affect client or pupil practices in particular instructional situations.

Proponents of the behaviorally-based feedback approaches provide an important alternative argument in response to these criticisms (Morris, 1992; Sharpe, 1997; Sharpe, Hawkins, & Ray 1995, 1998; Sharpe & Koperwas, 2003). The response arguments of those cited also provide an important foundation for the sequential behavior instructional strategy that is summarized and evaluated in this chapter. Response argument goes something like this: If, for example, a criterion-based framework is used to provide feedback and goal setting for teachers in training, then this activity would fall within what Morris terms *demonstration* (1992, p. 9). Using a demonstration approach, teachers are trained in a rule-governed manner (*i.e.*, told to exhibit certain behaviors or actions in a general way under the assumption that these behaviors and actions are generally effective) to demonstrate particular behaviors to criterion when practice teaching. If training stops with demonstration, it is argued that teacher-trainees may not come to an understanding of the functional relationships between what a teacher does and how it affects pupil behaviors in particular instructional situations. If a teacher-trainee does not leave the training program with adequate understanding of the setting specific nature of teacher–pupil interactions, then long-term use of effective teaching practices may not be realized.

An appealing alternative to a criterion-based approach, and one recommended by this chapter, is termed *discovery* (Morris, 1992, p. 9). In a discovery approach, teacher-trainees are first explicitly taught which behaviors and setting conditions may be strongly related to the use or nonuse of certain pupil behaviors. In behavior analysis terms, this is much like a *contingency-managed* approach to skill learning. If the specific time-based or sequential connections between what a professional (*e.g.*, teacher) does in a particular setting and how those activities impact on a specific clientele (*e.g.*, pupil) are explicitly taught, it is hypothesized that those professionals may then become more effective in determining which behaviors to use in certain situations to maximize their effectiveness in terms of desirable client behavior change. In a discovery approach to professional teacher preparation, instead of defining explicit criteria for certain behavior usage (*e.g.*, provide a minimum of three feedback statements a minute), a descriptive mapping of the many teacher and pupil behaviors that are used in a particular educational setting is first provided and is then analyzed in terms of the relative effectiveness of those teacher behaviors in relationship to the time-based connections with certain student behaviors within a particular educational situation. From this kind of analysis, a better understanding of just what works in particular educational situations may be discovered, and, from that discovery, objectives for future teacher behavior use may be defined and recommended for future instructional episodes.

Technology

One of the main difficulties of implementing a discovery approach to behaviorally based instructional feedback strategies lies in having access to capable and user-friendly direct observation descriptive mapping tools. Currently, many computer-based instruments have been developed and implemented to support the use of sequential behavior analysis and to facilitate the ability to collect and analyze multiple measurement types of multiple ongoing behaviors and events (Greenwood, Carta, Arreagamayer, & Rager, 1991; Sharpe, 1996; Sharpe & Koperwas, 2000). Many of these tools provide a primary focus on a sequential analysis, meaning that educational researchers have the capability to explicitly investigate how the behavior of the teacher affects the behavior of the student and in turn how actions of the student may change a teacher's behavior. Using sequential analysis allows supervisors to see the connections across time among these behaviors, and they may be made quantitatively explicit using amenable analysis techniques (Bakeman & Gottman, 1997; Sharpe, 1997; Sharpe & Koperwas, 2000). This capability is important to the analysis of a variety of interactive settings, in general, and instructional and therapeutic settings, in particular, given the importance of analyzing the relationship between what a teacher does and how a pupil responds. If successfully implemented, these tools provide an important next descriptive step for teacher education research and development. Researchers who take advantage of direct observation tools are beginning to find consistent results in areas previously not considered for quantitative analysis (Bakeman & Gottman, 1997; Sharpe & Koperwas, 2003). Examples include discovery of important time-based relationships among how babies learn to interact with their parents

in productive ways, how young children engage in productive social interactions, how marriages succeed or fail as a function of how spouses interact,
and how a variety of professionals succeed or fail in their interactions with a
variety of clientele. In this last regard, we feel strongly that computer-based
sequential observation techniques that include a thorough quantitative methodology provide an important set of scientific tools by which to discover much
more of the setting-specific functional relationships that characterize the
complex, interactive milieu that comprises most instructional settings.

A Sequential Analysis Illustration

When collecting data to illustrate the sequential connections (also known as
time-based connections) among multiple behaviors, it is first important to define
measures so that they explicitly capture the sequential character of behavior and
event interactions (*i.e.*, in the case of this chapter's teacher education illustration, teacher and pupil behaviors that describe how those teachers and pupils
interact in a variety of instructional and organizational situations). To illustrate
the difference, a *demonstration*-oriented investigation might look at the Off-Task
behaviors of pupils, and then monitor the teacher's treatment of Pupil Proximity
or Positive-Verbal Praise. A decision might then be based on the number of times
each pupil or teacher behavior occurs, or the relative percentage of class time
each behavior takes up. In a *discovery*-oriented sequential study, on the other
hand, a more global student measure might be used such as student Organizational Opportunities, with a variety of teacher behaviors monitored as a function
of occurring in time around those Organizational Opportunities. The most often
used measure in a sequential study is a conditional probability of occurrence of a
particular behavior. In other words, sequential investigations attempt to find out
the likelihood of a particular teacher behavior occurring given the recent occurrences of a targeted pupil behavior of interest (Bakeman & Gottman, 1997;
Sharpe, 1997; Sharpe & Koperwas, 2003). In this latter approach, the time-
based relationships among teacher and pupil behaviors are made explicit.
When this information is used as an instructional feedback strategy with
teacher-trainees after a particular practice teaching episode has concluded in
an instructional setting, it has been successful in (1) eliminating inappropriate
teacher behaviors that occur or tend to trigger undesirable pupil behaviors, and
(2) increasing appropriate teacher behavior around pupils who are experiencing
instructional or organizational challenges (Sharpe et al., 1995; Sharpe,
Lounsbery, Bahls, 1997; Sharpe & Lounsbery, 1998).

Providing a Database

In order to advocate using a sequential behavior approach in the field-based
or deliberate practice education of undergraduate teacher-trainees, it is
important to show empirical support for the educational method. In this

manner, a genuine science and technology of effective professional practice may be made available. In many respects, the creation of a database supporting sequential behavior techniques as applied to educational concerns may be perceived as a scientific return to the flurry of behavior analysis in education activity of the 1970s and early 1980s. While the principles we summarize here have been used before, we are showing an alternative way of looking at educational behavior in terms of the sequential patterns that tend to recur over time. From the data presented in this chapter we hope to convince readers that there is a lot to be gained from thinking about direct observational data in a time-based fashion. We also propose that when collecting behavioral data, omitting information related to sequential interactions is to potentially miss an important opportunity for discovery and evaluation. It is in this regard that we feel that the application described provides opportunity for significant impact on the future of training professionals, in general, and on educating future teachers specifically.

The study presented in this chapter is based on a line of research pursued in response to the criticisms of using behaviorally based instruction and feedback strategies in mainstream teacher education (Sharpe et al., 1995, 1997, Sharpe, Hawkins, Lounsbery, 1998; Sharpe & Lounsbery, 1998). Termed sequential behavior analysis (SBA) and sequential behavior feedback (SBF) when used as a feedback strategy with teacher-trainees, it provides an alternative behavioral approach to the direct observation and feedback provision process. To date, the immediate training and short-term maintenance effects of SBF on teacher and pupil behavior in the primary undergraduate practice teaching setting has been well documented (refer to Sharpe et al., 1997, for a complete description of these settings). In addition, studies have shown SBF to be beneficial to the improvement of the self-monitoring accuracy of experienced teachers working in public school settings (Sharpe, Spies, Newman, Spickelmier, Villan, 1996).

The next important questions to this line of research include:

- The amount that increased teacher-trainee proficiency as a function of SBF exposure generalizes to the first 2 years of on-the-job practice after exiting the teacher training program.
- The relative effectiveness of an SBF strategy when used as an on-the-job continuing education tool with professional teachers who have not been exposed to SBF strategies during their undergraduate training experiences.

These questions are particularly important to answer given that the long-term generalization of effective teacher practices that have been successfully trained during an undergraduate experience are not typically well maintained once an individual is teaching in a school setting (Graham, 1991; Lawson, 1991; Lawson & Stroot, 1993; Stroot & Williamson, 1993).

The purpose of providing the example data contained in this chapter is to observe and compare a matched group of teacher professionals currently working in public school settings to those who had been exposed to SBF strategies during their undergraduate experience and those who had not. An additional purpose of gathering the data provided in this chapter was to provide SBF to those teachers not previously exposed within their undergraduate training experiences to determine if a sequential behavior instructional feedback strategy was effective as a continuing-education activity.

SCIENTIFIC METHODS

Participants and Setting

Participants in this study included 6 male and 2 female teachers, all characteristically matched with the exception of exposure versus non-exposure to SBF strategies during their undergraduate teacher-training experiences. Each study participant began their first full-time teaching job with the onset of this study (Table 1). All participants were purposefully selected based on successful completion of a K–12 physical education teacher certification undergraduate degree within 4 years and with similar GPAs. Past teaching and coaching activities were also characteristically matched. Participants all matriculated through the same undergraduate program setting and were grouped and matched according to exposure versus non-exposure to SBF strategies (*i.e.*, experimental participants received SBF, and control participants received qualitative narrative feedback only). All undergraduate experiences were similar outside of SBF strategy exposure and included a core set of courses that combined educational theory with guided clinical practice activities in local public school settings.

All participants were purposefully chosen as a function of similarly positive letters of recommendation, of having accepted a full-time middle school

TABLE 1
Participant Information

Participant	Age	Gender	GPA	Experience	Certification
Exposed 1	22	M	3.3	YMCA youth sport coach	K–12, PE
Control 1	22	M	3.2	Middle school sport coach	K–12, PE
Exposed 2	23	F	3.6	Age-group swimming coach	K–12, PE
Control 2	23	F	3.5	Middle school basketball coach	K–12, PE
Exposed 3	22	M	3.1	Summer camp counselor	K–12, PE
Control 3	22	M	3.2	Summer camp counselor	K–12, PE
Exposed 4	24	M	3.7	High school football coach	K–12, PE
Control 4	23	M	3.6	High school football coach	K–12, PE

physical education teaching position the fall semester immediately following their undergraduate graduation, and all were within the same large metropolitan school district. Each physical education classroom used for observational purposes consisted of a well-equipped gymnasium and swimming pool setting in which team and individual sport skills (basketball, indoor soccer, volleyball, golf, flag football, and swimming) and fitness activities (flexibility, cardiovascular, and strength-training exercises) were taught in an individually prescribed, workstation format with end-of-class organized game activities.

Dependent Measures

In order to measure the differences between the two groups observed in this study, a set of dependent measures was implemented. Primary to this study was a sequential numerical measure of how a teacher behaved when an opportunity for instructional or organizational interaction presented itself during class time. Based upon an SBA framework (Bakeman & Gottman, 1997; Sharpe & Koperwas, 2003), the measures included:

- *Instructional opportunity* (IO), which represented an opportunity for a teacher to provide instructional action and was defined as a pupil or group of pupils who were having difficulty with the skills to be learned (*e.g.*, incorrect performance attempts) or were having difficulty discerning how to attempt a successful performance (*e.g.*, reading a task card for an extended period of time or passive observation of others practicing a skill).
- *Appropriate instructional action* (AIA), which provided an indication of whether a teacher took some form of appropriate behavioral action in the context of an IO incident; it was recorded if a teacher used a behavior in the context of an IO incident which clearly remedied that IO incident. To have an instance of AIA recorded, the teacher must have (1) implemented a behavioral interaction with a pupil or small group designed to specifically remedy the IO incident (*e.g.*, modeling a skill, explaining how to perform a task, providing skill information designed to encourage successful participation in an activity), and (2) the pupil or group involved in the IO incident must have returned to active and successful skill practice or activity engagement. If a teacher did not interact with a pupil or group in the context of an IO incident or a behavioral strategy was employed but the pupil did not return to successful skill or activity engagement within a 1 to 2-minute prescribed time period, then an AIA was not recorded.
- *Organizational opportunity* (OO), which represented an opportunity for a teacher to provide organizational or managerial action. It was defined as a pupil or group of pupils who were involved in an activity other than that prescribed for the day or were engaged in some form of disruptive behavior that required bringing that pupil or group back into appropriate activity practice.

- *Appropriate organizational action* (AOA), which provided an indication of whether a teacher took some form of appropriate behavioral action in the context of an OO incident; an AOA was recorded if a teacher used a behavior in the context of an OO incident that clearly remedied that OO incident. To record an instance of AOA, the teacher must have (1) implemented a behavioral interaction with a pupil or small group designed to specifically remedy the OO incident (*e.g.*, establishing close proximity to a pupil to encourage a return to the activity, verbally directing a pupil to return to the activity at hand), and (2) the pupil or group involved in the OO incident must have returned to active and successful skill practice or activity engagement. Similar to the recording of AIA, if a teacher did not interact with a pupil or group in the context of an OO incident or a behavioral strategy was employed but the pupil did not return to successful skill or activity engagement within a 1- to 2-minute prescribed time period, then an AOA was not recorded.

Two non-sequential measures of pupil activity were also used in this study:

- *Activity engagement:* A percentage of class time measure that was recorded when a pupil was engaged in practicing a skill or was participating in a fitness or game activity, according to the criteria set by the teacher for that lesson.
- *Off-task:* A percentage of class time measure that was recorded when any pupil was engaged in passive behaviors clearly not related to prescribed class activities or was engaged in any disruptive behavior that detracted from or interrupted the class activities prescribed by the teacher.

Observation Protocol

Participants given sequential behavior feedback during their undergraduate teacher training experience are referred to as the *exposed* group, and those without prior training in SBF are referred to as the *control* group. Each participant was observed for one complete 45-minute class period every other week over the course of four consecutive academic semesters. Each observed class period represented skill-based lessons in which teaching new skills necessary for successful team and individual sport participation was the primary focus. Data were collected by trained observers in real time using appropriate behavior analytic observational software run on laptop computers.[*] The data collection

[*] The computer-based data used for sequential behavior feedback and goal setting were generated using the Behavior Evaluation Strategy and Taxonomy (Educational Consulting, 4935 Buckhorn Butte Ct., Las Vegas, NV 89149); a free demonstration copy of the software tools may be obtained by contacting the primary author at sharpe@unlv.nevada.edu or www.skware.com) on IBM 360CS laptops (Sharpe & Koperwas, 2000). Data included: (1) lists of teacher and student behaviors and their number, average duration, percentage of total class time, and rate; (2) pie chart and bar graph representations of select teacher and student behaviors; and (3) sequential structures of teacher and student behavioral interactions.

method included the pressing and holding of alphanumeric keys that corresponded to the measures used in this study. Multiple keys could be pressed simultaneously, allowing the collection of overlapping event occurrences. A real-time recording format was used, generating the start and stop times of all recorded events as they actually occurred in each observational setting. From this time-based data record, an analysis program was used to extract a variety of measurement data, including the number and percentage data on all behaviors represented in the results section and related sequential data that reflected the time-based relationships among behavioral measures.

As noted previously, all IO, AIA, OO, and AOA data were recorded by pressing and holding alphanumeric keys on a keyboard as these behaviors actually occurred. Off-task data were recorded in the same manner for every off-task episode that occurred regardless of which pupil exhibited the particular episode. Recording off-task data in this manner provided a general percentage of time in relation to total class time in which off-task activity was occurring. To record activity engagement, pupils within each class being observed were rotated through a 2-minute recording schedule. Observers recorded the activity engagement for a particular pupil for a 2-minute period and then moved on to the next pupil to capture a general representation of the percentage of total class time pupils tended to devote to activity engagement.

Inter-Observer Agreement

Prior to collecting data for this study, observers were trained using a 50-minute criterion videotape of structured physical education settings not used for this study but which demonstrated repeated occurrences of the behavioral measures collected. Observers were trained to a minimum standard of .85 or greater agreement with the primary investigator on three consecutive 4-minute segments of the criterion videotape. Inter-rater checks were made once per experimental phase for each participant observed in this study. Checks at periodic intervals occurred between two independent data recorders during the data collection phase of the study. The formula (agreements ÷ [agreements + disagreements] × 100) was used to compare data records for observer training and inter-observer agreement steps, with occurrence data across all IO, AIA, OO, AOA, off-task, and activity engagement behaviors being aggregated and used for formula purposes. Mean observer training agreement was .96, with a range of .88 to 1.00. Mean inter-rater agreement was .92 with a range of .87 to .98.

Experimental Design

A multiple baseline design was used to compare relative changes in AIA and AOA in respective IO and OO contexts and relative changes in pupil activity engagement and off-task behaviors. In other words, change was analyzed as a function of exposure versus non-exposure to the sequential behavior feedback strategy treatment when used as a continuing-education or in-service teacher education strategy across all experimental and control participants. In addition, a social validation questionnaire was administered to all participants at the end of this study to determine the relative receptivity for the SBF strategy (see Table 2 for complete questionnaire instrument).

General Instructional Feedback Strategy Procedures

The feedback strategy treatment included the following:

- The direct observation of study participants for data collection purposes began with their first semester of professional practice in their first professional position and continued on an every-other-week basis for four consecutive semesters.
- Sequential behavior feedback was administered as an instructional feedback treatment in a multiple-baseline format according to the baseline, prompt, and maintenance schedules presented in Figs. 1 to 5: *baseline*, unobtrusive observation with no instructional feedback of any kind; *treatment*, sequential behavior feedback provided 3 days per week at the end of one class period per day for each treatment week; *maintenance*, unobtrusive observation with no instructional feedback of any kind.
- SBF treatments consisted of approximately 30 minutes of observer and teacher discussion of SBA data records of the teaching performance. Talks occurred immediately after one Monday, one Wednesday, and one Friday class period, constituting one full week of treatment. Data contained in Figs. 1 to 5 for treatment phases represent Wednesdays, or treatment week midpoints. Talks included the following for both exposed and control participants: (1) teacher responses to what they felt went well with their instructional lessons; (2) teacher responses to what they felt was the most challenging aspects of their lessons and how they might improve next time; (3) observer presentations of the IO, AIA, OO, AOA, activity engagement, and off-task data with time for teacher questions; and (4) provision of one to three goals for improvement that specifically related to the data records that were shown and discussed.
- Social validation data were collected from all exposed and control participants at the end of the study.

Treatment Implementation Training

Four trained data observers and SBF strategy treatment providers took part in the experiment illustrated. Each participating treatment provider completed a one-semester doctoral level course in SBA and SBF methods. The course

TABLE 2
Social Validation Questionnaire

Open ended

1. *What did you like most about the sequential behavior feedback and goal setting procedure?*
   - Clear and complete descriptions of what I was doing in the classroom and what my students were doing.
   - A method for measuring in very specific ways my daily teaching practices.
   - The objectivity and measurability of this type of feedback.

2. *What did you like least about the sequential behavior feedback and goal setting procedure?*
   - Nothing; loved it and wish we could do more.
   - Takes time from the current structure of our teaching day.
   - Makes me a better teacher but is challenging when I get lazy.

3. *What did you learn from participating in this study?*
   - How inaccurate my initial perceptions were of just what I and my students were doing behaviorally. I became a much better monitor of daily classroom events.
   - How to target students who need my attention and become a quick study of what to do for them.
   - How much is going on in my classroom in terms of what students are doing and how to make better use of my time with respect to interacting with students.

Likert scale				
Strongly agree	Agree	Neutral	Disagree	Strongly disagree
1	2	3	4	5

Rate the following questions:

1. Do you feel that the teaching behaviors targeted by the SBF procedure were important?
   .87   .13

2. Do you feel that the teaching behaviors targeted were effective in relation to student challenges?
   1.00

3. Would you incorporate the teaching behaviors targeted in your future classroom practice?
   1.00

4. Do you feel that you are more aware of student instructional challenges as a result of repeated exposure to SBF information?
   1.00

5. Do you feel that you are more aware of student organizational challenges as a result of repeated exposure to SBF information?
   1.00

6. Would you recommend the use of SBF as an ongoing instructional and evaluation tool for other teacher and public school administrator colleagues?
   .87   .13

included mastery of applied behavior analysis and sequential behavior analysis principles in relation to teacher training and assessment, training to criterion in the use of the software programs that generated instructional feedback and goal-setting data, and training to criterion in mock teacher feedback sessions with undergraduate student teachers who did not participate in this study. Each SBF provider in this study exited the course with an A and had ongoing graduate assistant responsibilities in the area of undergraduate practice teaching and student teacher supervision.

Treatment Integrity

An important, albeit little reported, feature of applied behavior analysis application and related data reporting is in the area of treatment integrity or treatment fidelity. Equally important to gathering reliable and accurate data when involved in direct observation activities is providing assurance in some data-supported way that a particular treatment is implemented in accordance with its operational description. To this end, and specific to the study contained in this chapter, a trained independent observer recorded numerical and duration data with respect to the SBA feedback procedure use during one feedback day (of the three days per treatment prompt phase) for each treatment phase for each study participant (33%). Table 3 provides a summary of treatment integrity data according to the observation system used for this purpose.

TABLE 3
Treatment Integrity Data Represented as Mean Time in Minutes Spent in Treatment Behaviors During Post-Observation Observer–Teacher Interactions (Ranges in Parentheses)

	Baseline	Treatment	Maintenance
Questioning, positive	.10 (.00 to .48)	5.6 (4.9 to 6.8)	.11 (.00 to .54)
Questioning, improvement	.00 (.00 to .00)	6.8 (5.1 to 8.2)	.09 (.00 to .51)
Data descriptions	.00 (.00 to .00)	10.3 (9.2 to 12.8)	.00 (.00 to .00)
Goal-setting	.00 (.00 to .00)	8.4 (6.9 to 11.3)	.00 (.00 to .00)
Interpersonal/other	6.8 (2.9 to 9.5)	2.4 (1.4 to 6.4)	5.4 (1.3 to 8.2)
Total post-class time	6.6 (2.9 to 9.5)	28.9 (27.6 to 39.6)	4.9 (1.3 to 8.5)

Note. For a complete list of operational definitions contact the primary author.

STUDY RESULTS

IO and AIA Data

Figure 1 presents IO and AIA data for the four study participants who were regularly exposed to SBF throughout their undergraduate program experience. Data are arranged as total number of IO incidents in relation to total number of AIA teacher responses to those IO incidents. Data are strikingly similar across each of the four exposed study participants. Baseline levels of IO were moderate for all participants with slightly lower AIA responses. With the exception of only a slight increase with the first maintenance phase for exposed teacher 1, a consistently sustained increase in both IO and AIA were evident across all participants for all consequent experimental phases. Specific to the sequential behavior focus of the SBA feedback strategy, the baseline to post-treatment exposure number of IOs that were not responded to with AIAs decreased markedly and were consistently maintained for all four teachers who were previously exposed to SBA feedback during their undergraduate activities.

Figure 2 presents IO and AIA data for the four study participants, termed *controls*, who received no exposure to SBF in their undergraduate preparation experiences prior to this study. The four control participants first showed a striking similarity in data patterns. In contrast to the data in Fig. 1, each control participant demonstrated markedly lower initial baseline IO and AIA data. With implementation of more frequent and extended exposure to the SBA feedback strategy than the exposed study participants received, all control participants exhibited a gradual increase over the course of the study in IO and AIA. However, IO and AIA improvement was much slower to reach levels similar to those for the Fig. 1 participants and required more frequent and more extended treatment exposure. In other words, familiarity with the SBF teacher and student-interaction information provided in treatment form was central to teacher reflection on and improvement of their interactions with their pupils in a variety of classroom situations. Control participant sequential data showed that the number of IOs that were not responded to with AIAs were greater during baseline for all participants when compared to the Fig. 1 data and relatively much more variable in improvement as a function of consequent treatment and maintenance phases.

OO and AOA Data

Figure 3 presents OO and AOA data for the four study participants who were regularly exposed to SBA feedback throughout their undergraduate program experience. Similar to Figs. 1 and 2, data are arranged as total number of OO incidents in relation to total number of AOA teacher responses to those OO incidents. Again, data were strikingly similar across each of the four exposed study participants. Baseline levels of OOs were low for all participants with

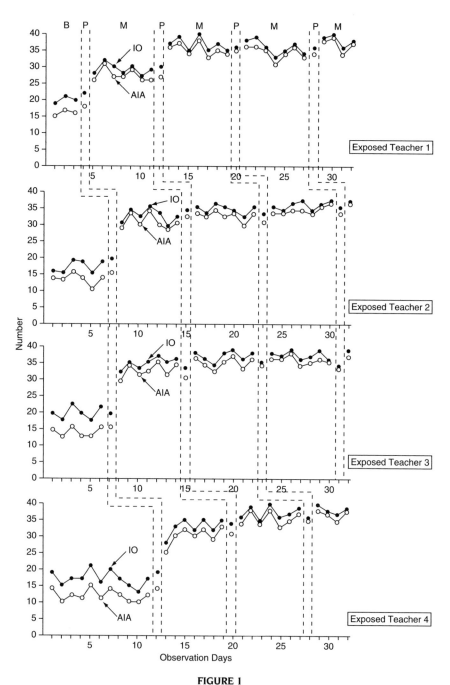

FIGURE 1

Number of appropriate instructional actions (AIAs) relative to number
of instructional opportunities (IOs) for exposed teachers (phase icons:
B, baseline; P, prompt; M, maintenance).

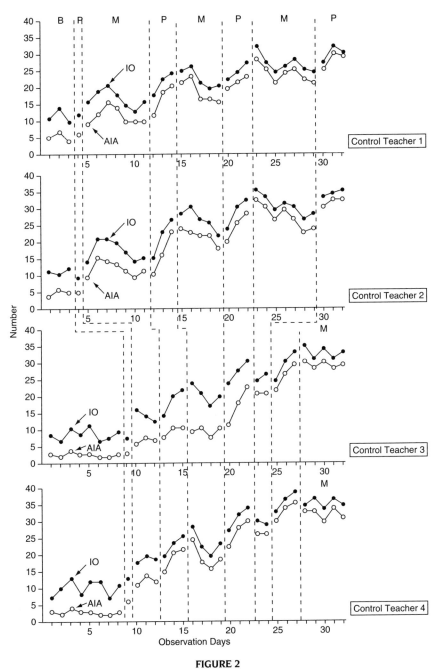

FIGURE 2

Number of appropriate instructional actions (AIAs) relative to number of instructional opportunities (IOs) for control teachers (phase icons: B, baseline; P, prompt; M, maintenance).

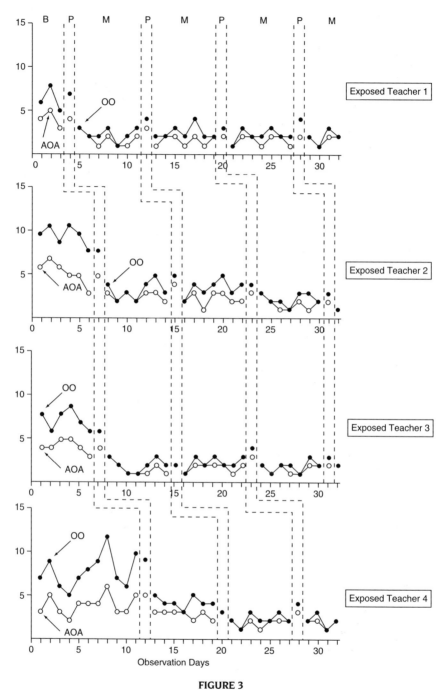

FIGURE 3

Number of appropriate organizational actions (AOAs) relative to number of
organizational opportunities (OOs) for exposed teachers (phase icons:
B, baseline; P, prompt; M, maintenance).

slightly lower AOA responses. With exposure to SBA feedback, each participant's OO and AOA incidents decreased from initial baseline levels and maintained a decrease for the remainder of the experiment. Specific to the sequential behavior focus of the SBF strategy, the baseline to post-treatment exposure number of OOs that were not responded to with AOAs decreased markedly and were consistently maintained for all four teachers who were previously exposed to SBF during their undergraduate activities.

Figure 4 presents OO and AOA data for the four study participants who received no exposure to SBF prior to this study. Again, data were strikingly similar across control participants. In contrast to the data in Fig. 3, each control participant demonstrated markedly higher initial baseline OOs, though similar AOA data patterns. With more frequent and extended exposure to the SBA feedback strategy, all control participants exhibited a gradual decrease in OOs over the course of the study. Again, as for the instructionally focused data (IO and AIA), familiarity with SBF information clearly improved teacher reflection on and improvement of a variety of effective teacher–pupil classroom interactions. However, as with the IO and AIA data for these participants, improvement was much slower to reach levels similar to those seen in the Fig. 3 participants and required more frequent and more extended treatment exposure. Control participant sequential data showed that the number of OOs that were not responded to with AOAs was greater during baseline for all participants when compared to the Fig. 3 data. The data showed relatively more variable improvement as a function of consequent treatment prompting and maintenance phases.

Discrete Pupil Data

Figure 5 represents activity engagement and off-task data for matched exposed and control teachers' pupils (previously exposed, 1, and control, 1; previously exposed, 3, and control, 3). Only two matched participant pairs were represented, given the similarity of the IO, AIA, OO, and AOA data within previously exposed and control participant groups. The baseline percentage of time pupils spent in activity engagement was much higher for the classes taught by participants previously exposed to SBF strategies within their undergraduate preparation experiences than for those not previously exposed. A small increase in activity engagement percentages was also seen in the exposed participants' pupils as a function of repeated exposure to SBF. In contrast, a relatively large increase in activity engagement was seen in the control participants' pupils over the course of the study, but not reaching that of exposed participants' pupil levels. The off-task percentages in the control participants' class settings were much higher in baseline then those of their matched exposed counterparts. A small and consistent decrease in off-task percentages was seen over the course of the study in the exposed participants' students as a function of repeated exposure to SBF, and a relatively large (but comparatively

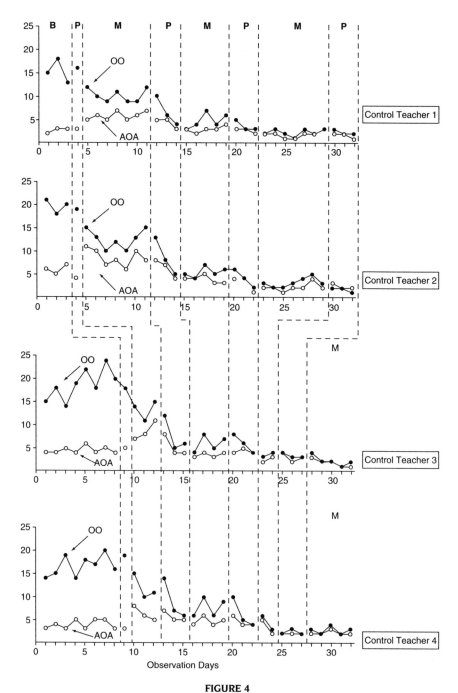

FIGURE 4

Number of appropriate organizational actions (AOAs) relative to number of
organizational opportunities (OOs) for control teachers (phase icons:
B, baseline; P, prompt; M, maintenance).

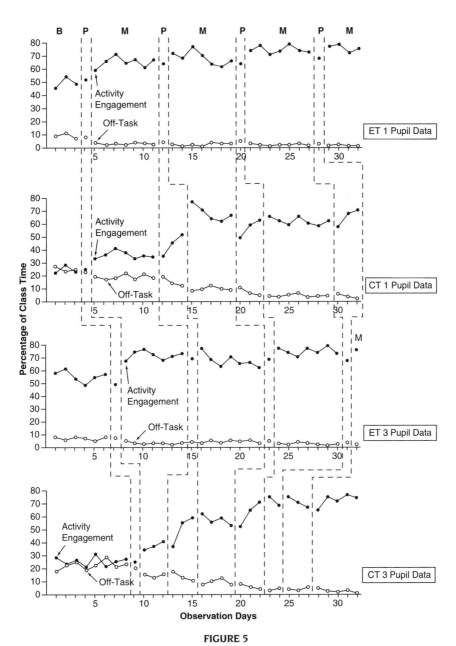

FIGURE 5

Comparison of exposed and control teachers on percentages of student classroom behavior as a function of the sequential behavior feedback (phase icons: B, baseline; P, prompt; M, maintenance).

slower to be realized) decrease in off-task behavior was seen in the control participants' students over the course of the study.

Social Validation Data

Social validation data were provided to demonstrate the potential receptivity for the SBF strategy on the part of professional teachers. These data were felt to be important given the limited literature providing participant response information in potential support of an ongoing professional education experience. Response information was consistently supportive of SBA feedback as a continuing education instrument (see Table 2 for questionnaire format and related response data). The end-of-study response data contained in Table 2 show that all participants, regardless of prior exposure to SBA feedback strategies in their undergraduate teacher training program, were supportive of SBA feedback as an ongoing instructional tool. They felt that they benefited in a variety of ways from interaction with sequential behavior descriptions of their classroom practice and the related practices of their pupils. The following participant quote provides a characteristic response:

> "Initially I was a bit leery of participation, not really knowing what would be expected of us. As I got involved in the activity, however, I found that the descriptions of my teaching in relation to what my students were doing and the challenges they experienced really helped me become a more accurate monitor of classroom activities, and really helped me improve what I did in the classroom in relation to how I interacted with my students."

IMPLICATIONS FOR EDUCATION
AND PROFESSIONAL TRAINING

The data contained in this chapter were first designed to demonstrate the appealing long-term generalization effects of one sequential behavior instructional feedback strategy on previously exposed teacher-trainees once they began their first professional position in a public-school setting. A second purpose of these data representations was to compare the effects of exposure to the SBA feedback strategy on teachers who had been exposed previously versus teachers who had not when used as an on-the-job continuing education tool. Third, pupil data were represented to determine any collateral effects on the pupils being taught by teachers exposed to SBA feedback. While pupil behavior data are only a correlate with important subject-matter achievement measures, the pupil data nonetheless provide important information in support of the effectiveness of the teacher behavior changes documented. Finally, social validation data were collected to determine the relative receptivity of participants to the SBA feedback treatment.

The results of the data presented in this chapter add substantially to an existing line of research by providing strong support for the effects of a specifically defined, sequential behavior instructional feedback and goal-setting procedure used within clinical professional practice settings. The preceding illustration demonstrated that teacher-trainees exposed to SBA feedback in their undergraduate practice-teaching experiences maintained the behavioral competencies initially learned when operating over long periods of time in their first professional teaching situations. This is an important finding in two respects. First, the data show that practicing teachers who had not been exposed to SBF during their undergraduate experiences did not exhibit the same levels of teaching practice in the context of IO and OO incidents. Second, the mainstream teacher-education literature points to the greatest challenge of teacher education programs being one of *negative socialization*. Negative socialization occurs when, upon exiting an undergraduate teacher preparation program, the new teacher tends not to demonstrate or utilize the teaching practices recommended within that preparation program (Lawson, 1991; Lawson & Stroot, 1993). In this regard, this study specifically points to the importance of behavior and sequential behavior instructional feedback strategies as a potential means of professional training to ensure the continued use of professional competencies well beyond the undergraduate preparatory setting.

The data presented in this chapter also demonstrate that the sequential behavior instructional feedback method, when used as an on-the-job continuing education activity, is an effective procedure in (1) improving upon previously exposed teachers' use of recommended behavioral strategies when faced with challenging instructional and organizational situations, and (2) improving the use of recommended behavioral strategies with those teachers who had received no SBA feedback exposure prior to their first job experience. This finding provides strong support for the use of specifically defined behavioral treatments for practicing professionals that are designed to continually improve their instructional performance when they are on the job. It also provides support for behavior-analytic strategies as appealing and productive methods for reversing what is perceived by much of the mainstream education literature as an insurmountable confound of negative socialization. This second finding is further supported by the social validation data that emphasized the consistent receptivity by all study participants for SBA feedback strategies when used as a continuing education activity.

The pupil data presented lend additional support for the effectiveness of the SBA feedback strategy when used as a continuing education activity. Our view is that while it is important to demonstrate long-term maintenance and generalization of professional practices as a function of a particular treatment, the ultimate indicator of the success of a treatment designed for professional practice improvement is in its corollary effects on the clients served (in this case, pupils taught) by those professionals who have been exposed to a particular treatment. In this regard, the consistent data changes in the areas of activity engagement and off-task behaviors in the indicated directions for all pupils involved in this study provide such support. Given that off-task behaviors are an arguable impediment to the effectiveness of a learning situation and that activity engagement has a strong correlation with student learning (Barbetta, Heron, & Heward, 1993; Greenwood, Hart, Walker, & Risley, 1994; Miller et al., 1995), these findings are consistent with earlier research and reinforce the need for continuing-education activities that include a SBF component. Of interest to future study in this area is the importance of correlating the potential effects of SBF on pupil grades received and a variety of academic skill acquisition indicators as a function of demonstrated teacher and pupil behavior change.

Of final importance, the data presented in this chapter lend additional support to the continued development of sequentially based behavior analysis methods designed to counter the technocratic criticisms of behavior analysis approaches to professional training, in general, and teacher training, specifically, that frequent the mainstream teacher education literature (Doyle, 1990). Consistent with earlier referenced studies conducted within this line of research, this chapter's data demonstrate that providing SBA feedback to teacher professionals working in public school settings is effective in increasing their targeting of, and responding to, challenging instructional and organizational pupil needs. When coupled with the generalization findings of the initial baselines of the previously exposed participants, a strong case is made for the effectiveness of SBA feedback in teaching teachers to recognize and ameliorate particular pupil situations. These data do not simply demonstrate isolated behaviors in an unconnected or potentially inappropriate manner, but rather are consistent with recommendations that connections between teacher and pupil practices in particular instructional situations be made explicit when developing teacher feedback strategies (Browder, Liberty, Heller, D'Huyvetters, 1986; Hawkins & Sharpe, 1992). Taking an illustration from Sharpe and Lounsbery (1998), stopping with the successful training of a teacher to criterion in the use of physical signals may ensure that a teacher consistently uses this behavior but may do little to ensure that this behavior is used at appropriate times and to the most effective result with regard to challenging pupil behavior. A representation, therefore, of how often a teacher takes appropriate action in a classroom in the context of particular pupil challenges is also needed.

Data findings represented in this chapter have several implications for future research and instructional activity when preparing professionals to acquire skills necessary to effective professional functioning. First, additional research is necessary to determine the relative effectiveness of SBF procedures for a variety of professionals when learning their respectively necessary behavioral skills in deliberate practice or residency-based practical situations. Second, longer range studies should be conducted to determine the differential time frames for optimal exposure and withdrawal of SBA feedback when used as a continuing education strategy. Questions of when SBA feedback is no longer necessary and how often this strategy should be used for optimal effects remain unanswered. Third, studies that correlate the effects of SBA feedback on teacher and pupil classroom behaviors with pupil subject-matter achieve-ment measures are necessary to determine the relative effects of this strategy on measures of pupil learning. In relation to this recommendation, it is neces-sary to use an SBA method specifically to map the form and character of different teacher responses to IO and OO incidents to explicitly determine the relationship between particular pupil challenges that occur in particular situations and just what a teacher does to ameliorate those challenges.

A FUTURE FOR SEQUENTIAL BEHAVIOR ANALYSIS

Using teacher education as an illustration, we hope we have presented an appealing data-based case for the use of a sequential behavior instructional feedback strategy when training undergraduates in practical settings and for the continued use of this strategy when providing continuing education for practicing teacher professionals. We find this strategy to be of potential appeal for a variety of professional training situations in which a deliberate practice or a specifically supervised residency-based component is necessary for effective professional preparation. Extrapolating from our teacher-training exemplar, we suggest that a case may readily be made for use of sequential behavior strategies in professional training areas such as medicine, school and clinical psychology, special education and rehabilitation, and a variety of other pro-fessional training areas that place a primary focus on ensuring the demon-strated and generalized use of interactive skills critical to effective professional practice. Additionally, we feel that a sequential behavior direct observation approach is amenable to a variety of other educational activities when preparing professionals for effective practice with the clientele they are being trained to serve. Appealing education opportunities include video-based and computer-supported laboratory experiences in which trainees learn to collect and analyze sequential data to (1) become accurate monitors of their potential professional surroundings, (2) reflect upon relatively effective versus ineffective practices in certain situations, and (3) formulate best-practice behavioral repertoires for use in actual professional practice settings. Another potential application is the development and implementation of simulated practical settings via video and computer technologies, in which professionals may participate in a virtual and predictive-choice laboratory reflecting the types of professional settings in which they will ultimately operate. Ray (Ray & Delprato, 1989; Ray, 1992) for example, has pioneered this second potential application with great success, with these developments discussed in detail in another chapter of this text.

What remains to us, and what we hope we have articulated, is that much remains to the thoroughgoing discovery and application of sequential behavior data in relationship to interactive settings, in general, and educational settings specifically. When endeavoring toward a new way of thinking—in this case, focusing on the temporal form of behaviors and events as they occur and recur over time—many opportunities for new discoveries of functional relationships among behaviors and events in effective and not-so-effective interactive situations are possible. With the advent of computer technologies designed to facilitate such data collection and analysis in user-friendly and time-efficient ways, what Barker presented over 30 years ago in his text, *The Stream of Behavior: Explorations of Its Structure and Content*, may become a reality in mainstream applied-science communities.

Acknowledgments

We would like to thank the many teachers and coaches in the Lincoln, NE, Public School; Tippecanoe County, IN, Public School; and Clark County, NV, Public School districts for their receptivity and enthusiasm to our approach to teacher training. Tom Sharpe, Ed.D., is the Sports Education and Leadership Program Coordinator and Professor at the University of Nevada, Las Vegas. Daniel Balderson is a doctoral student in the Sports Education and Leadership Program at the University of Nevada, Las Vegas. Hosung So, Ph.D., is an Assistant Professor in the Department of Kinesiology at California State University, San Barnardino.

References

Bakeman, R. & Gottman, J. M. (1997). *Observing interaction: An introduction to sequential analysis*, 2nd ed. New York: Cambridge University Press.

Barbetta, P. M., Heron, T. E., & Heward, W. L. (1993). Effects of active student response during error correction on the acquisition, maintenance, and generalization of sight words by students with developmental handicaps. *Journal of Applied Behavior Analysis*, 26, 111–119.

Barker, R. G. (1963). *The stream of behavior: Explorations of its structure and content*. New York: Appleton-Century-Crofts.

Browder, D. S., Liberty, K., Heller, M., & D'Huyvetters, K. K., (1986). Self-management by teachers: improving instructional decision making. *Professional School Psychology*, 1, 165–175.

Carnine, D. W. & Fink, W. T. (1978). Increasing the rate of presentation and use of signals in elementary classroom teachers. *Journal of Applied Behavior Analysis*, 11, 35–46.

Cooper, M. L., Thomson, C. L., & Baer, D. M. (1970). The experimental modification of teacher attending behavior. *Journal of Applied Behavior Analysis*, 3, 153–157.

Cossairt, A., Hall, R. V., & Hopkins, B. L. (1973). The effects of experimenter's instructions, feedback, and praise on teacher praise and student attending behavior. *Journal of Applied Behavior Analysis*, 6, 89–100.

Darst, P. W., Zakrajsek, D. B., & Mancini, V. H. (1989). *Analyzing physical education and sport instruction*, 2nd ed. Champaign, IL: Human Kinetics.

Doyle, W. (1990). Themes in teacher education research, in Houston, W. R., Haberman, M., & Sikula, J. (Eds.), *Handbook of Research on Teacher Education*. New York: Macmillan, pp. 3–24.

Graham, K. C. (1991). The influence of teacher education on preservice development: beyond a custodial orientation. *Quest*, 43, 1–19.

Greenwood, C. R., Carta, J. J., Arreaga-Mayer, C., & Rager, A. (1991). The behavior analyst consulting model: identifying and validating naturally effective instructional methods. *Journal of Behavioral Education*, 1, 165–191.

Greenwood, C. R., Hart, B., Walker, D., & Risley, R. (1994). Opportunity to respond and academic performance revisited: a behavioral theory of developmental retardation and its prevention, in Gardner III, R., Sainato, D. M., Cooper, J. O., Heron, T. E., Heward, W. L., Eshelman, J., & Grossi,

T. A. (Eds.), *Behavior analysis in education: Focus on measurably superior instruction.* Pacific Grove, CA: Brooks/Cole, pp. 213–223.

Greer, R. D. (1985). *Handbook for professional change agents at the Margaret Chapman school.* Hawthorne, NY: The Margaret Chapman School.

Greer, R. D. (1991). The teacher as strategic scientist: a solution to our educational crisis? *Behavior and Social Issues,* 1, 427–444.

Hall, R. V., Panyon, M., Rabon, D., & Broden, M. (1968). Instructing beginning teachers in reinforcement procedures which improve classroom control. *Journal of Applied Behavior Analysis,* 1, 315–322.

Hawkins, A. H. & Sharpe, T. L. (Eds.) (1992). Field systems analysis: an alternative for the study of teaching expertise [monograph]. *Journal of Teaching in Physical Education,* 12, 1–131.

Ingham, P. & Greer, R. D. (1992). Changes in student and teacher responses in observed and generalized settings as a function of supervisor observations. *Journal of Applied Behavior Analysis,* 25, 153–164.

Kamps, D. M., Leonard, B. R., Dugan, E. P., Boland, B., & Greenwood, C. R. (1991). The use of ecobehavioral assessment to identify naturally occurring effective procedures in classrooms serving students with autism and other developmental disabilities, *Journal of Behavioral Education,* 1, 367–397.

Landin, D. K., Hawkins, A. H., & Wiegand, R. L. (1986). Validating the collective wisdom of teacher educators. *Journal of Teaching in Physical Education,* 5, 252–271.

Lawson, H. A. (1991). Three perspectives on induction and a normative order for physical education. *Quest,* 43, 20–36.

Lawson, H. A. & Stroot, S. A. (1993). Footprints and signposts: Perspectives on socialization research [monograph]. *Journal of Teaching in Physical Education,* 12(4), 437–446.

Miller, A. D., Hall, S. W., & Heward, W. L. (1995). Effects of sequential 1-minute time trials with and without intertrial feedback on general and special education students' fluency with math facts. *Journal of Behavioral Education,* 5, 319–345.

Miller, S. P., Harris, C., & Watanabe, A. (1991). Professional coaching: a method for increasing effective and decreasing ineffective teacher behaviours. *Teacher Education and Special Education,* 14, 183–191.

Morris, E. K. (1992). ABA presidential address: The aim, progress, and evolution of behavior analysis. *The Behavior Analyst,* 15, 3–29.

O'Reilly, M. F. & Renzaglia, A. (1994). A systematic approach to curriculum selection and supervision strategies: A preservice practicum supervision model. *Teacher Education and Special Education,* 17, 170–180.

Page, T. J., Iwata, B. A., & Reid, D. H. (1982). Pyramidal training: A large scale application with institutional staff. *Journal of Applied Behavior Analysis,* 15, 355–352.

Ray, R. D. (1992). Interbehavioral methodology: Lessons from simulation. *Journal of Teaching in Physical Education,* 12, 105–114.

Ray, R. D. & Delprato, D. J. (1989). Behavioral systems analysis: methodological strategies and tactics. *Behavioral Science,* 34, 81–127.

Sharpe, T. L. (1996). Using technology to study daily teaching practices. *Teacher Education and Practice,* 12, 47–61.

Sharpe, T. L. (1997). An introduction to sequential behavior analysis and what it offers physical education teacher education researchers. *Journal of Teaching in Physical Education,* 16, 368–375.

Sharpe, T. L., Hawkins, A., & Ray, R. (1995). Interbehavioral field systems assessment: examining its utility in preservice teacher education. *Journal of Behavioral Education,* 5, 259–280.

Sharpe, T. L., Hawkins, A., & Lounsbery, M. (1998). Using technology to study and evaluate human interaction: Practice and implications of a sequential behavior approach. *Quest,* 50, 389–401.

Sharpe, T. L. & Koperwas, J. (2000). *Software Assist for Education and Social Science Settings: Behavior Evaluation Strategies and Taxonomies (BEST) and Accompanying Qualitative Applications.* Thousand Oaks, CA: Sage-Scolari.

Sharpe, T. L. & Koperwas, J. (2003). *Behavior and Sequential Analyses: Principles and Practice*. Thousand Oaks, CA: Sage.

Sharpe, T. L., Lounsbery, M., & Bahls, V. (1997). Description and effects of sequential behavior practice in teacher education. *Research Quarterly for Exercise and Sport*, 68, 222–232.

Sharpe, T. L. & Lounsbery, M. (1998). The effects of a sequential behavior analysis protocol on the teaching practices of undergraduate trainees. *School Psychology Quarterly*, 12, 327–343.

Sharpe, T. L., Spies, R., Newman, R., & Spickelmier-Vallin, D. (1996). Assessing and improving the accuracy of inservice teachers perceptions of daily practice. *Journal of Teaching in Physical Education*, 15, 297–318.

Stroot, S. A. & Williamson, K. M. (1993). Issues and themes of socialization into physical education [monograph]. *Journal of Teaching in Physical Education*, 12, 337–343.

Warger, C. L. & Aldinger, L. E. (1984). Improving teacher supervision: The preservice consultation model. *Teacher Education and Special Education*, 7, 155–163.

Grammar and Writing Skills: Applying Behavior Analysis

MARILYN B. GILBERT

Performance Engineering Group

Language is a cracked kettle on which we tap out crude rhythms for bears to dance to while we long to make music that will melt the stars. —Gustave Flaubert, *Madame Bovary*

NEGLECTED WRITING SKILLS

We have now had two decades of educational reform, focusing on two of the basic three R's, reading and arithmetic. The second R, writing, was left far behind. Most children in our elementary and middle schools are not fluent in grammatical usage and punctuation; they cannot spell, their vocabularies are poor, and they do not know the parts of speech well enough to take full advantage of a dictionary. But, perhaps we should not be surprised. Most students rarely write in school. Even the tradition of writing a research paper, once a rite of passage for high school seniors, is rarely observed. College professors and employers are alarmed and fear further consequences: The failure of American students to acquire proficient writing skills will affect every aspect of their lives—and ours.

In their report confirming the neglect of writing instruction, a prestigious panel of educators (National Commission on Writing in America's Schools and Colleges, 2003) has recommended that schools double the amount of time students spend on writing and that educators look for new ways to teach writing skills. A compelling concern is that both of the major college-entrance examinations, the SAT and the ACT, are being revised to include writing tests in 2005.

Yes, increased writing practice is essential, as are new teaching strategies. This chapter describes an approach in which the principles of behavioral science and the larger construct of performance are applied to improve instruction in both the process of writing and in its underpinnings of grammar, punctuation, mechanics, and style. Of the many valuable outcomes this application produces, two are major: First, writers learn a strategy for detecting errors or weaknesses in their own writing. Because few writers are lucky enough to have their own editors, self-editing is a critical skill. Second, writers become fluent in the underlying basic writing skills of grammar and punctuation.

Mastery of any discipline requires fluency in the basic skills, yet we educators allow many students to advance before ensuring they have acquired this degree of expertise. Behaviorists define fluency as a level of proficiency in which the skill is so well practiced that it is performed effortlessly and almost automatically (K. Johnson, personal communication). When students are fluent in the use of grammar and punctuation, they write with grammatical precision, and they punctuate their first drafts correctly as they write. In reading their drafts aloud afterward, they can discern an awkward phrase or confusing pronoun reference and make the revision. Any part of an essay that would confuse or mislead readers—or induce sleep—is called here a *reading alarm*. With enough practice, the number of reading alarms for punctuation and grammar diminishes, and writers write faster and more effectively. But, the primary value of fluency in basic writing skills is that it frees writers to explore the language so they can fit their message to their readers and convey it with some grace.

The principles of behavioral science were applied in earlier books on writing (Gilbert, 1984) and in a writing-improvement program (Gilbert, 1992) for Penn State University students employed as technical writers and course developers at a Salem, NJ, nuclear power plant. The principles and practices described here are applied in writing workshops for teachers of English in secondary schools.

METHODS OF TEACHING WRITING

Some educators contend that reading and writing are best taught together from kindergarten upward. This was the philosophy of R. B. Spalding in *The Writing Road to Reading* (Spalding & North, 2003), now promoted as the Spalding Method. Gilbert developed a program (1969) in which pre-kindergarten children were taught reading and writing together. He maintained that if children are taught to write, they will also know how to read, but that the obverse is not true; that is, children taught only to read will not also be able to write. Yet, most

Americans learn to read first and to write later. By the time they reach middle or high school, students with assorted writing skills show up in the same classroom. For teachers, the challenge is to manage this motley group so well that no one is left behind.

Traditionally, instruction in the process of writing and instruction in grammar and punctuation proceed as two separate activities. Because the writing activity is a management nightmare, however, teachers tend to make few writing assignments. When students *do* write original compositions, teachers may cover the papers in a jumble of red. Since they generally do not return the corrections until many days later, writers may not learn how well they have done until it is too late to matter. In some programs, students learn to use copyediting marks; with the teacher's guidance, they edit their writing and apply the changes in their rewrites. But, even those students do not write or edit their own work by themselves nearly often enough to learn how to write effectively.

Traditional instruction in the basic skills of grammar and punctuation follows an equally ineffective pattern. Students learn a series of actions to take, or responses (the grammar rules), for using each punctuation mark and each point of grammar. They learn to use commas to separate words in series, nouns in apposition, introductory words, city from state, and so on—one rule at a time. Next, they apply a rule to workbook examples and take a test afterward. When the rules for commas are exhausted, students proceed to rules for semicolons and repeat the process, rule after rule. Their instruction, however, does not provide them any direction for identifying the trouble spots these rules are expected to fix. This omission explains why so many students cannot make the leap to their own writing, and why they can apply only the most frequent usages of grammar and punctuation.

This labored instruction has other unwelcome consequences: It promotes repetitive sentence patterns, because students play it safe. If they are not confident about using a semicolon, they will not venture a structure they fear might require one. They will not delete cluttered or overblown text because they will not recognize it. Instead, they will rely on the clichés that come readily to mind.

An approach based on the principles of science turns the usual instructional methodology around 180 degrees. Students learn how logic can explain those conventions of usage and punctuation that seemed arbitrary when reduced to rules. First, they learn to review their own writing and recognize each reading alarm—the antecedent prompting a potential need; then they learn how to treat it. Some of the basic reading alarms are *subject and verb pair, name, title of creative work, end quote with other punctuation, negative tone, wordy of phrase,* and *wordy who, which, or that clause.*

Here is the caveat: The tags for these antecedents must be meaningful to the students' experience. For example, students encountering *Toledo Ohio* in their own work may not recognize it as a match to the reading alarm *two unrelated groups to define*. They may not have a clear view of the meaning of *define* in this context. They must also regard a city and its state as state as separate groups. *Groups to separate* might work better even though it is not as precise. So, tags for reading alarms are not meant to be set in stone; students may devise their own personal prompts.

The reading alarm *groups to separate* generalizes to four punctuation needs: separating the day from the year in a date, the city from the state, two nouns in apposition, and a noun in direct address from the rest of the sentence. All four are traditionally taught as individual rules to learn. With a behavioral or functional approach, one reading alarm often covers several specific occasions, thereby reducing the number of actions to master. This efficiency of fewer actions to memorize will also produce more effective learning.

WRITING AS A PERFORMANCE

Before applying the principles of behavior analysis to writing instruction, however, we must view the subject matter through the larger lens of performance so we can state exactly what we want to accomplish. Gilbert (1996) defines performance as a transaction between behavior and its accomplishment. Performance is behavior that produces an outcome we value—an accomplishment. Once this valued outcome is established, we can search for the behavior that can best produce it. In this chapter, the accomplishment can be an essay that makes its intended point with the emphasis needed to engage its readers. The standards we set are that this essay will be accurate, it will be complete, and it will be readable. The behavior required to produce this accomplishment to these standards is fluency in the set of basic writing skills discussed here and the means for identifying the rough spots in one's own writing.

The Behavioral Paradigm

The late B. F. Skinner did not invent the stimulus and the response. Skinner invented a functional statement of their relationship, known as the *behavioral paradigm*, which is invaluable to basic laboratory research and to its applications in schools and businesses everywhere. By applying this model to writing instruction, we can design a course based on the functions of the writing process and the writing skills rather than on content alone, as happens in traditional writing programs.

The behavioral paradigm forces us to define the antecedents of actions that students need to identify, and it reminds us to arrange the conditions so that students' efforts will be meaningful to them. Figure 1 is an example of a behavioral paradigm describing the main steps—called the *operants*—of the

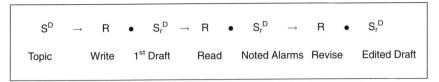

FIGURE 1

The steps in the process of writing.

writing process. It expresses environment–behavior relationships with a three-term contingency, which, for this chapter, would include (1) the antecedent stimulus, (2) the response, and (3) the consequence of the behavior. For those readers unfamiliar with these notations, the S^D stands for discriminative stimulus and represents the antecedent stimulus that prompts some action; in this case, the student writer discriminates the topic selected. The R represents the student's action, or response (here, the action to write freely). The S_r stands for reinforcing stimulus and represents the reinforcing outcome (here, the rough first draft, which we can call a *free-write*). Because this free-write is not expected to be perfect, it is also considered a discriminative stimulus that prompts the student writer to pursue a search for reading alarms to fix. These may be lapses in content, sequencing disorders, awkward phrasings, confusing details, incorrect punctuation, clarification needs, confusing references, cluttered prose, unnecessary commas or adjectives, or unorthodox sentence fragments. A careful writer checks everything, and each discovered alarm needs to be addressed.

Reading alarms are not necessarily instances of error, but they are always instances to check. For example, one reading alarm that writers are asked to examine is *owner/contraction*, which is intended to prompt a check of a possessive form. Because some possessives are often confused with contractions, students must determine if ownership or a contraction is intended and it is handled correctly. Writers must become reading detectives, searching their drafts for text that matches a reading alarm. As students become confident, they can address the basic alarms without effort, and they can move on; however, they must continue to look for flaws in content, style, clutter—and the mechanics—in everything they write. Anyone who has ever written anything will tell you this: Writing, like any art, can always be improved.

BEHAVIORAL STRATEGIES

Several principles and practices of behavioral science can be applied to the design of the writing instruction to make it more efficient and therefore more effective.

Shaping

The principal method of a behavioral approach to writing instruction is *shaping*, as it is in the instruction of many other highly developed behaviors in both animals and people. Shaping is defined as reinforced successive approximations to a desired outcome. In teaching a dog to jump to reach a line drawn high on the wall, for example, psychologists shape the dog's behavior by reinforcing (rewarding) smaller "accidental" behaviors first. When the dog scurries about and raises itself to reach a low point on the wall, experimenters immediately reinforce the behavior with food, but they withhold later reinforcement until the dog makes higher and higher jumps and finally reaches the goal. In writing, instructors do not seek some absolute of perfection, whatever that might be. Instead, instructors must shape their instruction so their students will come successively closer to their goal of writing proficiency.

Measurement

Measuring the performance of writing is not a simple task, however. In most writing instruction, teachers measure the results of students' tests on grammar rules, not on their proficiency in applying these rules to their own writing. Teachers may also evaluate students' compositions, but their evaluations tend to be subjective. In the early 1960s, the Indiana University satellite in Indianapolis conducted an experiment in which all instructors of English Composition 101 graded the same freshman composition. The grades they assigned to this essay ranged from A to F. Other English departments might have similar results. Since instructors are rarely given system-wide standards for measuring student achievement in writing.

The saying goes, "You get what you measure." We could measure accuracy alone and perhaps count the number of undetected writing flaws, but then we risk raising timid writers who are afraid to try out new arrangements or to play with words. We need firm evidence showing us how well our students have met our goals. For example, we can measure whether a student's essay has made its point. We can also evaluate how well the writing presents this point. Does it capture the reader's attention and hold it? We can also monitor and evaluate continued improvement in this student's writing skills.

Short-Term Feedback

As they learn to write, students should always know how well they are doing: what they are doing right, and what they could do better and how to do it. Short-term feedback (WISE), delivered in a positive tone, is critical:

- W stands for the need to focus on the *writing* itself rather than on other characteristics (*i.e.*, poor handwriting or sloppy-looking corrections).

- I stands for *immediate* feedback following the self-editing process.
- S stands for *specific* and *selective*, with feedback directed to the positive changes and two or three undetected reading alarms.
- E stands for an *educational* focus on the two or three alarms.

Teachers of writing can have a big stake in their students' progress by reviewing their work, noting and appreciating their small improvements, and teaching them new techniques. Their enthusiasm for the pursuit of writing improvement can be infectious. Students may continue to make errors and poor choices as they learn to discriminate between good and better changes, but they accept the challenge if they see their progress.

Long-Term Feedback

Because the acquisition of fluent writing skills is a long-term affair, students also need a larger view of their progress. To this end, student writers keep records of their achievements. One example of a student record is the progress plotter, which can have many different formats. Gilbert (1962a) described a simple progress plotter in which students plot the rising curve of their skill graphically to see their rate of progress toward a mastery criterion. Behaviorists emphasize the need to measure fluency by rate of response as well as by accuracy. In the approach to writing instruction presented here, however, a simplified matrix is used. The antecedents to grammar and punctuation needs are listed vertically: the horizontal axis shows the dates when students were taught each skill and when this teaching was reflected in their free-writes. This matrix is not a purely scientific assessment, and it does not measure rate of response; but it is an indicator of individual student success.

Discrimination Training

Results can be amusing when students confuse the punctuation rules. A letter from a car salesperson once addressed me as follows: *Dear, Marilyn* (comma before, not after, *Marilyn*). I guessed that the writer was taught two stylized rules: *Use a comma before a noun in direct address* and *Use a comma after a person addressed in a letter*. He obviously had not learned how to discriminate the stimulus for each rule. I would further guess that he had never confronted this discrimination.

Grammar and punctuation rules are just a huge group of *discriminations*, meaning similar stimuli that differ and so are treated in different ways. All behaviorists do not agree about how best to teach discriminations. I follow the logic that similar stimuli are best taught together so their differences are easy to identify. Students may also need some mediation—a mnemonic or other instructive device—to help them identify differences in the options to discriminate, so they can select the one that best fits . One example of a discrimination badly in need of a mediator is the set of mathematical symbols $>$ and $<$, meaning *greater than* and *less than*. If these symbols are presented together, their differences are clear, but how can we ever remember what each symbol means? If we examine the graphics, however, we can see that *more than* was initially designed as wide going to narrow and *less than* was designed to expand. Once we notice the designs, the meanings are clear. The same holds for grammatical discriminations.

Whoever designed English composition had a logical Framework in mind. Grammar rules may have masked this logic, but a behavioral approach restores it. As an example, suppose we are teaching students to attend to the reading alarm *two simple sentences in a row*, since this pattern can sound dull or choppy. More important, these sentences may have some significant relationship that is not apparent when they stand alone. By joining them, we can reveal this relationship. Do the two sentences provide separate or contrasting views? Does one sentence show cause and the other show effect? Does one sentence explains the other? Once students learn the logic, their choice is clear.

To teach responses to the discriminations, educators can look to the animal laboratory. Gilbert (1996) describes how to teach a rat to press a lever to get food whenever a light in its cage is turned on, but not to press the lever when the light is off. The sequence is first to teach the animal to discriminate the consequences of behavior: pressing the lever produces a click leading to food (S_r). Gilbert refers to this stage as *inductive*, because the animal is led (induced) into training and given a way of knowing the consequences of bar pressing. The second step is to teach the animal to discriminate the occasion (the light turned on) for responding successfully. This is the *skill*, or discriminative, stage of the training.

For training human beings, however, a step is missing. The rat performs in nearly unvarying situations—the cage and the light stay pretty much the same at all times. The rat has only two choices: when the light is on, it presses a lever; when the light is off, it does not press the lever. But, for human performance, occasions for responding in a specific way may occur in many forms. For illustration, suppose a lawyer is interpreting a legal contract. If the two parties agree on the terms of the contract, the contract is likely considered valid; otherwise, it is not. Although the situations facing the rat and the law student differ greatly in complexity, the discriminations are fundamentally identical—except in one respect. For the rat, the light is nearly always the same when it comes on, but legal contracts vary tremendously, both in form and style. Because the factors making a contract clear are not always obvious, the person has to develop a *concept* (genertalzation) for making the interpretation. Contracts have so many variants that not even experienced lawyers are expected to memorize them all. Something else is needed that will mediate the situation and the responses and will help lawyers remember or reason which response is correct. So, if law students are taught the intermediate behavior of checking whether the contract adheres to a set of general rules, they will be able to generalize such responses to many specific situations. Human beings need a concept to mediate their learning.

Let us return to our earlier example to see how we can teach the discriminations in constructing a compound sentence by joining two simple sentences and forming a compound sentence. Figure 2 shows the exercise model. By teaching students the differences in their options—with comma, semicolon, or colon—and addressing them, they can select the one that best fits their message. They can also choose the emphasis they wish to convey.

After presenting the inductive and the concept and demonstrating the *skill*, the instructor prompts students to punctuate several compound sentences from sets of simple sentences. Students then perform unaided. They may be asked to show how two clauses are related by joining them in each of the specific ways they learned, for example. The happy news is that after guided practice, students will not need to make these tedious decisions because the skills will be fluent.

[Inductive] Instead of writing two simple sentences (or independent clauses) in a row, writers can make their writing more interesting and informative by tying the sentences together. *[Concept]* The specific joiner writers select can tell readers how the two clauses are related.—and how important the information is.

[Skill] **EXAMPLE**: Mary saves stamps. Jose saves coins.

1. To show that the two simple sentences show separate detail, use the joiner *and* with a comma first. To be more formal or emphatic, use a semicolon alone. Or to be even more formal, use the very formal joiner *moreover* or *furthermore*.
   a) Mary saves <u>stamps, and</u> Jose saves coins.
   b) Mary saves <u>stamps;</u> Jose saves coins.
   c) Mary saves <u>stamps; furthermore,</u> Jose saves coins.

2. To show that the clauses have contrasting viewpoints, use the joiner *but* with a comma first. To be more formal or emphatic, use the joiner *however* with a semicolon first and a comma after.
   a) Mary saves <u>stamps, but</u> Jose saves coins.
   b) Mary saves <u>stamps; however,</u> Jose saves coins.

3. To show that the viewpoints in the two clauses are related by cause and effect, use *therefore* (or *consequently*) with a semicolon before and a comma after.
   a) Mary saves <u>stamps; therefore,</u> Jose saves coins. [She's "Mary, Mary, quite contrary."]

4. To show one sentence explaining the other, add a summary sentence and a colon. The first word after the colon isn't capitalized unless it is a proper noun or starts a quotation.
   a) Mary and Jose are collectors: Mary saves stamps, and Jose saves coins.

FIGURE 2

An exercise model for joining two simple sentences, or independent clauses.

These steps summarize the teaching of discriminations (Gilbert, 2003c):

- Introduce the skill, explaining what will be accomplished and why the skill is important to learn—and, sometimes, the consequence of *not* learning it. (*Inductive.*)
- Create a metaphor or generalized concept related to this skill that will serve as a framework guiding responses to particular instances (concept.)
- Use Gilbert's exercise model (1962c) of demonstrate, prompt, and release. Teachers may say, "I do it, we do it, you do it." (skill).
- Apply this learning in a real-world context—in this case, to one's own writing. (*Application.*)

As the behaviorists have always said (C. Ferster, personal communication), some good teachers may develop good teaching strategies on their own, because good strategies are often common sense and they are always logical. The value of a system of strategies is that all teachers can be more effective and all students will have the benefits.

Competition Analysis

A curriculum for teaching writing skills includes multiple discriminations, thereby raising many questions about how to arrange them in the best instructional sequence. Some decisions here were obvious, such as teaching prerequisite reading alarms first. But, a long list of infrequent skills is not practical. Students need some instruction for recognizing infrequent stimuli in their own work. If they forget a treatment, they can consult a good style manual (Sabin, 2001).

In designing an instructional sequence, Gilbert's (1962b) informal dictum was to "teach the hard things first, whenever possible." The logic for this principle is that it minimizes the competition for memory and the hard things become easier to learn and remember. So, what are the hard things? Gilbert described sources of competition, which he said was the primary cause of forgetting. To determine the sequence of instruction, as well as the tactic, Gilbert would set up a matrix of all the operants to be learned. He would then analyze their interactions—examine each operant and assess whether it would compete with or facilitate the learning of each of the other operants. My analysis for the instructional sequence of the reading alarms was more intuitive. The instruction described here favors early teaching of those reading alarms with a high potential for increasing the scope and variety of the students' writing, but a closer analysis of an instructional sequence for the reading alarms would be useful.

THE PROCESS OF WRITING

Ideally, perhaps, all grammatical usage, punctuation, mechanics, and style would be taught through the sentences that students write. But appropriate reading alarms do not show up naturally in a classroom setting or even in one-on-one tutorials. Teachers must initiate the learning by teaching parts and structures of grammar and their attendant punctuation first and then encouraging students to use the new features in their writing afterward. With the process of writing paired with instruction in writing skills, students are always practicing what they are taught.

My experience with writing programs has been with adults and in books, workshops, and classrooms; but the same principles apply with children—only the pace and tactics are different. Young children start with the definition of a sentence and then learn to discriminate between sentences and sentence fragments or run-ons. They write their own examples, thereby prompting the punctuation and mechanics needed to inform readers when a sentence begins and ends. Gradually, they learn to use phrases and other features within the simple sentence, and they check their writings for the reading alarms they learned. Once they can build simple sentences, they learn to build paragraphs. They also learn new sentence structures and the attendant punctuation. All along, they practice trimming their content and firming up their skills to fluuency.

With older students and adults, the instruction follows a more accelerated path and it can be more individualized. My tactic with the Penn State students was to give them a diagnostic test with at least two examples of the simpler and more frequent grammatical and punctuation reading alarms to identify and address. Students recorded the results of this test on progress plotters, so that instruction could proceed from individual baselines. But a diagnostic is not essential, however. Students may start by assessing their audience and writing a statement of the point they wish to make in a free-write, which they then produce. In a subsequent session, they self-edit their work by looking for matches to a list of reading alarms, and then making appropriate adjustments. Students can plot these results on progress plotters. Their prior experience is acknowledged, and no student will start the new writing program at zero.

Free-writing is a widespread practice intended to loosen people up and is often celebrated as a cure for writer's block. In Seattle, aspiring writers of fiction visit a special writing place—the Richard Hugo House on Capitol Hill—to free-write for a few hours once or twice a week. In a structured writing program, the objective of a free-write is to induce students to relax and let their thoughts take charge. Students have a stated period of time to produce a rough draft on a topic based on their studies or other interests. Their drafts are brief at first but become longer with practice. The term *free* means that students can write freely, without worry about anyone's opinion, as they apply whatever wording, grammar, or punctuation is fluent.

Using this free-write or working draft, students proceed to the self-edit, but not immediately. As many have observed, time is the best editor. Writers need time to reverse direction so they can review their work as if they are now readers. What makes readers so smart? They have had considerably more practice in reading than in writing. Readers come to rely on the consistent signals of composition they find in printed matter. If they do not get the signals they expect, they will stumble over the text.

As readers now, students start the self-edit by checking content and paragraphing—marking where each new idea starts and then shifts to something different. Next, they check to ensure that each idea is fully developed, with adequate examples. They check that paragraphs are in the proper sequence, as are the sentences in each paragraph, and they apply the edits needed. With content now secure, the objective is to note whether sentences are grammatically correct and whether some fat can be trimmed so wordings are sharpened. This closer look may require two or three readings. If possible, all readings should be aloud, so students can catch their own rhythm—hear whether the flow is smooth or labored. If they stumble as they read, they must stop to consider why they stumbled and what they can do about it. Afterward, the instructor reviews the changes and also teaches one or two new skills. Students then produce another free-write—this time, using the new techniques. The process is repeated, so that students are always learning new skills and practicing the old.

In doing their self-edits, students learn to use copyediting marks for editing hard copy or the Track Changes feature in the Tools menu of Word, for example, if they work on computers. Either way, the teacher demonstrates the method first, prompts the practice, and then lets students perform unaided.

Although free-writes are a major strategy for writing instruction, they are not the only source of writing practice. Students might write an essay intended for several diverse audiences, or all the students in the group might write from the same prepared outline of a familiar topic. Teachers will be surprised at both the differences and similarities in the resulting compositions. Another exercise for students is to write in the style of a specific author they are reading in school. High school students 50 or 60 years ago read and modeled the Roger de Coverley papers. Now, students can invent new adventures for Holden Caulfield and Harry Potter. Shorter practice exercises in key skills are beneficial—such as shortening sentences so they are more effective, expressing one idea in several different ways, or using some of the fine points of style. A challenging exercise is to cut the word count of an edited draft by half while maintaining its point. With usability gurus and information architects advising that Web writing should be 50% shorter than its print counterpart, severe word cuts do not sound so radical. Chances are that many students and adults will write on-line text, and learning to trim verbiage while maintaining the point and emphasis of the message is a worthy pursuit.

The Internet offers a multitude of opportunities to write; e-mail, of course, is one—even with its overall disdain for the grammar police. A more educational writing activity available to Web users is called Fan Press (formerly Fan Fiction). Teens write stories and post them on the Internet. Readers may ask their favorite authors to write on a special topic. Several other Websites (*e.g.*, Scholastic's) also publish student writing so that teens can see what others in their age group write. For the first time, they get rapid feedback from their peers. It is all great practice and an incentive for teens to write more often and to write better.

No setup for conducting a writing exercise works well with a really large group unless instructors make some accommodations. Instructors must be flexible managers—perhaps arrange for one group to write while another learns a new skill and a third self-edits. Instructors may encourage peer editing and use prepared editing and writing exercises. Quick fluency can pep up the class while firming their skills. The goal is keeping all students engaged. The finest achievement for any writing instructor may be to produce students who appreciate the beauty and elegance of language and like to experiment with words.

A LAST WORD

Few of us are as articulate in our oral communications as we can learn to be when we write. Writers must select the words and grammatical links that best convey their meaning. At the same time, writers must capture the nuances of speech—the smile, the frown, the indignation, the surprise, or the look-you-in-the-face confrontation. Writing is a dance between writers and their readers. Writers lead, and if their message is clear and gracefully constructed their readers will follow. Critics may say that writing is not like mathematics, and that a scientific approach to writing is too clinical. I believe that mathematicians, or at least a engineers, must have organized our grammatical structure from the Latin, and we benefit by learning the logic they applied. The behavioral principles help writers organize the conventions for translating oral speech into writing. They do not prevent writers from seeking full command of the English language so they can control the effects they elicit in their readers. That kind of mastery comes from knowing their readers, from achieving fluency in writing skills, from the ability to self-edit, from reading good writing, from learning about many different subjects, and from the leisure and desire to experiment. Our job as writing instructors is to encourage all students to learn the craft of writing. How they choose to use this craft will define them as artists.

References

Gilbert, M. B. (1984). *Clear writing: A business guide*. New York: John Wiley & Sons.

Gilbert, M. B. (1992). *A writing program*, unpublished course materials. Bainbridge Island, WA: author.

Gilbert, M. B. (2003). Clear writing starts with grammar and punctuation and Write for Your Readers. Eau Claire, WI: Otter Creek Institute.

Gilbert, T. F. (1962a). The progress plotter as a reinforcement device. *The Journal of Mathetics*, 1, 111–114.

Gilbert, T. F. (1962b). Mathetics I: The technology of education. *The Journal of Mathetics*, 1, 1–70.

Gilbert, T. F. (1962c). Mathetics II: The design of teaching exercises. *The Journal of Mathetics*, 2, 7–56.

Gilbert, T. F. (1969). A Beginning Reading Program, unpublished course materials. Bainbridge, WA: author.

Gilbert, T. F. (1996). *Human competence: Engineering worthy performance*. Silver Spring, MD: International Society for Performance Improvement (original work published in 1978).

National Commission on Writing in America's Schools and Colleges. (2003). *The neglected "R."* Chicago, IL: College Entrance Examination Board.

Sabin, W. A. (2001). *The gregg reference manual*, 9th ed. New York: Glencoe/McGraw-Hill.

Spalding, R. B., North, M. E. (2003). The writing road to reading, 5th ed. New York: HarperCollins (original work published in 1957).

Index